Multinational Democracies

Multinational Democracies is the first collaborative, multiperspective critical survey of a new and distinctive type of political association that is coming into prominence in the twenty-first century. These are democratic societies that are not only multicultural but also multinational: that is, they comprise two or more nations. Fifteen leading comparative political scientists and political theorists from Europe and North America clarify the complex character and tensions of multinational democracies by reflecting on four exemplars – the United Kingdom, Spain, Belgium and Canada. The work offers a new approach to the study, understanding and governing of multinational societies and, in so doing, of culturally diverse societies more generally. This volume will be of interest to those concerned with diverse societies, nationalism, struggles for recognition, federalism and democratic constitutionalism in conditions of pluralism.

ALAIN-G. GAGNON is Professor of Political Science at McGill University, Director of the Quebec Studies Programme and editor of *Politique et Sociétés*. His recent publications include *Ties that Bind: Parties and Voters in Canada* (1999 with James Bickerton and Patrick Smith), *Québec y el federalismo canadiense* (1998) *Québec* (1998) and *Comparative Federalism and Federation: Competing Traditions and Future Directions* (1993).

JAMES TULLY, FRSC, holds the Jackman Distinguished Chair in Philosophical Studies, Department of Philosophy, University of Toronto. He has held positions at the University of Victoria and McGill University. He is the author of several books including *Strange Multiplicity: Constitutionalism and Diversity* (1999) and *An Approach to Political Philosophy* (1993). He has also edited among others *Philosophy in an Age of Pluralism* (1994) and *Meaning and Context* (1990).

Multinational Democracies

Edited by

Alain-G. Gagnon
McGill University

James Tully
University of Toronto

CAMBRIDGE
UNIVERSITY PRESS

PUBLISHED BY THE PRESS SYNDICATE OF THE UNIVERSITY OF CAMBRIDGE
The Pitt Building, Trumpington Street, Cambridge, United Kingdom

CAMBRIDGE UNIVERSITY PRESS
The Edinburgh Building, Cambridge CB2 2RU, UK
40 West 20th Street, New York NY 10011–4211, USA
10 Stamford Road, Oakleigh, VIC 3166, Australia
Ruiz de Alarcón 13, 28014 Madrid, Spain
Dock House, The Waterfront, Cape Town 8001, South Africa

http://www.cambridge.org

First published 2001

Printed in the United Kingdom at the University Press, Cambridge

Typeset in 10/12pt Plantin   System 3b2   CE

A catalogue record for this book is available from the British Library

Library of Congress Cataloguing in Publication data

Multinational democracies / edited by Alain-G. Gagnon, James Tully.
    p.   cm.
Includes bibliographical references and index.
ISBN 0 521 80029 3 (hardback)   ISBN 0 521 80473 6 (paperback)
1. Nationalism – Case studies.
2. Minorities – Political activity – Case studies.
3. Federal government – Case studies.
4. Democracy – Case studies.
5. Pluralism (Social sciences) – Case studies.
I. Gagnon, Alain-G. Tully, James, 1946–
JC312.M854 2001
321.8′094′09045–dc21   00–065148

ISBN 0 521 80029 3 hardback
ISBN 0 521 80473 6 paperback

Notes on the contributors

DOMINIQUE AREL is Assistant Professor (Research) at the Watson Institute for International Studies, Brown University, and Program Chair of the Annual World Convention of the Association for the Study of Nationalities (ASN). His research has focused mainly on language politics and identity shift in Ukraine and on the various instruments by which states categorize their residents along identity lines. He is the co-editor, with David Kertzer, of *Categorizing Citizens: the Use of Race, Ethnicity and Language in National Censuses* (Cambridge University Press, forthcoming), as well as the author of 'Language and the Census', and the co-author of 'Census Categorizations and the Struggle for Political Power' in that volume. His work on language politics in Ukraine has appeared in *Post-Soviet Affairs*, *Nationalities Papers* and *The Harriman Review*, as well as in *Political Culture and Civil Society in Russia and the New States of Eurasia* (edited by V. Tismaneanu) and *Parliaments in Transition* (edited by T. Remington). He has taught at Yale University and McGill University.

MICHAEL BURGESS is Professor of Politics and Director of the Centre for European Union Studies (CEUS), University of Hull, England. His principal research areas include federalism and the European Union, Canadian federalism and constitutional politics, and comparative federalism. He has published widely on these areas, including *Federalism and the European Union, 1972–1987* (London: Routledge, 1989), *Canadian Federalism: Past, Present and Future* (ed.) (Leicester University Press 1990); *Comparative Federalism*, co-edited with Alain-G. Gagnon (London: Harvester Wheatsheaf, 1993); *The British Tradition of Federalism* (London: Cassell, 1995). His latest book is entitled *Federalism and European Union: the Building of Europe, 1950–2000* (London: Routledge, 2000).

DANIEL-PATRICK CONWAY is a PhD candidate in Political Science at Brandeis University, where he specializes in international relations. A graduate from Bristol University, he worked as a journalist in Buenos

Aires, hosting a daily current affairs programme on Radio Argentina. He has recently held research and teaching positions at Harvard University and Brandeis.

PIERRE COULOMBE is a political theorist whose research area is language policy. He has taught political science at McGill University, the University of Ottawa, the University of New Brunswick and the University of Western Ontario. His most relevant publications include: *Language Rights in French Canada* (New York: Peter Lang, 1995); 'Ford v. Quebec: the Language of Public Signs', in M. Westmacott and H. Mellon (eds.), *Political Dispute and Judicial Review: Assessing the Work of the Supreme Court* (Toronto: Nelson Canada, 2000); 'Citizenship and Official Bilingualism in Canada', in Will Kymlicka and Wayne Norman (eds.), *Citizenship in Diverse Societies* (Toronto: Oxford University Press, 2000); 'Federalism and Sovereignty: the Case of Quebec in (or outside) Canada', in Michelle Beauclair (ed.), *The Francophone World: Cultural Issues and Perspectives* (New York: Peter Lang, forthcoming).

ALAIN-G. GAGNON is Professor of Political Science at McGill University, Director of the Quebec Studies Programme and editor of *Politique et Sociétés*. His recent publications include *Ties That Bind. Parties and Voters in Canada* with James Bickerton and Patrick Smith (Toronto: Oxford University Press, 1999); *Canadian Politics*, 3rd edition, co-edited with James Bickerton (Peterborough: Broadview Press, 1999); *Quebec y el Federalismo Canadiense* (Madrid: Consejo superior de investigaciones científicas, 1998), *Quebec* (Oxford: ABC Clio, 1998); and *Comparative Federalism and Federation: Competing Traditions and Future Directions*, co-edited with Michael Burgess (London: Harvester Wheatsheaf, 1993).

DIMITRIOS KARMIS is Adjunct Professor in Political Science at the Université Laval (Quebec City, Canada). He taught previously at McGill University and Johns Hopkins University. He works in the fields of Political Theory, Comparative Politics and Canadian Politics. His research focuses on federalism, identity politics, citizenship and citizenship education in diverse societies. His publications include articles in *Ethnic and Racial Studies* (2001), *Politique et Sociétés* (1998), and the *Canadian Journal of Political Science* (1993, 1996). He is currently working on a book tentatively entitled *Between Nationalism and Cosmopolitanism: Reassessing the Potential of Normative Theories of Federalism in the Modern World*.

MICHAEL KEATING is Professor at the University of Aberdeen and the European University Institute of Florence. He has been visiting professor or research fellow in Spain, France, Italy, Norway, England and the United States. He is the author of *Nations against the State: Nationalism in Quebec, Catalonia and Scotland*, 2nd edition (London: Macmillan, 2001) and has co-authored with B. Jones, *The European Union and the Regions* (Oxford University Press, 1995); and, with John Loughlin, *The Political Economy of Nationalism* (London: Frank Cass, 1997).

ANDRÉ LECOURS is a PhD candidate in political science at Carleton University. His current research focuses on ethnonationalism and nationalist conflict management in western societies.

DAVID MILLER is an Official Fellow at Nuffield College, Oxford University. His recent publications include *On Nationality* (New York: Clarendon Press, 1995); he has edited *Liberty* (Oxford University Press, 1989); and *Pluralism, Justice, and Equality* (Oxford University Press, 1995).

LUIS MORENO is Senior Research Fellow with the Spanish National Research Council (CSIC). His main research interests are the welfare state and social policy, and territorial politics. Recent works in the area of territorial politics include *The Federalization of Spain* (London: Frank Cass, 2001); 'Multiple Ethnoterritorial Concurrence in Spain', *Nationalism and Ethnic Politics* 1 (1995), 11–32; and 'Multiple Identities in Decentralized Spain: the Case of Catalonia', *Regional and Federal Studies* 8, no. 3 (1998), 65–88.

WAYNE NORMAN holds a Chair in the Centre for Applied Ethics at the University of British Columbia. His is the co-editor, with Will Kymlicka, of *Citizenship in Diverse Societies* (Oxford University Press, 2000), and is writing a book entitled *Thinking Through Nationalism*. He is also the author of several articles, among which are 'Theorizing Nationalism (Normatively)', in R. Beiner (ed.), *Theorizing Nationalism* (Albany: State University of New York Press, forthcoming); 'The Ethics of Secession as the Regulation of Secessionist Politics', in M. Moore (ed.), *Self-Determination and Secession* (Toronto: Oxford University Press, forthcoming); 'The Ideology of Shared Values', in J. Carens (ed.), *Is Quebec Nationalism Just?* (Montreal: McGill–Queen's University Press 1995).

SHANE O'NEILL is Reader in Politics at Queen's University, Belfast. His recent publications include *Impartiality in Context: Grounding Justice in a Pluralist World* (Albany: State University of New York Press, 1997); *Reconstituting Social Criticism: Political Morality in an Age of Scepticism*

(Basingstoke: Macmillan, 1999); 'Liberty, Equality and the Rights of Cultures: the Marching Controversy at Dumcree', *British Journal of Politics and International Relations* 2, no. 1 (April 2000); 'The Idea of an Overlapping Consensus in Northern Ireland: Stretching the Limits of Liberalism', *Irish Political Studies* 11 (1996); and 'Pluralist Justice and its Limits: The Case of Northern Ireland', *Political Studies* 42, no. 3 (September 1994).

ALAN PATTEN is Assistant Professor of Political Science at McGill University. He is the author of *Hegel's Idea of Freedom* (New York: Oxford University Press, 1999) and articles in *The Monist, Nations and Nationalism* and *History of Political Thought*. His current research examines the relationship between liberalism and nationalism in normative political theory.

FERRAN REQUEJO is Professor of Political Science at the Universitat Pompeu Fabra, Barcelona. His main fields of research are theories of democracy, federalism and nationalism, and political liberalism and social democracy after World War II. In 1997, he was awarded the Rudolf Wildenmann Prize by the European Consortium for Political Research. Among his recent publications are *Democracy and National Pluralism* (London: Routledge, 2001); *¿Federalisme, per a què?* (Valencia: L'Hora del present 1998); *Zoom politic: Democràcia, federalisme i nacionalisme des d'una Calalunya europea* (Barcelona: Edicions Proa 1998); *European Citizenship, Multiculturalism, and the State*, co-edited with Ulrich K. Preuss (Baden-Baden: Nomos, 1998); and *Asimetría federal y estado plurinacional: el debate de la diversidad en Canadá, Bélgica y España*, co-edited with Eric Fossas (Madrid, 1999).

FRANÇOIS ROCHER is Professor of Political Science and Associate Director at the School of Canadian Studies at Carleton University. He has published several articles and book chapters on Quebec nationalism, Canadian federalism and the constitution, the impact of North American integration on intergovernmental relations in Canada and Canadian identity and political culture. He has co-edited *New Trends in Canadian Federalism* (Peterborough: Broadview Press, 1995) and edited *Bilan québécois du fédéralisme canadien* (Montreal: VLB éditeur, 1992). He is the former co-editor of the *Canadian Journal of Political Science/ Revue canadienne de science politique*.

CHRISTIAN ROUILLARD received his PhD in political science from Carleton University. He is currently Professor of Public Management at l'Ecole nationale d'aministration publique (ENAP) in Hull (Québec). His main fields of interest are organization theory, managerial reform and innovation, the transformation of the state, as well as Canadian and comparative federalism and constitutional politics. He has co-authored a number of journal articles on Canadian federalism.

RICHARD SIMEON is Professor of Political Science and Law at the University of Toronto. His writings on federalism in Canada began with the award-winning *Federal-Provincial Diplomacy: the Making of Recent Policy in Canada* (University of Toronto Press, 1972). More recent work includes *State, Society, and the Development of Canadian Federalism* with Ian Robinson (University of Toronto Press, 1991); *Rethinking Federalism: Citizens, Politics and Markets*, co-edited with K. Knop, S. Ostry and K. Swinton (Vancouver: University of British Columbia Press, 1996); *In Search of a Social Contract: Can We Make Hard Decisions if Democracy Matters?* (Toronto: C. D. Howe Institute, 1994).

CHARLES TAYLOR, FRSC, is Emeritus Professor of Philosophy, McGill University. His many publications include: *Philosophical Papers*, 2 volumes (Cambridge University Press, 1985); *Sources of the Self: the Making of the Modern Identity* (Cambridge University Press, 1989); *Multiculturalism and the Politics of Recognition: an essay*, edited by Amy Gutmann (Princeton University Press, 1992); *Reconciling the Solitudes: Essays on Canadian Federalism and Nationalism*, edited by Guy Laforest (Montreal: McGill–Queen's University Press, 1993); *Philosophical Arguments* (Cambridge, MA: Harvard University Press, 1995).

JAMES TULLY, FRSC, holds the Jackman Distinguished Chair in Philosophical Studies, Department of Philosophy, University of Toronto. He has held positions at the University of Victoria and McGill University. He is the author of several books, among which are *An Approach to Political Philosophy* (Cambridge University Press, 1993); *Strange Multiplicity: Constitutionalism and Diversity* (Cambridge University Press, 1995); *Une étrange multiplicité* (Sainte-Foy: Les Presses de l'Université Laval, 1999). He has also edited, among others, *Philosophy in an Age of Pluralism* (Cambridge University Press, 1994); and *Meaning and Context* (Princeton University Press, 1990).

Foreword

Charles Taylor

This excellent collection explores important new ground. The authors of these chapters examine the constitutive tensions at the heart of contemporary democratic societies.

These societies are in fact the site of two opposite tendencies. On the one hand, they require a new kind of unity and homogeneity which earlier, autocratic or hierarchical societies never needed. On the other hand, they are becoming more and more diverse. The need for unity comes from the conditions of legitimacy which belong to a democratic society. We can see this in a number of ways, three of which are especially evident.

First, democratic societies construe the ensemble of citizens as a 'people'; that is, as a unit of deliberation and decision. Yet, in order to sustain what can be recognized as a common deliberation, a people has to have a minimal common focus, a set of agreed goals, or principles, or concerns, about which they can debate, argue and struggle. Once they drift apart, with different segments focusing on different things, it becomes hard to construe the upshot as the answer to a common question. But then this upshot begins to lose legitimacy for those who no longer see it as the answer to *their* question.

If a minority, for instance, comes to see the majority as concerned exclusively for its good, rather than that of the whole, they will begin to feel that they are no longer included in this 'people'. Then, according to the very logic of democracy, they are no longer bound by the decisions arrived at without any concern for them.

Democracies need to be bonded in a common focus, what one could call a 'political identity'. This can be a set of common principles, as in the Republican tradition, but most commonly in the last two centuries, it has primarily centred on the nation.

Second, the need for unity and homogeneity can also be seen from another angle. A second crucial legitimating condition of modern democracy is the equality of the citizens. Any systematic inequality or mode of discrimination in a modern society is seen as a challenge to its right to exist, at least in its present form. Now equality is not homogeneity, although it has frequently been construed as such. In fact, differences frequently can be construed as entailing inequalities, and hence as something to be overcome in the name of democratic legitimacy.

From a third angle, the legitimacy of modern states, in an era in which the aura of traditional hierarchies has been dispelled, also depends on their efficacy, their ability to 'deliver the goods'. But this ability is often greater in societies with strong common purposes than in those which risk being paralysed by fundamental differences about their goals.

So, the modern state needs some basis for unity, yet this is getting harder to sustain. A common basis is the nation. This would suggest that a democratic world would be made up largely of nation-states, as in the Wilsonian dream. But there are just too many groups in the world which could legitimately construe themselves as nations. Not every one could have a state. In the past, many of these potential 'nations' did not see themselves as such, while in our day more and more are making demands for recognition.

We are moreover in an age of identity awakening. People are demanding that differences, not hitherto acknowledged, be recognized, along with a host of dimensions – gender, religious, linguistic and cultural.

And so the tensions rise. The three reasons for unity mentioned above remain true; they cannot be flouted. At the same time, it is becoming harder and harder to maintain this unity on the older bases, by homogeneous, difference-blind republics or homogeneous nation-states. Dilemmas arise which are hard to resolve.

This book attempts to tackle these dilemmas in a very important category of cases, that of multinational democracies. This is important, not only because national differences are among the most powerful and intractable; but also because the category of what can legitimately be called 'multinational' states is growing, as previously submerged groups begin to make identity demands.

Now in fact, in a number of societies which have been attempting to deal with these issues, new formulae are being devised. Some of these are examined in the chapters in this volume. This is a very considerable contribution, because not enough is known about these experiments. Furthermore, the authors attempt to explore the fundamental issues, normative and institutional, which the constitutive tensions of modern democracy raise for us. They try to cast these problems in a new light, even to the point of redefining the goal of mutual recognition.

It is this combination which makes this volume so valuable. Factually well-grounded, these studies also help us to see the dilemmas of our time in new ways. They are indispensable reading for whoever wants to understand the contemporary struggles for recognition.

Acknowledgements

The preparation of this book would not have been possible without the help of a number of people. First, we wish to thank our contributors for their collaboration throughout the many phases that go into putting together a book of this importance. This book has also benefitted greatly from the assistance of Can Erk, Raffaele Iacovino, John Provart, Luc Turgeon and Jonathan Havercroft. These graduate students in the Department of Political Science at McGill University, with the exception of the latter who is a graduate student at the University of Victoria, have been responsible for many important tasks during the preparation of the project.

We wish also to thank people involved in various capacities with the Quebec Studies programme at McGill for their continued support at all stages of the project, especially Stéphan Gervais, Damion Stodola and Luc Turgeon. They were particularly active in ensuring that the conference went smoothly.

We would also like to thank especially the Fonds FCAR (Formation de chercheurs et aide à la recherche) of the Quebec Government and the Social Sciences and Humanities Research Council of Canada (through its support programme established to provide financial support toward hosting international conferences) for their support of the activities of McGill's Research Group on Multinational Societies.

We would like to thank all the people involved in the activities of the Research Group on Multinational Societies for their remarkable contribution in making this project a rich intellectual experience.

We wish to thank everyone involved with the Research Group on Multinational Societies over the years for their continued contribution, but especially Dominique Arel, Pierre Coulombe, Guy Laforest, Pierre Noreau, Alan Patten, François Rocher and José Woehrling.

Finally, we are most grateful to John Haslam of Cambridge University Press for his unfailing support and encouragement.

ALAIN-G. GAGNON AND JAMES TULLY,
Montreal and Victoria

Introduction

James Tully

The aim of this volume is to present the first collaborative, multi-perspective and critical survey of a new and distinctive type of political association that is coming into prominence at the dawn of the twenty-first century – 'multinational democracy'. Multinational democracies are contemporary societies composed not only of many cultures (multicultural) but also of two or more nations (multinational). The Canadian Research Group on Multinational Societies brought together a team of leading experts from Europe and North America to clarify the complex physiognomy of multinational democracies by reflecting on four leading exemplars – Canada, the United Kingdom, Belgium and Spain – from the perspectives of history, comparative politics and political philosophy. This work thus strives to offer a new approach and contribution to the study, understanding and governing of multinational societies and, in so doing, of culturally diverse societies more generally.

We have sought to cast a new light on multinational societies by employing four methodological rules. Since multinational democracies are just coming into being in the present era it is not possible to present a definitive or comprehensive account. Rather than the crystalline purity of a theory of multinational democracy, therefore, we seek first of all to offer many, complementary, specific, theoretical and institutional sketches of the 'rough ground': that is, the activities, practices, dynamics, tensions, institutions, administrative arrangements, policies, procedures, structures, movements, citizenship, parties, struggles for and against recognition, obstacles, disagreements, laws, constitutions, shared sovereignty, values and norms that characterize these emerging polities. Next, although there are separate literatures on culturally diverse societies by political scientists and political theorists, there is very little dialogue between them. This is the first collection to bring together leading scholars from these two disciplines and to focus attention on four, exemplary democratic societies that have considerable experience with the complexities of struggles over the recognition and accommodation of both multinationalism and multiculturalism. While there are other multinational democracies in existence, and many more coming on line (such as the European Union), we decided to concentrate on these four, relatively mature cases for the sake of the coherence of the volume, the strength and testability of the comparisons and generalizations, and the broadly similar democratic cultures and institutions.

Furthermore, all the contributors have organized their analyses of various aspects of multinational democracies around the two types of question that are central to the emergence and reconciliation of these deeply diverse political communities: the more normative or theoretical questions of justice and recognition on one side and the more institutional or emprical questions of accommodation and stability on the other. These define, as Charles Taylor puts it in the Foreword, the 'constitutive tensions' of multinational democracies. Our aim is neither to subordinate one type of question to the other nor to resolve them in a higher synthesis, but to map their intricate lines of interaction and techniques of possible conciliation on the rough ground of actual exisiting politics. Finally, the studies are organized by three broad themes that also combine and juxtapose theoretical and institutional concerns, and these correspond to the three parts of the volume: (I) the interrelations between considerations of justice and stability in theory and practice; (II) the tensions between normative claims for and against recognition and institutional and procedural forms of accommodation; and (III) the normative and institutional dimensions of modes of reconciliation and conflict management.

What, then, is a multinational democracy? There is not one set of properties which uniquely defines multinational democracy, but rather, as with most complex political phenomena, a complicated network of overlapping and criss-crossing similarities and dissimilarities. It is the work of the volume as a whole to map this complicated network and its intricate details from various vantage points. Nevertheless, it is possible to draw from the studies in this volume four similarities which can then function as a provisional characterization of multinational democracies and as a guide to the more detailed investigations which follow.

First and foremost, multinational democracies, in contrast to single-nation democracies (which are often presumed to be the norm), are constitutional associations that contain two or more nations or peoples. The members of the nations are, or aspire to be, recognized as self-governing peoples with the right of self-determination as this is understood in international law and democratic theory. While some members of such a nation may seek to exercise their right of self-determination 'externally' – by secession and the formation of another independent, single-nation state – other members mobilize to exercise their right of self-determination 'internally' – by the reconfiguration of the existing constitutional association so its multinational character is recognized and accommodated. Since the nations of a multinational democracy *are* nations, their members aspire to recognition not only in the larger multinational association of which they are a unit, but also to some degree in international law and other, supranational legal regimes (as, for example, the four nations of the United Kingdom). Accordingly, multinational democracies are not traditional, single-nation democracies with internal, subnational 'minorities' seeking group rights within, but societies of two or more, often overlapping nations that are more or less equal in status.

Second, multinational democracies are not confederations of independent nation-states, plural societies of separate peoples or multinational empires. The citizens and their representatives participate in the political institutions of their self-governing nations and the larger, self-governing multination. Hence, multinational democracies standardly exhibit both federal and confederal features. The jurisdictions, modes of participation and representation, and the national and multinational identities of citizens overlap and are subject to negotiation.

Third, the nations and the composite multination are constitutional democracies. That is, the legitimacy of both the nations and the multinational association rests on their adherence to the legal and politicial values, principles and rights of constitutional democracy and international law. Hence the title, 'multinational democracy'. This feature is difficult to grasp because multinational democracies often emerge out of the cocoon of societies in which the majority tends to understand itself as a single-nation democracy, even when this is historically inaccurate, and to equate democracy with single nationhood. Consequently, multinational democracy appears to run against the prevailing norms of legitimacy for a single-nation democracy and it is condemned as unreasonable or abnormal by both the defenders of the status quo and the proponents of secession. But, a legitimate multinational democracy runs against the norms of single nationhood, not the norms of constitutional democracy, which are, fortunately for the future, contingently related to the old ideal of a single-nation polity.

Fourth, multinational democracies are also multicultural. Both the nations and the multinational association as a whole are composed of individuals and cultural, linguistic, religious and ethnic minorites who struggle for and against distinctive forms of recognition and accommodation of their cultural diversity. In response, the nations and the multinational association develop procedures and institutions for the

democratic discussion and reconciliation of these forms of diversity
with the unity of their respective associations (one way or another), in
addition to the procedures and institutions for the reconciliation of
their multinational diversity. The struggles over minority and multinational diversity overlap, compete, and undergo democratic negotiation as well.

These family resemblances among multinational democracies are
examined in the following sections of this Introduction. The Introduction is not a summary of the chapters that follow. Each of the three parts
opens with a short summary of the chapters. Rather, the introductory
sketch is a free-standing exposition of what I have learned about the
struggles over recognition in emerging multinational democracies from
my participation in this remarkable collaborative research project.
Nevertheless, it lays out major constituents of multinational democracies (the main political actors, the political options available to them, the
processes of mobilization, negotiation and reconciliation, and the democratic values at issue), and it provides references to the chapters in which
they are analysed in more detail. In a broad sense, then, it serves as an
introduction, as well as a contribution. For further guidance, the first
and last chapters are more synoptic than the others. Chapter 1 by
Michael Keating is a historical and comparative overview of existing
multinational democracies and chapter 14 by Richard Simeon and
Daniel-Patrick Conway is a critical survey of institutions of accommodation of multinational and multicultural diversity in democratic societies.
But the enlightenment of the whole derives from the specific light shed
by the individual parts. For the collection is a 'collection', a toolkit for
understanding the growing number of multinational democracies in
which we are trying to find ourselves and appropriate practices of
cooperation as the new century unfolds.

1   Freedom in multinational democracies

After fifty years of struggles over recognition and accommodation in
multinational and multicultural societies, we now have sufficient experience and research to begin to understand the characteristic dynamics of
this form of political association. The range of distinctive questions of
justice and stability raised and the range of solutions that can be
proposed are critically surveyed and analysed in this collection from a
variety of orientations and in a number of specific contexts. In the
remainder of this introductory sketch I would like to draw on the
experience of the last fifty years and the scholarship of this volume to
present and defend the following reflection on an important transition

that multinational (and multicultural) democracies are beginning to undergo.

The politics of recognition of multiple nations and cultures within a constitutional democracy has reached a historical limit and is passing through a transition to a new orientation; a new self-understanding of the citizens, politicians and civil servants involved. The limit is an impasse caused by the inability to resolve specific struggles definitively and permanently. The explanation of this inability is what I will call the 'plurality' of contests over recognition. This concept refers to two features of recognition politics: (1) struggles over the mutual recognition of identities are too complex, unpredictable and mutable to admit of definitive solutions, and (2) the intersubjective activity of striving for and responding to forms of mutual recognition is an intrinsic public good of modern politics which contributes to legitimacy and stability whether or not the form of recognition demanded is achieved. The intersubjective activity of competing over recognition (separate from the end-state of recognition at which it aims) is what I will call the activity of mutual disclosure and acknowledgement. Struggles *for* recognition are also struggles *of* disclosure and acknowledgement.

Recognition politics, understood as the activity of mutual disclosure, is an enduring feature of modern politics. As a result, the constitutive question is no longer the one that has defined these struggles since Kant and Hegel: what is *the* just and stable form of recognition that will end the struggle? As this collection shows, the question of just and stable forms of recognition must now be reformulated for the twenty-first century as an open-ended series of questions addressed to specific struggles and experiments with institutional solutions to them within the broader horizon of the politics of recognition as a long-term activity of politics, no different in this regard from other types of political activity (such as, say, struggles over distribution). The constitutive question around which struggles and critical reflection are now becoming reoriented concerns the framework in which the games of disclosure and acknowledgement take place: that is, what form of democracy enables the politics of recognition to be played freely from generation to generation, with as little domination as possible?

The primary question is thus not recognition, identity or difference, but freedom; the freedom of the members of an open society to change the constitutional rules of mutual recognition and association from time to time as their identities change. This is an aspect of the freedom of self-determination of peoples, one of the most important principles of modern politics from the American and French revolutions to the *United Nations Charter*. However, in its classic form the freedom of self-determination was understood as the determination of a people into a specific constitutional formation which all could accept as the just framework for politics – whether this was a uniform nation, a federation, or some other form. Amendment would be required only in exceptional circumstances, it would be difficult to initiate and achieve, and it would not affect the constitutional essentials (Tully 1995, pp. 58–70; Bellamy and Castiglione 1997).

This classic understanding of the freedom of self-determination has been called into question and discredited by the persistence of struggles for recognition in the very societies which were until recently legitimated by it, for the struggles demonstrate that the constitution is not acceptable to all. As a result, the question of the freedom of self-determination is raised anew. It is raised in the context of multinational societies whose members have passed through the experience of struggles over recognition and learned that these do not admit of a definitive solution (and so cannot be accommodated within the classic understanding of self-determination). Rather, these contests constitute an enduring dimension of modern politics: the public disclosure of misrecognized identities and the demand that the other members acknowledge these and respond. Accordingly, the new, second-order aim of these struggles is for a form of political association that takes this ongoing activity into account in its basic structure. The answer is that a multinational society will be free and self-determining just insofar as the constitutional rules of recognition and association are open to challenge and amendment by the members. If they are not open, they constitute a structure of domination, the members are not self-determining, and the society is unfree. Freedom *versus* domination is thus the emerging focus of politics in multinational societies at the dawn of the new millennium.

I present this argument in the following steps. Section 2 describes the relevant features of multinational democracies. Section 3 describes the relevant features of struggles over recognition and how they have reached a limit or impasse due to their plurality. The response to this impasse over the last two decades by means of democratic constitutional change is explored in section 4. This experience brings to light a second limit: current democratic constitutionalism is conceived under the same classic assumption that gave rise to the impasse in the first place; the assumption that under some considerations of justice and stability members will reach agreement on a definitive form of recognition for all affected. For reasons of 'plurality' this form of democratic constitutionalism is doomed to failure. The lesson to be learned from passing through this experience is taken up in Section 5. The form of culturally diverse democracy that will be both free and stable in the twenty-first century is one in which the prevailing rules of recognition are always open to challenge and modification by the diverse members, on the grounds that any' set of rules will harbour dimensions of injustice and non-recognition. This entails that the nations of multinational democracies should be treated as peoples with the right of internal self-determination.

The Supreme Court of Canada, in *Reference re Secession of Quebec* (1998), is the first court of a multinational society to acknowledge this condition of freedom and to articulate an appropriate account of democratic constitutionalism in response.[1] The Supreme Court argues that the members of a diverse constitutional democracy have the right to initiate political and constitutional change (up to and including secession) and the correlative duty to enter into political and constitutional negotiations with the member who invokes this right by a legitimate procedure. The right and duty constitute the key democratic device for the reconciliation of multicultural and multinational diversity with the requirements of unity in culturally diverse societies over time, as an ongoing activity. If a constitutional democracy does not embody this right and duty in its political and constitutional practices, and so allow struggles for and against recognition to be played freely, it is a closed structure of domination and unfree with regard to self-determination. Since the Supreme Court of Canada clarifies the revolutionary transition in self-understanding of constitutional democracy that Canada and other multinational democracies are struggling with in one way or another, I draw on the Court's exemplary reasoning in my own presentation.[2]

2 The 'problematization' of the constitutional identity of a multinational society by struggles over recognition

2.1 A multinational society

Canada is described as a 'free and democratic society' in section 1 of the Canadian *Charter of Rights and Freedoms*. For the purposes of this Introduction, a 'multinational society' or 'multinational democracy' is a type of 'free and democratic society' which includes more than one

---

[1] All references to the Supreme Court of Canada (1998) *Reference re the Secession of Quebec* 2 SCR 217 are to the numbered paragraphs of the text (SC 1998, para.). It is available at www.droit.umontreal.c/doc/csc-scc/en/index.html and reprinted in David Schneiderman (ed.), *The Quebec Decision* (Toronto: Lorimer 1999). For a more detailed defence of the interpretation I advance here, see Tully (2000a).

[2] For a broader, historical and theoretical introduction to this change in the understanding of constitutional democracy, see Tully (1995).

'nation', or, more accurately, more than one 'member' of the society demands recognition as a nation or nations. In the case of Canada, the present government of Quebec and many of the citizens demand recognition as a nation and the present leaders of the indigenous or 'aboriginal' peoples and the majority of aboriginal people demand recognition as 'first nations' or 'indigenous peoples'. For the sake of brevity, I will sometimes write simply that 'Quebec' and the 'aboriginal peoples of Canada' demand recognition as a nation and as first nations respectively. I mean by this shorthand that a majority of Quebecers and aboriginal people support these demands. A member of a multinational society that demands recognition as a nation may itself be a multinational society. Quebec, with eleven aboriginal peoples in and across its borders demanding recognition as first nations, is a multinational democracy.

To investigate the features of a free, multinational democracy let us start (not uncritically) from the classic liberal account of a reasonably plural, free and democratic society presented by John Rawls, in *Political Liberalism* (1996), and its careful and innovative extension by Anthony Laden, in *Reasonably Radical: Deliberative Liberalism and the Politics of Identity* (2001), to free and democratic, multicultural and multinational societies. Rawls and Laden describe a free and democratic society as one that has a high degree of self-sufficiency and a place for all the main purposes of human life (Rawls 1996, pp. 40–3). A multinational society, like all free and democratic societies, meets these conditions. Moreover, a multinational society, like all free and democratic societies, is a fair system of social, political and economic cooperation in the broad and thick sense given to this phrase by Rawls. It is the congeries of democratic practices in which we acquire, exercise, question and modify our identities as national and multinational citizens (Rawls 1996, pp. 15–22, 41, 222, 269; Laden 2001, chs. 5–8).

'Cooperation' is more than socially coordinated action. 'Cooperation is guided by publicly recognized rules and procedures that those co-operating accept and regard as properly regulating their conduct.' Cooperation also involves the idea of 'fair terms of cooperation' – 'these are terms that every participant may reasonably accept, provided that everyone else likewise accepts them' (Rawls 1996, p. 16). The fair terms of cooperation apply to the basic structure of the society, to its political, economic and social institutions, and they are expressed in the constitutional principles of the society (Rawls 1996, pp. 257–8, 269–71; cp. SC 1998, paras. 50, 54). Accordingly, a demand for recognition as a nation or nations and its mode of institutional accommodation within a multinational society must be compatible with conditions of a fair system of social cooperation, or what the Supreme Court of Canada calls 'unity', to be acceptable. Conversely, a demand for recognition is often supported by the claim that the prevailing terms of cooperation or unity are unacceptable in some respect, for example in the case of both Quebec and indigenous peoples.

A free and democratic society, whether multinational or uninational, is 'free' in two relevant senses. The members of the society are free and the society as a whole is free. That is, the members of the society not only act democratically within the rules and procedures of cooperation; they also impose the rules on themselves and alter the rules and procedures democratically *en passant*. Such a society is 'self-governing' or 'self-determining', not in the radical sense that its members will into being the conditions of association. Rather, the members are free to either accept the conditions of association or enter into democratic negotiations to change the conditions that can be shown to be unjust; or, if the second of these options is blocked, to initiate the option to negotiate exit (SC 1998, paras. 83–105, 111–39). This is one of the most widely accepted principles of legitimacy in the modern world: for example, (1) of a liberal society as a fair system of social, political and economic cooperation, i.e. the rules are freely accepted and regarded as appropriate by the participants themselves (Rawls 1996, p. 16); (2) of 'self-determination' as it is predicated of free societies or 'peoples' in international law (SC 1998, paras. 111–39); and (3) of a free and democratic society in which the sovereign people or peoples impose the rules of the association on themselves as they obey those rules (Habermas 1998, pp. 49–74, 129–54, 253–64; Rawls 1996, pp. 396–409). The rules and procedures are neither imposed from the outside nor from an undemocratic element within. A member 'nation' seeking recognition within the larger society itself will be free and democratic in these two senses as well, on pain of a performative contradiction (Tully 2000b).

A 'nation' is a 'people' with the right of self-determination. A multinational society is a 'people' composed of peoples, a multi-peoples society or a multination. The multinational democracies studied in this volume have been recognized as self-determining, single nations or peoples by international law for centuries. The nations that demand recognition within multinational societies also and *eo ipso* demand recognition as 'peoples'. The terms 'nations' and 'peoples' have been used in overlapping ways over the last two hundred years and they are used interchangeably in discussions over, say, the Quebec 'people' or 'nation' and the 'first nations' or 'indigenous peoples'. Since I wish to focus on the conditions of freedom and recognition in multinational societies, the concept of a people with the right of self-determination is appropriate, rather than the concept of a nation, which is appropriate for issues of nationalism (see chapters 1, 3, 12).

A multinational society is usually but not always a federation (see chapters 4, 5, 7, 10, 13, 14). Israel and New Zealand, for example, are binational but not federal. I will concentrate on multinational federal societies because I wish to draw on Canada and because they are more complex than non-federal multinational societies. If we can clarify the main features of freedom and recognition in multinational federations, the non-federal cases should not be difficult. A federation is a society in which democratic self-government is distributed in such a way that citizens 'participate concurrently in different collectivities' (SC 1998, para. 66) – in the democratic institutions of the society as a whole and of the federated members, such as provinces, states, nations or first nations. A 'confederation', in contrast, is an association, not a society, in which citizens participate only in their 'nation', not in the multinational confederation as a whole. The problem of multinational recognition in a confederation is correspondingly less complex and can be set aside for now.

2.2   *Four dimensions of constitutional identity*

When a demand for the recognition of one or more nations or peoples arises in a multinational democracy, it 'problematizes' the constitutional identity of the society. That is, the demand renders problematic the current (single-nation) constitutional identity of the society and proposes a change. Various solutions are then proposed to the problem in theory and practice. Looking back over fifty years of experience, three conflicting types of solution are standardly proposed around which citizens and governments mobilize: (1) defence of the status quo, with or without a degree of sub-constitutional change, (2) various forms of recognition of the nation or nations by changing the current constitutional identity, and (3) secession of the nation or nations and recognition as a new independent nation or nations, with or without some relation to the former society. As we see from the studies in this collection, each of the three types of strategic solution is defined by an evolving structure of argument which presents reasons for the justice and stability of its solution and the injustice and instability of the other two (see chapters 3, 4, 8, 13). Call the whole – including the reasons and causes of the demand, the proposals and solutions, the public discussions and negotiations, or refusals to negotiate, the amendments of the constitution and institutional changes, and the demands for recognition that this amendment in turn provokes – the 'problematization' of the constitutional identity of a multinational democracy (Foucault 1984, p. 389 and Tully 1999b for the concept of problematization).

The 'constitutional identity' of a multinational society, as of any free and democratic society, is its 'basic constitutional structure', what I called above the publicly recognized and accepted rules and procedures by which the members of the society recognize each other and coordinate their cooperation. In the words of the Supreme Court of Canada, the constitution 'embraces unwritten, as well as written rules', and includes 'the global system of rules and principles which govern the exercise of constitutional authority' (Supreme Court 1998, para. 32). The constitution is the present system of rules of mutual recognition that gives a society its constitutional identity.

There are four major dimensions of the constitutional identity of a democratic society. First, a constitution recognizes the *members* of a society under their respective identities and enumerates their rights, duties and powers. For example, the Canadian constitution recognizes 'citizens' with their rights, freedoms and duties, various types of 'minorities' (linguistic, cultural, and individuals or groups disadvantaged because of race, ethnic origin, colour, religion, sex, age and mental or physical disability), 'territories', 'aboriginal peoples' and their rights, 'provinces' with their legislative powers, the federation and its federal legislature, and the Canadian society as a whole. Second dimension, a constitution stipulates the *relations of governance* among the members, the rules and procedures that guide their conduct as members of a fair system of social cooperation (the totality of laws and regulations). Third, the constitution lays out a set of procedures and institutions of *discussion and alteration* of prevailing relations of governance over time. In Canada, these include the rights of public discussion, debate, assembly, voting, strike and dissent, courts, legislatures, procedures of federal–provincial renegotiation, the notwithstanding clause, treaty negotiations among first nations and federal and provincial governments, and procedures for amending the constitution. Fourth, the constitution includes the *principles, values and goods* that are brought to bear on the identification of members, the relations among them, and the discussion and alteration of their identities and relations over time. These principles, values and goods do not form a determinate and ordered set of principles of justice to which all the members agree. Rather, they are many, none is trump, different ones are brought to bear in different cases, and there is reasonable disagreement and contestation about which ones are relevant and how they should be applied in any case (SC 1998, paras. 49–54). Indeed, part of what makes the society free and democratic is reasonable disagreement among the members and their political traditions of liberalism, conservatism, socialism, republicanism, feminism, nationalism, multiculturalism, environmentalism and so on (Rawls 1999, pp. 140–3). These principles, values and goods comprise the public, normative warrants members appeal to in exchanging reasons over the justice and stability of their conflicting demands for and against recognition in any case (Rawls 1999, pp. 129–80; Laden 2001, chs. 5–7).

In cases of the recognition of nations in multinational societies, there are seven relevant principles. Following the Supreme Court, four principles are necessary (but not sufficient) to the 'reconciliation of diversity with unity' in cases of multinationalism: the principles of federalism, democracy, the rule of law and constitutionalism, and the protection of minorities (SC 1998, paras. 32, 49, 55–82). In thin liberal democratic theories, two principles – democracy and rule of law – are said to be co-equal and jointly sufficient for legitimacy (Habermas 1998, pp. 253–64). However, this is sufficient only for a subset of modern societies, those that are non-federal and do not acknowledge the protection of minorities as an independent principle.

In addition, three basic principles are indispensable to any free and democratic society: freedom, equality and distinctness. Free and equal are widely endorsed principles. By 'freedom' I mean not only the freedoms associated with private autonomy (the freedom of the moderns), but also, and of primary concern in this case, the freedom associated with public autonomy, the democratic freedoms of members to participate in their society in the twofold sense explained above (section 2.1). 'Equality' includes not only the relatively uncontentious formal equality associated with thin liberal democracy, but also the substantive equality associated with thicker liberal societies (such as Rawls' 'difference principle') and with social democracy (for example, social and economic rights for citizens and groups, and equalization transfers for provinces) (SC 1998, para. 64). Finally, it includes the equality of peoples (see section 5 below). Members standardly disagree over the ranking, interpretation and application of these three aspects of equality.

Finally, members not only recognize each other as free and equal but also as the bearers of 'distinct' or, as the Supreme Court puts it, 'diverse identities' (SC 1998, paras. 43, 58, 59, 60, 74, 79–82). The freedom of expression of individual citizens, the principle of non-discrimination, equity policies, proportional representation, the protection of individual and group identities, languages and cultures, aboriginal rights, self-government and some federal arrangements (such as the special provisions for Quebec) are often justified in part by the principle of diversity or distinctness. Again, support varies and is contested, but public recognition of some forms of diversity and of 'identity-related differences' is both unavoidable (language and culture being the most obvious examples) and good, either in itself or as a means to other goods, such as mutual respect.

2.3 The right to initiate constitutional change and the duty to acknowledge and answer

The constitution, therefore, is (1) the prevailing system of rules of mutual recognition of the identities of political actors, (2) the relations of cooperation among them, (3) the procedures for discussing, negotiating and altering the rules, and (4) the normative considerations that bear on the rules. However, we need in addition to see how these four dimensions of a constitution work together to compose and regulate a free, democratic, and efficient system of social, economic and political cooperation over time. Recall that the members, insofar as they are free, have rights and duties of democratic participation, as well as civic and social rights of various kinds (see chapter 11). These are democratic rights to enter into the processes and institutions of the third dimension of the constitution, either directly or indirectly through their representatives, to contest and seek to change any rule of recognition governing the members and the relations among them, by presenting arguments in terms of the principles, values and goods of the constitution. Insofar as the demand is reasonable, the other members of the society have a correlative duty to respond to the demand by means of the appropriate form and forum of discussion and negotiation.

These are the rights that nations invoke when they seek recognition in multinational societies by means of constitutional change. Although this is the type of case we are concerned with in this volume, it is important to notice that these rights are a subset of the kind of rights that any member invokes whenever he or she enters into public debate, joins a political party, votes, demonstrates, introduces a bill in parliament, enters into litigation, initiates treaty negotiations, or any other form of participation, with the aim of changing any of the rules of the society. A member demanding recognition as a nation is an instance of the general right and duty.

The Supreme Court explains this crucial democratic right of any member to initiate negotiations over a rule of recognition and the correlative duty of the other members to enter into negotiations if the demand is reasonable, first by presenting the general right and duty of all members to dissent and be acknowledged and addressed, and second by defining the more specific right of certain members, such as provinces, to initiate constitutional change:

[W]e highlight that a functioning democracy requires a continuous process of discussion. The constitution mandates government by democratic legislatures, and an executive accountable to them, 'resting ultimately on public opinion reached by discussion and the interplay of ideas'. At both the federal and provincial level, by its very nature, the need to build majorities necessitates compromise, negotiation, and deliberation. No one has a monopoly on the truth, and our system is predicated on the faith that in the marketplace of ideas, the best solution to public problems will rise to the top. Inevitably there will be dissenting voices. A democratic system of government is committed to considering those dissenting voices, and seeking to acknowledge and address those voices in the laws by which all in the community must live.

The constitution Act, 1982, gives expression to this principle, by conferring a right to initiate constitutional change on each participant in Confederation. In our view, the existence of this right imposes a corresponding duty on the participants of Confederation to engage in constitutional discussions in order to acknowledge and address democratic expressions of a desire for change in other provinces. This duty is inherent in the democratic principle which is a fundamental predicate of our system of government. (SC 1998, paras. 68–9)

Each member must possess this right to initiate rule change and the correlative duty to acknowledge and answer if the society is free and democratic. It follows from the 'democratic principle'. As a consequence, a free and democratic society is involved in 'a continuous process of discussion', a process which includes both the right to voice dissent and the duty to 'acknowledge and address those voices in the laws by which all in the community must live'. Any rule of recognition is thus in principle open to dissent, discussion, consideration and, if necessary, alteration, in accord with the totality of rules that are not in question in any particular case. As the Supreme Court summarizes:

Our democratic institutions necessarily accommodate a continuous process of discussion and evolution, which is reflected in the constitutional right of each participant in the federation to initiate constitutional change. This right implies a reciprocal duty on the other participants to engage in discussions to address any legitimate initiative to change the constitutional order. (SC 1998, para. 150)

This feature of a free and democratic society is difficult to grasp because the language of constitutionalism and struggles for recognition disposes us to presume that there is some definitive and permanent system of rules of mutual recognition, some definitive configuration of the first, second and fourth constitutional dimensions on which all agree (the present one, some renewed constitution, or secession and two new constitutional nations). But this is false. '[I]nevitably, there will be dissenting voices.' What is definitive and permanent is the democratic discussion and alteration of the rules over time. The members accept and respect this or that system of rules of recognition not because they agree on the system in virtue of some shared conception of justice, but because the rules are open to dissent, fair consideration and amendment. This free and democratic feature is expressed in and guaranteed by the right to initiate rule change and the duty to acknowledge and address legitimate demands for change. Now we need to ask why 'dissent' – the free play of this right and duty – is 'inevitable'.

3   The activity of struggling for and against recognition

3.1   The main features of a struggle over the recognition of a people

When a participant demands recognition of its identity, whether this is an individual in the workplace claiming discrimination and demanding an equity policy supported by public power or a member claiming recognition as a nation, the demand standardly involves four claims. The demand involves the claim that, (1) the present form of constitutional recognition of their identity constitutes non-recognition or misrecognition, (2) this state of affairs constitutes an injustice, (3) the proposed new form of recognition is just and well-supported by public reasons (drawn from the fourth dimension), and finally (4) recognition (and institutional accommodation) by the other members would render the overall constitutional identity of the society a just and stable system of social cooperation. As we can see, a demand for recognition problematizes not only the present identity of the member demanding recognition, but also the identities of all members and the relations among them. It calls into question the present arrangement of the first two dimensions of the constitution. (For example, the recognition of the province of Quebec as a nation and of aboriginal 'bands' as 'indigenous peoples' affects the identity and interrelations of minorities, provinces, territories, the federal government, and the rights, duties and freedoms of citizens in various ways.)

Hence, a demand for recognition is never 'merely symbolic'. Along the second dimension, it alters, in complex and often massive ways, the social, economic and political relations of power that constitute the present system of social cooperation, as has been noted, for example, in the analysis of proposals to add 'interpretive clauses' to the Canadian constitution (Riddell and Morton 1998). These four claims and the corresponding alterations in identities, in social, economic and political relations, and in related structures of interest, are taken up and struggled over by the three parties (status quo, constitutional change, and secession) in discussions and negotiations. These take place in the processes and institutions of the third constitutional dimension and appeal to the principles, values and goods of the fourth (see, for example, chapters 4, 8, 10, 12, 13).

To support their preferred solutions all three parties engaged in the struggles tend to simplify the situation by trying to eliminate from the discussion some of the other members that would be affected by the proposed change. Some defenders of the status quo either ignore Quebecers and aboriginal people who demand fundamental change or claim to speak for them. Some Quebec and aboriginal sovereignists ignore the members within their borders who disagree with their projects and reduce the other members of society to a homogeneous 'other'. By this tactic, they undermine the legitimacy of their own claim to recognition, for they misrecognize, or fail to recognize at all, the claims of others affected by their claim, precisely the injustice they are protesting in their own case. Such performative contradictions violate the first principle of recognition politics, the principle of reciprocity, mutual recognition, mutual acknowledgement or *audi alteram partem* (always listen to the other side). That is, every member affected by the proposed change should be acknowledged and have a say in the discussions and negotiations (Tully 1995, pp. 7–17, 115–16, 165–82). *Unilateral* defence of the status quo, unilateral constitutional change and unilateral secession are all unjust in the sense that they violate with respect to other members the very principle that is invoked to justify the act (SC 1998, paras. 86, 91, 95). Moreover, such unilateral acts are unstable, for the disregarded members are seldom silenced for long. All the force of the existing society or of the secessionist state cannot stabilize effectively the unjust situation or gain the recognition they need from others, as we have seen in many tragic cases.

Consequently, there is no just and stable way to bypass the complex situation as I have outlined it. We must pass through it freely and democratically – by means of negotiations in which all members affected have a voice – and abandon strategies of defending the status quo by ignoring demands for recognition or passing through to independence by ignoring conflicting claims to recognition of those affected. Any such unjust and unstable unilateral demand (or defence of the status quo) should be ignored because it is illegitimate. This is the central argument of the Supreme Court (SC 1998, paras. 85–96) and it was endorsed by all three parties (the prime minister speaking for the status quo, proponents of constitutional recognition of multinationalism, and the independentist premier of Quebec).

Taking this into account, let us examine the discursive space in which a demand for recognition is worked up, whether for constitutional change or independence. Any such demand will be acknowledged and addressed by the other members of the society. This is an obligation. They will respond to the demand in various ways and these responses will involve the claim that they be properly recognized in return. The legitimacy of a demand for recognition will be in part a function of the cogency in which the legitimate responses of other members are acknowledged and taken into account. Moreover, the demands for recognition will be of various kinds. A demand for recognition as a nation provokes responses from provinces, territories, aboriginal peoples, minorities, and individual citizens, each with recognized identities and relations they wish to either protect or modify in light of the initial demand. Thus, the appropriate way to acknowledge and respond fairly to the reciprocal claim of others in the course of elaborating and defending a claim for nationhood will be complex. For example, the demands of aboriginal peoples for recognition as first peoples are considerably different from the demands of Quebec and require different responses (Cook 1994; Cook and Lindau 2000; Gibbins and Laforest 1998). Finally, a demand for recognition as a nation in a free and democratic society must be generated and defended in a manner that takes into account the legitimate concerns, not only of other members in the larger multinational society, but also of individuals and minorities within the nation seeking recognition.

Accordingly, there are always three free and democratic *processes of identity discussion and formation* which occur simultaneously in the procedures and institutions of discussion (the third constitutional dimension). These are (predominantly) discursive practices in which citizens discuss, acquire, and negotiate the very identities they put forward for recognition. First, those mobilizing for recognition must convince a clear majority of their own diverse members that they are misrecognized under the current constitution and should be recognized as a nation (under some description). These members will often include (as in the case of Quebec) aboriginal peoples, linguistic and other types of minorities, and individual citizens with rights, duties and powers under the current constitution. Therefore, the discussion of a demand for recognition will involve public discussions and negotiations among these members in order to reach agreement on a clear formulation of what is meant by nationhood, one which shows responsiveness to the concerns of the dissenting minorities and citizens within (or the demand fails the test of reciprocity and can be ignored). The Supreme Court suggests that these conditions will be met and a demand will be recognized as legitimate if the demand for nationhood is formulated in a clear referendum question and receives a clear majority of votes (SC 1998, para. 87). This triggers the duty of other members to enter into negotiations on constitutional change (SC 1998, para. 89). These further negotiations will proceed in accordance with the four principles and so will in turn take into account the concerns of all members, both within the nation demanding recognition and those concerned members in the larger society (SC 1998, paras. 90–8, 103–4).

In Quebec, for example, these processes of identity discussion and formation have been in operation since 1976 (Maclure 2000). Various consultations, commissions, public negotiations and public discussions have been held in an effort to come to terms with the numerous issues involved: whether Quebec is an ethnic or a civic nation, if aboriginal peoples are to be considered equal nations, if linguistic minorities and multicultural citizens are to be recognized, if it is a neo-liberal or a social democratic nation, if French-speaking minorities outside Quebec are to be considered or ignored, whether the first nations and their territories may remain part of Canada, whether ridings voting massively against secession may remain Canadian, and so on (see chapters 1, 10, 13). No consensus has been reached and the majority has rejected three referenda on proposed definitions of the identity of the Quebec nation, in 1980, 1992, 1995 (Gibbins and Laforest 1998). Analogous processes of identity discussion and formation take place among aboriginal peoples. Disputations and negotiations exist between the national leadership and the native communities, among the over 600 native communities, between aboriginal men and women, those living on reserve and off reserve, among Indians, Inuit and Metis, and between generations (Canada RCAP 1996).

As this internal process takes place, the member demanding recognition enters into discussions and negotiations with the other members of the multinational society in order to amend the identity of the society as a whole in accordance with the recognition of nationhood. This constitutes a second process of identity discussion and formation as the participants argue for and against one or more proposal after another for reconstituting the rules of recognition of their collective identity. These discussions occur before and after the referendum that triggers the duty to negotiate. In turn, they provoke an equally important, third process of identity discussion and formation exclusively among the other members of the larger society (the 'Rest of Canada' without Quebec and 'non-aboriginal Canadians' in relation to aboriginal peoples).

For example, the other provinces, which are currently recognized as roughly equal in status to Quebec (with some institutional asymmetries justified on the basis of Quebec's linguistic and cultural distinctness), are asked by some Quebec nationalists to see themselves as one nation equal in status and power to the Quebec nation, thereby decreasing their status by a factor of ten and requiring a new 'fourth' order or superstructure of Quebec–Canada institutions. This proposed identity for the rest of Canada appears to be rejected by the majority of Canadians (Kymlicka 1998d, p. 40). The former Reform Party of Canada (now the Canadian Alliance Party) proposed in response that each province be recognized as equal in status to the Quebec nation, each taking from the federal government whatever powers Quebec takes (and so decentralizing the federation), while others suggest that the other provinces only need to be *offered* these powers to meet the principle of equality. Still others propose some sort of asymmetrical relationship, based either on the principle of Quebec's distinctness (such as the proposed 'distinct society' and 'unique society' constitutional amendments) or on the principle of equality, such that whatever powers Quebec patriates from federal jurisdiction to its National Assembly the federal members of parliament from Quebec abjure the right to vote on the exercise of these powers in the federal parliament The other provinces also present specific demands for the recognition of their equality or distinctness. Citizens, minorities and aboriginal peoples within the other provinces participate in these discussions, point out the adverse affects of these proposals on their constitutional identity and relations, and demand recognition (see chapters 1, 3, 10, 13, and compare 4, 7 and 12).

Finally, these three processes of identity discussion and formation interact in complex and unpredictable ways. Agreements or disagreements in the second process of the multinational democracy as a whole, for example, have enormous transformative effects on the self-understandings of the members engaged in the other two processes. In each of the three processes, the discussions tend to become structured around the three major strategic solutions (the status quo, constitutional renewal and secession) and this works against agreement. So, for example, even if a clear majority appears to converge on, say, a form of recognition by constitutional reform, as in the Charlottetown Accord of 1992, the defenders of the status quo and the secessionists will work from opposite sides to subvert it.

3.2   Plurality and the game of mutual disclosure and acknowledgement

We can now highlight four characteristics of the free and democratic activity of struggling over the recognition of the national identity of a member of a multinational society. The activity is intersubjective, multilogical, continuous and agonic. First, the identities of the member seeking recognition and of those members who are affected and respond are intersubjective. Their identities as members are shaped, formed and reformed in the course of the activity itself. There is no identity as a nation that precedes the activity and passes unaltered through the activity. The identities of the members are articulated, acquired and supported by citizens from a first-person perspective, and defended, criticized and reformulated over the time of the life of the society and its members as the three processes of identity discussion and formation interact. Even a claim that there is an authentic, pre-existing identity based on ascriptive characteristics is itself a claim that must be made good to and supported by other members of the purported nation by means of public discussions and debates in the available institutions – from talk at the bingo hall and on the bus, to history lessons, public demonstrations, grand commissions, aboriginal council meetings and public consultations.

Second, the intersubjective activity of struggling for and against recognition is multilogical. These complex struggles are not the idealized struggles between two actors (self and other) in dialogue that have dominated their representation in theory and practice since Hegel. This form of representation misrepresents what is actually happening, as this volume amply demonstrates, and in so doing violates the first principle of mutual reciprocity or *audi alteram partem*. These are discussions among many members of various kinds – 'multilogues'. Moreover, these multilogues involve not only deliberation but various forms of reason, rhetoric and visceral behaviour: deliberation, negotiation, persuasion, information-seeking, enquiry and eristic (Walton 1998 and Connolly 1999). Finally, the discussions, negotiations and contestations take place in a variety of practices and procedures, and the legitimacy of these is itself part of the discussion (Tully 2000b).

Third, the activity is 'continuous' (SC 1998, para.150). A demand is presented, others respond, the demand is reformulated in response, others respond to this, an agreement is reached or not, and this in turn gives rise to dissent and a new demand. Unpredictability, complexity and mutability are irreducible. Any form of mutual recognition should be viewed as an experiment, open to review and reform in the future in response to legitimate demands for recognition against it, and so viewed as part of the continuous process rather than as the telos towards which the activity aims and at which it ends. This is true even in the case of secession and the aim of recognition as an independent nation-state by the international community. To achieve this form of recognition,

Quebec would have to respond to the demands for mutual recognition of the eleven first nations within Quebec (who would appeal not only to Canada's constitutional obligation to protect them but also to the international law of indigenous peoples, the English-speaking ridings which would vote 'No' (who would campaign for partition or the continuation of their present minority rights under the new constitution), the French-speaking minorities within Canada (who require protection in the new Canada), the new economic and political relationship with an independent Canada, and the conditions it would have to meet to enter into the North American Free Trade Agreement (over which Canada has a veto).

The fourth feature is the contestatory character of the activity. The multiple struggles are 'contests'. The Greek term for a contest, 'agonism', has been revived to describe this feature and I will adopt it.[3] A great deal of what is going on in struggles over recognition is not aiming at recognition so much as it is making public displays of the intolerability of the present form of recognition and displaying another form of identity (nationhood). The other members respond in kind. It is a to-and-fro activity of mutual disclosure and mutual acknowledgement. The members say to each other with their words and deeds, 'don't see us under the present humiliating or degrading identity but under this or that respectful identity'.

The mutual disclosure and acknowledgement of the contests falls short of full constitutional recognition. What is disclosed in any given contest over recognition is partial and revisable, and the form of acknowledgement and response by other members is equally partial and revisable in the future. But this is far from trivial. It is a means of discharging *ressentiment* at the present structure of recognition (which might otherwise be channelled into anti-democratic ways); displaying how a member would like to be seen by the others; and generating pride in, solidarity with, and a sense of attachment to the disclosed identity. Both Quebec and the first nations have been successful in this form of activity, taking on and displaying many of the attributes of nations in their self-presentation to their own citizens, to other members of the society, and to the international community.

When this kind of disclosure is not recognized constitutionally by the other members, it is still acknowledged by others in the very act of

---

[3] The classic analysis of the agonic dimension of political activity is F. Nietzsche's short essay, 'Homer on Competitition', in Nietzsche (1994, pp. 187–94). The most influential analyses in the twentieth century are H. Arendt, 'What is Freedom?', in Arendt (1977, pp. 143–72; 1998, pp. 175–247), and M. Foucault, 'The Subject and Power', in Foucault (1982, pp. 208–27). See, Owen (1995, pp. 139–69), and Mouffe (2000, pp. 80–107).

accepting it and responding to it with public displays of their own. Holding referenda on renewed federalism and sovereignty, electing sovereignist parties provincially and federally, and accepting and answering these disclosures of nationhood by others are examples of this phenomenon. The 'struggle' itself is an intersubjective, multilogical game of disclosure acknowledgement. Although it is not formal constitutional recognition and accommodation, it is an important achievement in its own right for all the actors involved. Mutual disclosure and acknowledgement are absolutely central, for example, to the decolonization, rebuilding and revitalization of aboriginal communities after centuries of misrecognition, internal colonization and marginalization (Alfred 1998). The public disclosure of Quebec's identity as a nation and the defiant acknowledgement of that by refusing to grant formal recognition by the other provinces has in itself generated a healthy sense of self-respect and self-esteem among Quebecers. Nietzsche and other agonic theorists suggest that disclosure and acknowledgement, even when the acknowledgement takes the form of a counter-challenge, can generate the levels of self-respect and self-esteem that recognition theorists claim can come only with formal recognition.[4] If this is true, and there is considerable evidence for it in Canada, then the recognition theory of justice and psychological stability in terms of which these struggles are standardly analysed is mistaken.

These continuous contests of mutual disclosure and acknowledgement are also ends in themselves. They are the activity of democratic freedom itself, of participation in accordance with the rules laid down by the last struggle for recognition and the challenging of these rules against the principles, values and goods of the fourth dimension of the constitution (SC 1998, paras. 68–9). Moreover, although these games are serious, they contain an important play element, characteristic of most competitive games, which helps to explain their persistence generation after generation, even when the present structure of recognition appears to be reasonable from, say, the perspective of utility.[5]

---

[4] For a leading theorist of recognition, see Honneth (1995). Even he seems to suggest that the agonism itself may engender some degree of self-respect and self-esteem without full recognition (p. 164). Nietzsche argued that an agent or group is better off (freer and healthier) if it does not achieve full recognition. In his example, liberals were free as long as they were competing for liberal constitutions, but once they achieved formal constitutional recognition they lost their free way of life. They lost the struggle in which it thrives and became complacent. This seems to overstate the case. It is enough to realise that formal and definitive recognition is not a necessary condition of self-respect and self-esteem. Nevertheless, the constitutional system must not suppress demands for change and it must be open to demands when they arise.

[5] For the play element in political contests, see Huizinga (1950).

Finally, a theoretical distinction between acknowledgement and re-cognition cannot be drawn outside the struggles themselves. For some, the acknowledgement of Quebec's distinctness under the present system of rules or the present acknowledgement of aboriginal peoples' rights to land and self-government will be sufficient for recognition. For others it will be an intolerable humiliation. Even independence – with all the limits that would be placed on Quebec's sovereignty, the lack of positive acknowledgement by some members of the international community, and the dissent within – will seem less than appropriate recognition to some. Where to draw the line is not a question of theoretical but of practical reason, by the participants from within the ongoing processes of identity formation and discussion. In yet another respect, therefore, these are not struggles for some definitive recognition but struggles over what form of acknowledgement will count as recognition.[6]

Another example of the inability to distinguish between acknowl-edgement and recognition outside of the democratic process is provided by the first nations' quest for decolonization and freedom. From 1982 to 1992 the Assembly of First Nations and many aboriginal leaders argued that formal recognition as nations with title to their land and self-government should take the form of a constitutional amendment. When this strategy failed, they took the view that constitutional amendment, while desirable, was not necessary. They argued that the recognition of aboriginal peoples as self-governing first nations is already entrenched in the constitution, in sections 25 and 35 of the Constitution Act, 1982, and that this could be made explicit through litigation and treaty (Canada RCAP 1996, vol. 2, pp. 202–12 and vol. 5, pp. 117–33). Since 1992, they have concentrated on bringing the courts and the federal and provincial governments to acknowledge that this form of recognition already exists. This process has been marked by the 1997 Supreme Court Case of *Delgamuukw* v. *British Columbia*, which recognized abori-ginal title to land, and by ten treaty negotiations which involve land claims and self-government (Persky, 1998). The federal government and several provincial governments have responded by acknowledging their inherent right to self-government and aboriginal title to land to some extent. This in turn has brought about a partial reconceptualization of the constitutional identity of Canada as a whole, yet without any formal constitutional change.

---

[6] This is also the way Charles Taylor interprets the activity of recognition, as an ongoing dialogue of negotiating reciprocal acknowledgement (Taylor 1994, p. 34).

4   **The failure to reach agreements on forms of recognition
     of nations in multinational societies**

4.1   The turn to democratic constitutionalism in theory and practice

Given the characteristics of recognition politics, two central questions
need to be addressed: who decides if a demand for recognition as a
nation or first nation is legitimate? and, what are the procedures by
which the decision is made? The answers to these two questions marks
an important change in democratic thought and practice over the last
twenty years. It is no longer assumed that the forms of recognition of
members of a constitutional democracy can be determined outside the
political process itself, by theoretical reason discovering the *a priori*
forms of universal membership (individuals, nations, corporations,
provinces and so on). Also, it is no longer assumed that a consociational
elite is capable of making the determination by some form of accommodation behind the backs of citizens. It is now widely argued in theory
and practice that the identities worthy of recognition must be worked
out and decided on by the members of the association themselves,
through the exercise of practical reason in negotiations and agreements
(Tully 2000b).

The first reason for this is the significant deepening of the commitment to democracy in both theory and practice in the societies we are
considering. In theory, *Quod omnes tangit* (what touches all must be
approved by all), one of the oldest principles of western constitutionalism, has been revived and given a variety of multilogical reformula-
tions as a principle of democratic legitimacy. Because a demand for
recognition affects most if not all members of a society, it thus requires
their approval, or the approval of representatives they trust, through
actual discussion and agreement (Tully 1995, pp. 116–82; Bellamy
1999; Laden 2001). The second reason for the turn to democratic
procedures of negotiation to resolve disputes over contested norms of
action coordination is that this is the only way the legitimate concerns
of those affected can be heard and taken into account. A demand for
recognition as a nation affects members within the nation and other
members of the larger society in complex and variegated ways. Only
those inside the multilogue can develop an awareness of the diversity
of concerns of the members and work by the exchange of reasons
towards an acceptable compromise and accommodation (Tully 1994a
and 1995, pp. 99–116).

The third and most important reason for democratic dispute resolution follows from the nature of a legitimate collective identity such as a

province, nation or first nation. It is the people themselves who must experience the present system of recognition as imposed and unjust. A clear majority must come to support a demand for recognition as a nation from a first-person perspective. Moreover, they must respond to the concerns of other members and articulate a constitutional identity for the society as a whole which all the members can support from their first-person perspectives. All this requires discussion and negotiation across the three processes of identity formation by citizens and elected representatives. The demand for recognition as a nation and as a corresponding multinational society only counts as a legitimate (and stable) demand by one member and a form of recognition by others if it can be embraced and supported in this free and democratic way. If a demand is advanced by a political elite without popular deliberation and support, and if it is recognized by another elite or unelected court without passing through democratic will formation, then it is not likely to be supported on either side. It will be experienced as imposed, as misrecognition, and the struggle for recognition will be exacerbated rather than resolved.

This reason cannot be stressed enough. It is a basis of stability in multinational societies. The three processes of identity discussion and formation are processes of *citizenization*. Individuals and minorities *become* citizens of the nation demanding recognition by participating in these processes. As a result of participating, either directly or indirectly through everyday discussions, they develop a sense of belonging to and identification with the proto-nation. They, and the members of the larger society, *become* citizens of the larger multinational society by participating in the processes of identity formation and discussion of the proposed identity of the multinational democracy. As a result, they develop a sense of belonging to and identification with this larger democracy in which they have a say over its constitutional forms of recognition. It is not a necessary condition of the development of a sense of belonging and identification with the nation and the multi-nation that the citizens fully agree with the demand or that the demand be fully recognized. It is sufficient that the processes of identity discussion and formation be open to the participation of those who agree and disagree.

Two examples will suffice. Alongside their strong sense of belonging to Canada, the members of the English-speaking minority of Quebec have developed a strong sense of belonging to and identification with Quebec society over the last forty years by virtue of their participation in the public debate over Quebec's future. This is because they have taken part in the discussions and have played a participatory role in demands for renewed federalism. The moment they are shut out of the discussions, however, as during and after the referendum of 1995, and their demands for recognition as a minority fall on deaf ears, this sense of Quebec-citizen belonging and identification dissipates, many leave the province, and the hard-line demands of those who remain increase, such as partition in the event of secession. In a similar manner, Quebecers develop a sense of belonging to and identification with Canada, alongside their strong sense of identification with Quebec, precisely when their demands are taken up in the processes of identity discussion and formation in Canada as a whole. The moment these processes of citizenization are closed, as after the referendum of 1992 and during the current federal liberal government's policy of 'freezing' the constitution, their sense of belonging to Canada decreases and their exclusive identification with Quebec increases.

4.2   The procedures for reaching agreements

The procedures by which the members of a society reach agreement on a demand for recognition are free and democratic negotiations. There are two phases of negotiation. In the first a member works up a demand for recognition as a nation and for the corresponding change in the constitutional identity of the multinational society as a fair system of social cooperation. This demand is discussed by citizens and minorities within the member (province) and by listening to and taking into account the responses of other members of the society. At some point in this process of mutual disclosure and acknowledgement, the member or members come up with what they consider to be a clear and well-supported demand for recognition. This is then formulated as a clear question for a referendum.

It is fair to say that the question will be 'clear' just insofar as it meets the two conditions of informal practical reasoning with others who disagree. First, the demand should be internally cogent. By drawing on the principles, values and goods of the society, it should present reasons why the current form of recognition is unacceptable, reasons for the proposed form of recognition as a nation, and reasons for the proposed amendments to the constitutional identity of the society as a whole so it functions as a fair system of social cooperation. Second, the demand should be formulated by taking into account and responding in some way to the legitimate concerns of other members. This second condition is required by considerations of reciprocity and there is no reason to entertain a demand that does not meet it (Govier 1998, pp. 29–97; Ryan 1999).

The first phase ends with a referendum. If the question gains a clear majority, it is clearly well-supported and the other members are under an obligation to enter into the second phase of formal negotiations. The conditions of these negotiations are dependent on the specific question. However, as the Supreme Court argues, a number of conditions will apply in most cases (SC 1998, paras. 87–98, 103–4). The first four principles will apply to the negotiations: federalism, democracy, rule of law and constitutionalism and the protection of minorities (in less diverse societies the first and last may be irrelevant). The principle that 'what affects all must be approved by all' does not entail that the final arbiter is a majority will either within the province demanding recognition or within the society as a whole. The form and conduct of the negotiations should take into account the federal character of the society in some way (depending on the anticipated effects of the demand); the principle of democracy involves elected representatives and representative institutions as well as, or instead of, the majority will of individual citizens in referenda; the rules of law that are not under dispute in the demand are relevant considerations (by means of court challenges, for example); and the minorities who may be adversely affected by the demand and who have not been properly heard in the first phase should be consulted and protected in the negotiations.

As the Supreme Court argues, none of these four principles is trump and how they are brought to bear on particular cases of reconciling diversity with unity democratically is case-specific. For example, the treaty negotiations for the recognition of land title and self-government of the Nisga'a first nation have taken place for over twenty years with the chiefs of the Nisga'a Nation and negotiators for the federal government and the provincial government of British Columbia. Third parties have been consulted during the negotiations, a Parliamentary Standing Committee toured the province with a draft agreement to consult citizens over an eighteen-month period. The negotiators then went back to the table and reached agreement on a final draft of the treaty in 1998. The treaty was then put to a referendum within the Nisga'a Nation and received a majority vote of over 60 per cent. This triggered a ratification process which involved public discussion and debate in British Columbia and Canada and then successful votes in the federal and provincial parliaments. During the ratification period two court challenges to the treaty were initiated, on the ground that it violates the rights of non-aboriginal citizens, and a number of public protests by non-aboriginal citizens were staged. If the treaty survives the court challenges, or is successfully amended in the light of the Court's ruling, then it will form a constitutionally protected recognition of the Nisga'a Nation.[7]

One could reasonably argue that the Nisga'a treaty itself and the two phases of negotiation meet the conditions we have discussed. However, the opponents of the treaty argue that there should be a referendum of all the citizens of British Columbia at the end of the process, on the ground that democracy consists in 'having a say' (Campbell 1998). However, this would put the rights of a tiny minority (the 6,000 Nisga'a) at the mercy of the will of the non-aboriginal majority. Clearly in cases like these, where the demand for recognition involves a minority, the principle of democracy requires a referendum within the minority community (to ensure that the demand is well-supported and internal dissent is expressed in the formulation of the demand), a process of public consultation, debate and lobbying of one's elected representatives, and a public debate in the parliaments followed by a vote by the elected representatives. To go further and put the treaty to a referendum would be to treat the principle of democracy as the only relevant principle, to interpret it solely as the will of the majority expressed in a referendum, and to place no weight on the principle of the protection of minorities.

In addition to these factors, there are others which ensure that any 'agreement' is always less than definitive. First, there will always be 'reasonable disagreement' over any proposed norm of recognition or set of procedures (Rawls 1996, pp. 54–8; Bellamy 1999, pp. 91–140). Further, negotiations take place in real time and under real constraints. Not all members are heard and not all compromises are acceptable to all. The relations of power codified in the prevailing system of misrecognition structure the discussions and negotiations in unequal and unfair ways (this is one of the reasons for the demand in the first place). In some cases, a representative body will not unreasonably bring the negotiations to a close. At some point in these complex processes of democratic negotiation, as Chantal Mouffe argues, a *decision* has to be taken in the context of disagreement among democratic adversaries (Mouffe 2000, pp. 80–107). The dissenters may turn out on reconsideration to have been right after all. Moreover, any agreement can be interpreted in different ways, and this gives rise to disagreements over the institutions that are supposed to implement the agreement. As citizens experiment with the implementation of the agreement over time, conflicts will develop in practice that were not foreseen in the

---

[7] The details can be found in the text of the Final Agreement (Government of Canada, Government of British Columbia, and the Nisga'a Nation 1998b). For background, see C. Harris (ed.), *BC Studies*, 120 (Winter 1998–9).

agreement. In addition, the change in identities brought about by interacting in the new relations of mutual recognition will itself alter the participants' view of the agreement. By this time a new generation will enter into the three processes of identity formation and discussion and bring generational differences with them (Tully 1999b).

Taking all these factors of 'plurality' into account, there is no definitive and permanent form of mutual recognition of a nation in a multinational society to which all the members could reasonably agree by these procedures or any others. Any form of mutual recognition, within the society or by secession, will always involve reasonable disagreement and varying degrees of the injustice of misrecognition. The rules of recognition will always be unacceptable for some and dissent will be 'inevitable', as the Supreme Court succinctly puts it. Consequently, it is not to consensus on forms of recognition that we should look to find justice and stability in multinational societies, as current theories and practices incline us to do. Instead we should aim to place the free and self-determining activity of struggling over recognition within a continuous process of discussion.

The way through the current impasse of failures to reach agreement on recognition in multinational societies is to realize that such societies will be reasonably just and stable just insofar as the present constitutional identity is well supported in the three, free and democratic processes of identity discussion and formation (in which citizens develop a sense of identity and belonging to their federated unit and to the society as a whole) and, most important of all, insofar as the present constitutional identity is open to the exercise of the democratic rights of the members to challenge, discuss and amend it over time.

5   Conclusion: freedom as self-determination in multinational democracies

To summarize, one condition that renders a democracy free is that the rules by which the members recognize each other and govern their cooperation (dimensions 1 and 2) are negotiated, implemented, and amended by the members themselves in accordance with procedures and values that are also open to amendment (dimensions 3 and 4). In the words of the Supreme Court, a free and democratic society rests on continuous processes of discussion and evolution (cp. Shaw 2000 for the European Union). Hence, the members are always free to enter into negotiations over the reconciliation of the recognition and accommodation of diversity with the requirements of unity and stability in various sorts of political, legal and constitutional practices. These struggles are understood as enduring and valuable features because, for reasons of plurality, there is no definitive recognition of the diverse members. The very suggestion that a particular reconciliation is definitive (in theory or practice) is viewed with suspicion, as the voice of anti-democratic domination.

Due to the fact of reasonable disagreement, in any particular case of reconciliation there will be those who agree and those who disagree. Those who disagree will continue to identify with the democratic society, rather than become alienated and seek to secede, for two main reasons. First, in virtue of direct and indirect participation in the struggle of reciprocal disclosure and acknowledgement, they affect the outcome to some extent and they come to appreciate the reasons on the other side and the limits of their own. That is, they realize that there is no absolutely decisive, knock-out argument on either side. Even justices of the Supreme Court disagree on fundamental questions (SC 1998, para. 57). Yet, decisions must be taken. Dissent is inevitable. In addition to this democratic ethos the members acquire through engagment in such struggles, the dissenters remain attached to their democratic society because they know that the reconciliation they lost is in turn open to contestation, negotiation, and amendment in the future. While the dissenters do not see the reconciliation as 'just' from their point of view (this disagreement remains), for these two reasons they see it as 'legitimate' in the democratic sense. Like the heroes who, as the second day of battle breaks, welcome the dawn and their good fortune, they too assess their gains and losses, and begin again.

In multinational democracies, this condition of freedom is met if the nations or peoples have the right to initiate constitutional change and the other members have the duty to enter into negotiations over how to reconcile a well-supported demand with the requirements of unity. If peoples in multinational democracies do not have this right and duty, they are unfree because the background constitution is not open to democratic discussion and amendment. It is a structure of domination, a 'straitjacket' (SC 1998, para. 150). Moreover, the right and duty must be institutionalized in fair procedures of amendment that are flexible and effective. The members are not free if they have the right and duty in the written constitution yet are unable to exercise it in practice due to arbitrary constraints or unfair conditions which are all but impossible to fulfil in the real world. The members must not only possess the right and duty but also be able to exercise it in practice.[8] An effective right of

---

[8] To meet this condition the Supreme Court presents a simplified amending procedure of negotiations between representatives of the two majorities (Quebec and Canada as a whole). This bypasses the current, labyrinthine amending formulae yet still conforms to

a nation to initiate constitutional change concerning any powers of self-government (including secession) and the recognition of its distinct identity, correlated with the duty to negotiate, is equivalent to, or a domestic constitutional form of, the universal right of self-determination of a people in international law. Accordingly, a multinational democracy will be free and legitimate insofar as it ensures that its constituent nations possess and can exercise the right of self-determination of peoples in some appropriate form or other. This is the final argument of the Supreme Court.

The Court does not find it necessary to determine if Quebec constitutes a 'people', or if there are other 'peoples' in Quebec and Canada (that is: indigenous peoples), in order to address the question referred to it (SC 1998, paras. 109–10, 125).[9] The Court goes on to argue that Quebec, whether or not it constitutes a people or peoples, enjoys the right of self-determination under the Canadian constitution (SC 1998, paras. 109–39, 136, summary at 154). Canada and other multinational democracies are bound by the *Charter of the United Nations* and other documents of international law that affirm the full right of self-determination of peoples (SC paras. 113–21). This applies to peoples within multi-peoples or multinational states, not just to single-nation states (para. 124). That is, if there are peoples or nations in the constitutional association, then the constitution of multinational democracies must find a way to reconcile their exercise of the right of self-determination with the requirements of unity and with the other forms of diversity in the association. International law holds that the right of self-determination of people or peoples should be exercised normally within existing constitutional states. This is called the right of 'internal self-determination'. It consists in 'a people's pursuit of its political, economic, social and cultural development within the framework of an existing state' (SC 1998, para.126). Apart from oppressed and colonial peoples, it is only if a people is blocked from the 'meaningful exercise' of their right of internal self-determination that they are said to have a right to 'external self-determination': that is, to activate their right to secede (SC 1998, para. 134).

The 'meaningful exercise' of the right of internal self-determination

the four principles (SC 1998, paras. 84, 88, 93, 94; Greschner 1998; Tully, 2000a, pp. 28–9).

[9] The question is whether or not Quebec has the right to secede from Canada unilaterally. The Court answers that Quebec does not have the right to secede unilaterally because it can effectively exercise the right of self-determination internally or externally by means of bilateral constitutional negotiations. For the role of indigenous peoples in such negotiations, see Royal Commission on Aboriginal Peoples 1995, Grand Council of the Crees 1998 and Joffe 1999.

consists in exercising the powers of 'political, economic, social and cultural development' (SC 1998, para. 136). The meaningful exercise of the right of internal self-determination consists not only in the exercise of certain powers of political, economic, social and cultural development, by means of institutions of self-government, protection of distinctness, and federalism, but also in having a democratic say over what those powers are, how they relate to and are recognized by the other members of the multinational association, and to be able to amend them from time to time. If this were not the case, then the people would have a certain distribution of powers and recognition imposed on them by the constitution of the larger society, beyond their determination. The constitution would be a straitjacket and they would not be self-determining. They would be unfree according to the three democratic traditions mentioned earlier (section 2.1). The effective right to initiate constitutional change is, therefore, an essential feature of the meaningful exercise of the right of internal self-determination. As we have seen, this feature of internal self-determination is the central thesis of the Supreme Court's judgement in the Reference case. The Court can conclude that Quebec enjoys the meaningful exercise of the right of internal self-determination, then, because the right and duty are shown to exist in the arrangements and principles of the constitution, specifically in the Court's explication of the principles informing the Constitution Act, 1982, and to be applicable to any peoples (SC 1998, paras. 69, 136, 137; Tully 2000a, pp. 29–31).

The same analysis applies to indigenous peoples. They understand themselves as peoples with the right of self-determination under international law and there is a large body of scholarship that supports their claim (Canada RCAP 1996, vol. 2, pp. 163–244; Tully 2000c). A draft law on the right of self-determination of indigenous peoples is working its way through the committees of the United Nations (Venne 1998). However, at present they are not recognized in the Canadian constitution as peoples with the right of self-determination. Neither their right of self-government nor their right to initiate constitutional change is explicitly recognized in the written constitution. They are bound by a constitution that has been imposed on them and so are unfree as peoples. Their self-determination is blocked in two ways: they are constrained from the meaningful exercise of their right of internal self-determination and they are 'colonized' by the Canadian state. Yet, if aboriginal peoples are 'peoples', as the *Royal Commission on Aboriginal Peoples* concludes, then Canada is bound to recognize their right of self-determination internally and reconcile this with the requirements of unity (or else indigenous peoples have the right to initiate their right of external self-determination) (Borrows 2000). This would then enable indigenous peoples of Canada to exercise their right to initiate constitutional change effectively as they develop the capacity to share and exercise powers of self-government over their traditional territories and negotiate treaties of cooperation with provincial and federal governments (Tully 2000d).

A multinational democracy is free and legitimate, therefore, when its constitution treats the constituent nations as peoples with the right of self-determination in some appropriate constitutional form, such as the right to initiate constitutional change. This enables them to engage freely in negotiations of reciprocal disclosure and acknowledgement as they develop and amend their modes of recognition and cooperation, in conjunction with the fair reconciliation of other forms of diversity. One way in which the current Canadian constitutional identity could be brought in conformity with this enlightened argument of the Supreme Court is by the Assembly of First Nations and the Government of Quebec acting accordingly: that is, initiating separate referenda and negotiations for the explicit constitutional recognition of Quebec and first nations as peoples with the right of self-determination.

The Canadian response to struggles over recognition can be useful to other multinational democracies studied in this volume. Of course, the differences in history, legal and political traditions, and institutions have to be taken into account. This means that, while there is a universal right of self-determination that applies to all peoples, the formulation, institutionalization, and exercise of the right is always contextual. Hence the importance of the chapters that follow.

Part I

Justice and stability in multinational democracies

The first part deals with interrelations between considerations of justice and stability in theory and practice. In the wide-ranging historical and comparative first chapter, 'So Many Nations, So Few States: Territory and Nationalism in the Global Era', Michael Keating introduces the major themes. He argues that recognition and accommodation in multi-national societies are possible if we set aside the norm of a uniform nation-state. He points out that the nation-state has only existed since the nineteenth century, and as such is only one possible way of dealing with nationality issues. Through a rereading of the histories of multi-national societies, Keating demonstrates that there are traditions and practices in multinational societies which can provide a guide to present problems. These traditions and practices however, tend to compete against centralizing and unitarian doctrines. Turning to the multi-national states of the United Kingdom, Spain, Belgium and Canada, Keating argues that the states' ability to accommodate minority national groups has diminished, while the demands of these groups has in-creased. While some argue that this represents a decline of the state, Keating sides with others who argue that this situation actually repre-sents a need to renegotiate the terms of multinational unions. Such renegotiations could draw upon historic traditions of pragmatism and accommodation as well as a rethinking of sovereignty and the distribu-tion of powers.

In chapter 2, Dominique Arel seeks to identify stable institutional solutions to the conflicts in multinational societies over language and culture that are driven by a fear of, and resistance to, minority status. One side views cultural heterogeneity as a disadvantage for democratic stability, while the optimistic side believes in the benefits of cultural heterogeneity. Arel situates consociational democracy in this debate on stability within culturally divided plural societies, suggesting however that the institutionalization of differences involved in consociationalism can at times aggravate the conflict between groups. Arel also discusses the concept of the 'civic' state. Despite the differences between cultural community/nation and political community/nation, the author argues that all states are based on the political primacy of one culture. Culture is integral to the functioning of the state. Therefore, nationalist movements tend to differ in terms of their inclusiveness; but even the most inclusive ones are based on the primacy of one culture. The French and American states are called civic because the primacy of one culture has been established via a non-conflictual process, the author argues, while similar attempts have failed in Russia and Hungary. Consequently, Arel makes the point that the label of 'civic' depends on the success of the culturally hegemonic groups and the lack of challenge from minorities. At another level, Arel discusses group status and the primacy of languages. He argues that the process of political recognition of a language is related to its social status and that according a higher status to a language is less likely to lead to conflicts.

In chapter 3, 'Justice and Stability in Multinational Societies', Wayne Norman assesses the considerable obstacles to reconciling both justice and stability. He argues that the rival demands of justice and stability make compromises difficult to reach. More specifically, he shows that there is little room for a trade-off between justice and stability. Nonetheless he points out that the two concepts are interrelated despite the tensions between them. Many governmental practices that have traditionally been seen as stability-building measures (i.e. elite bureaucracies, nation-building processes and the like) are now seen as inconsistent with the notion of liberal justice. At the same time, however, the very notion of liberal justice has been enlarged to include the recognition of cultural diversity. A central problem for Norman is the contested nature of the concept of justice, i.e., the impossibility of reaching a consensus on its very meaning. Norman argues that justice presupposes the existence of a community, but at the same time a shared conception of justice is said to be a precondition of political community. Different conceptions of justice may conflict and lead to instability. Norman uses this framework to analyse various scenarios aimed at settling the conflictual relations between Quebec and Canada. He concludes that disagreements are often not about the degree of trade-off between justice and stability, but the very concepts of justice and stability themselves. Proposed solutions are often couched in terms of justice, while opposition to such proposals tends to emphasize stability.

In chapter 4, Ferran Requejo seeks to answer the difficult normative and institutional problem of asymmetry among members of multinational societies with reference to the case of Spain (see also chapter 13). The discussion in the first section of 'Political Liberalism in Multinational States: the Legitimacy of Plural and Asymmetrical Federalism' centres on 'political liberalism' and its relationship with the pluralism of national identities. The approaches of Rawls, Habermas, Kant and Hegel to liberal universalism and pluralism are examined and the Spanish federalization process is set within this broader framework. Requejo clarifies the association of symmetry with uniform federalism and asymmetry with multinational federalism. The implication of this argument is that in a homogeneous state, uniformity and symmetry enhance equality and citizen participation. And, in following a similar logic, asymmetrical arrangements are said to be able to settle questions of national identity better than symmetrical solutions. Requejo situates Spanish federalism within three different processes: democratization, the creation of a welfare state and European integration. He argues that one of the biggest design faults of the Spanish constitution is that it attempts to tackle the decentralization of the state and the articulation of its multinationality simultaneously.

So many nations, so few states: territory and nationalism in the global era[1]

Michael Keating

Introduction

Debates about the relationship of the state to the nation go back to the last century. The contemporary revival of nationalism and the emergence of new states, together with continental integration, have kindled new interest in the question. There is general agreement that there are more potential nations than possible states, yet the search for general principles which could define nationality and the conditions under which nationalities could qualify for self-government has proved inconclusive. Instead it is a matter of reconciling competing claims for nationality and the rights that go with it. Approaches to the normative questions of how to reconcile state and nation and the right of self-determination take two forms. Political theorists start from general principles and, using the language of rights, seek to determine which groups can have what rights to self-government under what conditions. The problem here is that the cases are too varied to fit into procrustean categories; that the language of rights lends itself poorly to compromise and bargaining, the essence of politics; and that very often the question of power is ignored. Specifically, once we take the issue out of the framework of the state (or existing legally entrenched supranational institutions) there is no regulator to legitimate or enforce rights. The second approach is that of conflict studies, which starts with the problem of competing claims and seeks to convert them into bargainable stakes. The problem here is that often ethical principles disappear altogether in the search for solutions that can work. Consociationalism, for example, has been widely criticized for stifling democratic participation, freezing ethnic boundaries, and placing excessive power in the hands of group leaders. So the principles of justice and stability may point in different directions. Too rarely are general norms placed in specific political, cultural and historical contexts (Requejo 1998c). This

---

[1] I am grateful to Richard Vernon, Dominique Arel and Damian Tambini for comments on earlier versions of this chapter.

chapter takes an empirical and comparative approach, examining the ways in which nationality and the state have been conceived in the four multinational states of the United Kingdom, Spain, Belgium and Canada, and the ways in which multinational polities have been managed. The findings are that the problem is less common in practice than in theory and that nationality claims are not arbitrary but emerge from a long process of political mobilization. If one puts aside the idea that the uniform state, an intellectual construction, should be the norm, then a reading of history and practice based on multinational accommodation is possible. It then looks at ways in which changing conceptions of the state and political order could help reconcile state and nation in the present era. Managing the nationality question then becomes part of normal politics, rather than a search for a definitive solution in accordance with fixed categories.

Nationalism and the state

It has often been claimed that nationalism is a form of zero-sum politics, as the claims it makes, to sovereignty and statehood, are non-divisible and non-negotiable. Closely related is the claim that nationalism is a product of modernization and confined to the modern era. Hobsbawm (1990) claims that the nation 'is a social entity only in so far as it relates to a certain kind of modern territorial state, the "nation-state", and it is pointless to discus nation and nationality except insofar as they relate to it'. Breuilly (1994, p. 2) does not go so far, merely insisting that the 'nation must be as independent as possible. This usually requires at least the attainment of political sovereignty'. Both locate nationalism in the era of nation-states and thus see it as an essentially modern phenomenon. To speak of nationalism in previous eras, they insist, would be an anachronism. On the other side are nationalist historiographers, who feel obliged to claim ancient roots for the nation and attribute to it a constant striving for statehood.[2]

Attempts to pin down nationality, nationhood and sovereignty in this way invariably come up against the fluid and indeterminate nature of these concepts and their historical malleability. While Breuilly (1994) is no doubt right to warn that 'a vague definition of nationalism which includes any statements about nations or ethnic groups would create an

---

[2] The Scottish Declaration of Abroach (1320) claims that the Scots are a lost tribe of Israel, arriving in Scotland after a transit through Spain. Sabino Arana, founder of modern Basque nationalism, had to invent a history of independent statehood to bolster claims advanced at the end of the nineteenth century. Belgian nationalists in the nineteenth century tried to claim ancient roots for their nation, just as Flemish nationalists did in their turn.

impossibly large subject', there is an equally serious danger of trapping ourselves in excessively rigid categories and so inventing conundrums which, by definition, have no solution. There are too many examples of things that look like nationalism in earlier ages to define it simply as the product of modernity, though it has taken distinct forms in the modern era. As for linking nationalism to the quest for statehood, this raises two objections. There are many movements which describe themselves and are described as nationalist in the present day which do not make such claims. Whenever this point is made, somebody counters that such nationalists are cunningly disguising their long-term ambitions behind short-term apparently moderate demands. This is an example of the tendency to ignore the evidence where it does not fit the theory or assumptions – nationalism is defined by the desire for one's own state so, in a circular manner, it is reasoned that nationalists must want their own state. Yet many scholars have now abandoned the search for a state as a necessary and defining feature of nationalism.[3] Secondly, the ideas of sovereignty and statehood themselves are increasingly recognized as problematic and changing. If we recognize that neither nationalism nor sovereignty is an absolute and that both can change and evolve over time, and that the nation-state as it has existed since the nineteenth century is merely one way of doing this, then we open up a large array of possibilities for managing nationality issues.

Some authors take a very broad view of nationality, equating it with the ethnic group, although, as Connor (1978) shows, this leaves us with an almost infinite number of nations. Even leaving aside the fact that ethnicity itself is almost impossible to define, it is clear that it is not always equivalent to nationality. Most observers have now accepted this distinction (Miller 1995; Keating 1996a), although there is still argument about the ethnic component in nationality (Smith 1986). Beyond that, however, we get into serious difficulty. Miller (1995) recognizes that the Scots are not just an ethnic group (in fact they are ethnically rather heterogeneous), but draws attention to the difficulty of calling them a nation, since there is also a British nation. Yet Scotland is one of the oldest nations of Europe and its nationality is as close as we can perhaps get to a 'sociological reality'.[4] At a meeting in Ottawa in 1998, agreement was reached on the proposition that Quebec is a nation, but almost came unstuck on the insistence by some of the Québécois

[3] Anthony Smith includes it in Smith (1971) but abandons it in later writings.
[4] Greenfeld (1992) claims that England, not Britain, was the earliest nation; Scotland has a claim to being not far behind. Colley (1992) argues that a British nation was created in the eighteenth century, but I would argue that the process was not completed until the twentieth, with the two world wars and the welfare state.

participants that it followed from this that Canada was not a nation. It does seem that the definition and content of nationality differ from one case to another, with some conceptions of it being more exclusive than others. So we need a category of nationality which is separate from that of the state-nation, but more than a mere cultural category, one that is broad enough to cover the diversity of cases, without being excessively wide. This is the category of the stateless nation – but what is this?

Kymlicka (1995) tries to separate ethnic group identity from nationality and provide a general basis for self-government claims by distinguishing between immigrants and national minorities, whose territory has been incorporated into a wider state, arguing that we should recognize the self-governing rights of the latter. This does help us limit the implications of recognizing self-government and allows for an argument which is historically rooted. It does not, however, travel well beyond North America or back in time. In Europe just about every ethnic and national group can be considered either immigrants or natives, depending on what the cut-off date is and who is doing the defining. The Normans came to Ireland with Strongbow in 1159 as settlers, although they assimilated within a couple of hundred years and no one considers them a separate group now. Irish Protestants, who arrived in the early seventeenth century, on the other hand, are a clearly distinct group but it is not clear whether they would be considered immigrants or natives. Scottish Catholics descended from Irish immigrants have until the last generation been a distinct community and maintained their own social institutions, but have now assimilated into the Scottish nation, sharing in the demand for a special place within the British state. Such settler groups existed widely around the fringes of Europe in the middle ages and their experiences of assimilation differ greatly.[5] The German diaspora across central and eastern Europe has sometimes made irredentist claims, sometimes made claims for self-government, sometimes assimilated, and sometimes retained the option of returning to the motherland which the law, until recently, kept very open. Prussia, often regarded as the heartland of German nationalism, was originally a German settlement among the Slavs. Kosovo, whose Albanians claim the right of self-determination, is regarded by Serb nationalists as their homeland. Across central Europe generally, the mixing of peoples, and individual and collective migrations make it impossible to distinguish between indigenous peoples and incomers, or between settlers and individual migrants. Matters are even more complicated in places where people can invent or reinvent ancient territorial

---

[5] For example, the Germans had distinct rights in the Baltic and central Europe; the Irish and Norman/English had different rights in Ireland.

identities, as in 'Padania' or Silesia. Nationality and rights claims on the West Bank of the Jordan pit the rival claims of Arabs, who have been there for some one and a half millennia, against those of Jews, who were dispossessed two millennia ago. It is not just in the past that groups have redefined their status and their demands. As we will see, nation-building and community-building projects are going on at present, giving rise to new types of demand. These may conjure up myths of a golden age of past self-government but they are no more than myths, that is, doctrines which may be true or false but whose power is quite independent of whether they are true or false.

If we treat the question of what is a nation as an empirical rather than a theoretical one, there is an infinity of answers. If it were merely a matter of cultural differences, we would hardly need the concept (except perhaps in the ancient sense of *natio*). Nationality involves more than this, but is a highly charged concept and cannot be defined descriptively, since it is essentially a series of normative claims. One such claim is that to self-determination. This does not mean, as often assumed, an automatic right to secession. Like other rights claims, it competes with those of other groups and individuals and so neither those making the claim nor those recognizing it have logically to believe that its expression and realization are unlimited. It may be no more than the right freely to negotiate one's position in a wider institutional order. Nationality claims are also essentially territorial. In medieval Europe, groups in ethnically mixed regions often had differentiated rights (Bartlett 1993) which tended later to disappear or be transmuted into territorial rights or differentiated systems of territorial government. In France, these survived until the Revolution (Braudel 1986) and in other parts of Europe lasted much longer. As we will see, these systems have remained part of the political practice of our four states. Finally, nationality claims are general in scope, presenting the nation as a broad system of social regulation or 'global society' rather than a fragment of a wider society, as is the case with ethnic or cultural particularism.

One way to advance these claims is by constituting an independent state, enjoying external sovereignty, with territorially defined boundaries and encompassing a set of governing institutions and civil society. There are still those, in countries like France, who can see the nation only in this way.[6] Modernization theorists, from Durkheim on, have generally insisted that the advance of the modern state, together with industrialization and the market economy, would in turn erode territorial differences. Integration theorists like Deutsch (1966) continued the argument

[6] For the French translation of my book, *Nations against the State*, the title had to be changed on the grounds that the distinction was meaningless in the French language.

in the postwar era. More recently, in a revamped version of modernization theory, some observers see the transformation of the state heralding
the end of territory (Badie 1995), as political identities are multiple and
rooted in groups whose spatial parameters may range from the very local
to the global. Others disagree, arguing that the management of plurality,
whether through consociational mechanisms at the centre, through
federal accommodation, or through territorial management, has been a
constant task of the modern state (Keating 1988; 1998a). In the present
era, the context has changed but the essence of the task has not.

If territorial management simply involved reconciling the competing
claims of existing units of people who had always been 'there', it would
be difficult enough. In fact, nationality is a dynamic concept; 'nations'
are created, reinvented and transformed all the time. In the late twentieth century, another process of restructuring is taking place as the
transformation of the state has weakened its capacity for territorial and
social integration. At the same time, we are seeing a reterritorialization
of politics, a process traceable to functional, political and normative
reasons. On the functional plane, in a global era, the process of
economic change has become territorially differentiated and there is a
substantial literature on the new regional development paradigm in
which qualities linked to the territory itself become a factor in the
productive process (Storper 1995; Dunford and Kafkalas 1992; Scott
1998). Cultural and linguistic policies, even in the age of mass communication, are increasingly territorialized. Politically, territory remains
the principal basis for mobilization, and there is an increased emphasis
on territorial, as opposed to sectoral, interests as the basis for political
competition. Normatively, territory remains the basis for most systems
of accountability and political representation. It has the advantage of
being inclusive and permitting civic equality among the inhabitants of a
given physical space and this accords with modern liberal democratic
principles (although the question of where the boundary is drawn is
crucial). It is this territorialization, or reterritorialization, of politics that,
along with historic experience, is at the base of nationality claims, since
a nationality is distinguished from an ethnic group, *inter alia*, by its
territorial basis or homeland. These are rarely invented from nothing,[7]
but usually follow existing cultural, political and territorial fault lines, or
at least use historical materials in forging their project. There are widely

---

[7] The nearest case to a movement of territorial contestation arising merely from the crisis
of the state in the context of internationalization is the Italian *Lega Nord*, but even this
has had to mobilize existing, usually very local, networks as part of its project to create
Padania. See Biorcio (1997). Like other ethno-nationalist movements, it has created its
own history as, in the words of a sympathetic account, 'the oldest community in Europe'
(Oneto 1997).

diverging interpretations of this phenomenon. For some, it is a case of reversion to 'tribalism', a premodern political identity based on affective group ties in contradiction to the modern or Enlightenment project of civil society. Others sees it as part of the condition of postmodernism, in which the oppressive structures of the centralizing state and capitalism, as well as forced and alienating individualism, are rejected in the name of more authentic group identities and values. Both of these interpretations are brought into question by the fact that, across western industrialized societies at least, values are in fact converging, at the same time as political behaviour is showing more territorial divergence (Keating 1998a). It is not necessary, and often not the case, that national minorities or minority nations espouse different values in order to have legitimate claims (McCrone 1992; Norman 1995). This brings us to a third interpretation, which sees the reconstruction of territory as part of the condition of modernity, insisting that neither modernity, nor the Enlightenment nor liberal democracy are necessarily tied to the form of the nineteenth-century nation-state (Keating 1996a). Within liberal democracies, minority nationalist movements can therefore often claim precisely the same kind of democratic and liberal legitimation as the larger nations within which they are presently contained. In this way we can separate the claims of national self-determination from the plethora of particularistic claims made for policy differentiation by cultural groups.[8]

Yet paradoxically, this very process may make accommodation more difficult than if we were merely talking about cultural or value differences, which could be accommodated with policy differentiation. Instead, we are seeing nation-like claims to general powers of social regulation and disputes over the constitution of the public domain within which political argument takes place. This is the basis of the stateless nation, a phenomenon usually rooted in old cultural or institutional materials but reforged as a sphere of action in the conditions of late modernity. Some Quebec intellectuals have argued that, given the incompatible nation-building processes in Quebec and the rest of Canada, the only option is secession (Langlois 1991a,b; Gagnon and Rocher 1992a; Laforest 1992b). Miller (1995) comes close to the same argument, but recognizes the problem with territorialization, that however you draw the boundaries, there will always be minorities left on the wrong side. The new dispensation is producing not a new, neatly defined set of national categories, but a complex order in which categories and identities overlap. Another way of putting it is that, in

---

[8] I am evading here the question of the native peoples of North America, a difficult question which I have not yet thought through.

places like Scotland and Quebec, there is a whole range of attitudes, from those who consider themselves exclusively Scottish or Québécois, to those (very few in number) who consider themselves exclusively British or Canadian. In between are a diminishing number who consider themselves Canadian or British, and Québécois or Scottish as a subset of this; and a growing number who consider themselves primarily Scottish or Québécois, with Britain and Canada seen more as instrumental identities than as primary ties. These are all territorially based national identities. They may be nested, in which case the problem is less acute, and can be accommodated through federal arrangements. They may compete, in which case there is a potential for conflict; or they may coexist. There is no way in which all of these groups can have their precise identities written into a constitutional document, but I would argue that there is no reason why, politically, they cannot coexist.

To return to an earlier point, very often this discussion is framed by an abstract model of the state in which unity and uniformity are assumed to be the norm and any deviation or distinctive treatment must be justified by reference to some universal and generalizable principle. Yet this does not correspond to political practice, even in the archetypal unitary state of France, still less so in multinational states.[9] My argument is that one reading of the history and constitutional practice of multinational states reveals traditions and practices of national-territorial accommodation which can provide a guide to the present, but which compete with centralizing and unitarian doctrines. Territorial management is a form of normal politics, found in almost all states, and not a temporary phase, to be overcome by a definitive constitutional settlement, allowing 'normal' politics to resume. In the final section, I argue that the new state dispensation opens up yet more such possibilities for this sort of politics.

Four states which illustrate this are the multinational states of the United Kingdom, Spain, Belgium and Canada. Here the state's capacity for accommodation has diminished, while the demands of the minority component nationalities have increased. From one perspective, this is seen as a crisis of the state, a reversal of trends to modernity, equality and universal values. From another perspective, however, it appears as a need to renegotiate the terms of a multinational union, drawing both on historic traditions of pactism and accommodation, and on the opportunities provided by the new state order to rethink sovereignty and the

---

[9] This is analogous to the assumption of many liberals that the atomized individual is both logically and historically prior to society and that therefore society needs a specific justification and explanation. As Ferguson (1767/1966) long ago pointed out, this is an intellectual construction that has no basis in human historical experience.

distribution of powers. Neither perspective provides any easy answers, but I will argue that the latter perspective at least provides a framework in which the issues can be addressed.

Models of the state

Rokkan and Urwin (1983) distinguish four models of the territorial state. The *unitary state* is built around one centre, with uniformity of institutions and policies. The *union state* has one centre of authority, but recognizes historic rights and infrastructures in various places. *Mechanical federalism* involves the division of the whole territory into federal units, with a single centre. *Organic federalism* is constructed from below, by distinct territories coming together, while retaining their own distinctive structures and severely limiting central control. So France is seen as a unitary state, while the UK and Spain are union states. Switzerland is an organic federation while Germany is a mechanical one. These distinctions are very important but for our purposes the key difference is between the unitary and mechanical federal models on the one hand, and the union and organic federal models on the other. In the former there is uniformity in institutions and a single focus of national identity, while in the latter there is variation, asymmetry and competing and overlapping foci of national identity. Within the union state, various parts are bearers of historic rights to self-regulation (Herrero de Miñon 1998), although these rights may be enshrined in constitutional law or merely be recognized by convention. Such historic rights have often been dismissed as irrelevant since the circumstances have changed since their enactment; as archaic, since they were enshrined in institutions that have little place in a democracy; or as reactionary since they represented privilege at a certain point in time and are incompatible with liberal equality. All these criticizms could be levelled at the nation-state itself, and the only people secure against them would be exponents of world government. So they perhaps reflect more the standpoint of the critics than any universal principles; and just as the nation-state itself, so historic rights can develop and democratize without losing their legitimating power. If we accept this idea, then mechanisms to recognize the rights and demands of specific territories can be justified. The state can be conceptualized as a pact, in which principles of territorial power need to be negotiated rather than imposed unilaterally. It is true that the pact in question is often implicit if not mythical but, once again, this applies to most forms of political authority, not least the nation-state. The history of our four states has lent itself to both unitary/mechanical federal and union/organic federal interpretations and it is precisely here that the problem of national accommodation lies.

The United Kingdom was created in stages, starting with the Act of Union with Wales in 1536, through the Union of the Crowns of England and Scotland in 1603, to the Union of the Parliaments in 1707 and the Union with Ireland in 1800. The unitary state interpretation of this process is associated with the Conservative constitutionalist A.V. Dicey, who argued that, the English Parliament having established the principle of parliamentary supremacy in the sixteenth century, the successive parliaments created through the unions were also supreme (Dicey 1912; Dicey and Rait 1920). Unionists do not deny the multinational nature of the UK. One the contrary, they stress this as an argument against home rule. Former Prime Minister John Major (1992), in his response to Scottish constitutional demands, conceded that 'no nation can be kept in a union against its will'; and opponents of Irish home rule in the nineteenth century and of Scottish home rule in the twentieth have usually given independence as their second preferred option after the unitary state. They therefore have drawn the conclusion that any concession of self-government to the constituent nations would be a repudiation of the union since the constituent nations would reassume sovereign rights and, sovereignty being indivisible, this would lead to separation (Dicey 1912; Wilson 1970). On the other hand, Liberal and Labour governments which have brought forth home rule measures have argued that moderate concessions would satisfy national concerns in the periphery, but at the same time insisted that home rule would not in any way diminish the sovereignty of parliament. So Gladstone (1886) was at pains to distinguish Irish Home Rule from a repeal of the Union as favoured earlier by Daniel O'Connell since, while neither would create a separate state, the latter would recognize sovereignty as lying in Ireland. Similarly, the Labour Party's Scottish devolution proposals of the 1970s and the 1990s have been accompanied by protestations that the sovereignty of parliament would be unaffected.

The competing interpretation is that the Union is a pact negotiated among nations. This is on weakest ground as concerns Wales, which was never an independent state and was legally incorporated into England at an early stage. It is on much stronger ground in the case of Scotland since the Acts of Union were negotiated voluntarily and included provisions of basic law. Both English and Scottish parliaments were abolished[10] in favour of a new parliament of Great Britain and, since the Scottish Parliament had never established the principle of absolute

---

[10] Scottish nationalists will insist that the Scottish Parliament was actually only prorogued. There was some talk of recalling it after the 1992 General Election.

sovereignty, it is difficult to see how it could have brought this into the new institution. There is a legal judgement upholding this view, *McCormick vs. Lord Advocate* 1953 (Mitchell 1996)[11] and the Scottish constitutional Convention of the 1980s and 1990s explicitly asserted the sovereignty of the Scottish people and its rights to negotiate its own constitutional settlement (CSA 1988).[12] Interestingly, the Labour Party signed onto this, blissfully unconcerned that its insistence elsewhere on Westminster sovereignty was in contradiction. The current Scottish devolution takes the form of an act of the Westminster Parliament, which in principle could be repealed at any time and there is a clause in the Scotland Act explicitly saying that the Acts of Union shall not be superior law above it. Yet, in contrast to the situation in the 1970s, there has been more willingness to accept a made-in-Scotland input through the Scottish constitutional Convention. There was a similar argument about Ireland in the nineteenth century. Unionists argued that the old Irish Parliament was not sovereign since, under Poynings' Law (1494), all its acts had to be ratified by the English Parliament. Nationalists insisted that Poynings was a law imposed by the Irish Parliament on itself and in any case had been repealed during 'Grattan's Parliament' in the late eighteenth century.[13] In the case of Northern Ireland, the sovereignty principle has come very close to being overturned altogether. Between 1937 and 1997 both the UK and the Republic of Ireland claimed sovereignty over Northern Ireland. Now under the terms of the Stormont accords, both have accepted that Northern Ireland, as a unit, has a right to self-determination and will decide freely to which state it wants to belong, with both states pledged to respect this choice. This follows general British weariness with the issue and earlier declarations that Britain had no selfish economic or political stake in Northern Ireland, a position far in advance of any that it has taken with regard to Scotland.

[11] The case concerned the Royal Titles Act, which gave the monarch the title of Elizabeth II, when there had been no Elizabeth I of Scotland. The case, and others like it, are of purely theoretical interest, since the courts declined to assume the right to overturn Acts of Parliament.

[12] The Scottish constitutional Convention was a civic forum dominated by the Labour and Liberal Democratic parties to draw up a scheme for home rule in the 1980s and 1990s. The Convention has a long tradition in Scotland and the deposition of James VII and the succession of William and Mary were undertaken by a Convention in 1689. In England, where the king ruled as James II, the deposition and succession were undertaken by Parliament. Home rule conventions had been summoned earlier in the twentieth century.

[13] They also argued that, although the old Parliament had been dominated by the Protestant ascendancy, it could have evolved into a popular assembly, a claim later rejected by republicans deriving their legitimacy from the essential nationality of the Irish people.

In the UK there was no jacobin project of national socialization as in France. There has never been a British national educational curriculum. When, a few years ago, the government wanted more direct control over the content of education, it adopted four separate 'national' curriculums for the four nations of the UK. Opposition to Europe on the part of the Conservative right is often no more than a disguised English nationalism, which finds much less echo in Scotland. As for the other symbols of nationality, Norman Tebbit's notorious 'cricket test', in which Britons of West Indian origin were asked which team they would support, ignored the facts that (a) cricket is an English game virtually unknown in Scotland and (b) many Scots tend to cheer *any* foreign team taking the field against England in any sport (but especially in soccer). In the last thirty years, as the factors that held the union together have weakened, nation-building has recommenced in Scotland and, to a lesser degree, in Wales (Keating 1996b).

In Spain there is a similar disagreement about the nature of the state. Unionists argue in the words of the 1978 constitution that the Spanish people is sovereign, the state emanates from it and in turn recognizes and guarantees the right of autonomy to its nationalities and regions. Parada (1996), for example, sees Spain as a unitary creation, founded on the Castilian language, product of a long process of integration, and sanctified by the defining moment of the constitution of Cadiz (1812).[14] Catalan nationalists espouse a very different view, drawing on their own traditions of shared sovereignty and compromise, rooted in the experience of pre-1714 Catalonia as a self-governing nation within a wider confederation. There are many permutations on this theme, but the common element is the belief that the Catalan people have a right to negotiate their own position within Spain and to project themselves more widely in the world and, especially, in Europe. This did not, however, prevent the moderate nationalists accepting the 1978 constitution and the statute of autonomy that was part of it. Basque nationalist traditions are different, since historically there was never a Basque state or a single government. Rather, Basque rights were rooted in the *fueros*, special provisions recognized in many parts of Spain after the Reconquista but of special importance to the Basque provinces. These involved limitations on royal power, and were a target for both centralizing monarchists and jacobin republicans before being finally eliminated in the 1870s, only the special fiscal arrangements remaining. It

[14] Parada does not help his case by arguing that Spain is 'a single nation like France, *Great Britain*, Germany or the United States' (p. 7), then on the following page criticizing his opponents for denying that Spain is 'a nation-state like France, Germany or *England*' (my emphasis).

was Sabino Arana who wove these into a theory of Basque nationality and sovereignty, claiming that the old Basque Country had been an independent entity in voluntary union with Spain (De La Granja 1995; Jaureguí 1996). So, in the high era of nationalism, a theory of medieval contractualism became a theory of national independence. This has remained the basis for Basque claims, with the moderate Basque Nationalist Party (PNV) refusing officially to recognize the 1978 constitution because it did not recognize the prior Basque claims, and the radical Herri Batasuna claiming that the Basques' future can be settled only by a referendum in the seven Basque provinces (three in the Basque autonomous community, the autonomous community of Navarre, and the Basque provinces of France). While the PNV have made use of the 1978 constitution and its autonomy provisions, they still see sovereignty as unfinished business (PNV 1995). They also recognize historic rights in the internal arrangement of the Basque autonomous community. The special fiscal powers of the *concierto económico* are exercised by the three provinces, and these are represented equally in the Basque Parliament, despite huge population disparities.

Spanish political practice since the transition has followed three tracks at various times. One is to accommodate the specific demands of the historic nationalities, as was done at the time of the transition, when provisions were put in place to try and limit autonomy to these three cases. A second is to limit autonomy, seek to recentralize and bring uniformity to the autonomy statutes, as with the LOAPA law of 1981 (Moreno 1997a). A third is to banalize the idea of nationality by measures such as allowing the autonomous communities of Aragon and Valencia to amend their statutes of autonomy to call themselves nationalities.

Belgium came much later to statehood than did its neighbours in France and the Netherlands. Up until the Napoleonic wars, it remained a congeries of territories under the overall jurisdiction of the Spanish and then the Austrian Habsburgs, each with its own privileges and special status. This typically premodern arrangement was radically disturbed by annexation to France under Napoleon, annexation by the Netherlands in 1815 and finally the establishment of a Belgian state in 1830. Belgium was organized on French unitary lines, with no recognition of intrinsic territorial rights, but coexisted with traditions and cultures which were inimical to this conception. Yet when the state came under challenge it was not from the old prestate units but from movements based on linguistic and cultural factors, starting among the Flemish-speaking part of the population. The state was then reconceptualized as a pact between two linguistic groups, to be reconciled through consociational arrangements (Lode 1996a,b). Since the interwar years and particularly since the 1960s there has been a further development in which the Flemish elites, and to a lesser degree the Walloon ones, have staked claims to nationality analogous to those made in Scotland, Catalonia or the Basque Country. Gradually the consociational arrangements at the centre have given way to autonomy, initially separately for the territorial regions and linguistic communities. In turn, the regions and communities have begun to merge, fusing their institutions on the Flemish side, with only the question of Brussels preventing the movement from being complete. Unlike the Scottish and other national movements, the Flemish movement is not based on a historic territory (Lode 1996b), but has had to invent that territory as a common home for Flemish speakers. The process is accompanied by claims that a Flemish nation is historically rooted, ignoring the differences in the use of the word Flemish in past ages or the fact that the territory of historic Flanders comprises only a small part of the present autonomous region (Kerremans 1997). Indeed, there have been many complaints that the Flemish government itself has been highly centralizing, reducing the scope for the provinces and municipalities which were the focus of traditional forms of autonomy. Another marked feature of the Belgian case is the fact that the pressure for decentralization has not come from below – indeed public opinion in both language communities has become increasingly centralist – but from the elites (Collinge 1987; De Winter and Frognier 1997). It is tempting to conclude from this that the whole process is invented by political leaders for their own convenience, except that the lack of resistance reflects a rather weak sense of Belgian identity, and a failure of nation building at the Belgian level. At the same time, the European context and Belgium's support for further measures of European integration have allowed a further diffusion of power and the transfer of contested functions.

So Belgium may be a case where the practice of accommodation, pactism and limited sovereignty has won out over the earlier attempts to impose a unitary conception of the state, but the units which engage in this bargaining and which are the recipients of shared power have changed radically in composition and definition. We cannot say that present-day Flanders has a right to self-determination because it is home to a 'people' who were in the past self-governing. We can say that there is a nation-building project that needs to be taken seriously and that the rival Belgian project is foundering. Indeed, it is now difficult to counterpose the component regions/nationalities and the state, since the state itself has been shared out between the communities, and there is almost no one left to speak for Belgium.

Canada was at one time often described as a union of two founding peoples, rooted in contract and accommodation and, although this had more resonance in Quebec than elsewhere, it became a widely accepted feature of Canadian political accommodation (McRoberts 1997a). Despite periodic efforts at assimilation, the francophone population of Quebec was generally allowed to maintain its own culture, language and religion and, with confederation in 1867 gained constitutional powers of self-government. Decentralization of power to Quebec, along with the other provinces, complemented practices of accommodation at the Canadian level which, while falling short of consociationalism, provided for Quebec participation in the central government. Although Canada did have a written constitution of sorts and a formal distribution of powers between the two levels of government, doctrines relating to the nation and the state were perhaps even more vague and ill-specified than in the United Kingdom. Crises such as those over conscription put the relationship to a considerable test and there were periodic resurgences of Quebec nationalism, but from the 1960s the issue moved centre stage. One reason was the co-existence of two modernizing, nation-building projects, one centred on Quebec and the other on Canada. In the era of the so-called Quiet Revolution, the Quebec government took on in-creased state-like powers and challenged the ascendancy of the tradi-tional and clerical elites who had maintained the distinctiveness of the 'French-Canadians' within Quebec and Canadian society. The ethnic division of labour was attacked, modernization took a distinctively Québécois form, and the ethnic group was transformed into a territo-rially based national society. At the same time, Canada was moder-nizing, asserting its independence both of Britain and the United States and equipping itself with such symbols of nationhood as its own flag. The clash of these two nation-building projects raised anew the question of just what sort of nation-state Canada was. Repatriation of the constitution in 1982 without the consent of the representatives of Quebec meant the rejection of the two-nations theory in favour of a majoritarian conception of Canada in which no one province could claim a special place. Federal bilingualism was a way of protecting the use of French while denying its status as a national language of Quebec. The Charter of Rights was seen by Quebec nationalists as an imposition from outside, and a way of undermining the cohesion of Quebec society itself (Laforest 1992b). Finally, the policy of multiculturalism was seen as a way of diluting Quebec's status as a founding nation by reducing it to the status of one cultural minority among many.

Consequently, three distinct doctrines of the Canadian nation-state have competed. One is the Trudeau vision, rooted in a form of mechanical federalism, in which all citizens have equal rights and the same relationship to the federal government. No province has special status and only individual rights are recognized. The second is the 'two nations' doctrine, now expanded to three nations with the recognition of the rights of native peoples. In this, Quebec and the native peoples are seen as nations,[15] with their own inherent rights, along with a third nation which is either Canada-as-a-whole or English Canada.[16] As a corollary, relations among these groups should be managed in the form of partnership (Laforest 1998). The third conception is even more complex, and involves accepting the claims of any self-defined group to recognized status, collective rights and self-government. This view received expression in the failed Charlottetown Accord, with its complicated lists of categorical rights and convoluted arguments about how they would relate to the recognition of Quebec. This bears comparison with the Spanish strategy of *café para todos*, in which everyone is allowed to be special and therefore nobody is.

So there are elements in the constitutional history and traditions of all four states which point to accommodation and the recognition of multinationality and shared sovereignty. Advocates of this view often find it difficult to define the units which will be parties to the pact or to produce a coherent justification for this. Yet if we see historic rights as a living principle rather than a strictly reactionary one, then it is normal that the depository of these rights should evolve and change without losing the central idea. So the legatee of the historic rights of the Basque provinces can indeed be the unified community of Euskadi, constituted as a nation (Herrero de Miñon 1998); the Flemish and Québécois can develop a territorial nationalism with a cultural/linguistic element while still insisting on the idea of shared and limited sovereignty. These visions still compete with unitary or mechanical-federal visions which insist that one size must fit all. Similarly, on the part of the national minorities, there are elements that espouse the traditional zero-sum view of nationality and independence, and others that look both backwards and forwards to ideas of shared sovereignty and complex authority.

---

[15] This is not to say that the native peoples are seen as a single nation, merely that their claims constitute a category.

[16] Many people refuse to accept that the third nation can be Canada as a whole, since this includes the other two and insist that, for symmetry and to engage in a proper dialogue with Quebec and, in due course, the native peoples, it must be English Canada (Resnick 1995). This seems to me an effort to force symmetry where it does not exist, although the project is not an impossible one. Most people in Canada outside Quebec do seem to consider themselves just Canadian and see no need for an intermediate identity at the level of 'English Canada', a sentiment which I share myself.

The transformation of the state

Nationality claims have never been simply about getting one's own state. Self-determination has never been simply a matter of secession, but has involved the assertion of rights within a specific context, often as a matter of negotiation. Nowadays this is even more the case as the state itself is transformed. This transformation complicates nationality claims but also presents new opportunities for resolving or managing them. The idea of the state has been with us a long time, but the nation-state, in the form in which we know it, is a rather recent phenomenon. It represents the coincidence in space of a number of principles of social and economic organization. It is the primary focus of collective identity, reinforced and transmitted through culture and socialization. This collective identity in turn provides the basis for social solidarity. The state is the framework for internal and external security. It frames an economic system, allowing us to talk of national economies, with definable, if not impermeable, boundaries. It is a set of institutions and mechanism for policy making. In this sense, the nation-state is the product of the modern era. It is not, *pace* most international relations scholars, the product of the Peace of Westphalia in 1648. The only European state that has the same boundaries in 2001 as in 1648 is Portugal, and that has lost an empire which profoundly shaped its internal politics. If we look at the internal construction of the nation-state, this is even more clear. The substantive content of the nation-state is largely the product of state and nation building since the nineteenth century. The nation-state has always been in transition, and the present era is no exception, sparking a renewed debate on the 'end of sovereignty' (Camilleri and Falk 1992). It is being transformed institutionally from above, by the rise of international regimes, notably, in the four cases discussed here, the European Union and the North American Free Trade Agreement (NAFTA); and below by territorial assertion. Its functional capacity remains high, but interdependence is limiting its autonomous use of this. Its scope for autonomous economic management is being eroded from above, by globalization, capital mobility and the rise of the multinational corporation; laterally by the advance of the market; and from below by forms of economic restructuring rooted in local and regional specificities. The three-directional erosion of the nation-state from above, from below, and laterally in the face of the market, has broken the link between economic change and policy making and between policy making and representation. It has weakened social solidarity and made difficult the old class compromises and trade-offs which underpinned the west European welfare settlement of the postwar era. It has undermined old strategies of territorial management based on the distribution of economic resources and state monopoly of the links between regions and the global market. It has even threatened economic efficiency, by militating against the production of public goods and the social cooperation which is the essential counterpart to competition in a market economy.[17]

So we are in a world where multiple spheres of authority coexist with multiple systems of action. As we have seen, these tendencies have always been present, albeit neglected in unitary accounts of the state. They recall an earlier era of overlapping authority, multiple identity and complexity, before the rise of the modern state (Tilly 1990, 1994) but, as noted, there are continuing elements in the constitutional practice of the four states that would enable us to grasp this new politics. I have argued that politics is in some respects reterritorializing and that minorities are able to claim various forms of self-government rooted in historic rights and practices. Yet territorial devolution is not always the answer, since there is still the problem of internal minorities or minorities-within-minorities; and the fit between territory and function is still somewhat tenuous and varies from one function to another.

Unpacking sovereignty

While simply returning to a past of shared and overlapping sovereignties is not, therefore possible, there are elements in the new global order which may permit us again to unpack the functions of the nation-state, allowing differentiated forms of autonomy and differentiation of policy spheres. Many of these depend on the development of supranational forms of political order, especially where substate groups have direct access to them. Gradually, if tentatively, the idea has spread that the state is not the only subject of international law, modifying traditional conceptions of sovereignty (Held 1995).

One area in which conflict has been generated is that of human rights, with nation-states insisting that they provide the only framework for defining and enforcing them. This produces the paradox that universal rights are defined in a national framework, itself determined by the state majority. Minority nationalists frequently object to the assumption that universal rights are not safe in their hands. This is an area in which international jurisdiction has developed considerably. It has gone furthest in Europe, where the European Convention on Human Rights has been incorporated into the legal system of many states. It is

---

[17] These issues are discussed at greater length in Keating (1996a and 1998a).

noteworthy that the 1998 Scotland Act and Northern Ireland Act provide that the Scottish Parliament and Northern Ireland Assembly will be limited, not by a UK Charter of Rights but by the European Convention, allowing the courts to strike down laws passed by the devolved bodies if they infringe the Charter. Similarly, devolved governments in Spain and Belgium are subject to the European Charter, though in these cases there is also a national constitution, which has been used in Spain to limit the scope of the autonomous communities in matters of language law. In Canada, on the other hand, the Charter of rights is rejected by many in Quebec as the imposition of a unitary conception of Canadian nationality on the Quebec people (Laforest 1992b); this is not the same as a supranational system as operated in Europe. Europe has gone much less far in defining and entrenching collective rights such as those of linguistic groups. There are charters of minority languages and the Council of Europe has been active in the field of cultural minorities, but this work is more exhortatory. The point I am making is that as the question of individual rights is taken out of the hands of the state it is divorced from nationality so that national minorities can subscribe to universal principles without surrendering their identity. This also removes an excuse used by states to reject asymmetrical constitutional arrangements, on the ground that this would allow devolved governments to impinge on universal individual rights.

European Union law, largely aimed at creating a uniformity of market conditions, may serve a similar purpose in limiting the ability of devolved governments to discriminate. The 1998 Catalan language law, for instance, is carefully phrased to avoid conflicting with European single-market regulations. In some cases, indeed, Europe has guaranteed a greater equality of rights than exist within the state, as illustrated by two recent cases. In 1997, the British government stipulated that students from England, Wales and Northern Ireland would pay higher fees at Scottish universities while those from the other fourteen states of the EU would qualify for the lower Scottish rate.[18] In the same year, the European Court of Justice ruled that the special fiscal privileges available to investors domiciled in the Basque Country investing in Basque industry would have to be extended to other citizens of the EU, but not necessarily to those of other regions of Spain.

---

[18] The origins of this bizarre circumstance lie in the fact that Scottish honours degree courses are of four years' duration while elsewhere in the UK they are of three years. The Scottish Office decided to use its budget to ensure that Scottish students would only have to pay the same total amount for their degrees as students studying elsewhere in the UK, but was not prepared to use its money to subsidize non-Scottish students for the four-year course. Further complications arose in 2000 when the new Scottish Parliament abolished the fee.

This search for political spaces beyond the nation-state is not new. Catalan nationalists in 1932 proclaimed an independent Catalan republic within the 'Iberian federation'. Since there was never any chance of the Portuguese surrendering their statehood to bring such a federation about, this was a pipe-dream; but it had the attraction of offering a common framework free of the accumulated weight of Spanish nationalism. More recently, the British and Irish governments have invented the idea of the 'islands' (no longer referred to as the British Isles) as a forum for bringing together on conditions of equality a variety of sovereign, semi-sovereign and non-sovereign bodies (see below).

A great deal has been written on the opportunities presented by global and regional free trade for substate entities to enhance their autonomy (Keating 1992). States have lost many of their old powers of macroeconomic regulation, and attention has shifted to the importance of regions and localities for economic change and restructuring. Ohmae (1995) argues that global free trade is leading to the rise of 'regional states'. Although his argument can be criticized as ill-informed, simplistic and economically determinist and many people would find his rigorously neo-liberal trading order unattractive, there is a growing literature on the way in which substate territories are positioning themselves in the global economy (Scott 1998).

Another feature of global change and continental integration, especially in Europe, is a blurring of sovereignty. In the European Union, sovereignty is shared, although not all member states have come around to this. None actually mentions membership of the European Union in its constitution, although the German Basic Law now contains a provision giving the *Länder*, through the Bundesrat, a veto on the transfer of sovereign powers to international bodies, which in effect means the EU, and the proposals for constitutional reform in Italy would explicitly embrace the European dimension and the regions' place in it (Bicamerale 1997). In the UK, the new devolution settlement for Scotland and Wales are based on the continuing sovereignty of Parliament. In the case of Northern Ireland, however, British governments have gone a long way to accepting shared sovereignty with the Republic of Ireland. The idea is to allow the two communities in Northern Ireland to express their different national identities through the creation of new over-arching institutions. The 1998 Stormont Agreement provides for a North–South Ministerial Council to link the Republic with Northern Ireland, a British–Irish Intergovernmental Conference to recognize the stake of the two 'sovereign' states, and a British–Irish Council in which the Republic of Ireland, the UK government, the Northern Irish Assembly, the Scottish Parliament, the Welsh Assembly and constitutional oddities like the Channel Islands and the Isle of Man would all be represented. European integration has not acted directly to erode the border through encouraging economic exchange, as a functionalist approach might suggest, since the issue is not fundamentally economic. Yet the existence of the European project with the reality of eroding sovereignty, and the participation of both states in European institutions, has created a new context greatly encouraging to this kind of accommodation. The breach in the principle of state sovereignty caused by European integration has been exploited heavily by minority nationalists in Spain and Belgium, arguing that the principle of sovereignty is an archaism and does not correspond to contemporary reality, although Basque nationalists have a more traditional understanding of sovereignty than the Catalans. Belgium's 1993 constitution skates around the question of sovereignty. While declaring that the Chamber of Deputies represents the entire Belgian people, it also says that Belgium is a federal state composed of communities and regions, where the previous one talked of it being divided into subunits. It also gives the communities and regions full international competence in their respective spheres, subject only to some overriding Belgian foreign policy considerations.

The new global order also creates new political spaces for substate actors and, again, Europe is the most developed case. A great deal has been written on the Europe of the Regions (Hooghe 1996; Petschen 1993; Bullman 1994; Jones and Keating 1995) and on the scope for minority nations in this perspective. Initial enthusiasm has now given way to a hard-headed realization of the limits of regional actions within the European political space, given the domination of decision making by state governments, but the argument has not ceased. Some minority nationalists and strong regionalists have also sought to detach themselves from the group of regions as a whole, most of which are defined functionally and administratively, and lack a nationalist dimension. So the Flemish government has been promoting the concept of Europe of the Cultures (Foundation Europe of the Cultures 1996), seeking to carve out a space for regions with a cultural or historical identity. The Spanish minority nations have taken a more pragmatic approach, seeking every opportunity to penetrate European institutions and to use Europe as a platform to promote their aspirations, without producing blueprints for the future. Recently, the Catalan nationalist coalition CiU has been pressing for a recognition of the concept of 'shared sovereignty' within Spain and Europe. The European dimension has been a central part of the Scottish home rule debate since the 1980s, recalling the debates of the nineteenth and early twentieth centuries, when home rule was invariably placed in the context of the British Empire. While European political space is not as open as minority nationalists would want, there is almost nothing at all comparable in the North American Free Trade Agreement. NAFTA is a strictly intergovernmental pact, limited to economic issues and with environmental and social chapters included only at the insistence of the American Democrats. It is widely supported by political leaders in Quebec as a means of loosening the Canadian framework, but does not itself provide new spaces for political entrepreneurship by non-state actors. Quebec's membership of the *La francophonie* does give it an international platform, although Canada could concede this only by including New Brunswick as well, so diluting the significance of Quebec's membership. The possibilities of an international presence have symbolic as well as substantive importance, as recognition by the world community is one reason why nationalists so often insist on their own state (Taylor 1993b). The growth of paradiplomacy at the substate level thus provides an important means for satisfying national aspirations without breaking up existing states (Aldecoa 1999).

A more radical option is to use the existence of over-arching systems like NAFTA and the EU to allow minority nations to become independent and accede directly to the supranational order. This is the policy of the Scottish National Party and the Parti Québécois. The problem is that it does not really allow us to get around the issue of sovereignty, since only sovereign states can accede to NAFTA and the EU. Both parties, moreover, recognize the need to retain special links with the old state, even in the proposed sovereign future. In the case of Quebec, proposals have usually involved various forms of association, even if the term 'sovereignty-association' is no longer used, and the degree of association proposed does vary. Jacques Parizeau, for example, believes that Quebec can manage with much less than do some other sovereigntists. In the case of Scotland, nationalists talk from time to time about the need to retain the 'social union'. They also favour an intergovernmental rather than a supranational Europe. Catalan and Basque nationalists are divided. Some favour independence, and these usually call for the unification of the Basque and Catalan lands, including those in other autonomous communities of Spain and in France, a prospect imaginable only in a Europe so advanced that the old states disappeared altogether. Most nationalists, however, talk vaguely of advancing further to home rule in step with further European integration. This theme is echoed in Flanders, where there is a widespread feeling that the Belgian state will be unable to survive the arrival of the single currency, since it will have been stripped of practically all its state-like functions, and will live on, if at all, as an empty shell or, at best, a convenient arrangement for blurring the issue of Brussels and managing intercommunity relations.

Given the fragmented nature of the European opportunity structure, stateless nations do not have a slot to fit into the new order, but a variety of channels, to be used as appropriate. What is more important, however, is the role of Europe in fostering a new nationalist discourse. It provides a fairly neutral political space within which a variety of claims can be articulated, challenges the idea of absolute sovereignty, and facilitates nation building by allowing stateless nations a field of action beyond the state. It also allows them to rebut charges of 'separatism', insularity and parochialism and, indeed, to portray themselves as more internationalist and universalist than their host states, trapped as they are in a restrictive state nationalism of the nineteenth century. This is a powerful theme in the discourse of almost all stateless nations in western Europe. The symbolic importance of nationality has been consistently underestimated by state elites and by many observers. In Canada, the Meech Lake Accord came to grief essentially because of the unwilling-ness to recognize Quebec as a 'distinct society', let alone a nation. Spanish political parties have been tied to a unitary conception of the Spanish nation which finds it difficult to comprehend the multinational principle.[19] Within the new transnational order, stateless nations may find the symbolic sustenance for their nationality claims.

Conclusion

Since the nineteenth century, groups seeking the right of self-determina-tion have invoked the principle of nationality, precisely because of its normative loading. This continues in the late twentieth century. Yet, despite the open-ended nature of the principle, nationality claims are hard to make and there is not an infinite number of nations waiting to escape the state and set up on their own. The right of self-determination does not necessarily entail secession; the costs of secession militate strongly against this. Indeed it may be that secession is more likely in conditions in which the right to self-determination is denied, thus forcing nationalists into more extreme postures (Jauregui 1997). It is unionist as much as nationalist ideology in the UK and Canada that has insisted that anyone claiming the right of self-determination must secede, there being no room for any intermediate position. The issue of

---

[19] The UK has always better understood this symbolic dimension. While my Canadian passport bears the single word 'Canada', my British one carries the description, 'European Community. United Kingdom of Great Britain and Northern Ireland'.

who counts as a nation is largely answered by political practice. To put it perhaps rather simplistically, nations are those who make successful cases and these, given the needs of mobilization around nationalist themes, are not easy to make. In the historic nationalities of Spain, nationalist leaders, while still insisting on historic rights, now emphasize more strongly the extent of support for nationalist parties as the basis for their claims (BNG-PNV-CiU 1998). Certainly, this is a great deal more practical than engaging in a debate over who in the past was self-governing over what. I have argued above that the general principle of territorial self-government does find grounding in the historic political practice of the four states. This is an argument not for universal principles to determine who is entitled to what, but for a different form of statecraft, sensitive to the political realities of nation and nationality and their lack of correspondence to the state. The definition and delimitation of the groups and territories to which it applies is a change-able matter, the result of politics. This does not mean, as reasoning from general principles might indicate, that anyone can and will make claims to national self-determination. Only in the case of a breakdown of central state authority have we seen a generalized resort to the right to self-determination (in the former Soviet Union and former Yugoslavia). It is true that, in reaction to the demands of minority nations, other territories are making competing claims of their own but these are essentially different. So when Albertans or British Columbians claim that they are entitled to the same consideration as Quebec, this is justified on the grounds that Quebec is a province like the others, not that Alberta is a nation. People in Madrid frequently concede that the Basques can have powers to run their own affairs, just as long as they accept that they are Spanish like themselves. Nationality claims are not an absolute and there are borderline cases, in which some people insist that they are a nation and others dispute it. Padania comes to mind. These claims command legitimacy and will be taken seriously to the extent that the leaders in question succeed in nation building and political mobilization around it. So far, the promotors of Padania have had a very limited success. Aragon has succeeded in persuading the conservative government in Madrid to recognize it as a 'nationality' like Catalonia, the Basque Country and Galicia but, far from enhancing the status of Aragon, this has merely banalized the term and left the three historic nationalities looking for something else. So the question of what units are nationalities and thus entitled to special treatment is resolving itself politically, as nation-building processes are converting historic senses of identity into modern systems of action.

At the same time, separatism is becoming increasingly irrelevant in an interdependent world, opening up a range of intermediate solutions. This chapter has not considered the ideology, strategy or support base of minority nationalist movements – topics that I have covered elsewhere. It is apparent, however, that they command greater legitimacy both internally and externally to the extent that they are inclusive rather than exclusive and recognize internal pluralism. Hence the insistence by many minority nationalists that theirs is a 'civic' project shorn of ethnic exclusiveness. These have also, in many cases, come much further than state nationalists in accepting the limitations of sovereignty. It is therefore no longer the case that nationalist claims must be zero-sum. I have reviewed the historical experience of the four countries not to show that this can simply be reproduced in modern circumstances – the context has obviously changed – but to show that there are other ways of thinking the state. Yet the idea of the multinational state, of nations within nations and of asymmetrical loyalties, comes with great difficulty to many theorists. Looking backwards and forwards, I am also arguing that there is more than one way of securing justice and stability. This is not to present a general formula; one theme of this chapter is that it is very difficult to start from general principles and work to individual cases. Rather the theoretical and empirical approaches must complement each other.

This chapter has argued for an approach to the issue of multinational states, not for a grid to determine absolutely how to treat particular categories of territory or claim. It points to asymmetrical arrangements both in the state and in supranational regimes like the EU (Requejo 1996; Keating 1998b). There still problems and no tidy categorization is as yet possible. Nation building is more successful in some places than others; some of these units are more territorially integrated than others. There is no argument at all about the land boundaries of Scotland,[20] and fairly little about who is a Scot.[21] In the Basque Country, these issues are wide open. One group seeks a territorially integrated community within the Autonomous Community or Euskadi while another dreams of a wider Basque nation. Wales is still divided, as the 1997 referendum showed. Although, in sharp contrast to 1979, a majority for home rule was obtained, there were negative majorities in the areas of English settlement and in Cardiff. In Northern Ireland, the conflict is

---

[20] I say land boundaries because the maritime boundary, which would determine the division of offshore oil reserves, is still a matter of contention.

[21] Nobody denies that everyone born in Scotland is a Scot, although in the past sectarian conflicts meant that the Irish Catholic community was somewhat apart. The SNP accepts the non-Scots born as Scots if they are living there and, while this is not always accepted socially, there is really no such thing as an 'English minority' in the way that there historically was in Ireland.

precisely over how to define the political unit that has a right to self-determination. Recent debates in Quebec have similarly posed the question and rival claims to self-determination are in conflict. There is a nation-building process under way in Flanders, although it is at best a partial success and agreement on the borders is prevented by the issue of Brussels, historically Flemish but now with a francophone majority, and located within the boundaries of Flanders. In these cases, a simple territorial solution, by self-government for the territory concerned, is not possible but nor, *a fortiori*, is secession appropriate. Here we need some functional as well as territorial unpacking of sovereignty,[22] but political practice does give precedents for this. The real intellectual problem arises from the doctrine of the unitary or uniform/mechanical state in which every deviation from uniformity has to be justified by reference to a general and universalizable rule. This is more of an intellectual fiction than an account of politics in any real state, still less in the new global order.

We can therefore see a future in which territorially based minorities can bargain for particular types of autonomy within the state and international order. Forms of asymmetrical government need to be refurbished (Requejo 1996). In some cases, past state practice and theory can be refurbished to serve the needs of the new complex order, notably the idea of territorial rights and pactism. This is a great deal easier in territorially integrated places like Scotland than in divided societies, where more complex forms of unpacking sovereignty will be necessary. Multiple national identities can, and do coexist, although appreciation of this is often lacking in majority communities.

Finally, the normative argument that only nation-states can guarantee the conditions for equal rights and democracy is undermined by the increasing separation of rights from the state and the construction of new spaces of democratic discourse. These spaces can no longer be confined to the uniform nation-state, nor can they easily be carved out at the supra-state level. Instead, the task must be to sustain and encourage them at multiple levels, corresponding to the multiple levels of functional government.

---

[22] This is a complex issue in itself, discussed further in Keating (forthcoming).

2 Political stability in multinational democracies: comparing language dynamics in Brussels, Montreal and Barcelona

Dominique Arel

Can multinational states be stable in the long run? The question has long interested philosophers and social scientists. For over a century, liberals and socialists shared the assumption that *intra*-state cultural identities were transitory, characteristic of a specific stage of historical development and would lose their salience with the onset of modernization or socialism. Even the Soviet socialist leaders, who actually institutionalized cultural differences in the 1920s by creating 'ethnically' defined republics, did so with the belief that economic equality under developed socialism would inevitably make the political status of cultures irrelevant (Connor 1984). Among those who assumed, on the contrary, that the non-conflictual blending of sundry cultures into a state-sponsored, 'nationwide' culture is not the only path to state building, two traditions formed regarding the stability of states in a multicultural setting. They could be called the pessimist and the optimist schools.

The pessimist school can be traced back to J. S. Mill's classic statement that a multilingual population cannot generate a united public opinion, a necessary condition for the maintenance of a representative government (Mill [1860] 1995). Almost a century later, Almond (1956) incorporated this insight in his typology of political systems, with the assumption that political stability requires cultural homogeneity. In a colonial setting, a similar argument was developed in J. S. Furnivall's concept of a plural society, where cultural segments display incompatible values and can only cohabit politically through externally-induced order, i.e. a colonial government (Furnivall 1948). A generation later, Rabushka and Shepsle (1972) argued that multinational states inexorably descend into cultural polarization and disorder because of a rational, and therefore irresistible, incentive for elites to appeal to the narrowly defined interests of their cultural constituency, and to keep upping the ante for fear of being outbid by challengers from within their own ranks.

The optimist school goes back to a contemporary of Mill, Lord Acton, who, in an oft-cited rebuttal, wrote that public opinion is in fact strengthened and invigorated by the co-habitation of several cultures within one polity (Acton [1862] 1996). Forty-five years later, challenging the hegemonic socialist view which reduced 'nationalism' to a tactical ploy of the bourgeoisie inimical to the real interests of the working class, the Austro-Hungarian Bauer ([1907] 1996) argued that cultural groups were autonomous from classes and would become even more differentiated under socialism. Socialism would bring stability by decoupling culture from the economy and granting non-territorial self-determination to the nationalities.

In the postwar era, by far the most influential statement of the optimist school has been Lijphart's development of the Dutch model of consociation into a theory of political stability in plural states. The key to stability in the Netherlands and three other postwar cases (Belgium, Switzerland and Austria), he argued, was the willingness of elites to share power, through policies of coalition, proportional representation, mutual veto and autonomy, as long as a certain number of 'facilitating conditions' were in place (Lijphart 1968b, 1969, 1977).

Lijphart's model generated a vast body of literature in the 1970s, much of it devoted to its applicability to other cases of 'deeply divided societies'. Increasingly, the model was criticized on three grounds. First, Lijphart was accused of constantly oscillating between a normative and a predictive reading of his theory, which led him to state that elites should engage in consociation regardless of whether the background conditions are favourable or not, on the grounds that consociation is the most optimal (read: desirable) solution most of the time (Laitin 1987). Second, he was criticized for imputing a selflessness to elites, a willingness to sacrifice their own interests for the good of the cause, which jars with the growing consensus in political science that actors pursue their own interests and that political outcomes result from the clash of conflicting interests, not necessarily economically defined.

Third, it became increasingly clear that Lijphart's theory had been built on cases where the main cleavages were not ethnic, but ideological (combining religion and class). However, most divided societies nowadays appear to have ethnicity as their main cleavage, including Belgium – one of consociationalism's foundational cases – since the 1960s. And one could add that most have language as a key identity component. The point has been made that ethnic conflicts are less amenable to accommodation than religious or class conflicts (Barry 1989). This is so not because of some irreducible 'essence' of ethnicity, but due to a

structural requirement: non-territorial solutions are much more difficult
to attain when language is the main dividing marker than when religion
or class acts as the main marker.

This brief review of the literature on multinational polities suggests
that the pessimist and optimist schools disagree over two core issues:
whether cultural demands can be decoupled from politics, and whether
durable incentives can be found for elites to compromise. The philosopher Mill and the anthropologist Furnivall believed that culture
formed the bedrock of politics and that therefore a culturally heterogeneous political system was, on its own, untenable. The philosopher
Acton and the socialist Bauer thought, on the contrary, that politics
could stand *above* culture(s). The pessimists (Shepsle) argued that
culturally driven politics inexorably leads to an outbidding within
cultural groups, with the most radical and polarized views winning out.
The optimists (Lijphart) believe that elites have, on the whole, a
propensity to compromise, realizing that polarized politics can lead to a
worse outcome for all.

At the end of the twentieth century, a solid majority of analysts find
themselves in the optimist camp, with few advocating secession or
partition as the optimal solution where ethnocultural politics dominate a
given territory/state. The fact that Huntington's civilizational thesis,
with its claim that states 'cleft' along a religious–civilizational axis are
secession-prone, has been roundly attacked aptly reveals the prevailing
mood (Huntington 1996, p. 138). With Lijphart's consociational model
in disrepute, however, another model, that of the 'civic' state, has gained
in popularity. The model is not new, but it has become, perhaps anew,
the ideal against which multinational states should strive, in the eyes of
analysts. The model of the civic state, as discussed in the literature,
stands firmly in the Bauer tradition, which maintains that culture *can* be
isolated from politics and that various cultures can be preserved within a
state.

This chapter examines the relationship between the multination (a
political community made up of at least two demographically significant
ethnic groups) and political stability. It seeks to demonstrate, in the first
section, that the model of the civic state is in fact profoundly misleading
and obscures much more than it reveals. To think that culture can be
removed from politics is to miss the whole point about ethnonational
politics. This is not to say that Furnivall was right and that cultures are
in their essence politically incompatible.

The point is rather that, in assessing the prospects for political
stability in particular cases, it is ultimately more fruitful to look at
psychological factors, namely the social status of cultural groups,

whether there are trends indicating a change in groups' perceptions of themselves and the other, and the likely political implication of these changes. The argument is not that all that counts in cultural politics is the 'intangible'. As the second section of this chapter will try to make clear, the psychology of group perceptions is very much dependent on tangible factors such as economic power. And, in certain cases, they can be significantly affected by political arrangements. Yet the same political devices, in a different psychological climate, i.e. a different configuration of group statuses, can yield very different results. Stability in one case can become instability in another.

In discussing these two theoretical points (the civic state and group status), the chapter will rely on three of the main cases featured in this volume: Quebec, Catalonia and Flanders. In all three cases, language has become the main marker of identity among the two groups battling for public space (Quebec francophones and anglophones, Catalans and Castilians, and Belgian French and Dutch speakers), nationalist parties have spawned language revivals among the three historically-dominated groups (Quebec francophones, Catalans and Flemings) and the political-linguistic battleground has been and remains the big city. The analysis in the second section will thus centre on the political implication of language dynamics in Montreal, Barcelona and Brussels.

In all three cases, moreover, democracy rules and violence have been largely avoided. No doubt, the consolidation of democratic values has much to do with the non-violence. Some scholars, such as Nordlinger (1972, pp. v, 11–13), equated stability with the absence of mass violence and repression. This definition, however, excludes non-violent cases where the boundaries of the polity are being contested, as with the three cases under study. One could argue that a looming challenge to the territorial integrity of a state by a peaceful autonomist/secessionist movement certainly brings an element of instability into the political system.[1] Even though Quebec has by far the strongest secessionist movement of the three cases under review, one of the findings of this chapter is that Belgium is actually the least stable of the three cases, perhaps more likely to lead to a partition of the state in the not so distant future. Catalonia appears to be the most stable.

---

[1] This is closer to Lustick's (1979, p. 325) definition of stability, which goes beneath the threshold of violence by focusing on the expectation that 'key patterns of political behavior' will persist in the future. This could be labelled the 'minimum' version of stability, as opposed to the maximum version proposed by Nordlinger.

The civic state: panacea for stability?

While scholars tend to use the adjectival form 'ethnic' neutrally when the word refers to a 'group',[2] the term acquires a negative connotation when conjoined with 'nationalism.' The message is unequivocal: ethnic nationalism is bad, while its alternative form, 'civic nationalism', is far better. In the past decade, with nationalism once more on the rise in Europe, countless analyses have argued that the accommodation of cultural differences would be far more manageable, and a better guarantor of stability, if undertaken in 'civic' garb.

The dichotomy civic/ethnic is not new. Since the French Revolution and the powerful impact it had on German thinkers shortly thereafter, 'nation' has come to mean either a *political community* (French version) or a *cultural community* (German version). The nation as a political community was the revolutionary concept of a *citizenry*, of a body of people endowed with equal rights and collectively embodying the attribute of sovereignty. Political power was not exercised in the name of God, tradition, or a dynastic lineage, but in the name of the people, of all the inhabitants residing on a given territory. Individuals could only be free if they formed a political nation (Smith 1993, p. 9; Pierré-Caps 1995, p. 59).

The concept of the nation as a cultural community embodied the revolutionary idea that culture is crucial in determining the *boundaries* of political organization. Political sovereignty did not reside in a group of people inhabiting a territory arbitrarily defined, but rather in a group of people *sharing certain cultural traits*. Using the primordial language of a God of Nature endowing the garden of humanity with a flora of nations, the German philosopher Herder, at the turn of the nineteenth century, gave philosophical standing to the cultural nation. The idea that 'natural' nations have *political* rights quickly followed – and caught fire.[3]

The key distinction between the concepts of the nation as a political community (civic nation) and the nation as a cultural community (ethnic nation) lies in their *principle of legitimacy*. The former is legit-imized by the principle of *equality*: the Déclaration des Droits de l'Homme legitimized the French nation and delegitimized the *ancien régime*. The latter is legitimized by the principle of *cultural distinctness*. Woodrow Wilson's endorsement of 'self-determination' legitimized the

---

[2] Ethnicity, in this case, denoting a group of people who feel ancestrally related, are bound by self-described identity markers, are attached to a territory which they perceive to be theirs historically, and believe that they form a community larger than one resting on face-to-face contact.

[3] Herder equated national identity with linguistic distinctness. Put differently, he saw language as the necessary marker of national identity. See Breuilly (1995, p. 105).

Czech quest for independence and delegitimized the Habsburg imperial hold on Bohemia.[4]

Ethnic nationalism acquired its bad name in the highly influential work of Hans Kohn, at the height of Nazism. Kohn (1967) argued that ethnic nationalism was an 'eastern European' (then including Germany) phenomenon and a reaction against the basic western values of individual liberty and reason. What these eastern European nationalisms extolled, he wrote, were the 'primitive and ancient depth of [their] traditions'.[5] The view that ethnic nationalism is essentially illiberal informs much of the contemporary debate. Yet it conveniently omits, often out of blissful ignorance, the *western* ethnic nationalisms that have developed since the 1960s, as in Quebec, Catalonia and Flanders.

These nationalisms may be seen as 'ethnic' since their principle of legitimacy is based on the cultural distinctness of the titular group, i.e. the group claiming a territory as its historic 'homeland'. Yet they are not illiberal. In all three cases, nationalist parties have been in power for long periods and their electoral practices have not been less democratic than elsewhere in the west. In a sort of litmus test, in 1995, a solid majority of Quebec francophones (close to 60 per cent) voted for Quebec independence, but the Yes vote fell short by a hair (49.5 per cent) due to the near unanimous vote of non-francophones. Despite some rumblings, no public figure challenged the verdict. The golden rule of democracy – one adult, one vote, irrespective of ethnic background – is firmly entrenched.

Nationalist policies in our western cases are often accused of violating individual rights. Yet the contested rights are cultural in nature, specifically pertaining to the public use of a minority language. In celebrated cases, three Quebec anglophones appealed to the United Nations Human Rights Committee in the early 1990s over the right to use English in commercial public signs, and a Belgian francophone petitioned the Council of Europe in 1997 over the right of francophones at the outskirts of Brussels, in officially unilingual Flemish territory, to use French in schools and in their dealings with authorities. The anglo-

---

[4] Wilson's use of the term 'self-determination' was itself ambiguous and he actually referred to the 'peoples' of Austro-Hungary (Wilson [1918] 1995). The point is that his call was interpreted by leaders of culturally based national movements in central Europe as an endorsement of their cause.

[5] Kohn's view that nationalism is anti-western can be found in contemporary debates within western states containing strong nationalist movements. Thus, the Canadian psychiatrist Vivian Rakoff, author of a devastating study on Quebec nationalist leader Lucien Bouchard, declared that 'instead of abiding by the Universal Declaration of Human Rights by creating a rational, pluralist and respectful society, there exists in Quebec a longing for a German theme: the Counter-Enlightenment, the *Volksgeist*' (as reported by the Canadian Press, in *La Presse* [Montreal], 27 August 1997).

phones won their case and the francophone lost his,[6] but the broader point is that the whole issue of how minority rights relate to individual rights has become salient only fairly recently, being essentially a phenomenon of the 1990s, and actually goes against the grain of the dominant interpretation of classical liberalism.

Liberals are concerned about discrimination against an individual's access to education and equal economic opportunity, but they assume that the language of life chances is the language of the state. In this view, the French state must not discriminate against those of non-French mother tongue, as long as they publicly adopt French. This rigid conception of the linguistically homogeneous nation-state may be changing, and an international law expert could argue that the Quebec and Flemish governments *are* violating rights, but this has nothing to do with infringing the precepts of the 'civic' or 'liberal' state as they have been traditionally conceived. One can not argue at once that ethnicity (language) is strictly 'private' in an ideal civic state (see below) and that an 'ethnic' state is wrong to prevent the public use of non-titular languages.

Ethnic nationalism is also associated with the repellent image of *exclusion*. As Brubaker (1992) pointed out, German nationalists in the late nineteenth century opposed extending citizenship to non-ethnic Germans, such as the Poles of East Prussia, because they could not conceive of a political community in terms other than a community of common descent (thus, ethnic). French nationalists, by contrast, believed that all could join the political community, irrespective of lineage (Parekh 1995, p. 28). While it would be difficult to argue that this German stance is not 'ethnic', and fundamentally different from that of France, applying the citizenship criteria to contemporary cases does not prove very fruitful. In western Europe, many states, besides Germany (and including Belgium), do not automatically give citizenship to children of immigrants. Does this make most western states 'ethnic'? In eastern Europe, where ethnic violence is much more prevalent, states have *inclusive* citizenship policies, with a few exceptions. Ironically, the

---

[6] In Quebec, the language law had banned the use of English signs, except by cultural and educational institutions, and offices of federal jurisdiction, such as post offices. The UN Commission ruled that the state could make the use of a language (French) mandatory in commercial signs of the private sector, without however preventing the use of a second language; United Nations, Human Rights Committee, Communications Nos. 359/1989 and 385/1989, 31 March 1993. In Belgium, francophones were protesting against the attempts by the Flemish government to curtail the right of francophones to use French in their dealings with authorities. A report by a Council of Europe investigator (*rapporteur*) had recommended that the Flemish decrees to that effect be repealed, but the Council's General Assembly rejected the recommendation; see Dubuisson 1998d.

two states that disenfranchised most of their minority (Russian-speaking) populations, Estonia and Latvia, are actually considered to be the most liberal among post-Communist states, since the rule of law is more entrenched there than elsewhere in the east. These two Baltic states legally deprived almost half of their populations of the right to vote. Should we consider them more 'ethnic' than, say, Romania, which gives citizenship to all, but whose government recently included extreme nationalists in its coalition?

Arguably, the appeal of the civic state model lies in its premise that the best way to cope with ethnicity is to remove it from the political realm. In this view, the maintenance of minority cultures is 'purely private' and therefore 'depoliticized' (Nathan Glazer, quoted by Kymlicka 1995, p. 4; Snyder 2000). The state acts as an 'ethnically neutral' agency (Burg 1996, p. 196). However, as Kymlicka demonstrated, the state cannot be linguistically neutral, and thus ethnically neutral whenever language acts as a marker of identity. While citizens can enjoy their religious freedom in private within the framework of a religiously neutral state, language cannot be analogously separated because it is integral to the functioning of the modern state.

That state, in Gellner's powerful prose, requires a working force literate in a 'high culture', able to disseminate and receive context-free information (Gellner 1983). The high culture rests on a standardized language, and this language, notwithstanding the efforts of Esperanto enthusiasts, cannot be devoid of ethnic foundations, that is, of the culturally preexisting repertoires of *particular* groups. The United States uses English, the language of early British settlers, but not the language spoken by the settlers of Pennsylvania, Minnesota or Louisiana. France uses French, a language spoken by less than half of the population of France at the time of the 1789 Revolution. The Soviet Union finally admitted, in the early 1950s, that the language of the postnational era would be Russian, and not some supra-ethnic construction, as theorized in the early decades of Sovietism.

Even when a state legitimizes itself by appealing to the nation *cum* community of citizens, it cannot avoid having to make decisions that will inevitably privilege one culture (and therefore one group) over another. In the words of Kymlicka, 'Government decisions on languages, internal boundaries, public holidays, and state symbols unavoidably involve recognizing, accommodating, and supporting the needs and identities of particular ethnic and national groups' (Kymlicka 1995, p. 108). The so-called 'civic' state has in fact a strong cultural component. Remarkably, liberal theory has no justification for the use of the politically dominant culture as the culture of public life. It is simply taken as a given. Once more, the boundary of the civic and ethnic models is unclear. In *both* cases, the aim of the state is to consolidate the public domination of a single culture. The principle of legitimacy is different, but culture is at the core of both projects.

Two arguments can be made to mitigate the claim that civic nationalism is also about the primacy of one culture. The first is that the adoption of the public culture of the civic state by citizens of other cultural backgrounds is voluntary and non-conflictual. Comparative historical analysis, however, shows that similar attempts to establish one central language, on rational and non-ethnic grounds, can produce both non-conflictual (France, USA) and conflictual (Imperial Russia, late-nineteenth-century Hungary) outcomes. In each case, the intent was the same: to rationalize the state by making its citizens publicly adopt the language of the state (Laitin 1989, p. 309). Yet the French/American model is called 'civic' because the process proved non-conflictual in the end, while the Russian/Hungarian model is never called 'civic' since it engendered conflicts. Seen comparatively, however, it becomes clear that the French and the Americans did not succeed because they separated culture from politics, they succeeded because cultural minorities did not successfully challenge the culturally hegemonic French/ Anglo-American project.

What this suggests is that the instability generated by a project of linguistic primacy has to do more with the micro-foundations of particular cases, rather than the legitimizing principle (civic vs ethnic) of a state carrying out a language policy. As will be argued in the last section of this chapter, the contemporary Catalan language project is largely non-conflictual, very much unlike the Flemish and Quebec counterparts, even though the aims and policies of the three nationalist movements are similar.

A second argument in support of civic nationalism as a superior form concedes that culture cannot be dissociated from politics. The claim is, rather, that it is possible to accord equal status to more than one culture in the public realm, thereby not privileging one group at the expense of another (Burg 1996, p. 196). The examples of Canada, Belgium and Switzerland are traditionally cited to buttress the point. These states have granted official status to more than one language (three, in the case of Switzerland). What this argument obscures, however, is the fact that one culture virtually always predominates at the substate, *territorial* level. Most Swiss cantons are either German unilingual or French unilingual; Dutch and French are the exclusive official languages of Flanders (excluding Brussels) and Wallonia; and French is the sole official language in Quebec, while English has *de facto* supremacy in all but one of the other provinces. The official bi- or multilingualism characteristic of central policy more often than not translates into official unilingualism at the bottom. Even here, the 'civic' bi- or multicultural state cannot dissociate culture from politics.

All these outcomes resulted from conflictual processes: the French-speaking portion of the Jura canton separated itself from the dominant German-speaking portion to join a hegemonically French canton of Switzerland in the 1970s; Dutch progressively supplanted French, the former high culture of Flanders, following the adoption of the principle of territorial unilingualism in the 1930s;[7] and official unilingualism in Quebec has remained controversial, while the curtailment, if not outright banning, of the use of French in public domains of English-Canadian provinces, particularly in the west at the turn of the century, was anything but non-conflictual.

There are certain 'zones of contact' within disputed territories that may resist the movement towards official unilingualism. As hypothesized in the last section, this resistance may occur when the social status of languages remains persistently out of synch with their official statuses. Greater Brussels is a case in point, with its language question remaining very much unstable more than three decades after the linguistic territorial borders of Belgium were supposed to have been solved once and for all. Barcelona, on the other hand, while much more bilingual in its daily life, has a Catalan-first language policy which does not appear to create much dissension among a population which is nearly half of non-Catalan origin.

There is a third school of thought which promotes the idea of the civic nation. Contrary to the first two, however, this emerging school, which is strongly represented in Quebec intellectual circles, expressly envisions the nation as a project that can only be sustained by the political primacy of one culture against competing cultures. The core idea of this school is that an ethnic nation is one that fundamentally *excludes*, while the civic nation has an *inclusive*, integrationist character. Exclusion in this case, contrary to the German tradition discussed above, does not pertain to deprivation of citizenship, but to a refusal to integrate or assimilate the other. Raymond Breton, in analysing the evolution of English-Canadian nationalism (and by extrapolation, American nationalism), actually uses the label 'ethnic' to describe its original stage, even though the construction of nations from settlers' communities in North

---

[7] A principle staunchly defended by the French-speaking Walloons who, despite the fact that they inhabited an already hegemonically French area, feared the possible intrusion of a 'foreign' language [Dutch] had pan-state territorial bilingualism been adopted as a means of protecting the French minority of Flanders (Sonntag 1993, p. 16).

America is commonly referred to as civic projects based on notions of individual rights and civil equality.

Breton's point is that the Anglo-Saxon settlers, whose cultural markers and institutions served as the crucible into which later waves of settlers were expected to assimilate, had a very strong sense of cultural superiority, and were concerned about uncouth newcomers, such as eastern and southern Europeans, vitiating the cultural values of the national core. However, as the core gradually became de-Anglo-Saxonized, and with the growth of the multiculturalist idea emphasizing the contribution of non-European cultures to the mainstream, English-Canadian and American nationalisms shifted from an ethnic to a civic 'orientation' (Breton 1988, pp. 88–93).

This insight is shared by Quebec scholars who take strong exception to the charge that 'the objective of Québécois nationalism is, as was the case in the 1960s, the creation of an ethnic state in Québec' (William Johnson, quoted in Rocher 1996). The French-Canadians, as they referred to themselves before the 1960s, used to be an insular group, intent on preserving their traditional Catholic and rural values. Yet with modernization, the Quebec francophone nation is no longer closed to the integration of people whose religious and racial heritage differs from that of the descendants of the original French settlers, the so-called *francophones de souche* (indigenous francophones). In this view, the only difference between Quebec and Anglo-Canadian or American 'nation building' is that the 'common public culture' into which immigrants are assimilating is not English, but French (Rocher 1996; Laforest 1995a).

The Québécois, in the cultural national sense, are becoming less Catholic and also less white, but share a common identity by virtue of the fact that they speak French as a first language, the same way that the Canadians outside Quebec are becoming less Protestant and less white, but continue to adopt English as a mother tongue intergenerationally. According to this argument, governmental regulations to ensure that the common public culture remains French are not aimed at ensuring the predominance of a narrowly defined ethnic group (the indigenous francophones), but at serving the interests of a linguistic majority which is very much inclusive of peoples of all backgrounds. This brand of nationalism is thus deemed inherently pluralist.

Yet an inclusive project may still appear to exclude. A nation may be genuinely inclusive and outward-looking and yet be faced with the counter-project of a group, who also sees itself as a nation, and thus wants to have its culture recognized as an alternative 'common public culture' in the political space and, eventually, as the legally hegemonic culture (language) on a given territory. In the early modernization period, the francophones of Belgium were inclusive of the Flemings, as long as the latter adopted French as their high culture. Flemish nationalism was precisely a reaction against this form of 'civic' inclusion. The Flemings wanted to carve out their own exclusive high cultural domain, and they succeeded – up to the contested borders of the capital. The French-Canadian/Québécois national movement made identical demands and certainly did not consider Lord Durham's brief for assimilation in the 1830s as an all-inclusive civic project![8]

N.B.

The point is that, in these cases – and arguably in the majority of cases where religion does not act as a salient ethnic marker – exclusion is directed at the public identity of a group, not at the putative members of the groups as *individuals*. Thus, the Turks refuse to consider the Kurds as a nation, but this does not mean that they wish to exclude *individuals* of Kurdish background (Kymlicka 1993). The Turkish conception of the nation is, in fact, a carbon-copy of the French model of the nation: *all* citizens form the nation and partake in one common public culture. No linguistically-defined group can be granted political rights. Kurds who adopt a Turkish identity will be considered full-fledged Turks (an option that has been quietly taken by millions of Kurds).[9]

This conception of the nation is certainly very inclusive, as long as Flemish-speakers became 'Belgians,' the descendants of French settlers became anglophones, and Kurds adopted the Turkish language. But this is not at all how those Flemings, French-Canadians or Kurds who perceived their group as a nation saw it. For nationally-minded individuals, the aim of the politically dominant nation is not inclusion, but *assimilation*, and assimilation is seen as the greatest threat to the nation's survival. From this perspective, there is nothing 'civic' in promoting the language of the dominant public culture. The anglophone Québécois who object to the public restrictions in the use and status of their language are not inclined to see the francophone national project as civic, since they perceive the gradual assimilation of immigrants to the French language – reversing a historic trend – as a threat to the survival of their community.

Like in a game of shifting mirrors, the civic nation to some becomes the ethnic nation in the eyes of the other. This is so because ethnicity cannot be driven out of politics by ideal political arrangements. The concepts of the nation as a political community and the nation as a

---

[8] In the wake of the failed rebellion of French 'patriotes', the Durham Report found 'two nations warring within the bosom of a single state' and recommended the assimilation of French-Canadians as the solution (Levine 1990, p. 28).

[9] The Greeks share exactly the same attitude towards the Macedonians ('There are no Macedonians in Greece, only Greeks with a Slavic mother tongue'). The examples are countless.

cultural (ethnic) community cannot be empirically dissociated in concrete cases, since, in the words of Smith (1993, p. 13), at the heart of
every nationalism lies a 'profound dualism', The Quebec state may be
ethnic, but non-francophones democratically and peacefully prevent
francophones from declaring independence. The USA may be civic, but
does not try to use Spanish in California schools. Ethnic cleansing is
horrific, but it is no more the norm of 'ethnic' states than the bloody
American war of secession is the norm for 'civic' states. Nationalism can
be violent or non-violent, liberal or illiberal, expansionary or respectful
of the sovereignty of other states. Most of the time, though, it is both
civic and ethnic, depending on some its aspects, and depending on the
perspective of particular groups. As an all-encompassing conceptual
tool and set of practices pointing towards an elusive stability in multinational states, 'civic' nationalism is, essentially, useless.

Group status and the fear of minorization

A major driving force of nationalism is the fear of minorization. Nationalism thrives on the perception that the culturally defined nation is in
danger of becoming a minority on its 'own' territory (the homeland),
due to birth rate differentials, immigration flows, or assimilation. Representatives of the nation may disagree about whether the danger is real
and what to do about it, and indeed much of nationalist politics takes
the form of intra-group tensions over policies. Yet as long as the fear of
minorization has mobilizing potential, an element of instability persists
at the core of the political system. The locus of the perceived process of
minorization is the big city. Nationalist politics is about 'reconquering'
the urban metropolis. In Belgium, the fear of minorization used to apply
to Flanders as a whole, at a time when the urban bourgeoisie was
French speaking, but since the 1930 compromise establishing a unilingual Flanders, it has revolved around the fate of Brussels. In Quebec
and Catalonia, it is directed essentially at demographic trends in
Montreal and Barcelona.

Flanders, Quebec and Catalonia share this in common: in each case,
nationalism arose against the domination of the language of the 'centre'.
Brussels, Montreal and Barcelona had historically been founded by
speakers of the titular languages – Flemish, French and Catalan. In the
postwar decades, however, the 'public face' of these cities was resolutely
French, English and Castilian (the name given both by linguists and by
Catalans to what is commonly referred to as 'Spanish').[10] It is worth

[10] The public use of Catalan was actually banned by the fascist Franco regime.

noting that the predominant use of the language of the political centre is the norm of the 'civic' state. It can only lead to a stable outcome, however, if speakers of peripheral languages assimilate intergenerationally without mobilizing. Once nationalist mobilization sets in, as occurred in Flanders and Quebec in the 1960s, and in Catalonia in the 1970s, maintaining the predominance of the central language becomes politically perilous. Under these conditions, official bilingualism becomes the second preferred choice of liberals, even though it jars with the core precept of a single 'common' language in the 'ethnically neutral' civic state.

Official bilingualism, or the equal legal status of two languages, however, when enforced in the linguistic zone of 'reconquest', i.e. the big city, is not conducive *as such* to a politically stable outcome. The argument here is not philosophical, but empirical. Languages have social prestige, which to a large extent depends on the career opportunities they might provide. Prestige, or status, is a relative concept, since a higher status socially conferred upon a language can only mean lower status for another. A crucial point is that the *social* status of a language may not coincide with its legal, or politically conferred, status (Woolard 1989, p. 92). Even when the law gives equal status to two languages, one of them may still be perceived socially as lower in rank. As long as the language of the group attempting a reconquest of the city maintains a low social status in the city, while the group's nationalist movement is able to keep a mobilizing base (not necessarily in the city), the potential for instability remains. This argument will be buttressed by a comparison of Flanders, Quebec and Catalonia.

Comparing our three western cases is theoretically fruitful, since the outcome in each case is expected to differ. As will be argued below, the fundamental language trends point to a strong potential for stability in Catalonia, a strong potential for instability in Belgium, with Quebec standing in between, although increasingly pointing to a stable outcome. Stability, in this analysis, is inversely related to the fear of minorization. The more the fear has mobilizing potential, the more instability prevails, with, as a probable final outcome, the deconstruction (partition) of the larger state.

Our three cases also differ in two key variables: religion and economic power. Religion acted as a barrier against linguistic assimilation in societies where religious mores were strong, whenever the language and the religion of two groups were not the same. This was the case in Quebec, but not in Catalonia or Flanders. Economic power is a strong component of the social status of a language. Yet it is does not always coincide with political power. It did in Flanders and Quebec, but not in

Catalonia, where the bourgeoisie was historically of Catalan mother tongue, even during the Franco era. The particular configuration of these variables, and their propensity for change, has important implications for long-term political stability. Before pursuing the point, however, a brief outline of the three cases is in order.

Flanders

The two public languages in Belgium are French and Dutch. The state is comprised of two unilingual territories – Flanders (Dutch), in the north, and Wallonia (French), in the south – with the capital, Brussels, officially considered bilingual. Until the turn of the century, the state functioned strictly in French, the universities were French, and the Flemish bourgeoisie assimilated to French. In 1930, after universal suffrage made Dutch speakers a political force, elites had to choose between making Dutch, in addition to French, mandatory in state offices everywhere in Belgium, or making Flanders and Wallonia officially unilingual, with Brussels as an exception. The Walloons were totally opposed to any introduction of Dutch on their territory and, in effect, abandoned the French speakers of Flanders (Sonntag 1993). Territorial unilingualism was adopted and the French presence, within generations, virtually disappeared from the Flemish hinterland.

Brussels, however, happens to be located in Flanders with historically Flemish-speaking areas separating it from Wallonia. The city was only one-third French-speaking in the middle of the nineteenth century, a proportion which grew to approximately half by 1910, and to more than two-thirds by the end of the Second World War (Hooghe 1991, p. 16). At the time of the 1930 compromise, twelve communes (districts) of Brussels had French majorities and the law stipulated a threshold of 50 per cent of French speakers for the communes around Brussels (by then located in officially unilingual Flanders) to be granted an official bilingual regime and be attached to Brussels (Van Velthonen 1987, p. 40).[11] The next census, in 1947, revealed that seven more communes had acquired French-speaking majorities. The 1930 formula became untenable as Flemish nationalists balked at the steady territorial inroads of French in Flanders from one census to the next.

The compromise, in 1960, was to freeze once and for all the linguistic boundaries of Belgium and, thus, of Brussels. The seven communes were attached to officially bilingual Brussels but no more communes

---

[11] A threshold of 30 per cent granted 'external bilingualism' (language of institutional correspondence with citizens); a threshold of 50 per cent – 'internal bilingualism' (language of administration).

could be added in the future and the census would no longer record the language of respondents. As a result, the state would no longer know the proportion of French speakers in the communes outside of Brussels. An additional compromise, in 1963, allowed the French speakers of these latter communes to have French schools and use French in their relations with authorities, even though, officially, these communes had a unilingual regime. These communes became known as the *communes à facilités* (communes with facilities).[12]

Thirty-five years later, French is now spoken by at least 85 per cent of Belgian citizens in Brussels proper, and up to 95 per cent if all residents are included.[13] Meanwhile, the proportion of French speakers has reached perhaps up to 80 per cent in some of the *communes à facilités* and apparently an important proportion in other communes at the outskirts of Brussels where there are no *facilités* (Villers 1998).[14] The political freeze of the linguistic boundaries has done nothing to prevent the spread of French beyond the official boundaries of the capital. Since 1996, Flemish officials have attempted to curtail the use of French in government relations with residents in the communes. Their stance, solidly backed by Flemish public opinion, is that the *facilités* were transitory and the francophones must integrate.[15] Francophone activists retort by using the language of minority rights, demanding that the use

[12] The law also prevented parents of Flemish mother tongue in Brussels proper from sending their children to French schools. Flemish parents protested and after the law was repeatedly flouted, the freedom of choice ('la liberté du père de famille') was restored in 1971 (Witte 1987, p. 56). The Flemish nationalists were thus thwarted in their attempt to develop Flemish-language schools in Brussels by *Flemish* resistance. In the communes outside of Brussels, however, only children whose father is of French mother tongue can be enrolled in French schools.

[13] According to Swennen (1998, p. 19), 85 per cent of francophones is the usual estimate given by Belgian analysts, but this curiously excludes the large number of international immigrants. The latter may not yet be citizens, but they are unlikely to leave in the future and they assimilate almost exclusively to French. In 1996, the newspaper *Le Soir* reported that 95 per cent of cases in the correctional tribunal of Brussels were conducted in French (Borloo 1996). Even though immigrants are probably over-represented in this pool, the figure is likely to be close to the current linguistic picture of the capital. In the municipal elections of 1995, using proportional representation, the Flemish list obtained ten seats out of seventy-five, approximately 13 per cent of the citizens' vote.

[14] These can only be estimates, as the census no longer records the native language of respondents. Four of the six *communes à facilités* now have a majority of francophone councillors in the communal council. This strongly suggests that these communes have francophone majorities (Columberg 1998).

[15] The 1996 Circulaire Peeters, a decree named after a Flemish minister, ruled that, in order to receive documentation from the commune in French, francophones will have to request it each time, as opposed to having their language preference entered permanently in the system, as it had been until then. As Minister Peeters candidly explained in a television debate: 'We want a just interpretation of the facilities, which are temporary and must disappear by themselves' (Dubuisson 1998a).

of French be extended to other communes and even floating the sacrilegious idea of annexing the communes to Brussels. The Flemish response is peremptory: calling into question the linguistic boundaries means the end of Belgium.

Quebec

The two public languages of Quebec are French and English. Although at the federal level, both languages have been official languages since 1969, only French has official status in Quebec, since 1977. French was the language of the original European settlers. After the British conquest in 1763, the French speakers were allowed to keep their institutions: church, schools and civic code. Montreal acquired a majority of English speakers in the first half of the nineteenth century, after which the majority shifted again to French speakers. The economic pulse of the city, however, was English. Someone visiting downtown Montreal generally had little idea that the majority of Montrealers were actually of French mother tongue. Until the 1960s, the great majority of French-Canadians lived in rural areas. The Quebec provincial government was run by French-Canadians and, by tacit agreement, it did not interfere with anglophone institutions. The Quebec anglophones had virtually complete autonomy.[16]

The belated modernization of Quebec in the 1960s led to a severe decline of the role of the Catholic church and to an intense migration of the new generation to Montreal. For the first time, young French speakers wanted to make careers in industry and finance, a milieu that was almost entirely English. At the same time, a spectacular decline in the birth rate of French-Canadians brought to the fore the question of the survival of the nation (culturally defined). Until the First World War, most migrants to Quebec came from Great Britain, and French-Canadians migrated en masse to New England in search of work, but their extremely high birth rate preserved their proportion of the population at approximately 80 per cent. Later, immigration from overseas shifted to non-English speakers, mainly Italians and Greeks, particularly after the Second World War, and the overwhelming majority sent their children to English schools.[17] In the late 1960s, riots broke out in St-Léonard, a suburb of Montreal with a growing population of Italian immigrants,

---

[16] Education comes under provincial jurisdiction in Canada, but before 1960, the Quebec government did not have a Ministry of Education and the anglophone school network (Protestant School Board of Greater Montreal) 'was virtually a self-governing body' (Levine 1990, p. 48).

[17] By 1961, one Montrealer out of five was of non-French, non-British background (Levine 1990, pp. 9–10). By the late 1960s, over 92 per cent of children of immigrants

when the local school commission decided that all instruction would henceforth be in French.

The school question rocked Quebec politics for almost a decade and spawned three language laws. The last law, enacted by the secessionist government of the Parti Québécois in 1977, no longer allowed children of international immigrants to attend English schools (at the elementary and high school levels; the law does not regulate colleges and universities). English schooling was reserved for children with a parent educated in English in Canada. The law also regulated the use of French in the workplace and banned English from public signs. The latter clause was struck down by the Canadian Supreme Court in 1988 and finally amended in 1993 following a report of the UN Human Rights Commission.[18] Since 1976, the Parti Québécois has won four elections and lost two referenda over the independence of Quebec. The last referendum was so close, however, that the secession option remains very much alive. The Quebec anglophones still reject the language law in principle, but have learned to accept it in practice.[19]

Catalonia

The two public languages of Catalonia are Catalan and Spanish, known as Castilian. Catalonia, located on the southeast border of Spain, was an independent principality in the Middle Ages, before gradually coming under the influence of the Kingdom of Castile (Madrid) in the fifteenth century. The language of the higher classes gradually shifted to Castilian, but reverted to Catalan when Catalonia experienced an industrial boom in the second part of the nineteenth century. The Catalans recoiled at the high trade tariffs imposed by an economically more backward centre and demanded greater autonomy, which they obtained in the early 1930s. Catalonia was a bastion of anti-fascism during the Spanish Civil War and was severely punished by the victorious Franco regime. The Catalan language was banned from all forms of public expression and Catalan schools were eliminated.

Nonetheless, Catalonia prospered economically after the war, attracting a vast cohort of working-class Castilian speaking migrants,

(of non-French, non-English mother tongue) were enrolled in English schools (Levine 1990, p. 56).

[18] See footnote 6.

[19] A 1998 public opinion poll revealed that more than 80 per cent of Quebec anglophones still believe that immigrants should have the freedom to choose the language of instruction of their children; see Bauch 1998. Interestingly, among these very children, i.e. children of immigrants who had to go through the French school system, more than 60 per cent *agree* with the school provisions of the language law; see Norris 1997a.

mostly from the nearby province of Andalusia. The migration was so significant that the number of Castilian-speakers reached almost half of the population of Catalonia by the 1970s.[20] These migrants lived compactly in districts surrounding Barcelona and had a poor active command of Catalan. With the transition to democracy in the late 1970s, Catalonia, along with the Basque land and Galicia, obtained an autonomous status and set out to regulate the public use of languages. In a 1983 language law, Catalan and Castilian were both assigned the status of official languages, but Catalan was also proclaimed Catalonia's 'own language' (*llengua propia*),[21] whose usage should 'predominate' in state offices. A 1998 law strengthened the use of Catalan in packaging and in the media.

The situation in schools experienced a complete turnaround. Since 1983, the main language of instruction, up to university level, is Catalan, with Castilian taught as a second language and sometimes used for a particular topic, such as geography.[22] Children of Castilian mother tongue and Catalan mother tongue are thus not separated in principle by the Catalan Department of Education, although residential patterns probably lead to lopsided majorities of Castilian speakers in particular schools. Thanks to an electoral system of proportional representation, the Catalan nationalist party Convergence Catalonia has been in power for twenty years and its federal wing even joined a coalition government in 1994 in Madrid. Convergence is an autonomist party which does not advocate the secession of Catalonia, but more powers for the Generalitat (the official name of Catalonia) and a greater autonomous presence within the European Union. The secessionist movement within Catalonia remains weak.

Analysis

As was mentioned earlier, the fear of minorization can be politically activated if the proportion of 'titulars' is perceived to be decreasing as a result of at least one of three factors: significant birth rate differential among language groups favoring the non-titular group, assimilation of immigrants to the non-titular language group, or linguistic assimilation

---

[20] In 1910, only 5.4 per cent of Catalonia's population was of immigrant background. The proportion reached 47.7 per cent in 1970 (Laitin 1989, p. 302).

[21] *Llengua propia* literally means 'proper language', in the sense of 'proper name' (Woolard 1989, p. 126).

[22] With certain restrictions, parents residing in Catalonia have the freedom to choose the main language of instruction of their children. Yet Rees (1996) reports that in 1994–95 'Of 248,000 children seven years of age or younger legally entitled to receive instruction in Spanish, only 79 opted to do so.'

of titulars to the non-titular group. In Flanders, Quebec and Catalonia since the 1960s, the birth rate of the two major linguistic groups barely differs and is not a factor. In Flanders, however, the assimilation of Flemish speakers has been, and remains (in the Greater Brussels area), the fundamental problem, while in modern Quebec and Catalonia, the key question pertains to the linguistic assimilation ('integration') of immigrants.

Brussels became a French-speaking city because Flemish migrants to the city assimilated to French. According to estimates, approximately half of Brussels francophones are of Flemish descent (McRae 1983, p. 296). By contrast, a negligible proportion of French-Canadians who migrated to Montreal assimilated to English.[23] In both cases, the language of economic mobility (French in Brussels, English in Montreal) differed from the mother tongue of rural migrants, and yet the French-Canadians did not become anglophones. This had to do with religion. Both Flemings and French-Canadians came from conservative Catholic societies where interconfessional marriages were taboo. Most Montreal anglophones were Protestant, but virtually all Brussels francophones were Catholic. Since linguistically mixed marriages constitute perhaps the key factor behind inter-generational linguistic assimilation (McRae 1983, p. 300), the French-Canadians, by continuing to marry within their religious group even in the city, preserved their language, while the Brussels Flemings lost theirs, since francophones and Flemish-speakers shared the same religion. Barcelona was different, since the rural migrants were not the titular group (Catalans) but the Castilian-speakers and the language of economic mobility, contrary to the situation in Belgium and Quebec, was not the language of the centre (Castilian), but Catalan. Even with their language publicly banned for four decades, the Catalans did not assimilate.

The Catalans, however, faced the prospect of becoming a demographic minority on what they consider their homeland. The stepping stone of their language revival project consisted of making Catalans out of Castilian-speakers, that is, of reaching the point where the children of Castilian-speaking immigrants would adopt Catalan as their language of identity or, in the vocabulary of sociolinguists, would experience a language shift towards Catalan, using Catalan as their preferred language of private life. These children of Castilian speaking immigrants would probably retain a command of Castilian, the same way that most

[23] In the 1981 census, only 3.2 per cent of respondents with French as a mother tongue in metropolitan Montreal reported using English in their home (Levine 1990, p. 213). Demolinguists define linguistic assimilation as the shift from mother tongue to a different language used at home.

Catalans are able to speak Castilian, but the crucial point is that there would be less and less of a difference between children of Castilian-speakers and children of Catalan-speakers: both would use Catalan as a native language. In the 'civic' definition of Québécois intellectuals, the Catalans would have 'integrated' the Castilian speakers.

The language revival project of Quebec francophones is similar, with the proviso that the group targeted for linguistic assimilation is comprised of international immigrants, the overwhelming majority of whom have neither the language of the centre (English), nor the titular language (French), as their mother tongue. As indicated above, until the 1977 law which closed English schools to them, nine immigrants out of ten assimilated to English. English being the language of economic mobility in North America and, moreover, in Montreal at that time, it was perfectly rational for immigrants to choose an English-language education for their children. Twenty years later, the reversal of the assimilation trend in Montreal is no less impressive than the reversal of the school situation in Barcelona. Among immigrant children (called 'allophones' in Quebec) educated in French since the passage of the law, two out of three who had linguistically assimilated by 1991 assimilated to French (Jedwab 1997).[24] One out of three did not even know English as a second or third language.

In Brussels, as in most western European capitals, the presence of international immigrants (from Africa and the Middle East) is massive, reaching a quarter of the residents of Brussels (but not of the electorate, as the immigrants do not have citizenship). Linguistically, they have

[24] This figure has not impressed several francophone demolinguists, who have pointed that the actual cohort (post-1977 allophone children who have experienced a language shift) is small, that a majority still shift to English among all allophones who linguistically assimilated, and that the census authorities changed their data-gathering technique in 1991, rendering comparison with previous censuses problematic. The first two points are true, but they do not contradict the key trend which is central to our argument. The pre-1977 cohort of allophones, having been massively educated in English, are 'lost' to francophones in terms of eventually adopting French as their first language. To include them in the aggregate figure is beside the point. The number of post-1977 allophones who have experienced a language shift (i.e. using a language other than their mother tongue at home) is necessarily small, since linguistic assimilation is an intergenerational phenomenon and most of these allophones still report neither French nor English as mother tongue and language at home. But these allophones will eventually assimilate to a 'local' language, as all children of immigrants to North America do. And the trend shows that an outstanding number choose French. The trend has been confirmed by several other studies. These reveal that, among allophone siblings, the proportion using French over English is two to one (Comité interministériel sur la situation de la langue française 1996, p. 139), and in all but one of the French-language school boards of Greater Montreal, of those allophones experiencing a language shift, the proportion choosing French to English was nine to one in 1994 (Jedwab 1996, p. 101). These non-census findings render the methodological point, mentioned above, moot.

been entirely 'lost' to the Flemings, with all children of immigrants enrolled in French schools. And the assimilation of Flemings, probably through interlinguistic marriages, does not seem to have abated in the suburbs of Brussels.

Why have the Flemings been unable to reverse the linguistic tide in their capital, while the Catalans and Quebec francophones are apparently winning the linguistic battle of the future? The answer lies in the social status of languages and their resilience, or capacity to change. Perhaps unique among the language-based nationalisms of the last century, Catalan was actually the language of prestige, or high-status language, of Barcelona when Catalan nationalism rose after the death of Franco. Quoting Weinreich, Woolard defined prestige as the 'value of a language for social advance,' and social advance as 'promotion to a status that is *consensually* [our emphasis] validated as higher by the larger social system of which the minority linguistic group in question forms a part' (Woolard 1989, p. 91). The Catalans felt like a political minority in Spain, but the Castilian-speaking immigrants felt like a social minority, since the good jobs were held by Catalan-speakers. As a result, these immigrants wanted to learn Catalan. As Woolard reports from her field work of the late 1970s, 'I was surprised to learn that most of my high school informants in the immigrant suburbs endorsed monolingual Catalan schooling' (Woolard 1989, p. 86). When the government announced that all schools would teach Catalan as a first language, the (quiet) resistance actually came from the Catalans themselves who had grown accustomed to a bilingual world (Laitin 1992, p. 157). From the immigrants themselves, there was no outcry.

In Montreal, by contrast, the language of prestige was the language of the (Canadian) centre – English. An influential sociolinguistic study in 1960 revealed that French-Canadian schoolchildren concurred with their English-language peers that English was the high status language (Lambert 1960, pp. 44–51).[25] Back then, French-Canadians ploughed the land while the English owned the economy. Four decades later, most businesses in the private sector and the huge corporations of the semi-private sector, such as Hydro-Québec, are owned by francophones. Media ratings of the most influential businessmen in Quebec routinely place only a handful of anglophones. The salary gap among francophones and anglophones, which used to be considerable, has now vanished.[26] The proportion of anglophones who know French used to

---

[25] The unexpected finding was that French-Canadians also rated themselves lower than the English on the 'solidarity' dimension, i.e. pride in one's group.

[26] Anglophones earned 51 per cent more than francophones, on average, in 1961; Levine 1990, p. 3. A recent study by Vaillancourt (1996) shows that the average salaries are

be one out of three in 1971. Twenty-five years later, it had reached 83 per cent among college-age anglophones (Norris 1998). And French is everywhere to be seen on public signs. A 1986 study found that French still had a lower social status, but the language behaviour of allophones (assimilating to French) and anglophones (learning French as a second language) renders plausible an eventual reversal of the status (Genesee and Holobow 1989).[27]

In Belgium, a reversal also took place, with the once economically backward Flanders becoming the economic powerhouse of the country after the Second World War, while Wallonia was languishing with its ill-adaptable smokestack industries. As a consequence, the wealthier Flemings contribute more to social security and end up subsidizing the Walloons. Remarkably enough, the Flemish economic success story appears to have had no impact on the language question. This is so because language is a problem in Brussels, not in Wallonia, and because the social standing of Walloons and Brussels francophones is quite different. In Brussels, the economic establishment has remained solidly francophone. As Deprez and Persoons noted in 1984, 'As a group, [Brussels] francophones have attained a higher level of education, enjoy higher incomes and therefore have greater social status. Consequently, they still feel socially and culturally superior to the Flemings' (Deprez and Persoons 1984, p. 278). Current debates in the Belgian press reveal that the Flemings still resent the francophones' sense of superiority. The editor of *Standaard*, the main Flemish-language paper, considered it 'obvious that a good number of Brussels francophones have contempt for anything that is Flemish' (Achten 1998). The bottom line, for Flemish speakers, is that Brussels francophones, after all these years of official bilingualism, still refuse to make the effort to learn Flemish (Dubuisson 1998b).[28]

Conclusion

Cultural insecurity can be a potent factor of political instability. It has generated a strong secessionist movement in Quebec and produced the

now virtually equal, as long as francophones are bilingual. Another study, reported by Norris 1997b, suggests that Montreal allophones have higher earning prospects if they first learn French, rather than English.

[27] This study also revealed that Quebec francophones now rate themselves higher than anglophones on the solidarity (pride) dimension.

[28] In a bilingual debate between two prominent Flemish and francophone politicians, the fact that the latter could not function without simultaneous translation was seen by Flemings as one more symbolic proof that francophones do not want to learn Dutch (Dubuisson 1998c).

politics of permanent renegotiation of autonomous powers for 'nationally' defined subterritories in Belgium and Spain. The foregoing analysis points towards an eventual lessening of cultural insecurity in Catalonia and Quebec, but not in Belgium, where the sentiment that Dutch is 'losing' vis-à-vis French is as acute as it was four decades ago. Catalan and Quebec nationalists would probably disagree, and strongly, that the language question is stabilizing in their favour. Catalonia, after all, passed a new language law in early 1998 introducing sanctions against the excessive use of Castilian in certain sectors, while several Quebec demolinguists have raised the spectre of francophones becoming a minority in Montreal, a claim which has been largely coopted by the governing Parti Québécois.[29]

The trends which we have identified, however, are *long-term* trends, especially since a gap is generally occurring between changes on the ground and the political perception that changes have taken place. Once a politically critical mass of Catalans and Québécois will internalize the fact that a stable equilibrium has been reached on language, that is, once they perceive that the Castilian speakers and allophones are 'becoming' Catalan and francophones, the question will lose its saliency. Although this chapter did not discuss the point, we assume that there is a linkage between the 'internal' cultural insecurity problem, i.e. the perception that the titular group is in danger of becoming a minority on its territorial 'homeland', and the 'external' problem of the status of the homeland within a larger state. The more unstable the internal problem, the more unstable the external problem.

In Quebec, it is often argued that, since immigrants are needed to replenish the population, the secessionist movement will inevitably decline because there will be fewer francophones around. This implies a primordialist understanding of ethnicity, whereby children of immigrants somehow keep their immigrant genes and can never identify with a nationalist project. What is likely to happen, instead, is that the collective realization that immigrants are routinely becoming francophones will make the secessionist project less and less urgent.

In Belgium, on the other hand, even though almost every conceivable political and legal compromise has been tried in the past decades, the fundamental linguistic problem has not changed, except for the worse, since Brussels is becoming almost entirely French. Francophones are

---

[29] Their point is that allophones will become the majority and would be less induced to adopt French if indigenous francophones are in the minority. As Jedwab (1996, p. 95) pointed out, however, 'the decline in the share of francophones on the Island of Montreal has not resulted in the reduction of transfers of allophones to the French language in Montreal Island French schools'.

not learning Dutch (the subject is no longer mandatory in schools) and the linguistic 'oil spills,' to use a well-known Flemish expression, keeps expanding in Flemish territory. Once considered totally beyond the pale, the partition of the country is now routinely discussed, if not brandished, in the press. The Flemings now believe that, since the francophones of the periphery (i.e. those outside the official boundaries of Brussels) do not want to voluntarily adopt Dutch in their surroundings, they will have to be given no legal choice. The high-status francophones, contrary to the low-status Castilian-speakers of Barcelona, vehemently object. In a partitioned Belgium, the status of Brussels proper would be hugely contested and a compromise could be to make the capital of the European Union a 'European' city. The francophones of the periphery, however, would, in such a scenario, most likely be left behind, as the Flemings will never agree to compromise the territorial integrity of Flanders, as established since 1960.

We began this chapter by asking whether multinational states can be politically stable. Our answer is that they can, but not because of the deceptively appealing concept of the civic state, which glosses over the important issues. States can be stable when a national group which perceives itself as a minority and fears for its cultural survival is successful in reversing assimilatory trends and develops a sense of cultural security. This can be obtained through 'politically incorrect' means, such as closing all Castilian-language schools in Barcelona and eliminating freedom of choice in the language of instruction for immigrant parents in Montreal. These nationalist measures may actually defuse nationalism in the long run. Sometimes, however, institutional arrangements are unable to affect the source of instability, as in Belgium. The Quebec francophones were able to change assimilatory trends through legislation – and a whole battery of language regulatory devices – but the Flemings were unable to do the same because they were unable politically to convince their own (residents of Brussels of Flemish background) to change their behaviour.

3   Justice and stability in multinational societies

Wayne Norman

I   Introduction

The first line of the first section of the first chapter of John Rawls's monumental first book thunders in a way that almost none of the subsequent lines ever do: 'Justice is the first virtue of social institutions, as truth is of systems of thought' (Rawls 1971, p. 3). Although he will apologise in the second paragraph for probably stating his convictions too strongly, he allows himself the rest of the first paragraph to reveal the radical idea he has in mind.

A theory, however elegant and economical, must be rejected or revised if it is untrue; likewise, laws and institutions, no matter how efficient and well arranged, must be reformed or abolished if they are unjust. Each person possesses an inviolability founded on justice that even the welfare of society as a whole cannot override. For this reason justice denies that the loss of freedom for some is made right by a greater good shared by others. It does not allow that the sacrifices imposed on a few are outweighed by the larger sum of advantages enjoyed by many. Therefore in a just society the liberties of equal citizenship are taken as settled; the rights secured by justice are not subject to political bargaining or to the calculus of social interests. The only thing that permits us to acquiesce in an erroneous theory is the lack of a better one; analogously, an injustice is tolerable only when it is necessary to avoid an even greater injustice. Being first virtues of human activities, truth and justice are uncompromising. (Rawls 1971, pp. 3–4)

For Rawls this paragraph is a shot across the bows of utilitarianism and intuitionism,[1] the two then-dominant normative theories that his theory of justice would try to displace. By beginning with this declaration Rawls makes clear that his basic critique of his rivals is that they are willing to sacrifice justice and individual rights for the sake of other basic political values – a move that Rawls wants to rule out of court.

[1] Intuitionist moral theories, as Rawls defines them, have two features: 'first, they consist of a plurality of first principles which may conflict to give contrary directives in particular types of cases; and second, they include not explicit method, no priority rules, for weighing these principles against one another: we are simply to strike a balance by intuition, by what seems to us most nearly right' (Rawls 1971, p. 34).

The debate about whether justice can or must on occasion be compromised for the sake of political stability is an interminable one in multination states. As radically pluralistic societies – where not simply values and beliefs, but also identities and political traditions and discourses, diverge – democratic multination states betray compromise from their founding treaties and constitutions to the selection of their current crop of cabinet ministers. To be successful for any length of time, political leaders must be masters at finding compromises while appearing to be guided by unwavering principles; and then selling these compromises to diverse constituencies in order to 'reconcile the solitudes', to recall the title of a recent collection of essays by Charles Taylor (Taylor 1993a). In advanced multination states of the sort discussed throughout this volume, minority national communities have considerable degrees of autonomy, usually as the majority in a federal or quasi-federal subunit (e.g. province, canton, autonomous region, linguistic 'community'). And they typically demand *more* autonomy. They also must share power with a central government, and coordinate many of their activities with both the central governments and the other subunits. All of this provides on-going opportunity for conflict, which erupts periodically into full-scale constitutional crises. In short, while there are certainly considerations of justice that are relevant to the basic constitutional and institutional arrangements in a multination state, rarely can such arrangements be seriously discussed without considering the implications for political stability and national unity (to use an inherently controversial term within states that embody competing national identities). And this inevitably leaves many observers of and participants in these debates believing that justice has been compromised for the sake of stability or unity. Some (let us call them *pragmatists*) believe that this is a perfectly sensible way of dealing with conflicting values, goals and identity politics in a multination state; while others, like Rawls in his opening paragraph (in this context only, let us call them *puritans*) reject or regret any attempt to sacrifice justice for the sake of what they consider to be political expediency.

Of course, in the politics it is not uncommon to find people who are pragmatists when it comes to compromising *others'* basic principles, and puritans when *their own* principles are under attack. This is indeed part of the story about the interplay of justice and stability in the politics and political philosophy of the multination state; and it gets a lot more complicated than that. But let us start with the basics.

Although general concerns about stability and unity arise in the political discourse of most states, they arise in a very specific and often very acute way in multination states. It is only in states with national minorities concentrated on their own homelands that we find the continued existence of the state and its current frontiers threatened from within. In the past two centuries there is not a single example of a serious secessionist movement that was not based on ethnic difference.[2] In unitary states there are occasionally revolutions and civil wars where one ideological faction tries to overthrow the current regime and take control of the state itself. But even in otherwise mature democratic multination states like Canada, the UK, Belgium or Spain – where the idea of such a revolution is no longer thinkable – it is entirely within the realm of plausibility to believe that within a decade a large chunk of the state's territory and population will have seceded to form a state of its own. I do not mean to imply that it is *likely* that this will happen in any of these states (within a decade, at any rate), but only that this possibility is on the minds of all political actors when dealing with major institutional and constitutional issues. It is always feared that the wrong institutional change, or the failure to implement the right change, will set in motion a dynamic process leading to the break-up of the state. Indeed, when the demands for (or against) institutional change come from a national minority[3] itself, there is often an implied or explicit threat that failure to do as it wishes will alienate that group from the larger state, and thereby make secession more likely.

In this chapter I will be looking at the relations and tensions between justice and stability in the multination state; and I shall do this, in large part, by examining the way arguments from justice and arguments about stability are used (or ought to be used) in the public justification of major institutional and constitutional provisions. These issues typically include debates over the following sorts of questions:

- Should a minority nation be formally recognized as such in the constitution of a multination federation?
- What should be the primary identity of citizens in a multination state?
- What powers should the subunits of a federation have?
- What representation should they have in central institutions?
- What role should they have in amending the constitution?
- Should the powers of various federal subunits differ if some, but not all, are controlled by minority national communities?
- Should there be a legal procedure for allowing federal subunits or minority nations to secede from a just democratic state?

[2] I am ignoring the comic-opera attempted secessions in Western Australia and Nova Scotia, and also the secession attempt that provoked the US Civil War and which is sui generis in most respects.

[3] In this chapter everything that I say about minority nations or national minorities in general is meant to apply to those rare cases where the group seeking autonomy or independence is actually, like the Flemish in Belgium, the majority.

- If so, what should be the terms of such a procedure?
- Should there be a system of transfer payments from wealthy to poorer regions?
- And so on.

It should be obvious to politically aware citizens of multination states why taking a stand one way or another on issues such as these may have implications for the stability and continued existence of a multination state. Indeed, there are possible implications for either answer, in some cases, and we may not be sure which would be most serious or most likely. Consider, for example, the first question. In some situations, the constitutional recognition of a national minority might strengthen the national identity of the members of that group, and thereby weaken their attachment to the larger state. Or conversely, this symbolic gesture might make the members of the group feel more at home in a state that no longer pretends that they do not exist. Even looking at a specific case in its historical context (such as the attempt to recognize Quebec as a 'distinct society' in the Canadian constitution in the early 1990s), it may be difficult to predict which consequence of constitutionally recognizing the national minority would be most likely. For the moment, however, my only point is that for issues like this, everybody grants the relevance of the stakes in terms of stability and national unity. But as I have noted already, it is also the case that in any serious constitutional debate about issues such as these, both (or all) sides in the debate will draw on principles of justice to make their case. This sets the stage for potential conflicts between considerations of justice and stability, as well as attempts to trade off one consideration for the sake of the other.

In what follows I shall try to throw light on the relations and tensions between justice and stability from three different angles. First, *qua* analytic philosopher, I shall look briefly at what an analysis of the concepts themselves tells us about their interrelations. Then, *qua* political sociologist, I shall examine the way these concepts tend to be used in live political debates about institutional and constitutional change in multi-nation states. And from these two discussions I shall finish, *qua* normative political philosopher, with some recommendations for how we might conduct our constitutional debates more fruitfully in multination states.

2   The concepts of justice and stability

Justice

'Justice' is what political theorists used routinely to call an 'essentially contested concept' (Gallie 1956; Connolly 1983). That means, roughly, that even reasonable and informed persons are never going to agree on a theory of justice or on all of their judgements about which policies and institutions are just. This is true even in the primary domain of justice, concerning the nature of basic liberties and equality rights for individuals. In diverse societies, however, we see another realm of disputes about justice – even between people who agree about individual rights – as soon as discussions turn to questions about justice between groups and political entities such as states, nations and provinces. This is not to deny the existence and legitimacy of a variety of group rights, but only to note that they are inherently contested. There are multiple reasons for this. First, until quite recently there has been much less attention paid to group rights by political philosophers and in the political discourse in general. Second, many of the most important kinds of group-rights claims are made for such large-scale, *sui generis* kinds of political relations that it is often difficult to ground or refute competing intuitions. I am thinking, for example, of claims to rights of national self-determination, self-government, or for particular kinds of powers or representation rights in a federation. And third, exacerbating this problem, the intuitions behind these rights claims often tend to divide over the very lines that separate the membership of the groups in question (more about this in the next section). For all of these reasons, views about the justice of relations between political and cultural communities are likely to diverge and conflict in multination states. Moreover, the fact that disputes about intercommunity relations and arrangements are conducted in the language of justice heightens their intensity, raises the stakes, and makes principled compromise-solutions harder to find.

I have still not said much about the concept of justice *per se*, except that its content and application is, and will remain, inherently controversial. We can add, without controversy, that 'justice' is a normative concept. Can we also assume general agreement on roughly what distinguishes a concept of justice from other moral concepts, such as 'right', 'good', 'fairness' and 'equality'? For those of us raised on Rawls, Robert Nozick and Ronald Dworkin, it is difficult not to think of a conception of justice as a 'set of principles for assigning basic rights and duties and for determining . . . the proper distribution of the benefits and burdens of social cooperation' (Rawls 1971, p. 5). Let us call this, for the purposes of this discussion, the *social-cooperation conception of justice*. It is worth noting that this view of the general realm of justice can be agreed upon by theorists (say, on the left and the right) with very different views about what the basic rights and duties are, and about how the benefits and burdens of social cooperation should be distributed.

But it is also worth reflecting on the fact that even this very general claim about justice seems inconsistent with some of the discourse of justice heard in multination states over the sorts of institutional questions mentioned earlier. Consider, again, the first question, about whether a national minority should be recognized as such in the constitution. While defenders of such recognition may consider the lack of recognition to be a source of injustice, it is difficult to see how recognition *as such* can be regarded as a benefit of social cooperation to be distributed to the group in question. (Of course, it could be argued in some cases that recognition is a first step to rectifying historical injustices against the members of a group, but this instrumental argument is not the principal one used by advanced minority nations like the Catalans, Flemish or Québécois.) For a case like this we must decide between, on the one hand, expanding the concept of justice beyond the limits of the social-cooperation conception; or on the other, retaining the social-cooperation conception of justice, and accepting that many of the claims of intergovernmental and identity politics are not grounded in considerations of justice. I do not think that this choice is merely semantic. There are costs, in terms of clarity of thought and effective discourse, to expressing all serious political demands in the language of justice. Rawls is not alone in seeing justice as the first, and uncompromising, virtue of social institutions; political advocates and activists naturally incline to this 'puritan' view. So as the number of kinds of claims of justice increases, the chance of finding reasonable trade-offs between competing claims decreases. I will discuss other advantages to sticking to a narrower, social-cooperation conception of justice throughout this chapter.

Before leaving the discussion of the concept of justice, it has to be said that many of the great institutional issues in a multination state (including some of the ones I listed earlier) are, to varying degrees, directly concerned with classical matters of justice. Indeed, one of the most exciting developments in political philosophy over the past decade has been the project of trying to show that many of the group rights traditionally claimed by minorities can be grounded in an essentially Rawlsian conception of justice which places a high value on individual autonomy.[4] To take only a couple of the more obvious examples, consider the question of whether richer regions or subunits should transfer wealth to poor ones. Equalization payments of this sort are a standard feature of most multination federations (as well as the European

---

[4] Ground zero for this project is, of course, the work of Will Kymlicka. See, e.g. Kymlicka 1989, 1995 and 1998a. See also Buchanan 1991; Baker 1994; Tamir 1993; Phillips 1995; Carens 2000; Kymlicka and Norman 2000.

Union), and they can serve important functions for promoting pan-state identities and social cohesion. But they are also a way to make for a more just distribution of the benefits and burdens of social cooperation; in short, by making the worst off better off. The same can be said of demands by minority nations or smaller subunits to have enhanced representation in the central government: this can be seen as a defence against the 'tyranny of the majority' which tends to ignore the interests of the minority in ways that are manifestly unjust. Finally, there are other institutional issues in multination states that may or may not fall within the realm of the social-cooperation conception of justice, depending on what kind of justification is given. This is true, for example, of the question of whether minority nations or federal subunits should be given a constitutional right to secede. If the claim is that they are a nation, and that all nations have an inherent right to self-determination, then it is not clear how this could qualify as a claim about justice. After all, they are claiming a right to secede even if they are receiving a fair share of the benefits and burdens of social cooperation in the larger state. They are, in effect, asking for a right not to have to cooperate, not a right to more of the benefits of their cooperation; and this seems different. But not all justifications for a constitutional right to secede rely on this idea of national self-determination.[5] Others argue that groups should have a right to secede if, and only if, they have been victims of systematic discrimination, oppression or exploitation. These are, of course, classical forms of injustice; so a constitutional secession procedure designed to enable groups with just cause to secede could be perfectly consistent with the social-cooperation conception of justice.

Let us summarize a few points about justice before turning to the concepts of political stability and national or social unity. The foregoing discussion has certainly gone beyond what once was called conceptual analysis. We noted that justice is an inherently controversial moral concept, all the more so when we consider various proposals for collective rights, and claims about the justice or injustice of a variety of major constitutional provisions in multination states. Some of these claims seem to be based more on the significance of identity than on grievances about inequality or the distribution of the benefits and burdens of social cooperation. A political discourse that expresses all political values in the language of justice will tend to blur this distinction; and I shall return in sections 3 and 4, below, to consider the implications of this.

---

[5] I discuss at length three general normative theories of secession, which I call 'national self-determination', 'choice' and 'just-cause' theories, in Norman 1998.

Stability and unity

For the purposes of the questions at hand, I shall often use terms like 'political stability' and 'unity' interchangeably. It may on occasion make sense to think of political stability as a function of the political system, and unity as a function of the integrity of the political community. But in practice, for the sorts of issues I am discussing here, the two will tend to go together or disintegrate together. At the existential limit, we are asking about the connection between, on the one hand, the justice of relations between individuals and between political and cultural communities, and on the other, the ability of these communities to continue cooperating within the bosom of the same multination state. For my purposes, then, we might say that an event or change is destabilizing to the extent that it increases the prospects of secession or even a major political stand-off between the central government and one or more regions, subunits or cultural minorities. This is not to deny that there are many other conditions that can properly be called instability in a polity. But in this chapter I am concerned with how arguments from justice and stability are used in multination states to prevent this particular kind of instability (or in the case of some minority nationalists, to justify increasing the instability to the point of secession).

Now, even as I have rather stipulatively defined the notion of stability, or the sense of political stability that I shall be discussing here, we cannot say that 'stability' is a wholly descriptive concept. In other words, in practice there is likely to be considerable disagreement among political actors and political scientists about whether or not some particular political system is or is not stable. And at least some of this disagreement has normative roots. In this sense, political stability is a bit like beauty; the eye of the observer will betray certain preferences. A dictator is likely to see nothing but turmoil and instability in the rough-and-tumble of politics in democratic states, with ruling parties coming and going, not to mention periodic strikes and demonstrations. Those democrats, however, are likely to look at the neighbouring dictator's regime as inherently unstable, even if it lasts for decades, because it is propped up by coercion which cannot keep the will of the people suppressed forever. Similarly, there is no question that political actors and observers within democratic states are inclined to see evidence that policies they oppose are leading to a breakdown in social cohesion, and vice versa. This normative bias in the concept of stability takes hold in large part because of the limited ability of social scientists to predict accurately the medium- to long-term dynamics of political and social systems in general, and the consequences of institutional change in particular. Consider, for example, how few specialists of Eastern European or Soviet politics predicted the imminent collapse of the Soviet bloc in the late 1980s and early 1990s; or how divided experts are about, say, the long-run implications of the decision by the British government to grant a Scottish parliament.

So the assessment of both the justice of institutions and their implications for stability and unity both permit significant room for disagreement, even among sincere political philosophers. This fact will become significant in sections 3 and 4, below, where we try to grapple with the fact that most theorists' own assessments of justice and stability tend to converge. The room for disagreement that both of these concepts permits, in short, seems to provide more than enough space for wishful thinking. In principle, however, 'justice' and 'stability' must be independent variables. There is no logical inconsistency in thinking that a certain institutional change would be just, but nevertheless destabilizing; or conversely, that it would promote stability despite denying justice to some individuals or groups. Indeed, the very possibility of this kind of trade-off is what makes the opening paragraph of *A Theory of Justice* such a powerful idea.

Before turning in section 3 to the sociology of justice and stability talk (so to speak), I will round out this 'conceptual' section by looking at a series of general relations and tensions between justice and stability.

Relations and tensions between justice and stability

Justice and stability are mutually reinforcing in several ways, and so too are injustice and instability. That is, very loosely, justice institutions and behaviour tend to attract support, while unjust behaviour or institutions tend to generate opposition. Claims of this sort are empirical or causal, not conceptual, and I shall describe a few variations on these themes presently.

There is one important relation between justice and stability that is genuinely conceptual, at least within the context of a normative theory. In social-contract traditions of moral theory, the achievement of political or social stability will be a crucial consideration when the parties agree to accept a conception of justice to order their social relations. This is clearly true even of Rawls's theory, the opening paragraph of *A Theory of Justice* notwithstanding :

It is . . . a consideration against a conception of justice that in view of the laws of moral psychology, men would not acquire a desire to act upon it even when the institutions of their society satisfied it. For in this case there would be difficulty in securing the stability of social cooperation. It is an important feature of a conception of justice that it generate its own support. (Rawls 1971, p. 138)

Or as Rousseau put it, his *Social Contract* is meant to take men as they are and laws as they might be. This conceptual link between justice and stability by no means guarantees that the best conception of justice will in fact generate its own support in any given situation. In other words, it is not true that any social order that is unstable and lacking support is *by definition* unjust. But it does show that considerations of stability are relevant to debates about the justice of institutions, especially for debates conducted at a fairly abstract, general level.

In one way or another, most great political theorists in history have believed that, in favourable conditions, there is a causal link between justice and stability (and between injustice and instability). This belief can take at least three different, though related, forms.

First, it is hoped that a fair degree of political stability and social unity can be considered as an *empirical precondition* for free and fair democratic cooperation and just redistribution. Without a widely shared sense of social solidarity, it is argued, people or peoples will be less likely to make the sacrifices and display the trust necessary for a just and democratic society. (This is a central assumption for J. S. Mill in his *Considerations of Representative Government* and for David Miller (1995).)

Second, it is hoped that just arrangements will give rise to voluntary, mutually advantageous social cooperation. Or to put the point more clearly, the absence of justice in social relations leads to grievances that call into question the freedom in social arrangements and the stability of the political system or social unit that allows the (perceived) injustice to persist.

Third, at the heart of a number of modern political theories and ideologies is the faith that shared sentiments and conceptions of justice can provide a secure basis for social unity. Rawls believes that the modern era is characterized by a shift in the basis for social unity, from a shared conception of the good (religion) to a shared conception of justice. Something similar is at work in the faith of liberal nationalists and many constitutional patriots: namely, the belief that shared principles of justice can provide the basis for a shared identity that will unite a political and cultural community. These are variations on a more general belief that social unity is based on the sharing of common values (rather than, say, identities), and that the value of justice can serve this purpose. (See Norman 1995 for an analysis and critique of this general view, especially in the context of a multination state.)

By the same token, there are at least two potential tensions between justice and stability that have been voiced periodically in the history of modern political thought. First, conservatives and communitarians have always worried that justice (or at least liberal justice) may demand that governments grant a degree of freedom and autonomy to individuals that undermines the bonds of community and ultimately political stability. Or similarly, that a concern for justice to the neglect of other political and social virtues may accord individuals rights and freedoms without the sense of responsibility they need to maintain the bonds of community. Second, supporters of existing states and strong central governments have always feared that justice may require that governments grant a degree of autonomy to cultural or social groups that encourages or allows them to separate – politically or socially – from the larger state community. Something like this fear is currently responsible for making federalism an unthinkable concept (and an unspeakable F-word) in the multination states of eastern and central Europe, even among good liberals who are impressed by the federal autonomy available to linguistic minorities in countries like Switzerland, Canada and Spain.

Finally, it is clear that there is what we might call a 'meta-tension' between justice and stability; namely, the fact that the existence of many divergent conceptions of justice – especially when they are held by different cultural, religious or regional communities, or by different social classes – can exacerbate political instability or disunity by perpetuating arrangements that are perceived by many to be unjust.

3   The politics of justice and stability: a case study of Canada–Quebec relations

Given that most of the interesting relations and tensions between justice and stability are causal or contingent, and not conceptual or necessary, the preceding subsection has been as much an abstract exercise in political sociology as it has been a philosophical analysis. Using the categories and mechanisms introduced in that section, I would now like to present a comprehensive set of paired normative and empirical claims about justice and stability in the institutional choices of a multination state. The aim here is to see how views about justice and stability in the real world tend to line up rather more neatly than we should expect given (a) the difference between these concepts, and (b) the relatively loose or weak causal mechanism that links them. For the sake of illustration, I will look at a particular case study, the debates about the status of Quebec within Canada as they crystallized in the late 1980s and through the 1990s. Virtually all of the proposals alive in Canadian constitutional debates over the past two decades fit within these five broad categories (S1–S5).

I think that this is an instructive example for a number of reasons. It is about some of the classic institutional demands in a multination state, and the various positions staked out have been refined by sophisticated (and also not-so-sophisticated) political thinkers and actors over two or three decades. Throughout this period the 'marketplace of ideas' (subsidized by countless government commissions and private foundations) has been receptive to the emergence of new or better ideas. For these reasons I think that there are some generalizable lessons from these debates for understanding the political cultures of other democratic multination states, such as the UK, Belgium, Switzerland, Spain and elsewhere. This is not to say that I think that these other states will or should be considering the particular institutional options that figure prominently in the Canada–Quebec debate (indeed, they would be well advised to avoid some of these debates if at all possible), but rather, that these debates tell us something interesting about the dynamics of normative political discourse where the notions of justice and stability figure prominently.

Here, then, are five options for defining the status of Quebec inside or outside of the Canadian constitutional regime.

S1   Status quo, Charter patriotism

This is, if you will, the solution instituted by the government of then Prime Minister Pierre Trudeau in the constitutional reform of 1982. Supporters of S1 hope that in the long-run most Canadians, including most Quebecers, will come to cherish and identify with the terms of equal citizenship as laid out in the *Charter of Rights and Freedoms* (the bill of rights added to the Canadian constitution in 1982). Supporters of this strategy evince the kind of ideological faith, described above, where unity will be grounded in a shared conception of justice. They also believe that other proposed solutions giving Quebec special status amount to unjustifiable violations of the requirements of equal citizenship and thus are trying to buy stability at the expense of justice. Some of the more extreme proponents of the status quo fear, or claim to fear, that other solutions which strengthen the autonomy of the Quebec government would endanger the rights of individual members of the anglophone, allophone and Aboriginal minorities in Quebec. (The most ridiculous version of this argument warned that a Quebec government protected by a constitutionally entrenched 'distinct society clause' could take away abortion rights in order to increase the francophone population.) Some less ideological supporters of the status quo do not think that special status or recognition for Quebec is necessarily unjust, but they fear that such recognition would fuel a dynamic of nationalism that would come to demand ever more unreasonable and unstable degrees of autonomy for Quebec.

Virtually all opponents of the status quo opt for one of the following solutions, and their critiques of the status quo are implicit in their arguments in favour of an alternative.

S2   *Formal recognition of Quebec's distinctiveness along with some additional concrete features of autonomy*

In the terms familiar to observers of Canadian constitutional politics, this is 'Meech', 'Meech-plus', 'Charlottetown',[6] and at the very outside, the Calgary Declaration (though this latter is close to the status quo).[7] Some positive supporters of this position believe that this kind of recognition is appropriate from the point of view of an enlightened conception of justice, or at any rate, from an enlightened political morality that includes such considerations as core principles along with justice. These supporters were (at least up until the demise of Charlottetown) also inclined to believe that such recognition would satisfy the demands of enough Quebec nationalists that it would also promote

---

[6] 'Meech' is short form for the Meech Lake Accord, an ill-fated constitutional amendment agreed to by the leaders of all of the provinces as well as the federal government in 1987. It was designed to secure Quebec's consent to the constitution of 1982, but it failed to get entrenched in the constitution when two provincial legislatures refused to ratify within the three-year time-limit (unanimity of all provincial legislatures, as well as the federal Parliament is required for this sort of amendment). Among the more contentious features of the Accord were (a) the formal recognition of Quebec as a 'distinct society', and (b) the effective granting of a veto on constitutional amendments to all provinces. Meech did not transfer any formal powers from the federal government to Quebec, and so arrangements are sometimes called 'Meech-plus' if they propose a more nationalist recognition of Quebec than merely as a 'distinct society', or if in addition to the provisions in Meech, they propose transferring powers from the federal government to Quebec or to all provinces. 'Charlottetown' refers to the Charlottetown Accord, which followed the Meech Lake Accord and essentially included all of its provisions along with a number of proposed amendments demanded by other groups and regions in the country, including changes to the federal parliament, to satisfy outlying provinces, and Aboriginal self-government. This proposed amendment also came to naught when it was rejected in a country-wide referendum in 1992. There have been no serious constitutional discussions in Canada since the demise of Charlottetown.

[7] The Calgary Declaration is a non-constitutional statement of principles agreed to by the premiers of the anglophone provinces in the summer of 1997, as a gesture of good intentions to Quebec following the referendum on secession which failed in that province in 1995. It is usually considered to be a watered down version of Meech, recognizing Quebec as merely having a 'unique character', and insisting on the fundamental equality of all provinces in a way that seems to preclude asymmetrical solutions to Quebec's special aspirations.

long-term stability. Other pragmatic supporters, especially during the Meech Lake and Charlottetown constitutional rounds, were less inclined to see recognition as a requirement of justice or political morality, but worth granting formally because its denial was likely to fuel even stronger nationalist demands. To the extent that these pragmatists actually find recognition regrettable from the point of view of justice, they are willing to trade off some amount of formal justice for stability (this may be Prime Minister Jean Chrétien's post-Meech position).

Opponents of S2 include Trudeauites who think it violates the demands of justice as equal citizenship *and* would fuel nationalist demands and thus lead to instability; and so-called 'hard-line' nationalists who believe that a nation like Quebec has a right to a more glorified form of recognition (e.g. as a nation or a founding people) and a more substantial and concrete degree of autonomy. I cannot recall any major political leader or opinion maker who opposed S2 because of a belief that S2 is demanded by considerations of justice, but ultimately ill-advised because it would promote instability.

S3   *'Meech-plus-plus': the recognition of Quebec as a nation and a refounding of Canada as a multinational federation*

Again, naturally, the strongest supporters of such a solution are inclined to see it as both consistent with, or even required by, the demands of justice (and perhaps legitimacy) *and* the best hope for a united Canada. In general, the more pragmatic supporters of such an idea, as well as its opponents, will tend to defend their positions along the lines sketched in S2.

S4   *Outright secession of Quebec from Canada*

Virtually all serious supporters of this position are sovereigntists from Quebec. Some because it is preferred to the above three solutions as well as the one to follow, and some because it is preferable to the status quo or anything else that is likely to be offered by the rest of Canada. In either case, they believe that Quebec secession is consistent with justice (usually citing a right to national self-determination, or a breach of the federal contract in 1982); and while obviously creating disunity for Canada as a whole, it is also sold to both Quebecers and Canadians (not to mention Americans and international bankers) as the best long-term solution for political and economic stability for the peoples north of the forty-ninth parallel.

Since secession is in essence the enactment of disunity, there are obviously not going to be opponents who think it is a just solution but not preferred because of its impact on unity. There are, however, those who believe that secession would be justified but ill-advised because of the amount of political and economic instability that would accompany it in the short to medium term. Such people, however, presumably also think that not seceding is justified or consistent with justice, so they are not trading off considerations of justice and stability. If anything, they are claiming that considerations of justice overall, including economic implications, militate against secession. Other opponents simply believe that secession itself goes against the dictates of justice or just international law.

S5   *Sovereignty-association, confederal partnership*

There are two major kinds of supporters for this option: cynical Québécois nationalists who believe that pursuing this option is the best strategy for achieving outright independence for Quebec (e.g. then-Premier Jacques Parizeau circa 1995), and more idealistic nationalists who think that it is both justified as an exercise of Quebec's right to self-determination and the best long-term solution to political stability north of the forty-ninth parallel. These idealistic supporters must also believe that a two-party, European-Union-like arrangement is itself likely to be stable, or they would opt for either a more moderate (S3) or a more radical (S4) solution. There is only a tiny amount of support for this idealistic justification outside of Quebec.

Some opponents of this solution consider it to be tantamount to secession and unjustified for reasons given in S4. Others may accept a right of Quebec to secede but oppose this solution because they are convinced that a two-partner confederation of this sort could not possibly be stable. In general, concerns about the stability of such an arrangement have made it a virtual non-starter in political and academic circles outside of Quebec.

I certainly do not pretend to have articulated all of the possible arguments for and against these positions, though I do think I have given voice to most of the basic positions of opinion leaders in Quebec and Canada over the past decade or so. What general lessons about the relations or tensions between justice and stability can we learn from this plethora of positions and arguments? Here are four general observations from the sidelines of these debates.

First, as noted already, the above arguments betray a fairly high degree of faith on both sides that (a) the solutions one finds just will lead to more stability, and (b) the solutions one believes to be unjust will lead to instability. Given the general weakness of the causal links between justice and stability, this convergence within each perspective is quite striking. It also would seem to have no special relation to the Canadian debates; it seems to be a natural ideological faith of a sort we should expect to emerge in similar debates in other multination states.

Second, relatedly, what we do *not* generally find in examining these debates are situations in which both sides agree about what would be just and what would promote stability, but disagree about how these goals should be traded off. Instead, for any given proposed solution supporters and opponents tend to be in significant disagreement about either its justice, its stability implications, or both.

Third, for the middle-ground options between the status quo and secession (i.e. the options for which there is at least some hope of a consensus inside and outside Quebec) there is a tendency for proposals to be supported with arguments emphasizing justice or other moral considerations, and a tendency for opposition to emphasize considerations of stability. In some sense this should not be surprising since the impetus to move from the status quo comes primarily from Quebec nationalists, and since resistance comes from those (e.g. Canadian nationalists) who are not terribly dissatisfied with the status quo.

Fourth (this is speculating beyond the data, so to speak), there is a tendency on both sides of the argument to treat what we might call 'identity-based political desires' as claims of justice. Demands for constitutional recognition of Quebec's distinct or national status is an example of this. So are some demands that citizenship status must be uniform for all Canadians, a view typically accompanied by a desire that all citizens put their Canadian identity above their cultural or provincial affiliations. It is time now to look at some of the consequences for politics and political philosophy of working with a notion of justice for constitutional issues that departs significantly from what I earlier called the social-cooperation conception of justice.

4   Justice and stability in public justification

It is impossible to provide a comprehensive argument here for why many of the normative issues involved in the politics of a multination state (e.g. the sorts of issues raised in the Canada–Quebec case, above, or in settling the institutional questions I cited in section 1, above) are not primarily matters of justice; for two reasons. First, because there is not space here to look at each of these issues and decide whether a particular institutional change would significantly alter the rights and duties of citizens and the distribution of the benefits and burdens of social cooperation. (Although I did sketch this form of argument for some institutional issues in section 1.) But second, because there is unlikely to be a decisive argument for limiting talk of justice to that permitted by the social-cooperation conception. Indeed, this is what it means to say that 'justice' is an essentially contested concept.

It is possible, however, to show why the quality of political argument may be improved for all parties if fewer claims were couched in the language of justice. I will conclude now by briefly sketching reasons for taking 'identity-based' claims seriously, while nevertheless avoiding collapsing all of them into the concept of justice.

The first reason for sticking with a narrower conception of justice, like Rawls's social-cooperation conception, follows from the uncompromising nature of justice claims, as voiced in the opening paragraphs of this chapter and of *A Theory of Justice*. If the public justifications both for and against a constitutional change make the positions seem like matters of justice, then the supporters of each side will come to believe that they must take a stand against any form of compromise, even if some modifications could make the change much more acceptable to both sides (more about this in a moment). The situation of such debates is that much more unfortunate when, as is often the case, the supporters and opponents of the change are using rather different criteria or conceptions of justice.

A second, and related, reason for shying away from justice talk for some constitutional issues in a multination state is that such language naturally makes stability considerations appear less relevant and less morally worthy. But surely it is irresponsible not to consider seriously the long-term consequences of major institutional change. Indeed, if Rawls and Rousseau are right about the intrinsic relation between justice and stability, it is irresponsible from the point of view of justice itself not to worry about whether an institution will gain broad support from citizens. Instability is in nobody's interest in a multination state (apart from fanatical secessionists and revolutionaries eager to see the state falter), and can be quite costly in political and economic terms – and also, therefore, in terms of the most basic considerations of justice. A state lurching from one constitutional crisis to the next because its institutions are unstable is unlikely to be a state in which political leaders have the time or energy to work toward an optimal distribution of the benefits and burdens of social cooperation. There is all the more urgency to find stable, self-legitimizing solutions to *constitutional* problems, since constitutionalized provisions are often very difficult to change or rectify in multination federations.

A third reason for developing a political discourse that allows considerations of justice, identity and stability to be treated on equal footing, so to speak, is suggested by the first two. Different groups in a multination state may be much more willing to agree to implement constitutional changes that are primarily in the 'identity' interest of another group or region (e.g. granting recognition or autonomy to that group) if they can be satisfied that the proposed change will be stable and not harm the legitimate interests of their own members. In order to satisfy these conditions, it may often make sense to look beyond the particular demands of a minority group and to simultaneously enact measures to make each group secure in its interests.

Perhaps an example will make this idea clearer. Let us consider the issue of stability in its starkest form: namely, the avoidance of a process making secession more likely. I have already noted that one of the main reasons supporters of existing states hesitate to grant recognition and autonomy to ethnocultural minorities is that they fear that these 'concessions' will be used in nation-building projects at the minority level that will only lead to further demands for autonomy, backed up ultimately with threats to secede. But when minority leaders are making the initial demands for recognition and autonomy they are most likely to be arguing that these are just and legitimate demands and should be granted for that reason. The other regions or the central government may question the sincerity of the minority leaders, or they may think that, sincere or not, it is simply naïve to think that autonomy, say, will not eventually create the conditions for demands for further autonomy. In a case like this, however, there may often be a solution consistent with all groups' stated desires for identity, justice and stability. Recognition and autonomy could be granted along with other measures that would help secure stability in the long term. These could include reforms that integrate the newly autonomous region more successfully within the institutions and political culture of the larger state (say, by making their language an official state language, or by enhancing their representation in the central parliament). Or, more innovatively, such measures could include securing agreement by the minority group to concrete provisions that would make secession more difficult; say, by requiring a supermajority (e.g. 60 per cent or two-thirds) for secession, or by allowing only one referendum on secession to be called within a fifteen-year period.[8] An agreement on a procedure that would make secession difficult but not impossible would work not primarily by blocking

---

[8] I have discussed a number of possible 'hurdles' that might be incorporated into a constitutional secession clause, as well as the reasons for believing that such a clause might meet the demands of justice, in Norman 1998 and Norman (forthcoming).

secession attempts; it could simply make it less likely that regional political leaders would decide to use secessionist politics to bolster their demands for more autonomy. At the same time, the central government might be willing to accord more autonomy to the region in the first place if it could be assured that this would not make secession more likely. At any rate, my point here is not to get lost in the details of this example, but rather to suggest that *when considerations of identity, justice and stability are all given equal footing in the public deliberation of constitutional negotiations there should be a greater chance of finding acceptable solutions for all parties.*

The last sentence, above, could easily serve as the conclusion of this chapter. But since I began with Rawls and have kept him in the shadows throughout, it is worth returning to some of the points he raises in that first paragraph of his magnum opus. I cited his paragraph because it is a particularly forceful expression of a very noble and common view: the idea that justice cannot be compromised. I have tried to show, however, that it is unfortunate, if not disastrous, in multination states to retain this view about justice while (a) expanding the range of issues that a concept of justice is supposed to pronounce upon to include all or most of the major constitutional issues of a multination state, (b) conducting public constitutional discourse in a language of justice. I have tried to suggest that there are good reasons for resisting both (a) and (b). It is noteworthy that when Rawls himself is claiming that justice is the first virtue of social institutions, such that it cannot be sacrificed for other goods, he is explicitly talking about a conception of justice based on individual rights. He is not claiming that whatever you end up calling a matter of justice, it is *ipso facto* the first virtue of social institutions! It is quite likely that many of the institutional changes that are debated in the constitutional politics of multination states are more or less neutral in terms of their impact on the basic civil and political rights of individual citizens.

Rawls's first paragraph also reminds us of how many of the basic issues in the 'basic structure' of the multination state do not even show up on the Rawlsian radar screen, so to speak. For example, he refers to the 'liberties of equal citizenship' in a just society, as if this idea were not problematic in a federal state where citizens living in different subunits can have substantially different civil, political and social rights. As some Rawlsians have pointed out when they have sought to adapt his political theory for diverse societies, we simply cannot take for granted that society is a 'cooperative scheme in perpetuity', in which 'membership is a given' and 'fixed', and in which the citizens 'will [all] lead their [entire] lives' (Rawls 1971). It is precisely because we cannot take these things for granted in a multination state that most of the major constitutional issues arise. And when they do arise, we realize that justice cannot be the *only* first virtue of political institutions. It is arguable that the current citizens of Belgium who reside in Flanders would live in a state that was equally just, whether or not Flanders seceded from the Belgium; and likewise for the Scots, the Québécois, the Catalans and so on. It matters not just that one's state is *just*, but also that it is *one's* state, the state one can identify with. And given that we live in a world with radical pluralism of both values and identities, where there will continue to be states in which citizens have competing identities and competing views about justice, it also matters that the major institutions designed to regulate political contests be stable.

4   Political liberalism in multinational states: the legitimacy of plural and asymmetrical federalism

Ferran Requejo

This chapter deals with normative and institutional concerns about the legitimacy and suitability of establishing asymmetrical agreements in multinational societies. In it, I will defend the notion of *asymmetrical plural federalism* for both the recognition of identities it engenders and the possibilities for self-government of national federal units it affords. After a brief discussion of political liberalism and federalism in cultural pluralist contexts (section 1), I put forward an application of plural federalism for the Spanish *estado de las autonomías* taking into account its membership of the European Union (section 2).

1   Two initial comments on multinational states and federalism

1.1   Political liberalism and cultural pluralism

The recent debate between political liberalism and cultural pluralism is helping to achieve two things: (1) a better understanding of the cultural limitations of the liberal tradition, both in normative theory and in the institutional practices of democracies, including federalism; and (2) the fuller realization of those very same 'universal' values of democratic liberalism, without the cultural and ideological biases of yesteryear.

The first aspect highlights and corrects the tendency of the liberal-democratic tradition to treat cultural differences as particularist trends or deviations. Like other political theories, political liberalism starts from a specific set of questions, concepts and values which are only laterally relevant when dealing with cultural phenomena of a plural nature, such as political accommodation in multinational states. Hence cultural questions related to identity cannot be made to fit the usual liberal-democratic approaches to individual political rights, pluralism, liberty and equality. Regarding cultural issues, what is sometimes wrong in this tradition is not what is said, but what is taken for granted, i.e. the 'statist' cultural assumptions of state-led nation-building processes that impregnate the symbols, languages, institutions, decision-making processes and powers of liberal-democratic states. Despite the usual liberal defence of a *laissez faire* approach to cultural matters, experience indicates that the state has not been, nor can it be, culturally neutral. The practical result of liberal-democratic development has often been the marginalization of cultural differences in favour of an extremely partial interpretation of equal citizenship and non-discrimination.[1]

In order to guarantee the most impartial implementation of the rights of citizenship in the 'moral' rules of democratic systems, it seems necessary to make an 'ethical' interpretation, in intercultural terms, of those rights.[2] To demand an intercultural interpretation does not imply the promotion of a multicultural equidistance or an ethical relativism, but rather advocates an optimization between plural normativities that breaks with the traditional versions of liberal universalism. Otherwise, liberal universalism may be resistant to decisive aspects of pluralism when it puts into practice 'ethical' aspects of a cultural nature that are denied access through the front door of theoretical fundamentation. Given the inevitable agglomeration of particularities that cultural pluralism entails, progress in this direction will require a greater acceptance of *modus vivendi* type agreements to regulate the interaction of collective rights and other liberal-democratic values. Liberal democracy is neither unique, nor can it be defined by reference only to abstract conceptions independent of the actors involved in cultural pluralism.

The second aspect highlights the emancipating nature of liberalism when it combats the tendency present in all societies to think that there is only one way of being rational and moral, both in the private sphere (personal relations, sexual practices, types of family, etc.) and in the public realm. At the same time, it also corrects the inclination to assess universal values with simple evaluative scales. The revision of liberal-democratic norms, with the aim of proceeding towards a more impartial implementation of their own premises in multinational contexts, entails paying more attention to the cultural components of individuality in the 'moral' rules of each political association. This is a revision that encourages greater normative 'negotiation' and 'recognition' among differ-

---

[1] For a typology of different kinds of cultural pluralism movements based on five discriminatory criteria, see Requejo 1999.

[2] I maintain the distinction between the 'pragmatic', 'ethical' and 'moral' dimensions of practical rationality as they are usually understood in contemporary political philosophy. I develop this point in Requejo 1998a, sections 1 and 2.

ent cultural traditions and which any sort of federalism that is to be suitable for those contexts cannot afford to ignore.

I believe that it is no longer appropriate to consider there to be a conflict between a universalism based on the egalitarian components of human 'dignity' and a particularism based on the intersubjective communitarian dimension of cultural identity acquired in the process of socialization. This is because the former is also part of many particular identities, while the latter influences the modern concept of 'dignity' in a pluralist society.[3] On the other hand, a distinction between universalist and particularist elements in liberal democracies must be distinguished from the way these two elements are applied.[4] To sum up, this is a question of 'filtering' cultural particularisms from a 'negative' perspective based on universal 'moral' criteria. At the same time it also involves establishing an 'affirmative' perspective of the 'ethical' particularities that de-particularize the statist assumptions that the hegemonic cultural groups have imposed on each one of those spheres under an homogenizing notion of 'democratic citizenship'.[5] In this sense, multinational states show a complex form of national identity that is difficult to legitimize in terms of a monist statist nationalism (Taylor 1992c).

A normative refinement of liberal democratic theory would view pluralism as a value worth protecting and not simply as a fact to be tolerated. The normative and institutional movement towards 'advanced democratic societies'[6] implies, in the case of multinational states, a superior accommodation of component national identities in the symbols and democratic institutions of the different political collectiv-

---

[3] Nowadays, the political regulation of cultural pluralism can no longer maintain an anti-discriminatory attitude of an 'integrationist' nature. While it is difficult to defend, for example, a national particularism that wishes to be 'shielded' from a universalist 'moral' imperative, it also appears to be difficult to deny that the latter should regulate agreements that are relevant and accepted by the different national groups that make up the political collectivity.

[4] In the legitimation processes for the rights, institutions, policies, etc., of democracies, neither universality coincides with applicative impartiality nor particularity with partiality. See Miller 1995, ch. 3; Stocker 1992; Nagel 1991. See also Parfit 1984. In my opinion, the criticism that universalism directs at particularist positions is no more and no less valid than the particularist critique of universalism (Tully 1994b; Requejo 1999).

[5] An alternative approach, in terms of Kohlberg's conception of moral reasoning, would be to consider the legitimacy of the decisions of western democracies as an articulation of preconventional, conventional and postconventional stages of moral reasoning. From this perspective, the conventional terms have usually remained hidden, especially in liberal-democratic domestic politics. See 'democratic citizenship' in Kymlicka and Norman 1994. A critical analysis of the monist concept of the demos in liberal theories can be found in Requejo 1998a, section 1.

[6] The expression 'to establish an advanced democratic society' is from the introduction of the current Spanish constitution (1978), alongside clear statist references to a single and sovereign Spanish nation.

ities individuals belong to. And this, in turn, suggests that a reformulation of federal agreements in multinational societies is necessary.

1.2 Political liberalism and federalism: liberal federalism is neither decentralization nor subsidiarity

At the beginning of the twenty-first century, it is clear that a gulf exists between political theories of democratic liberalism and those of federalism and decentralization. The latter tend to focus on structures, actors, and federal procedures and processes. Studies of democratic theory, on the other hand, have tended to avoid extended reflection on federalism, particularly in those works with a rigorous philosophical base. This is a deficiency that can be found in both 'liberal' democratic theory and in political theory of a more 'republican' nature.[7]

In relation to whether it is possible that multinationalism can be articulated satisfactorily by means of federal agreements or regional decentralization schemes, my answer is that it is difficult to expect such a thing if we remain within the institutional framework of regional states or symmetrical federations. The latter have shown that they have the capacity to create and consolidate a uninational reality, but their institutionalization in multinational contexts has tended to be much more precarious in terms of legitimation. In fact, the 'pluralism' considered in classical theories of federalism was not even related to cultural pluralism. I believe that a possible escape route towards a more stable federal regime in societies with multinational demos is provided by the introduction of confederal and asymmetrical agreements that break with the statist nationalism of traditional uninational federations.[8] The question remains, however, whether there are some kinds of federal agreements capable of articulating states with complex territorial and national

---

[7] It is possible to identify at least four groups of theories in analyses of democratic legitimacy which should, in my opinion, be considered when addressing federalization and decentralization. First, the classical theories of liberal-democratic legitimacy, from Rawls's work onwards (including the debate between 'liberal', 'communitarian' and 'deliberative' conceptions of democracy); this is a tradition that has, in general, not been particularly attentive to analyses of federalism and decentralization. Second, the theories relating to cultural pluralism, above all those linked to the relationship between liberalism and nationalism. Third, theories of practical rationality and its relation to different types of political legitimation. And finally, the conceptions of decentralization and federalism, which had not generally shown themselves to be particularly inclined towards the normative discussion of democratic legitimacy until a few years ago. See Requejo 1998b, chs 1 and 2.

[8] In the interest of conceptual clarity it is advisable to distinguish, as Ronald Watts does, between the more general area of federalism, the more institutional and descriptive area of federal agreements, and the much more restricted area of federal states (Watts 1995). An empirical perspective can be found in Burgess and Gagnon 1993 and Elazar 1991.

identities from a liberal perspective of political recognition. This is currently one of the most important challenges of federalism (Katz and Tarr 1996; Webber 1994; Burgess 1996; Seidle 1994, Jeffery and Savigear 1991; MacCormick 1996; Boismenu 1996, Milne 1991).[9]

Before dealing with the case of Spain, I would like briefly to point out two general considerations that are sometimes confused in the debate about federalism in some states of the European Union (EU): the difference between federalism and the notions of decentralization and subsidiarity.

A. Decentralization. As many scholars (including Elazar, Watts and McRoberts) have pointed out when dealing with the legitimacy of states with federal structures, there are at least two different perspectives in analyses of comparative politics which are frequently mixed up: non-centralization and decentralization. This is a distinction which goes a long way beyond its apparently scholarly nature, as it is able to provide a rough and ready framework for understanding the implications of pluralist and monist conceptions of the demos for different federal models.

In the liberal tradition, federalism is based on the principle of a territorial division of powers. This principle, originally associated with a constitutional agreement on the centralization and non-centralization of specific functions, is clearly different from other organizational principles used by democracies, such as participation, efficiency, or equity. It is true that the central governments of some federations have been taking over functions that were formerly the responsibility of member states. The increase in the number of concurrent powers in other federal systems is also well known, especially with the development of the welfare state. However, despite these tendencies towards 'co-operative', 'organic', or 'executive' models, liberal federations uphold two fundaments: first, regardless of how powers are divided between the constituent units and the centre, the extant distribution of powers cannot be altered without mutual agreement; and second, that the original pact be drawn up between the different units on equal terms (Elazar 1987, p. 166).

Decentralization, on the other hand, starts with a single political unit and consists of dispersing power outwards from the centre to other centres. Because this arrangement presupposes the existence of a centralized structure before any constituent agreement can take place, the demos can be seen in more uniform monist terms in this model than in the traditional federal interpretation. We might say that the unity of the demos is based more on democratic than liberal logic in this case, for it

---

[9] The first reference to the concept of asymmetrical federalism can be found in Tarlton 1965.

displays a greater tendency towards a levelling use of the notion of 'democratic citizenship'. In short, depending on the dominant perspective adopted, we can observe different practical consequences, especially in the symbolic and institutional spheres, which are fundamentally important for the recognition of national pluralism in liberal-democratic systems.

In principle, traditional normative universalism offers a good basis upon which to evaluate the legitimacy of the decisions made by both levels of government in a federation, each one within its own sphere. However, in the event of conflict between the two levels, this universalism (operationalized by statism) offers bigger advantages to the central power. This is due to the federal government's ability to present its policies as being imbued with 'common democratic values', such as the 'absence of discrimination based on territory' for all the citizens of the federation. Following from this logic, demands made by the subunits for recognition or for greater self-government can be portrayed as being based on 'particularist interest'. Thus, from the perspective of traditional democratic federalism, a federal unit seeking recognition (i.e. the respect and guarantee of its national collective specificity) will probably have difficulty explaining to the citizens of other subunits that this claim is not inconsistent with equal citizenship, but only with standardizing interpretations of equality. Similarly, it will also be difficult to explain that denying recognition of multinationality within the framework of the federal state is tantamount to discriminating against one national identity in favour of another, the latter being just as particular as the former but couched in universalist rhetoric. In other words, the uniform treatment of distinct and different realities often associated with traditional normative universalism does not really promote the equality that constitutes one of the foundations of liberal democracies. In fact, the pretended cultural neutrality evident in most declarations of constitutional rights has tended to promote standardizing versions of state nation building.

B. Subsidiarity. Since the Maastricht Treaty became part of the symbolic landscape of the European Union, the notion of 'subsidiarity' has increasingly been invoked to define the relationship of EU organs and the institutions of member states. It is a term that has multiple meanings, but is most commonly used to connote an organizational and territorial principle requiring that decision making, or at least its implementation, be carried out in a sphere that is as close as possible to the citizen. Subsidiarity has thus been understood to refer to a technical distribution of powers between different administrative levels that is designed to guarantee efficiency and proximity to the citizen.

As has been previously stated, the original liberal conception of federal organization is linked to the territorial division of powers, rather than to the efficiency and proximity of decision making to the citizen. In other words, the division of powers is the starting pistol for federalism, not the finishing line. To question or to subordinate this division to 'efficiency' criteria (supposedly related with subsidiarity) or homogenizing 'democratic' criteria is thus to continue to reason in monist or unitarian terms. Or at least in nationalist monist terms.

Upon first glance, then, subsidiarity may appear to be a principle that is closely related to federal philosophy, and thus characterized by a decentralizing urge and a favourable disposition towards local autonomy. But on closer inspection, the hasty association of subsidiarity and federalism can be seen to be based on a serious conceptual confusion which may have grave practical repercussions. In fact, invoking subsidiarity in federal discourse may result in the erosion of the federal principle (Noël 1998).[10] What is more, this erosion may be particularly serious in the case of multinational federations, especially when their 'federal' structures are vaguely defined or poorly developed, as is the case of the present-day Spanish *estado de las autonomías*. It can be said that the difference between the principles of subsidiarity and federalism lies not in what we are looking at, but in how we look at it. Even a territorial organization characterized by a high degree of municipal decentralization, for instance, like that which currently exists in some Nordic countries, is a long way from the true spirit of federalism. In those states in which the federal principle has an important role to play, subsidiarity tends not to fit very well.

Subsidiarity may be useful as an organizational principle for a variety of levels of self-government conceived either in functional terms of efficiency or economies of scale. It may also be useful as a 'democratic' principle, not necessarily linked to efficiency, but rather aimed at bringing decision making closer to the citizens of a strongly united demos. But subsidiarity is not useful in designing political mechanisms to articulate multinational realities when these consider themselves to be distinct demos. Given this assessment, it can be seen that only a few federal models or agreements are aimed in the right direction. Here, democratic and liberal logic follows different paths to the normative and institutional principles of western democracies.[11]

---

[10] See also Lemieux 1996; Brown-John 1988.

[11] I have developed the contrast between liberal and democratic logics in Requejo 1994, chapters 5 and 6. For a revision of the Federalist Papers, see Abbott 1996. See also Sanders 1997; Stark 1997.

2   Plural and asymmetrical federalism: the Spanish case

Is the federal state a good model for regulating democratic citizenship in multinational societies? In earlier works, I have situated my answer to this question somewhere between a 'no' and a reluctant 'maybe', arguing, in the case of Spain, for the introduction of asymmetrical regulations (Requejo 1999 1998b).[12] Here I would like to enlarge on my reasons for suggesting these regulations from three perspectives: an analysis of the limits of the current constitutional model when it attempts to articulate the multinationality of Spanish society (section 2.1); by the distinction between what I have called the primary and secondary uses of state nationalism (section 2.2), and by the introduction of what I shall call 'agreements of plural federalism' in the context of the ongoing construction of the European Union (section 2.3).

2.1   Spain's estado de las autonomías: the regional model of the 1978 constitution

In general terms, it can be said that Spain has displayed a variety of frustrated attempts at nation building in contemporary times. The construction of an inclusive and legitimate Spanish nation-state has never been the successful outcome of Spanish nationalism. Non-state nationalisms, on the other hand, especially in the Basque Country and Catalonia, have been unable to consolidate a nation-building process based on obtaining their own state or federal structures. Up until the post-Franco period, the Spanish state's organization was based on the French model: there were two administrative levels – a dominant central power and a municipal level with a very low degree of autonomy – and an extremely centralized conception of the state. All attempts to articulate the state from more 'regionalized' premises, some of a very moderate nature, failed for different reasons: the First Republic (1873), the 'mancomunitats' of the Restoration period, and the 'integral' state of the Second Republic (1931–9).

The territorial model included in the 1978 Spanish constitution has evolved in very different conditions compared to those of past periods: (1) the transition from authoritarian to liberal-democratic rule; (2) the development of the Spanish welfare state; and (3) the ongoing process of European integration.[13] The result has been the *estado de las autonomías*, a new model of a fundamentally regional nature that establishes a

---

[12] See also RVAP 1997; IEA 1995; Moreno 1994, 1997a; Agranoff 1995; Fossas 1995.
[13] Public spending went from 23 per cent to 48 per cent of GDP in the 1972–96 period. Spain joined the European Community (today's EU) in 1986.

number of substate self-governing regions (autonomous communities or 'ACs') based on a process of 'variable geometry' determining the configuration of each.

I maintain that the *estado de las autonomías* is not a federal model, but a regional one. Despite the fact that in some works of comparative politics (Elazar 1991; Watts 1996) Spain often appears classified with the 'federal' states, there are many arguments that would suggest a more appropriate classification amongst 'regional' states. Spain is not an 'incomplete federation' (Agranoff 1995; Moreno 1994) but a highly decentralized regional state when compared with other regional states. Furthermore, the Spanish polity does have one thing in common with federations: decentralization is designed for all the territorial subunits (autonomous communities) and not only for some of them. Put together, all of the territories which enjoy constitutionally guaranteed political autonomy – currently seventeen ACs plus two cities in North Africa, Ceuta and Melilla – make up the whole of the territory of Spain.

However, there are also many elements which distance the current Spanish model from federations:

1. Constituent units. The autonomous communities are not constituent entities. The Spanish constitution establishes 'the indissoluble unity of the Spanish Nation' (article 2) and defines the 'Spanish people' as subject of the 'National sovereignty' (article 1). Some of the ACs did not even exist before the 1978 constitution.

2. Division of powers. The decentralization of legislative powers is unclear. The central power maintains its hegemony through the so-called *leyes de bases* (special constitutional laws), which are the same throughout the state. There are also overlappings between the regulations of central and 'autonomous' powers in the majority of areas of responsibility.

3. Judicial power. Unlike the legislative and executive powers, the *estado de las autonomías* has had practically no effect on the structure of the judiciary, which continues to be that of a centralized state.

4. Constitutional Court. This is an organ of the state and not an organ of the central power. The ACs are not involved in the appointment of its judges, which are only appointed by the parliament, the judiciary and the government of the central power.

5. Senate. The upper chamber is not linked to the federated units. The majority of the senators are elected by the 'provinces', a set of administrative divisions which date back to the nineteenth century.

6. Taxation. The *estado de las autonomías* is a long way from any model of fiscal federalism. Almost all taxes are collected by the central power, which proceeds to return an amount equivalent to that which the

ACs need in order to finance the services they provide. The Basque Country and Navarra are the exceptions to this rule as they enjoy an asymmetrical fiscal agreement with the central power. This special arrangement is based on a number of 'historical rights', and is regulated under terms which are more confederal than federal. By means of the so-called 'economic accord' (*concierto económico*), these two communities collect taxes and pass on a percentage to the central power to pay for the services that the latter provides for the community.

7. European Union. The ACs are not considered to be political actors in relation to the principal institutions of the European Union, in contrast to the federations of the EU (Germany, Belgium). The central government has resisted giving any important role to the ACs in relation to European issues.

8. Constitutional reform. The ACs do not participate in the process of constitutional reform. This is in the hands of the central parliament and of the citizens of the state through referenda.

The general conclusion is that the current Spanish *estado de las autonomías* can hardly be called a 'federation', even when one makes a very free interpretation of the 1978 constitution. Despite the fact that the ACs possess a high degree of autonomy in some areas, the basic characteristics of the model are grounded in a regionalizing perspective a long way from federal logic. The most important issue to be resolved is, however, quite different: the political accommodation of a multinational reality.

In my view, the biggest design fault of the Spanish constitution is that it attempts to achieve two distinct objectives at the same time: the decentralization of the state, and the articulation of its multinationality. Although both of these desirable objectives must be regulated within the constitutional framework, they can hardly be regulated with the same mechanisms.

This regional constitution establishes two ways of achieving self-government, depending on whether the community in question has enjoyed autonomy in the past, under the Second Republic.[14] In this way, a transitory asymmetry of powers is established to achieve the highest level of self-government. However, the final design for the distribution of powers is of a potentially symmetrical nature, if the autonomous communities wish to achieve the highest level of self-government, with the exception of the regulation of certain differences (*hechos diferenciales*: own languages, insularity, civil law, historical rights,

[14] Second transitory clause; art. 151, 143, 144 of the Spanish constitution of 1978.

etc.). This complex constitutional design becomes more complicated when one establishes the possibility that the central power can devolve powers to certain communities.[15] On the other hand, the most asymmetrical legal characteristic is the economic agreement enjoyed by the Basque Country and Navarra, which is based on the so-called 'historical rights' which predate the 1978 constitution.[16]

It is possible to identify three phases in the development of the Spanish *estado de las autonomías*:

I. Constituent phase (1978–81). This period corresponds to the negotiation of the constitution and the *estatutos de autonomía* (statutes of autonomy) for the communities possessing national characteristics. The articulation of the state's multinationality does not take the form of a 'constitutional solution', as this matter had not been resolved politically during the period of political transition. The result could be described as a procedural framework for decentralization, which could develop in a variety of ways.

II. Autonomous agreement phase (1981–92). During the 1980s, the main political parties with representation throughout Spain (UCD, PSOE, PP)[17] sign two pacts concerning the autonomous communities, the first in 1981 and the second in 1992. Centralism came to dominate autonomous development through the passing of the constitutional 'basic laws' *(leyes de bases)* by the central political institutions (such as, laws governing the universities, the civil service, and local government). One of the consequences of this was the increasing judicialization of autonomous development in the first half of the 1980s, which resulted in the constitutional Court playing an important and leading role. The final event marking this period was the establishment of a homogenizing model of political development, inspired in part by the German model, which is at present far from being consolidated.

III. The phase characterized by parliamentary agreements with the Basque and Catalan nationalist parties (Partido Nacionalista Vasco (PNV), Convergència i Unió (CiU)) (1993–2000). This phase is marked by the absence of majority governments, forcing the largest parliamentary parties (PSOE between 1993 and 1996, PP since 1996) to look for support from other parties in order to guarantee the stability of the central government (governability). The confusion between decentralization and multinationality that characterized the two preceding

---

[15] Article 150.2, used by the devolution of powers in the cases of the community of Valencia and the Canary Islands.

[16] First additional clause of the Spanish constitution. An analysis of 'historical rights', in Herrero de Miñon 1998.

[17] UCD: Unión del Centro Democrático (centrist); PSOE: Partido Socialista Obrero Español (centre-left); PP: Partido Popular (conservative).

phases has yet to be resolved. This confusion provides the setting for the two basic perspectives from which the autonomous model is perceived by different political actors:

(a) Decentralization perspective. Spain is conceived of as a single national reality divided into seventeen autonomous communities. Although these ACs clearly differ in terms of powers, they are viewed as belonging to a similar conceptual framework as the fifty-two administrative provinces of the earlier centralized model. From this perspective, it is suggested that the most suitable federal techniques are those designed to achieve a multilevel but homogeneous polity. With this perspective, uniformity and symmetry are considered the most suitable procedures whose legitimacy is based on democratic 'equality' and 'citizenship'.

(b) Multinational perspective. Spain is conceived as a society made up of diverse nations that should be constitutionally recognized and politically articulated. From this point of view, the suitability of political arrangements is to be judged on how well they promote the national diversity of the Spanish polity. This makes it convenient to introduce legal asymmetries or agreements of a confederal nature in those areas relating to national symbols, institutions and powers.[18]

Despite its success in decentralization, the Spanish constitutional model continues to pose an unresolved question concerning the regulation of multinationality. The present-day *estado de las autonomías* is obviously an improvement in relative terms, especially when it is compared with the illiberal and undemocratic constitutional regulations of Spain's recent history. But this relative improvement is unable to conceal serious shortcomings in the regulation and fit of its national realities, in symbolic, institutional and self-government terms. It can be said that the *estado de las autonomías* worked relatively well when it had to decentralize the institutions of Franco's authoritarian state; but it is a model that has been far less successful at recognizing and accommodating the multinationality of the contemporary Spanish state. It is somewhat contradictory to treat the different national demos as if they were just ordinary 'Spanish autonomous regions' like the others. My

---

[18] This perspective is currently being elaborated by the two parties that govern Catalonia in coalition. In 1997, both the CDC (Convergència Democràtica de Catalunya) and UDC (Unió Democràtica de Catalunya) drew up internal documents on how to best express the multinationality of the Spanish state institutionally: 'Per un nou horitzó per a Catalunya', CDC; 'La sobirania de Catalunya i l'estat plurinacional', UDC. The concept of 'shared sovereignty', meanwhile, which is defended almost single-handedly by Catalan president Jordi Pujol, takes the polity existing in the Spanish territories before the Catalan defeat in the War of the Spanish Succession (1716) as its main point of historical reference.

conclusion is that something essential, not just procedural, has been left unresolved in the current Spanish political model.[19]

2.2   The question of national identities

One of the main difficulties one faces when trying to reconcile the decentralization and multinationalist perspectives is the use of the word 'nation' in the expression 'Spanish nation'. In this instance, the word has two levels of connotation, primary and secondary. The primary level is that which defines the national identity of citizens over distinctive criteria of affinity including language, culture, sense of group history, desire to belong to a specific collectivity, and so on. Despite the existence of a spectrum of mixed identities, the primary use of the term 'nation' in Spain generally implies four basic types of identity: Spanish, Catalan, Basque and Galician. In this primary sense, to see oneself as having a 'Spanish' national identity demonstrates the affinity that is shared by residents of Zaragoza, Seville and Madrid, for instance. While some of the citizens of Galicia, Catalonia and the Basque Country might also share the 'Spanish' national identity in its primary sense, many Galicians, Catalans and Basques prefer to think of themselves as belonging to their own nations in the primary sense of the word. Although the primary conception of the Spanish 'nation' might be shared by a majority of the citizens of the Spanish state, then, it is a long way from being a conception that is 'common to all Spaniards' as the constitution states. Spanish nationality in its primary sense thus constitutes what we may call the 'hidden nationality' in arguments about the multinational nature of the Spanish polity. In descriptive terms, one cannot regard Catalonia, Galicia and the Basque Country as mere subunits of a Spanish nation which, understood in this primary sense, does not exist as a common point of reference for all citizens.

The secondary use of the term 'Spanish nation' regards Spain as a 'nation of nations'. This usage attempts to include all citizens of the Spanish state within the nation, regardless of what their dominant national affinity, understood in the primary sense, may be. The expression 'nation of nations', however, is not very precise. Paradoxically, it is

---

[19] To dilute multinationality within the wider concept of 'differences' (*hecho diferencial*) is not of much help when dealing with this question. The nationalist forces of the three 'historical minority nations' (Catalonia, the Basque Country and Galicia) have pointed out the need to proceed towards a reform and a reappraisal of the Spanish constitution in multinational terms. The concepts of self-government and 'shared sovereignity', which had been left out of the debate until now, have been given new impetus in the political arena.

acceptable to both state and non-state nationalist forces alike, as long as it is not defined.

On the one hand, Spanish nationalists usually prefer to emphasize the first part of the expression, that of the 'nation', sometimes written with a capital 'N' as it appears in the constitution. They also tend to use the term exclusively in its primary sense, neglecting its secondary meaning despite the fact that the 'nation' here refers to all the citizens of the state. This Spanish nationalism thus restricts the second part of the expression, the nations, to Catalonia, the Basque Country and Galicia, excluding the primary sense of a Spanish nation. Instead, these three 'nations' are to be tolerated in different ways, ranging from considering them as interesting but always subordinate elements of the 'Spanish nation', to believing that it is simply better to ignore them as much as possible, while wishing they did not exist at all.

On the other hand, Catalan, Basque and Galician nationalists generally prefer the second part of the expression 'nation of nations'. Here, however, it is the notion of 'nations' which tends to be most controversial and confusing, especially when it comes to deciding whether to include the Spanish nation in its primary sense. The notion of an umbrella Spanish 'nation' in the secondary sense of the term, meanwhile, is tolerated as well as it can be by most Catalan, Basque and Galician nationalists. But they tend to view this conception of the Spanish nation as either a fictitious, rhetorical and artificial construction, built on an unreal state nationalism, or as an existing but largely irrelevant reality hindering the recognition and self-government of the minority nations in the primary sense.

One has to conclude that the expression 'nation of nations' is very confusing indeed when nationalists of different stripes mix primary and secondary versions of the term 'nation' when they refer to Spain. This confusion is also implicit in the constitution,[20] which hinders the construction of a secondary notion of the Spanish nation that is acceptable to all the citizens of all the national demos in this multinational polity.[21] To these difficulties we must also add the existence of

[20] This is the case of the well-known article 2: 'The constitution is based on the indissoluble unity of the Spanish Nation, common and indivisible homeland of all Spaniards, and it recognizes and guarantees the right to autonomy of the nationalities and regions that it is composed of and the solidarity between all of them' (translated by the author).

[21] More than sixty years ago, Azaña, the president of the Second Spanish Republic, was already stating that 'in order to solve this, it is not enough to change the political system; we must change the politics of the system . . . the last state in the peninsula that was part of the old Catholic monarchy which succumbed under the weight of the despotic, absolutist Crown was Catalonia, and there is no doubt that the defender of Catalan liberties could reasonably say that he was the last defender of Spanish liberties

the seventeen territorial units under the current model. These units are subsumed in a regional model with federalizing features that has failed to develop the potential asymmetries existing in the constitution of 1978.[22] These asymmetries would be well-suited to facilitating a recognition of the pluralism of national identities in Spain, thus modulating different ways of belonging to the Spanish polity. I think that without asymmetrical regulations allowing for the development of national symbols, institutions and powers, it is more than likely that the secondary sense of the Spanish nation will remain an unresolved matter for the Spanish democratic system for a long time to come.

2.3   *Multinationality and federalism: plural federal agreements, European citizenship, and 'regions'*

The increasing complexity of a world that is becoming more and more globalized at the international level, and more and more plural at the domestic level, also requires greater complexity in new federal agreements. One of the potential advantages of these arrangements is their flexibility and adaptability to specific situations of territorial cultural pluralism. At present, the history of federations has been characterized mainly by symmetrical models. These are models that are very closely linked to uninational realities and their statist conceptions, which are associated with the process of building a single nation. Nevertheless, in multinational polities like Spain, in which different processes of nation building coexist with the construction of the European Union, it is time to start thinking about regulating specific jurisdictions through asymmetrical agreements. This process, in turn, offers one of the main avenues of renewal for the future of federalism: the establishment of different types of agreements depending on the sphere which is to be regulated, and according to the characteristics of each level of government involved. That is to say, the aim should be to implement what might be called plural federalism.

In the light of past experience, agreements of an asymmetrical or confederal nature will be most relevant in those spheres that are closely related to national identities and to their cultural expression. The growing complexity of intergovernmental networks demands that we

. . . the assimilatory policies of the Spanish state really began in the nineteenth century. The policies of the kings of the House of Austria were not assimilatory; but the liberal, parliamentary and bourgeois politics of the nineteenth century were' (Azaña [1932] 1977, pp. 34–5) (translated by the author).

[22] One case is the distinction between 'nationalities and regions' expressed in article 2 of the Spanish constitution, which is not mentioned in the rest of the text as it is subsumed by the more general notion of 'autonomous communities'.

overcome the statist rigidities of traditional constitutionalism. I am not suggesting that we pit a form of symmetrical global federalism against asymmetrical federal arrangements in multinational states, but rather that we choose which type of agreement turns out to be most suitable in a given sphere in order to optimize the regulation of national plurality. When the national reality of a state is plural and asymmetrical, establishing symmetrical federal agreements is ill-advised.[23]

The following is a synthetic example of plural federalism for Spain that I think would accommodate the multinationality of this state to a far greater degree than current arrangements. It involves envisaging three kinds spheres – a symbolic-linguistic sphere, an institutional sphere, and one related to powers – along with three types of federal agreements – one relating to the recognition of a general pluralism of national identities, the second to asymmetrical or confederal accords, and the third to symmetrical agreements. The first and second type of arrangements represent the core of plural federalism. In general terms, pluralist agreements for national identities result in regulations that support the multinational character of the state as a whole, by means of its symbols, linguistic regulations, educational curricula and international representation.[24] Plural federalism attempts to improve the articulation of the moral, ethical and pragmatic dimensions of practical rationality. In symbolic and linguistic spheres, this relates to questions like the content and use of flags and national anthems, or the regulation of multilingualism. In the Spanish case, other examples would include things as simple as the use of the four state languages on coinage (whether this be Spanish or EU coinage), identity cards, passports and so on. This is something that is relatively easy to implement, and it would represent a tangible example of movement towards an equality of

---

[23] To remain within the perspective of regional decentralization models or the perspective of 'subsidiarity' will be even less appropriate when we try to accommodate multinational and asymmetrical realities. Again, this accommodation implies thinking in terms of different democratic demos that have to be constitutionally articulated based on their own cultural characteristics and their expressed will for self-government. It is not a question of a decentralization process. For an analysis of the suitability of asymmetrical agreements in multinational contexts, see Requejo 1999, section 3.

[24] This seems to me a mechanism that should be introduced even if the seventeen autonomous communities were reduced in number. I believe that this is a procedural mechanism that is preferable to reducing the number of senators from the autonomous communities of the national collectivities in relation to the number of senators from other communities, or to a mechanism of fixing a series of spheres in which those senators were not allowed to vote as they would be dealing with questions over which the autonomous communities had exclusive jurisdiction. Other questions in the institutional sphere would include the broadcasting of autonomous television stations throughout the territory of the state (or EU), or plurilingualism on private TV stations (Requejo 1999, Watts 1991, Michelmann and Soldatos 1990).

citizenship and a pluralist understanding of the Spanish nation in its secondary sense. Within the institutional sphere, asymmetrical mechanisms must be established in the upper chamber of the central parliament, such as the right of veto in certain circumstances for the representatives of the national minorities. On the other hand, asymmetrical and confederal agreements are related to matters that are crucially important for the self-government of national entities. Table 1 below summarizes a possible regulation of this type of federalism in the case of Catalonia (I exclude the symmetrical or mere decentralizing agreements).

The fundamental question for the regulation of the three spheres mentioned above in a multinational state is, above all, a question of application. It is a question of a more practical than theoretical nature, which must be accompanied by *modus vivendi* agreements between the political actors involved in each specific case. In Spain's case, the great advantage of the present situation compared with past experiences is the existence of the EU.[25]

Since the 1992 Maastricht Treaty of European Union (TEU), the image of the EU as a union with clearly federal elements has been reinforced, in contrast with the preceding European Community's image as a series of intergovernmental relations of a purely economic nature. The EU may be characterized as the pragmatic construction of a set of political (and also fragmented) sovereignties led by the executive institutions of member states. It is a 'postmodern' union, in that it has no established final design and because it goes far beyond the European order established by the Treaty of Westphalia. In short, Maastricht represents a turning point in the construction of a European polity (McKay 1997). I want to focus here on two elements of the TEU, notably its recognition of both the concept of a European citizenship and the importance of regions in Europe. Along with the other more visible trappings of European statehood (including the single currency, common foreign and security policies, the common market and social cohesion), these two features mark the beginning of a unique new political framework. On the one hand, this new arrangement plays down secessionist aspirations within the states of the Union. On the other hand, however, it gives shape to new ways of overcoming the implicit statism of liberal democracies by trying to find a place within EU institutions for the distinct national realities of the continent to express

---

[25] This is a framework that means that Spain even has a relative advantage compared to other multinational polities, such as Canada, which are more evolved democratically, but also more polarized (McRoberts 1997a; Gibbins and Laforest 1998; Karmis and Gagnon 1996; MacCormick 1996). For the Canadian case and asymmetry, see also Weber 1994; Vipond 1995; Burgess 1996; Seidle 1994; Boismenu 1996, Lenihan, Robertson and Tassé 1994; Milne 1994.

Table 1. *Plural federalism: a proposal for the Spanish case*

	Regulation of state national pluralism	Confederate or asymmetrical regulations concerning Catalonia's link to the state, the EU and in the international sphere
Symbolic-linguistic sphere	• Constitutional recognition of equality of linguistic and national cultures • Plurilingualism: – Official name of state – Coinage – *Documents, personal iden-ity cards (passport, identity card, driving licence etc.) – Stamps • Plurinational state symbols (anthem, flag, etc.)	• Control over uses of anthems flags (of Catalonia, the state and the EU) • Own national teams. Catalonia's representation in international sporting events (world and European Championships) • Official recognition of the COC (Olympic Committee of Catalonia) • Register of births, marriages and deaths, mercantile register and land register in Catalan • *Optional monolingualism in personal identity cards • *Optional monolingualism in official documents
Institutional sphere	• Plurilingualism in central parliament (documents and oral speeches) • Plurilingualism in embassies and consulates • Plurinationality in the state's cultural policies abroad	• International representation according to the plurinationality of the state • Differentiated representation in the EU and the Council of Europe • Generalitat delegations in international sphere • Own representation in EU for own powers • Own representation in UNESCO • Possibility of agreements between communities (extendable to all state communities) • Single electoral constituency for Catalonia in Spanish general elections and those of the EU • Only two administrative authorities: Generalitat and local authority. Suppression of state peripheral administration • Senate: – 2nd-level election by communities – senators of minority nations have right of veto – symmetrical bicameralism

Table 1. *contd.*

	Regulation of state national pluralism	Confederate or asymmetrical regulations concerning Catalonia's link to the state, the EU and in the international sphere
		• Right of veto for Generalitat of regulations of central power that affect Catalonia exclusively • Constitutional Court: composition with specific appointment for national minorities • General Council of the Judiciary and Tribunal de Cuentas (econ. control court): specific composition • Supreme Court of Catalonia: last court of appeal for own powers, regulations of the Generalitat and local authorities • Own organization of judiciary and its government
Powers sphere	• Inclusion of plurinationality and plurilinguism in educational curricula (primary and secondary education) • Creation of language and cultural departments of the national minorities in the state's universities • Plurilinguism in the central power's policies directed at all the citizens	• Confederal regulations: own legislation and policies (local power, civil law, universities, infrastructures, internal and external electoral regulations, language, culture, foreign policy, concerning own powers) • Asymmetrical regulations (with state coordination): own legislation and policies in economic, fiscal, education, European, immigration, health, social security and communications, (powers to control own telecommunications), domestic affairs

Note:
* Alternative regulations of the Generalitat (Catalan self-government institutions)

themselves and be recognized. It is true that these formulations are as yet timid and vague. But their very existence indicates a movement towards a political, and not merely economic, formulation of the foundations of the Union from premises that are no longer exclusively based on the state.

The first thing that must be said about 'European citizenship' is that it is a vague concept. It is characterized by a constant dualism, which hesitates between falling back on member states' different notions of citizenship and the will to establish a status common to all the citizens of the Union, independent of which state they belong to (Preuss and Requejo 1998; Everson and Preuss 1995; Martiniello 1995). As has occurred in other spheres in which agreements have been established, it seems that the first aspect will be dominant in the development of European citizenship, at least in the first phase (Dahrendorf 1994). The basic reason for this lies in the precarious existence of the present institutions of the EU (Martiniello 1995; d'Oliveira 1994). Because of this, the regulation of a series of rights common to all European citizens will be limited. The enlargement of these rights would also go beyond the limits specified by the Maastricht Treaty.[26] When the matters included in this 'citizenship' are enumerated, then, it becomes clear that most of the elements are of relatively low political profile: freedom of movement between member states and the right to reside anywhere in the Union, participation in municipal and European elections in the state of residence, the right to protection from the diplomatic and consular authorities of any member state in non-member countries, the right of petition before the European parliament, and access to the European Ombudsman.[27] There is nothing in the Treaty approaching a declaration of rights.

Based on these foundations, European citizenship will essentially continue to be defined by member states rather than European-level institutions, while political identities will continue to be articulated around national components of both a state and non-state nature (Keating 1988 1996a). Without a wide range of common rights, the chances of developing a European identity seem to be slim. From the point of view of national pluralism, however, this result has ambivalent consequences. On the one hand, the statist components of the liberal approach to interpreting European citizenship are maintained. On the other hand, the fact that this is a gradual process will most likely permit a future fit not only of states, but also of 'regions' within the institutions and processes of collective decision making of the Union. In contrast to past Community clauses stemming from the Treaty of Rome, Maastricht has permitted the EU to begin to regard 'regions' as legitimate political

---

[26] Treaty of Maastricht, section I, Common Provisions, articles A and B.

[27] Treaty of Maastricht, section II, second part, articles 8, 8A, 8B, 8C, 8D. This low profile is reinforced by the low level of internal migration among European citizens (about 1.4 per cent of the population, Eurostat, 6/1993: 1–10; quoted by Everson and Preuss 1995, p. 27).

actors, as the principle of territoriality has gradually pluralized itself and escaped the monopoly of state control. From the moment that the Committee of Regions was created, also under Maastricht, European regions began to enjoy direct representation within the institutions of the EU for the first time. But it is an institution with little real power as yet. Most notably, the Committee lacks elected representatives and is restricted to advisory functions. Moreover, regions share their representation with municipalities on the Committee. And finally, the well-known principle of subsidiarity, also introduced by Maastricht, may not necessarily be applicable to the case of the state subunits. In Spain, for instance, subsidiarity is usually understood to apply only to the relations between member states and the EU.

The future political construction of Europe will most likely include more federal features, of both a symmetrical and an asymmetrical nature. The successful institutional articulation of a 'liberal politics of recognition' on a European scale, however, will also require the reduction of the state's organizational hegemony and a diminishing of the tensions generated by competing nationalisms in multinational states. The EU is partially succeeding in this respect, but minority nations in multinational states – such as United Kingdom, Belgium and Spain – will also have to situate their struggle for recognition and self-government within the framework of the EU, probably through asymmetrical mechanisms and common European networks. There is no doubt that the ongoing dilution of statism that has characterized the European order since the Treaty of Westphalia will continue to be a slow process full of stops and starts. But I am optimistic that European-level regulation of national pluralism and the elaboration of an effective European citizenship will be two parts of the same process by the second half of the present century. When one is dealing with political processes, of course, nothing is certain. It is therefore important that those organizations that make Europeanism a central part of their political programmes, and which work towards pluralism and the recognition of national identities, are ruled by up-to-date elites that are able to tackle the new problems that arise with new concepts and attitudes. This is for the very good reason that 'art begins where imitation ends'.

3   Conclusions

In this chapter I have highlighted some aspects of the current institutional revision of democratic legitimacy in multinational states, presenting an application for the Spanish state by means of the notion of plural federalism which includes asymmetrical and confederal regulations.

In the first section, I have shown that the implicit statism of traditional political liberalism establishes particularist cultural biases in its pretended universalism. I have defended the suitability of accommodating the different 'ethical' components of practical rationality that exist in multinational societies in the constitutional framework, as well as the suitability of breaking the monist uniformity of the concept of the demos that is usually implicit in political liberalism. The general objective is to promote the 'universal' values of democratic liberalism by minimizing the cultural biases of yesteryear. It suggests that we should focus more on the suitability of *modus vivendi* type agreements. This is a key point in order to obtain a stable and legitimate framework supporting a 'liberal politics of recognition' in multinational societies. Finally, in this first section I have focused on some of the shortcomings of the territorial division of powers when it is confused with the perspectives of decentralization or subsidiarity. The latter are organizational principles regarded in more monist (and 'democratic') terms than in the federal (and 'liberal') perspective.

In the second section, I have presented an institutional revision based on the aspects mentioned in the previous section. I maintain that the current Spanish *estado de las autonomías* can hardly be called a 'federation'. Despite the high degree of autonomy achieved in some areas by the 'autonomous communities', the basic characteristics of the model are predominantly based on a regionalizing perspective which is a long way from federal logic. I have clarified the concept of the 'Spanish nation' by distinguishing between the primary and secondary uses of this concept.

I believe that the biggest design fault of the Spanish *estado de las autonomías* is the attempt to tackle two very different issues at the same time: the decentralization of the state, and the accommodation of its multinationality. These different objectives need different institutional and procedural mechanisms. Plural federalism is arguably a better way to articulate normative and institutional relations between the demos of different national collectives, which are based on a mutual 'liberal politics of recognition'. The core of plural federalism is based on regulations in the national pluralism of the state, and on confederal and asymmetrical federal regulations. I have put forward an application of both kinds of regulations for the current Spanish case, and have presented a potential reform of the Spanish *estado de las autonomías* after establishing three different regulatory spheres. This proposal also takes into account Spain's membership of the European Union, and the potential and ambivalent possibilities contained in the concepts of European citizenship and European regionalism which were introduced by the Maastricht Treaty of European Union.

Part II

Struggles over recognition and institutions of accommodation

Part II examines the tensions between normative claims for and against recognition and institutional and procedural forms of accommodation. In chapter 5, Dimitrios Karmis and Alain-G. Gagnon use a comparative study of Canada and Belgium since the 1960s to demonstrate both the high importance and the major difficulties of reaching a federal balance between unity and diversity in multinational societies. They argue that neither the pan-Canadianism strategy adopted by Trudeau in Canada, nor the constitutionalization of cultural and linguistic *cloisonnement* in Belgium, have led to a balance between unity and diversity. These processes, they suggest, have led to identity fragmentation, in Canada's case by an overemphasis on universalism, and in the case of Belgium by an excess of particularism. In short, neither outright denial nor ad hoc accommodation seems to be able to provide long-lasting just solutions. Attaining this delicate balance between universalism and particularism requires a thorough political engineering and a political will that are lacking at the present time.

In chapter 6 François Rocher, Christian Rouillard and André Lecours examine how political parties reflecting specific national identities have developed to challenge the constitutional and institutional frameworks of their states. They also argue that the transformations that these nationalist parties make to party systems may be an enduring source of instability. Specifically, they analyse the political reforms in Belgium, Spain and Canada in terms of the checks and balances installed to attain political stability. They come to the conclusion that not all reforms succeed in such a quest. The authors proceed from different perspectives in evaluating federal reforms in these countries. Rocher, Rouillard and Lecours, follow two lines of argument – one based on horizontal and vertical cleavages in terms of identities, and a second one based on shared spaces. From this, they conclude that Belgium's national identity is being eradicated, that in Spain there is an hierarchy of identities, and that in Canada one is faced with conflicting identities.

A complementary interpretation of Spain is provided by Luis Moreno in chapter 7, 'Ethnoterritorial Concurrence in Multinational Societies: the Spanish *Comunidades Autónomas*'. Moreno is concerned with the checks and balances that constitute the foundations of successful federal arrangements. Moreno claims that a characteristic of the Spanish case has been the existence of a dual identity, or compound nationality, which has contributed to the stability of the political system. Following the enactment of the 1978 constitution, the recognition of diversity in Spain has not only significantly decreased conflicts. It has also enhanced democracy by creating civic channels for citizen participation.

In chapter 8, Shane O'Neill discusses 'Mutual recognition and the Accommodation of National Diversity: constitutional Justice in Northern Ireland'. The argument made by O'Neill to resolve instability and injustice in Northern Ireland is both innovative and straightforward. To achieve the purported goals, one would need to be able to deconstruct hierarchical patterns of power relations that have developed over the years and to seek an inclusive political culture. Tackling the conflict in Northern Ireland from a philosophical perspective, O'Neill argues that nothing less than an egalitarian form of bi-nationalism can end injustices and political instability. It is suggested that egalitarian bi-nationalism can be accomplished through a constitutional settlement that would make both Britain and Ireland jointly sovereign. The author discusses the 'Good Friday Agreement' of 1998 from this critical perspective and concludes that, even though this accord indicates that some significant progress has been made, the proposed arrangement does not put an end to hierarchical relations between unionists and nationalists. An inclusive political culture has still to be achieved.

In chapter 9, 'Federalist Language Policies: the cases of Canada and Spain', Pierre Coulombe's focus is on language rights in multinational federations. He argues that competing claims over language policy are often based on the symbolic issues associated with language policy. This reality, in turn, is reflected in the state's response to claims of justice and to power struggles among linguistic communities. Discussing the cases of Canada and Spain, Coulombe argues that the liberal tradition is unable to account for diversity and suggests that there are two strands of liberalism which inadvertently justify the denial of diversity. For Coulombe, cultural identity is important for the individual as he/she is situated within a collective group. He thus asserts that cultural rights must be considered in conjunction with the traditional liberal conception of individual rights. Coulombe makes the point that cultural rights, such as the right to the preservation of one's language, are now frequently presented side-by-side with traditional individual rights, such as the right to freedom of expression and the right to physical integrity.

In addition to this universal right of cultural identity, the force of a particular claim often depends on the historical grievances involved. Therefore, state intervention in the market of cultures and languages is not only about regulating and managing intercommunal conflict; it is also about a moral obligation. Coulombe views the multilayered and dual belonging that is associated with multinational federations as a welcome situation in which federal citizens may belong to two nations and refuse to rank their loyalties. He concludes that a mutual acceptance of the legitimacy of language policies between Quebec and Ottawa can help attenuate the tensions emerging from the coexistence of policies, while in Spain he finds no recognition of linguistic diversity at the federal level.

Michael Burgess closes the second section in chapter 10 with an analysis of 'Competing National Visions: Quebec–Canada Relations in a Comparative Perspective'. He starts by making a distinction between uninational and multinational federations. Burgess contrasts two different federal settings in which justice and stability interact. He compares the uninational federalism devised by the *Federalist Papers* with the federalism used to bring together people with different descent, race and culture. He follows this with an interpretation of Canadian federalism as an example of the second type of federalism. Burgess analyses five dimensions of Canada–Quebec relations – language politics, the 'distinct society', centre-periphery relations, asymmetrical federalism, and the structure and process of constitutional reform – and concludes that there are two competing national visions in Canada and Quebec.

5 Federalism, federation and collective identities in Canada and Belgium: different routes, similar fragmentation[1]

Dimitrios Karmis and Alain-G. Gagnon

As exemplified in the simultaneous presence of rising trends towards atomization, economic, political and cultural integration, the proliferation of nationalist movements, and the multiplication of identity-based demands, the early twenty-first century is marked by tensions between universalism and particularism. These tensions tend to result in a growing polarization of political and theoretical positions, most often expressed through a debate on citizenship. Between the discourses of homogenizing universalism, exclusive nationalism, and postmodern hyperfragmentation or atomization, little space is left for a balance between unity and diversity. In this context, despite the recent collapse of federations in central and eastern European countries, most of those who believe in the suitability and feasibility of a balance between unity and diversity still consider federations – or some other type of federal system – as one of the most valuable options (see Kymlicka 1998b; Smith 1995a; Forsyth 1994, pp. 22–3; Norman 1994; Taylor 1993a; Gagnon 1993a, pp. 21–31). By way of a comparative study of the evolution of federalism, federation and collective identities in Canada and Belgium since the 1960s, this chapter seeks to demonstrate both the high importance and the major difficulties of reaching a federal balance between unity and diversity in multinational and polyethnic countries.[2]

---

[1] This chapter is a translated and revised version of an article previously published in French (see Karmis and Gagnon 1996). We wish to thank Raffaele Iacovino, PhD candidate at McGill University, for his assistance in translating the original version of this text.

[2] On the distinction between multinational and polyethnic, see Kymlicka (1995, pp. 11–26). Both the high value and the problematic nature of federalism in deeply diverse states are well captured by what Kymlicka calls 'the paradox of multinational federalism': while it provides national minorities with a workable alternative to secession, it also helps to make secession a more realistic alternative by reinforcing the belief that the group is able to exercise full sovereignty. According to Kymlicka, the fact that federalism is not likely to remove the issue of secession from the political agenda – 'indeed, it is likely to form the benchmark against which federal systems are measured' –

A balance between unity and diversity – within a single multinational and polyethnic country – may be defined as the institutionalization of both the plurality and the asymmetry of allegiances in compatible ways. Such a definition means that a balance may be reached through very different institutional forms, varying from one spatio-temporal context to another (for converging definitions, see LaSelva 1993 and Dumont 1989).

We shall see that even in Canada and Belgium, where the conditions are among the most favourable[3] and where contrasting federal formulas have been adopted for thirty years, the outcome is a similar identity fragmentation. Neither the pan-Canadianism stemming from Pierre Trudeau's vision, nor the constitutionalization of cultural and linguistic *cloisonnement*, or partitioning, in Belgium have led to a balance between unity and diversity. On the contrary, they have often contributed to processes of identity fragmentation already in course, the former by excess of universalism, the latter by excess of particularism. From a strictly practical point of view, the result has been an increase in political and social fragmentation, along with the instability which comes with it. From a moral perspective, the access to primary public goods such as political liberty and social solidarity has been considerably affected. In the first part of the chapter, a history of the evolution of collective identities in both countries will serve to contextualize the federal solutions introduced over the last thirty years. In the second and third parts, we shall see how and to what extent both federal solutions have contributed to identity fragmentation and its problems. Finally, we shall evaluate the implications of our findings for the normative theorizing of citizenship, particularly in the case of multinational and polyethnic states.

It should be noted that the concept of collective identities will be used in a particular sense. It will refer to the diverse ethico-political definitions and redefinitions of a country (our unit of comparison) – at once products and sources of sentiments of belonging – in competition in the public sphere. To be more precise, we could speak of 'global' collective identities, in the sense that such identities are constituted by definitions

---

is no reason to reject federal solutions, because 'federalism is often the only option available for accommodating conflicting national identities within a multination state. And, even if a federal system eventually dissolves, it may bequeath important lessons regarding the nature and value of democratic tolerance. So federalism is certainly worth trying' (Kymlicka 1998b, p. 142).

[3] In Canada and Belgium, the economic conditions, the political culture and the history of intercommunity relations make it reasonable to assert that the cultural and linguistic tensions are more firmly grounded within the democratic process than in most other countries.

and images of the global political entity of belonging – the country being the political entity inclusive of the whole social diversity which characterizes a territory (gender, sexual orientation, generation, class, region, nation, ethnicity, language, religion, etc.). Global collective identities are the various and often conflicting imaginary representations which are made of this diversity (multicultural state, community of communities, indivisible nation, community of solidarity, etc.).[4] The evolution of the relationships between global collective identities, federalism and federation will be studied through comparative historical sociology,[5] and the relations between state and society will be considered as dialectical (see Simeon and Robinson 1990, pp. 13–16 and 1994, pp. 369–71).

Two historical routes

The history of Belgium is generally analysed through the evolution of three cleavages: clerical/anti-clerical; capital/labour; French/Dutch speakers. These cleavages have affected the country with variable intensity since the revolution of 1830 (Miroir 1990, pp. 13–14; Mabille 1986, pp. 101–2, 137–40, 169–70, 175–6, 243–7, 319–34, 346–7, 379–89). In the nineteenth century, the primary source of conflict was philosophico-religious. From the turn of the century to the 1960s, class conflict became most important. It is only in the recent period that language conflict – communitarized and territorialized – has become predominant.[6] Mapping the history of this third conflict helps to clarify the gradual fragmentation of global collective identities and the emergence of federalism and federation in Belgium.

A Belgian identity emerged from a shared experience over the turmoil of the dynastic wars of the seventeenth and eighteenth centuries (Vos 1993, pp. 128–32, 143; Stengers 1989; De Schryver 1981, pp. 15–25, 31–2). Attempts at independence failed in 1789–90, 1792 and 1814. In 1815, the Congress of Vienna decided to bring both the Northern and

---

[4] This definition allows for the inclusion of identity discourses which challenge the political boundaries of the global entity of belonging, either in the sense of secession (e.g. Quebec) or in the sense of extension (e.g. Europe, the world). It is important to specify that our study is confined to the fragmentation *between* these global collective identities, to the incompatibility which characterizes several definitions of the same political entity. This choice should not be considered as a negation of the diversity existing *within* each of the identities in question.

[5] For a general survey of the virtues and limits of comparative historical sociology, see Badie (1992).

[6] As Luc Huyse pointed out, class and religious conflicts are henceforth mediated by the community conflict (Huyse 1981, pp. 122–3). It is therefore more appropriate to talk about a *superimposition* of cleavages than about a simple *succession*.

Southern Netherlands together, after two centuries of separation. In the context of a regime dominated by the Dutch elite, the differences between the two parts of the new United Kingdom of the Netherlands promptly proved to be problematic. As Jean Stengers wrote, '[the Dutch and the Belgians] were separated by religion and even, to a large degree, by language, because half of Belgium was French-speaking as were, in addition, the upper classes in the Flemish part. . . . They were still more separated by a feeling of otherness' (Stengers 1981, p. 51). In addition to these differences, liberalism was more present in Belgium. In 1828, liberal and Catholic Belgians allied in order to push their respective objectives forward. As a result of the combination of religious, linguistic, economic and political conflicts, the 1830 revolution led to the political independence of Belgium.

In 1830–1, the National Congress opted for a unitary state and adopted a constitutional provision protecting the freedom of individuals to express themselves in their chosen language (article 23). These decisions proved to be fundamental for the future of Belgium and must be contextualized. Three main factors explain the choice of a unitary state. The first key element to mention is the pressure of the international environment. A small state having achieved independence against the will of its powerful neighbours, Belgium had an evident interest in making conformist choices and building a strong state (Beaufays 1988, p. 64). Second, in 1830, the Belgian identity was dominant. Sociologists and historians have firmly established that while the terms *Flamands* (Flemings) and *Wallons* (Walloons) were part of the vocabulary in 1830, they did not yet refer to actual sentiments of belonging (among sociologists, see Zolberg 1974 and Huyse 1981, pp. 128–33; among historians, see Stengers 1989, pp. 30–3; Stengers 1981, pp. 47–57; De Schryver 1981, pp. 22–33). In a similar vein, geographers have shown that the current territories of Flanders and Wallonia are essentially products of the postrevolutionary period (see Murphy 1988). Thus, in 1830, the state of the allegiances ran clearly towards the creation of a unitary state. Third, the characteristics of the elite of the constituent assembly did not favour the attribution of any political significance to language differences. During that era, French was the language of political and economic power; it was the language of a social class more than the language of a people. The Belgian elite was francophone – the Dutch-speaking members of the elite were generally bilingual, while the francophone members were unilingual – and based in Brussels.[7] Moreover, the voting system restricted political participa-

[7] It should be noted that French was easily adopted as the language of the constituent assembly.

tion to this elite and it was still difficult to know the exact linguistic composition of the population. In such a setting, it was far from easy even to imagine the creation of a federal state (Covell 1987, pp. 60–1). Article 23 on linguistic liberty is also illustrative of the characteristics of the elite and of the consequent non-politicization of the language differences among the working classes.[8] The political and economic imbalance between the French and Dutch languages was not considered problematic. The choice of French as the language of governmental publications was justified on utilitarian grounds, notably its greater uniformity. Janet Polasky pointed out that the members of the National Congress came to consider language as a purely individual matter, without distinction between state officials and ordinary citizens. Having in mind the 'Hollandization' policy of the United Kingdom of the Netherlands, their primary concern was to guarantee the right of the Flemish elite to speak French (Polasky 1981, p. 43). In addition to reflecting the interests and preoccupations of the elite, this measure can be further explained by the liberal convictions of a large number of delegates (Polasky 1981, pp. 42–5). Belgium thus became a unitary state, and, in principle, the linguistic question was removed from the public sphere.

In practice, considering the sociological properties of language, article 23 established the domination of French much beyond the matter of governmental publications. As Aristide Zolberg emphasized, 'language issues . . . cannot be processed by separation from state, since the state can make itself "blind" but not "deaf-mute"'. Furthermore, the individual capacity to transfer from one language group to another makes likely a certain assimilation among the individuals belonging to a sociologically disadvantaged language group (Zolberg 1977, p. 140). Thus, in Belgium, in addition to being the language of economic life, French became the language of the state and the language of education. In its relations with the public administration, the Flemish-speaking population was often constrained to use French. Clearly at the source of this inequality, article 23 – coupled with the governmental order of 18 November 1830 – constitutes the first cause of the politicization of language in Belgium. It favoured the emergence of a community and regional consciousness in the northern part of the country, where the Flemings were concentrated. Inspired by the work of Zolberg, Huyse

---

[8] It is important to note that as of 18 November 1830, an order of the interim government had affirmed the principle of linguistic liberty in dealings between the administration and citizens and the use of French as the sole official language of governmental publications. Article 23 of the constitution simply confirmed these initial choices (see Mabille 1986, pp. 125–6).

identified three additional factors for the period 1850–1914. First, industrialization increased the costs of the linguistic imbalance and made Flemings more aware of their disadvantage. Second, in recognizing the principle of equality between the French and Flemish languages,[9] the language laws provoked a rise in expectations among the Flemings, without ensuring them an equivalent rise in social mobility. Finally, beginning in 1893, the gradual establishment of universal suffrage allowed the Flemings to make political use of their demographic superiority (Huyse 1981, pp. 109–12). These factors explain the evolution of the demands and justifications of the Flemish movement. Originally, the emphasis was placed on the introduction of bilingualism in the north of the country and such a claim was justified in the Belgian language of individual rights. As De Schryver remarked, 'there were demands neither for separatism nor for federalist reorganization of the Belgian state' (De Schryver 1981, p. 27). From the beginning of the twentieth century, a more collectivist discourse claimed unilingualism in public administration and education in Flanders, supported by arguments focusing on ethnicity and the principle of territoriality. Starting from a strictly linguistic, liberal and Flemish-Belgian character, the nationalism of the Flemish movement intensified and distanced itself from the Belgian identity (Vos 1993, pp. 136–7). In southern Belgium, the political nature of the Walloon movement was essentially the result of the emergence and hardening of the Flemish movement. In its origins, the Walloon movement mainly sought to revitalize the Walloon culture and dialects. It came to politicize when confronted by the linguistic laws, largely perceived as the threat of a Flemish takeover of the state. From that point to the 1940s, the movement argued for the preservation of the Belgian state of 1830 and sided with the politically dominant nationalism of the time, that is to say, the pan-Belgian nationalism of the francophone elite of Brussels.

From the point of view of the evolution of collective identities, two events marked the First World War: on the one hand, the collaboration with the German occupying forces was mostly Flemish; on the other hand, Flemish soldiers often had to deal with officers whose language they did not understand. With regards to collaboration, the Flemish movement was discredited, while the pan-Belgian nationalism strengthened and became more Jacobin. Coupled with the tragedies experienced by certain Flemish soldiers, this Jacobinism accelerated the separation process of the Flemish identity from the Belgian. Politically speaking, the Flemish movement consisted of a 'radical' wing proposing feder-

---

[9] First in Flanders in the 1870s, then in the rest of the country with the 'equality law' of 1898.

alism or secession, and of a more moderate one maintaining a stance of unilingualism in Flanders. Territorial unilingualism was finally recognized by the 1930s laws, but strong francophone resistance would considerably slow down its implementation.

During the period extending from the Second World War to the constitutional reform of 1970, the linguistic/cultural/regional cleavage came to be more important than those of class and religion. Three developments fostered this outcome. First, the war was again marked by a (mostly) Flemish collaboration with the German occupying forces. The ensuing anti-Flemish reaction was more intense than in 1918. Clinically dead in 1945, the Flemish movement was revived by a wave of infractions to the linguistic laws of the 1930s. The movement gradually repoliticized and the Flemish identity came to crystallize in an ethnolinguistic and territorial definition. Second, a shift in economic superiority to the advantage of Flanders favoured a strengthening of the Walloon identity on socioeconomic and territorial grounds. Thus, the two identities would come to take form and oppose on different bases. Finally, the consociational methods and their educational and social pacts allowed for a relative neutralization of religious and class conflicts, paving the way for an increasing institutionalization of the 'community' conflict throughout the 1960s. This increasing institutionalization took form in three different ways. To begin with, the importance of the linguistic laws of 1961, 1962 and 1963 must be emphasized. They did not only sanction the principles of the 1930s' laws – unilingualism in Flanders and Wallonia, bilingualism in Brussels – but they also modified the linguistic boundary and achieved the homogeneity of the provinces and administrative districts (Mabille 1986, pp. 329, 331).[10] They firmly established the principle of territoriality and constituted a first step towards federation (Senelle 1989, p. 57). Second, the institutionalization of the community conflict found

---

[10] It is important to point out that the 1960s' linguistic laws allowed special measures for what came to be known as the *communes à facilités*: 'special Dutch-language facilities and rights were guaranteed in four communes just to the south of the language line, and special French-language facilities and rights were guaranteed in twelve communes, six just to the north of the language line and six others immediately adjacent to Brussels' (Murphy 1995, p. 84). However, these half-measures departing from the principle of territoriality were inadequate to respond to the practical requirements of very complex situations. For example, there were several cases of populations forming the majority at the local level, the minority at the regional level, while living close to either a bilingual region or a region where their language is the majority one. The inadequacy became especially obvious in periods of intercommunity tension, when the special measures were enforced without flexibility. Finally, we should also point out that the whole bilingual province of Brabant remained an exception to the linguistic homogenization until the constitutional reform of 1993 (see Fitzmaurice 1996, pp. 59–60).

expression in the increasing number of regional political parties as well as in the beginning of a regionalization of the three major parties. The latter trend would eventually end in the absence of any political party whose field of action is the whole Belgian territory. Finally, the 1960s witnessed a growing number of projects for federalization. Thanks largely to a series of governmental crises, these projects led to a first major reform in 1970. On 18 February, Prime Minister Gaston Eyskens made a statement reflecting the evolution of Belgian society: 'The unitary state, as still governed by the laws in its structures and operation, is overtaken by facts. Communities and regions must take their place in the reformed structures of the state, better suited to the specific situations of the country' (Gaston Eyskens, cited in Mabille 1986, p. 370; our translation).

Meanwhile, beginning in the 1930s, Belgium followed an immigration policy that would prove to be an additional factor of identity fragmentation. Initially at the request of the coal mining companies, the Belgian state allowed for the institutionalization of a limited guest-worker status in order to make up for the mining sector's difficulties to attract Belgian workers. In view of the economic advantages of importing cheap labour restricted to a specific sector of the economy, other sectors of production got the same privilege and guest workers gradually became 'an indispensable element of the Belgian economy' (Roosens 1981, p. 65). As Eugeen Roosens noted, prior to the 1970s, the identity implications of the guest worker status were seldom if ever pointed out: 'immigrants were seen simply as cheap labor for less attractive jobs' (Roosens 1981, p. 66). And when Italians became too expansive, Belgian companies started to look further to the south, particularly to Turkey, Morocco and Tunisia. In the short term, the guest-worker policy proved to be a factor of fragmentation in the sense that it favoured the persistence of a precarious and uncomfortable status, from an identity perspective as well as from legal and economic perspectives. It made first-generation guest workers – especially those from non-European countries – a very particular category of semi-citizens: they were culturally and economically marginalized; they had very few incentives to apply for naturalization and to try to integrate into Belgian society; they were unlikely to acquire full citizenship, even if they applied for it; yet the majority society expected them to pay taxes and to behave as any good citizen should do. In the third part of the chapter, we will see that, in the long term, the guest workers policy came to affect the identity of the children of the first-generation guest-workers and even to have a certain impact on the tensions between the Flemish and the francophone populations.

We have seen that a multitude of societal and state factors favoured a gradual identity fragmentation in Belgium. From a dominant pan-Belgian identity, there was an evolution towards a complex panorama: a more and more separate Flemish identity, ethnolinguistic and territorialized; a Walloon-Belgian identity in process of territorialization and mostly socioeconomic in character; a pan-Belgian identity mostly shared by Brussels francophones. Without being an inevitable outcome, such a federalization of the state was very likely in the context of the 'federalization' of Belgian society. In comparison with the history of collective identities in Belgium, Canada presents a strongly contrasting starting point, but a rather similar finish.

Soon after the British North America Act (BNAA) of 1867, Canada differed from 1830 Belgium on many aspects. Beside the preservation of a semi-colonial link with London, two fundamental differences must be highlighted: the plurality of identities was manifest; the Canadian differences were integrated through a federal settlement.

In the years preceding the BNAA, the plurality of identities expressed itself through two cleavages. First, the British dominion of North America was divided into several distinct politico-administrative entities, laying the foundations of a plurality of relatively strong regional identities: the United Canadas, Nova Scotia, New Brunswick, Prince Edward Island (PEI) and Newfoundland. Second, the English-Canadian and French-Canadian populations differentiated on the bases of religion, ethnic origin and language.[11] This second cleavage was deeply rooted. In the seventeenth and eighteenth centuries, under the French colonial regime, a distinct Canadian identity was already emerging. With the British conquest of 1760 and the subsequent arrival of Loyalists defeated by the American revolutionaries, a distinction between Canadians and English – and later between French-Canadians and English-Canadians – began to take form.[12] Major conflicts arose after the Constitution Act of 1791, which granted representative institutions to the colony – although without responsible government – and divided it into Lower Canada and Upper Canada. The French-Canadian *petite bourgeoisie* controlled the Assembly of Lower Canada – where French-Canadians made up the overwhelming majority – , but the absence of responsible government deprived its members of the economic and political power to which they would have had access in a non-colonial context. Combined with the economic crises, this situation steered the French-

---

[11] The situation of the aboriginal population will be addressed later, as they were not included in the negotiations surrounding the BNAA.

[12] The survival of a community whose religion was Catholic and language French was made possible by the collaboration between English authorities and the decimated Canadian elite, notably through the Quebec Act of 1774.

Canadian *petite bourgeoisie* towards the rebellion of 1837–8.[13] Following the failure of the uprising, in a perspective of assimilation inspired by Lord Durham's report, London took strong measures to counteract the French-Canadian threat to unity: the two Canadas became the United Canadas and were granted the same number of parliamentary seats, even though the population of Canada East (previously Lower Canada) was larger; English became the sole official language of the new entity. Although unity seemed to be saved for a while, the attempt at assimilation was both a failure and a source of identity fragmentation. First, the alliance of the Reform leaders of Canada West (previously Upper Canada) with those of Canada East allowed simultaneously for the advent of responsible government (1848), the access of French-Canadians to administrative and ministerial appointments, and the abrogation of the provision making English the only official language. In addition, as the 1851 census demonstrated, Canada East's population had become significantly smaller than Canada West's and was henceforth taking advantage of the equal number of seats. Finally, the clergy's reaction to the threat of assimilation – the ideology of messianic *survivance* – proved to be much more than an effective defence against assimilation: it froze the French-Canadian identity into a narrow ethnic definition which proved to be a major source of fragmentation in years to come.

In the context of the early 1860s, the dual fragmentation of identity had not decreased and appeared to be problematic in three respects. First, in the United Canadas, the combination of class and ethnolinguistic conflicts led to a political impasse. Second, on the economic front, the end of British preferential rates towards British colonies and the non-renewal of the reciprocity agreement between the United Canadas and the United States made necessary the development of a domestic market among the British colonies of North America. Third, the threat of military invasion from the United States continued to hang over the colonies, which were separately vulnerable.

The combination of a dual fragmentation of identity with increasing needs for unity explains the union of 1867 and the decision to implement a federal formula. However, the founding elites of Canada rarely showed an equal preoccupation with the requirements of unity and diversity. On one side, there were those, like John A. Macdonald, who sought and foresaw the weakening of regional/ethnolinguistic loyalties and the evolution towards a unitary system. On the other side, there were those who interpreted the BNAA as a 'treaty' or a 'compact' between the

---

[13] The claim for responsible government also led to a rebellion in Upper Canada.

original colonies or between two ethnolinguistic communities. For the latter, 'Confederation was primarily a device for the preservation and development of its member communities' (Simeon and Robinson 1990, p. 21). Such differences are deep and had major implications. First of all, no compromise could manage to get the support of PEI and New-foundland. Furthermore, a significant opposition persisted in Nova Scotia, New Brunswick and Quebec. Finally, the final compromise included ambiguities potentially conducive to identity conflicts. Two such ambiguities concerned essential matters. Simeon and Robinson highlighted the vagueness of the BNAA with regards to the type of federal regime and the delimitation of jurisdictions (Simeon and Robinson 1990, pp. 23–7). More generally, they pointed out that the character and the collective identity of Canada remained 'unclear and controversial' (Simeon and Robinson 1990, p. 21). Linguistic issues would be particularly affected by this early ambiguity.

The period ranging from 1867 to the end of the nineteenth century was marked by regional oppositions to Macdonald's quasi-federalism and by the decline of French outside Quebec. On the former front, the combination of provincial initiatives with the economic context produced a more classic variant of federalism (Simeon and Robinson 1994, pp. 374–5).[14] On the linguistic front, the provisions of the BNAA proved to be inadequate to protect the French language and they contributed to the aggravation of identity conflicts. The provisions concerning bilingualism in article 133 were restricted to parliamentary and judiciary institutions in Ottawa and Quebec, providing no linguistic protection for French-Canadians outside Quebec.[15] The results were unequivocal: '[t]he abolition of education rights for the francophone minorities in New Brunswick (1871), the Northwest Territories (1892) . . . , the hanging of Riel in 1885, the elimination of French from the Manitoba Legislature in 1890' (Waddell 1986, p. 75).[16] Thus, in English Canada, regionalism and a nationalism tinged with British imperialism led to a dominant multiregional conception of federalism allowing very little institutional space to French. Among French-

---

[14] On the importance of regional identities in Canada between 1867 and 1945, see Jenson (1995, pp. 103–7).

[15] Although it defines the right of school minorities in religious terms, Article 93 on the federal protection of minority education could have been used for linguistic purposes. For lack of political will, it was not the case. We should add that from a purely demographic perspective, bilingualism would have been much easier to justify in 1867 than in 1969.

[16] According to Waddell, there was a 'systematic opposition in English Canada to the extension of French language rights and of an articulate French presence beyond the boundaries of the province of Quebec and the Parliament in Ottawa', actively or tacitly supported by the federal government (Waddell 1986, pp. 75–6).

Canadians, the decline of French outside Quebec became a source of resentment and contributed to the rise of a nationalist movement whose dominant inclination was to advocate binational federalism and bilingualism from a perspective of *cloisonnement*.

The first half of the twentieth century was marked by a more pronounced polarization of the two nationalisms. There were efforts to forge a unified Canadian nationalism, but the compromises of Prime Minister Laurier tended to displease both sides more than to unify them. On the one hand, English-Canadian nationalism proved to be highly influenced by the rise of British imperialism, with the result of a persistent decline of French in the provinces (e.g. the promulgation of Regulation 17 in Ontario, in 1912). On the other hand, French-Canadian nationalism – whether of liberal or clerical trend – was increasingly inclined to politicize the question of French-Canadian rights. It is partly in this way that one should interpret its opposition to participation in the Boer War as well as to any conscription during the two world wars. In short, in both languages, the two nationalisms appeared to become more and more exclusive.

During the period from 1945 to 1968, a 'transformation of the Canadian symbolic order' started to take place (Breton 1986, pp. 27–41). To begin with, we should point out that the Statute of Westminster had confirmed the political independence of the country in 1931. From an identity perspective, the Canadian situation could then be described as follows: with recently arrived waves of immigrants to assimilate[17] and carrying the burden of the American cultural threat, the country was destined to enter a period of redefinition. Canada managed to distance itself from Great Britain through a series of governmental initiatives, with the aim of constructing a pan-Canadian identity: cultural and scientific institutions were built, the Canadian Citizenship Act was passed (1946), the Supreme Court of Canada was made the final court of appeal in all matters (1949), a Canadian was appointed governor-general for the first time (1952), a Canadian flag was adopted (1965). In addition, as Josée Bergeron remarked, the combination of the economic crisis of 1929 with the Second World War and the rise of Keynesianism favoured an unprecedented expansion of the activities of the central government, one of whose main objectives was Canadian nation building and Canadian unity (Bergeron 1997, pp. 375–8).[18] In the context of such transformations, Quebec went

---

[17] From the nineteenth century to the reforms of the 1960s, the Canadian immigration policy selected immigrants on the basis of ethnic criteria, in order to favour their assimilation and to maintain the ethnic structure of the country.

[18] As Jenson noted, while addressing Canadians primarily as individuals, Keynesian

through its own dynamics of change. Between 1945 and 1960, criticizms of the clerical nationalist ideology dominating the Duplessis regime came to be increasingly visible, numerous and deep.[19] In the wake of the *Refus Global* manifesto, two groups of intellectuals proved to be particularly influential for the long term political future. Both were opposed to the dominant anti-statism of the regime and to the genealogical identity coming with traditional nationalism, but they clashed over their alternative projects. Mostly anti-nationalist, the first group gathered round the journal *Cité Libre* and believed in the possibility of a pan-Canadian identity including respect for cultural differences. Neonationalist, the second group sought to fight the identity battle where it seemed more likely to be won – within Quebec – and by distancing itself from the means and language of dominant traditional nationalism. It would soon come to argue for a shift from the French-Canadian identity to a Québécois identity. This new identity would be built upon the Quebec state and would combine liberal democratic values with certain features of the French-Canadian identity, whose choice and interpretation is still currently the subject of a major debate (see Karmis 1994). Both groups contributed to the election of Jean Lesage's Parti libéral du Québec (PLQ) in 1960 and to the subsequent speeding-up of the modernization of the Quebec state. However, as the connection between Quebec policies and the definition of a Québécois identity became more and more evident, most of the *citélibristes* came to concentrate their activities around the federal government. In 1963, in the context of the double shaking of Canadian federalism by Lesage government's demands for provincial autonomy and particular status and the parallel rise of a Quebec independence movement, the federal government responded with the creation of the Royal Commission on Bilingualism and Biculturalism (B&B Commission). The mandate of this commission was to 'recommend what steps should be taken to *develop the Canadian Confederation on the basis of an equal partnership between the two founding races*, taking into account the contribution made by other ethnic groups to the cultural enrichment of Canada and the measures that should be taken to safeguard that contribution' (ministerial order of July 19, 1963, cited in McRoberts 1997a, p. 40). From 1968, it was up to the government of Pierre Trudeau to decide on the fate of the report of the B&B Commission.

The identity evolution of aboriginal peoples has not been integrated

---

policies reflected the growing influence of the labour unions and a partial transfer from regional identity to class identity (Jenson 1995, pp. 107–8).

[19] On the widening gap between the clerical nationalist ideology and Quebec society between 1867 and 1945, see Roy (1993, pp. 47–92).

into the preceding historical account because these peoples were left on the margins of the Canadian federal system. Not conquered, yet decimated by the first contacts, they had remained relatively autonomous until Confederation. In accordance with the Royal Proclamation of 1763, the British Crown both recognized the existence of aboriginal rights and committed itself to protect them. While there were attempts at 'civilizing' the Natives through a reserve system beginning in the 1830s, it was only with the 1857 legislation that the official objective of protection gave way to one of assimilation (Tobias 1991, p. 127–30). The latter objective became clearly dominant once the fiduciary powers of the Crown were transferred to the Canadian government in 1867. Such an imperialist perspective was systematically applied from the adoption of the Indian Act in 1876 to the 1970s, although the methods of assimilation varied (for examples, see Tobias 1991, pp. 131–41). Without attaining its ultimate objective, it managed to put an end to aboriginal self-government and to the cultural coexistence it preserved. In the 1960s, the Native peoples were politically and culturally in an advanced state of decline.

In sum, one century after the BNAA, the Canadian forms of federalism and federation were far from having reduced identity fragmentation. The 1960s map of allegiances may be described in the following way: the English-Canadian majority was divided between its overseas roots, its identification with the new Canadian symbols and a plurality of regional identities; in redefining their identity through an emerging quasi-citizenship in Quebec, the Franco-Québécois distanced themselves not only from English-Canadians, but also from French-Canadians outside Quebec; as for the aboriginal peoples, they were struggling between the extremes of genealogical identification and outright eradication; finally, despite the objective of assimilation of the Canadian immigration policy, Neo-Canadians began to make claims for an institutional recognition of their differences. The BNAA harboured latent conflicts regarding the nature of both the federal system and the collective identity of Canada. The Canadian nation-building project initiated over the Second World War began to impede British and regional identities, but its orientations remained ambiguous. They would soon be clarified under the Trudeau regime.

Pan-Canadianism and fragmentation: thirty years of Trudeauism

In the recent history of Canada, Trudeau holds an unequivocal importance. An academic and a co-founder of *Cité Libre*, he was an active participant in the battles against Duplessism during the 1950s. Over the 1960s, faced with the Lesage government's autonomist claims and the rise of a secessionist neo-nationalism, Trudeau listened to the call of politics. Initially close to the New Democratic Party, Trudeau became a member of the Liberal Party of Canada (LPC), was first elected to the federal parliament in 1965, and became Prime Minister of Canada in 1968.[20] His understanding of nationalism and federalism as well as his vision of the country came to have an enduring influence over Ottawa's identity policies, leaving an indelible mark on the institutions and political culture of the country.

On the question of collective identities and federalism, Trudeau went through a marked evolution. At the beginning of the 1960s, as an academic, liberal individualism of the cosmopolitan type seemed to be the driving force behind his thinking. Faced with the simultaneous challenges of autonomist and secessionist neo-nationalisms in Quebec, Trudeau contrasted 'sociological nation', emotion, nation-state and particularism on the reactionary side, with 'juridical nation', reason, federalism and universalism on the progressive side. From this perspective, he wrote that, 'the history of civilization is a chronicle of the subordination of tribal "nationalism" to wider interests' (Trudeau 1968, p. 156). In his eyes, the principle of the nation-state slowed down the process of civilization. Recognizing the existence of the nation in a sociological sense, he considered that it produces an emotive and particularistic attachment contrary to human reconciliation. As the foundation of the state, the sociological nation is said to lead to fragmentation and never-ending wars (Trudeau 1968, pp. 151–9). Hence, Trudeau concluded that the openness to 'universal values' was threatened by Quebec neo-nationalism (Trudeau 1993, p. 72), because he considered that any sociological nationalism was the first step towards secessionist movements based on the nation-state model.[21] Trudeau proposed the idea of a 'juridical nation' – a political entity founded on reason – as the basis for reconciliation, unity and peace. First, it would permit diverse sociological entities to cohabit within a 'multinational' state (Trudeau 1968, pp. 165–6). Second, the internal diversity of such a state would favour a greater reconciliation and unity between states. For Trudeau, federation represented the most accom-

---

[20] For a more detailed analysis of the development of Canadian political parties, see Bickerton, Gagnon and Smith (1999).
[21] Throughout the 1960s, Trudeau showed an even-handed severity towards English-Canadian nationalism, deploring the fact that the federal government had all too often been used as its instrument (see Trudeau 1968, pp. 159–67 199–200).

plished form of the juridical nation and embodies the exercise of reason in politics (Trudeau 1968, pp. 195–6).

The plea for reason in politics, however, was mitigated in Trudeau's political practice. He came to believe that the triumph of his universalist ideals could only be guaranteed by marrying rational politics with a pan-Canadian sense of belonging. As a theorist, he wrote that there was no reason to believe that one nationalism could supersede another. And he added that '*in the last resort* the mainspring of federalism cannot be emotion but must be reason' (Trudeau 1968, p. 194). In practice, in order to unify Canadians, Trudeau increasingly relied on emotional appeals to pan-Canadian nationalism. However, he continued to insist that this brand of nationalism was founded on *universal* values. Such values would find expression in a purely civic identity of juridical type. They appeared in the LPC platform for the 1968 election under the slogan of the 'just society': individual liberty and the equality of opportunity required for its exercise (Trudeau 1990b, pp. 381–2).[22] The 'just society' programme came out against the recognition of any particular collective status funded on historical, cultural or territorial claims. It addressed solely individuals and attempted to shift the priority of their allegiances towards the Canadian 'juridical nation'. Linguistic and cultural rights were seen as compatible with liberal values only to the extent that they were given to individuals and justified as necessary for individual autonomy. In other words, Trudeauism wished to separate the sociological differences from the collectivities, territories and institutions which constitute them. In such a vision, sociological differences are strictly individual attributes, protected from sea to sea by a central state invested with a sense of its own moral superiority.[23] The identity policies stemming from this pan-Canadianism, however, did not provide the social and political effects expected by Trudeau.

In June 1968, when the proponents of the 'just society' got the mandate to form a majority government, the situation in Quebec

[22] We should point out that Trudeau's and Trudeauist cosmopolitanism would rapidly come to be superseded by a seemingly more pressing objective: the destruction of Quebec neo-nationalism. This has become particularly evident over the last few years. For instance, the federal government has persistently and arrogantly presented Canada as 'the best country in the world', implicitly depreciating the rest of the world. Furthermore, during a meeting organized by the PLQ prior to the 1994 Quebec election, the Canadian Finance Minister found a new way to oppose pan-Canadianism and cosmopolitanism. In a classic piece of neo-liberalism, Paul Martin asserted the Canadian will 'to conquer global markets' and 'to win the economic world war', trying to convince Quebec voters that Quebec competitors are not the other Canadian provinces, 'but Japan, Germany . . .', that is to say the true 'other'.

[23] Guy Laforest rightly remarked that such a programme is not necessarily incompatible with a decentralized form of federation. However, it does require centralization in the symbolic realm (see Laforest 1995c).

seemed increasingly explosive: the autonomist nationalism of the governments of the 1960s and the B&B Commission's *Preliminary report* had heightened the expectations of francophones; the Front de libération du Québec had been active since 1963; two small independentist parties had received close to 9 per cent of the votes in the 1966 election; René Lévesque was seeking to gather together the democratic forces for independence. Already obsessed by the threat of separation, it was in this context that Trudeau and his team undertook the task to reform the Canadian federation. Three identity policies were simultaneously planned at the outset of their first mandate: the constitutional entrenchment of a charter of individual rights and freedoms, the White Paper on Indian affairs and the Official Languages Act. The policy of multiculturalism was added along the road.

The White Paper on Indian affairs revealed the most extreme version of Trudeau's ideas. In 1967, the Pearson government – of which Trudeau was a member – announced its intentions to revise the Indian Act. In July 1969, the Trudeau government – whose Minister of Indian Affairs and Northern Development was Jean Chrétien, the current Prime Minister of Canada – took over and introduced a revolutionary proposition that was essentially contrary to the positions expressed by Native organizations. While these organizations sought a transition towards more collective autonomy, the White Paper rather proposed to gradually eliminate the so-called 'Indian' status, because it was considered to be discriminating (to Indians themselves as well as to other Canadians). In other words, Natives were proposed to be Canadian individuals like all others, a measure implying the end of the protection of their land reserves and the definitive rejection of their historical territorial claims. More generally, the federal government attempted to abdicate its fiduciary role with respect to First Nations' collective rights. The radical character of such a proposition can be explained in various complementary ways: Trudeauists' individualist convictions; the belief that the existence of any special status might serve Quebec nationalists' ambitions; the political, economic and demographic weakness of the First Nations (see Weaver 1981, pp. 53–6). Surprised by the vigorous reaction of Native organizations, the government finally withdrew its project in 1971. However, the effects of such a project on aboriginal mobilization and organization were much more than temporary and were opposite to the expected results: '[t]he White Paper became the single most powerful catalyst of the Indian nationalist movement, launching it into a determined force for nativism [sic] – a reaffirmation of a unique cultural heritage and identity' (Weaver 1981, p. 171; see also Miller 1989, pp. 230–2 and Karmis 1993, pp. 73–4). Since then, after some significant and uneasy gains, the First Nations of Canada have been going through a period of cultural revival and the temptation to define themselves in opposition to other Canadians has been very strong. The Trudeau government not only failed to impose his view of Canadian identity, but favoured the development of an aboriginal neo-nationalism largely characterized by resentment, and whose very low desire to secede has a lot to do with pragmatic reasons.

In the same period, without waiting for the final report of the B&B Commission, the Trudeau government sought to settle the 'national unity' question via a policy of bilingualism that would rectify the short-comings of the BNAA. The government's eagerness and the separation of the notions of bilingualism and biculturalism were not particularly surprising. As early as 1963, Trudeau suggested to the B&B Commission that it should limit its inquiry to the issue of language. Two years later, faced with the dualistic orientation of the *Preliminary report*, Trudeau and five other *citélibristes* adopted a very critical point of view, inter-preting the recognition of cultural duality as the road towards a par-ticular status for Quebec as well as the first step towards independence (Oliver 1991, pp. 341–2). Moreover, in its 1967 volume entitled *The Official Languages*, although it was still defining Canada as a bicultural country, the B&B Commission itself proposed a policy of bilingualism neglecting the territorial and collective dimensions of the problem. As Waddell contends, it was the individual who was at the heart of the recommendations:

Confronted by the choice between a *territorial* and a *personality* . . . approach to the provision of language services and rights, it finally opted for the latter. Such a vision dictated that institutions be bilingual, with individuals having the right to be served in their language wherever they may be. Hence, the commissioners came down in favour of integral coast-to-coast bilingualism . . . At the same time they admitted to the problems inherent in the application of such a concept and proposed four levels of intervention: that French and English become the official languages of the Parliament and Government of Canada; that New Brunswick and Ontario imitate Quebec in becoming officially bilingual; that bilingual districts be established throughout the country in areas where the minority is sufficiently numerous to be viable as a group; and that the federal capital area should accord equal status to French and English. Again – and it cannot be too strongly stressed – the model referred to throughout is that of Quebec, a model that Quebec itself was no longer satisfied with. (Waddell 1986, p. 90)

Such recommendations contained all the elements to satisfy Tru-deau's individualist pan-Canadianism.[24] Trudeau and his team made

[24] In January 1968, he declared that 'if minority language rights are entrenched throughout Canada then the French-Canadian nation would stretch from Maillardville

them their own and passed the Official Languages Act as early as 1969. With the exception of the two official language minorities, the law was not very well received. The reaction of English-language Canada was mostly negative, particularly in the west.[25] Resistance from the provinces impeded the creation of bilingual districts. Today, some thirty years later, with the exception of New Brunswick – whose bilingual status was recently constitutionalized and whose 30.5 per cent of francophones (Statistique Canada 1997, p. 10) proved to be difficult to marginalize – the results of the policy of bilingualism in Canada outside Quebec remain equivocal.[26] Opposition was not much less intense among the francophones in Quebec. On their way towards the building of a territorialized autonomous identity, an increasing number of Franco-Québécois came to believe that the survival and flowering of their identity was only possible through either one of two options: particular status within Canada or Quebec sovereignty. One hundred years after the BNAA, the combination of the economic inferiority of the French language in Quebec with its demographic decline outside Quebec seemed to call for another path than bilingualism. Henceforth, equality had to be achieved by asymmetry or independence. Thus, the Gendron Commission and the successive Quebec language laws came to gradually define a Quebec whose first language was French.

The Official Languages Act contributed to identity fragmentation in at least two different ways. First, it significantly increased the lack of understanding between Franco-Québécois and other Canadians by undermining Quebec legitimacy to adopt language policies that fit for its very particular linguistic situation in North America. Second, by acting eagerly without consulting the provinces in such a politically sensitive

in BC to the Acadia community on the Atlantic Coast . . . Quebec cannot say it alone speaks for French-Canadians . . . Mr. Robarts will be speaking for French-Canadians in Ontario. Mr. Robichaud will be speaking for French-Canadians in New Brunswick. Mr. Thatcher will speak for French-Canadians in Saskatchewan. Nobody will be able to say, "I need more power because I speak for the French-Canadian nation"' (Trudeau, cited in McRoberts 1993, p. 122).

[25] Behind most of the criticizms was the erroneous belief that Canada was on the way towards an integral bilingualism that would leave unilingual citizens out in the cold. In the west, this belief was coupled with an increasing discontent with central Canada. For an overview of the initial opposition to the Official Languages Act, see McRoberts (1989, pp. 148–50). On the evolution of western Canadian discontent and claims, see Gibbins and Arrison (1995).

[26] In his 1995 report, the Commissioner of Official Languages concluded that even in the federal administration, where the progress of French is much more noteworthy than in the anglophone provinces, French still did not have a fair status as a language of services and work (see Hébert 1995). Furthermore, the 1996 census showed that the historical pattern of assimilation among francophone minorities has not yet been overcome (see Statistique Canada 1997, pp. 9–11).

area, the federal government failed to underscore the positive potential of bilingualism.

In 1971, the Trudeau government adopted a policy of multiculturalism whose foundations were very similar to those of the Official Languages Act. This new identity policy was partly intended to meet the grievances of Canadians whose origins were neither French nor British. From the very beginning of the B&B Commission and still more after the Official Languages Act, these Canadians demanded to have some say in the redefinition of the country. However, as Raymond Breton (1986, pp. 45–8) argued, the demands for a policy of multiculturalism extending beyond a merely symbolic affirmation were strongly encouraged by the institutional opportunities offered by the central government. The will of the latter to reject the concept of biculturalism endorsed by Quebec autonomist nationalists was a major factor in the adoption of such a policy. Both the Official Languages Act and the policy of multiculturalism were mainly justified in the language of individual rights and were presented as a step towards more universal allegiances. Moreover, while the former did not distinguish the needs of French-language speakers from those of English, the latter did not distinguish the Franco-Québécois and aboriginal national aspirations from the more modest aspirations of the other groups. And once again, the effects of the new policy would not be in accordance with the expectations of the Trudeau government.

On the basis of individual cases, it might be tempting to conclude that the policy of multiculturalism as a whole has been a source of increasing *cloisonnement* between the nations and the ethnocultural groups of Canada. Neil Bissoondath (1994) rightly pointed out that the policy of multiculturalism has often been understood as an encouragement to ghettoization and to excess of cultural relativism. However, as Kymlicka (1998a, ch. 3) convincingly demonstrated, we cannot – as Bissoondath and others tend to do – talk about a general trend because the policy of multiculturalism is part of a body of various citizenship policies that tend to balance each other. This does not mean that the policy of multiculturalism has not been a factor of identity fragmentation in some important areas, notably by neglecting the crucial distinction between nations and ethnocultural groups. Such an omission has undoubtedly undermined the legitimacy of aboriginal and Franco-Québécois national claims and, even, to a certain extent, the legitimacy of the Official Languages Act. Why English and why French? A policy of multiculturalism – or preferably interculturalism – could be built in very different ways.

From the Trudeau government's perspective, the repatriation of the

Canadian constitution and the entrenchment of a charter of individual rights and freedoms were the most important pieces of the puzzle. However, the federal government failed to reach this objective on several occasions – in 1971, 1975–1976 and 1978–1979 – because he was unable to come to an agreement with the provinces on such key issues as the amending formula, the content of the charter and a new division of powers. During the Quebec referendum campaign of 1980, Trudeau came to promise that a No vote would mean 'change'. After the defeat of the sovereigntist option, the table was set for a new attempt at repatriation. In the fall of 1981, after a legal dispute between the Trudeau government and eight provinces opposing the terms of its project, the political manoeuvring of the central government managed to split the coalition. Repatriation took place, yet without the consent of Quebec. With regards to identity, the modifications with the most serious consequences were the following: the amending formula stated the principle of equality among provinces for certain major changes and excluded the idea of special status; the Charter protected most of the classical individual rights (articles 2–15 (1)) as well as the principles of the Official Languages Act (articles 16–20, 23) and of the multiculturalism policy (article 27); these rights would be subject to judicial review; several provinces managed to obtain the inclusion of a nothwitstanding clause (article 33), but the federal government succeeded in limiting it to articles 2 and 7–15; both the charter (article 25) and the constitution (article 35) granted special status to aboriginal peoples, but without any precise definition;[27] and finally, the new constitution stated the principle of equality of economic opportunities (article 36), notably through a commitment towards equalization payments to cope with regional inequalities. As Peter Russell remarked, these measures were the result of a political compromise that was not totally in accordance with the Trudeau's government plan, but the notwithstanding clause and the articles on aboriginal rights were the only elements to be really contrary to the spirit of Trudeauism (Russell 1996, pp. 98–100).

The assessment of the 1981–2 episode clearly indicates an increase in identity fragmentation. In the first place, the recognition of undefined aboriginal rights has led to a situation of deep uncertainty with negative effects on the relationships between Native and non-Native populations. The Trudeau government increased the expectations of the First Nations while being fully aware that he would never accept to meet their

---

[27] On aboriginal major difficulties to obtain such a recognition, see Hawkes and Morse (1991, pp. 164–5).

main demand – the inherent right to self-government.[28] In 1983, the Trudeau government rejected the report of the Special Parliamentary Committee on Indian Self-Government (the Penner report), which was largely favourable to the idea of an inherent right. In 1983 and 1984, two constitutional conferences on aboriginal rights reached a deadlock. The outcome was no more conclusive after the end of the Trudeau era in 1984, although the aboriginal cause did make some progress along the road to the Charlottetown Accord of 1992 and the 1997 report of the Royal Commission on Aboriginal Peoples. Today, while the Canadian government – led by one of the fathers of the 1969 policy of assimilation, Jean Chrétien – has recently made public his response to the Royal Commission report – including apologies 'for past actions of the federal government' (Government of Canada 1998a), but nothing concrete on sensitive issues requiring the provinces collaboration (self-government and the many unsettled land claims) – First Nations continue to affirm their inherent right to self-determination and tend to define themselves in opposition to non-Native Canadians.[29] Moreover, although largely symbolic, the 1982 constitutional recognition has had significant effects on the courts' interpretation of Native rights and has produced some backlash, especially in provinces facing major aboriginal land claims. And most often, the new constitution itself has fuelled the discourse of Native rights opponents. For instance, in British Columbia, civil society opponents to Native rights have made use of the principles of equality among provinces and equality among individuals to argue that the Native population has no right to special status.

The Constitution Act, 1982, has also been detrimental to relations between Franco-Québécois and other Canadians. On the formal plane, both the autonomist nationalists of the PLQ and the sovereigntist nationalists of the Parti Québécois (PQ) have considered the adoption of profound constitutional modifications without the consent of Quebec to be illegitimate. This common stand has found expression in several votes held in parliament, in the subsequent constitutional platforms of the PLQ and, more generally, in both parties' public discourse. In terms of content, aside from the constitutionalization of pan-Canadian multiculturalism and bilingualism, two complementary principles have been considered to be problematic: the numerical – rather than proportional

---

[28] Trudeau admitted that his government never deemed acceptable the granting of special collective status addressing simultaneously a sociological group and a bounded territory (see Trudeau 1990b, p. 389).

[29] The rather negative response of aboriginal leaders to the reconciliation statement of the federal government has shown how difficult it is to forgive for a policy of assimilation whose disastrous socioeconomic consequences are still deeply felt every day (see Anderssen and Greenspon 1998).

– equality among provinces; the priority of individual rights over the claims of territorially based sociological groups. Contrary to Trudeau- ists' beliefs, the discontent did not disappear after 1982. The Meech Lake Accord of 1987 and the Charlottetown Accord of 1992 sought first and foremost to satisfy the PLQ government's proposals for constitu- tional change and to secure Quebec formal consent to the new constitu- tion. On both occasions, the ex-Prime Minister Trudeau and his supporters intervened vigorously in order to keep intact the fabric of 1982 (see Trudeau 1990a and 1992). Their position prevailed, but it also helped the autonomist and sovereigntist nationalisms to gain a major revival of popularity. As Simon Langlois remarked, the Canadian homo- genizing pressure has fuelled the Quebec building process of a franco- phone 'global society' – a society where Franco-Québécois can give a majority status to their language and culture – launched in the 1960s by the creation of a parallel network of social and state institutions (Lan- glois 1991a, pp. 101–3). In Quebec, pan-Canadianism has generally been interpreted as a negation of this francophone space of conversation in North America.

The vision of Canada entrenched in the charter has been much more positively received by the 'English-Canadian' majority. The principle of (numerical) equality among provinces, the normative superiority of individual rights and, to a lesser extent, the policy of multiculturalism, have come to constitute the heart of a dominant political culture considering the recognition of any special status to territorially based groups to be unjust.[30] The members of both official language minorities and the members of ethnocultural minorities have generally shared this charter identity, except for the fact that the former have laid emphasis on pan-Canadian bilingualism, while the latter have focused on pan- Canadian multiculturalism. Thus, Trudeau and his allies got a consider- able audience when they argued against Meech and Charlottetown.

Finally, it is important to note that while regional allegiances were slightly declining over the first decades of the 'transformation of the Canadian symbolic order', the federal government's policies of the last thirty years seem to have had a different impact as far as the west is concerned. The combination of the Official Languages Act with the National Energy Program (1980) and the persistence of constitutional

[30] The fact that 'English Canada' has no specific definition of itself and has repeatedly sought to absorb other nations in a pan-Canadian definition reveals a unitary more than a federal mentality. As Philip Resnick argued, Canada does 'need a term to differentiate the pan-Canadian sense of Canada as a federation including Québécois, Aboriginal People and English-speaking Canadians, from the more specifically English- Canadian society (i.e. non-Québécois, non-Aboriginal) within Canada' (Resnick 1994b, p. 74).

discussions paying little attention to the main concerns of the west have led to increasing regional discontent and to the creation of the Reform Party of Canada.

In short, the identity policies of the Trudeau governments not only failed to bring victory to the pan-Canadianism of the 'just society', but they also contributed to identity fragmentation. They were relatively successful with respect to regional identities and linguistic and ethnocultural minorities, yet they fuelled both Native and Quebec nationalisms. As Russell noted, the problem is not to have people who give a different meaning and attach a different value to Canadian citizenship: '[m]aintaining a political community, worthy of the name, for a citizenry with multiple identities may not be the easy way, but increasingly it is the way of the world, and it is certainly the only Canadian way' (Russell 1996, p. 105). The problem occurs when identities are not only different, but refer to incompatible (fragmented) visions. And a persistent constitutional crisis is in itself a cause of fragmentation (Russell 1992, p. 193). The recent episodes of Meech and Charlottetown have shown that Canada finds itself with a plurality of conflicting identities that seem still less compatible than they were in 1968.

In such a context of fragmentation, the virtues and duties of citizenship are the first to be affected. This is particularly true with regards to political liberty. In the area of relations between various ethnocultural and national groups, the combination of identity fragmentation with a process of judicial review may further the gradual desertion of the common political spheres for the field of legal confrontations. This is increasingly the case in Canada. On the one hand, citizens of various groups come to feel so much different from each other – and sometimes come to feel so resentful towards each other – that they are less and less able to have a dialogue, to settle their disagreements in the political spheres and to undertake together important political tasks for their future. As a result, an increasing fragmentation of social and state institutions makes the contacts less frequent and not easy. The increasing regionalization of political parties and votes at the federal level is an example of such a process. On the other hand, for the very same reasons, the various ethnocultural and national groups are increasingly inclined to make use of judiciary means to settle their disagreements. These are indicators of a political culture on the road to depoliticization.[31]

---

[31] We do not mean that the courts have no role to play in matters of intercommunity relations. We mean, rather, that their role should be twofold: (1) making sure that unambiguous constitutional rights are respected; (2) calling for political deliberation when there are deep disagreements regarding the existence of a constitutional right, or when there is no clear legal answer, or when the solution to a problem cannot be first and foremost a legal one.

Moreover, combined with an economic success above average, the exacerbation of the feelings of otherness and resentment may also come to threaten the exercise of the duty of solidarity. As soon as dissatisfied groups see themselves as providing the largest part of 'others'' welfare without receiving fair compensation, their solidarity is likely to weaken. While one cannot maintain that Canada has reached such a stage, one might well argue that it could happen very soon in provinces combining constitutional discontent with constantly high contributions to equalization payments. In addition, intercultural solidarity seems still more at risk in a context of macro-structural pressures threatening the achievements of the welfare state.

Devolutionary federalization and the temptation of *cloisonnement*: *belgitude* in crisis

In Belgium, the problem of identity fragmentation was approached quite differently. Two differences are particularly worth stressing. First, there were no guiding principles behind the institutional reforms. As Hugues Dumont pointed out, federation was generally conceived as a mode of pacification, rarely as a political project (Dumont 1989, p. 108). In the words of Zolberg, Belgium is a case of 'federalization without federalism' (Zolberg 1977). Apart from the fact that there was no Belgian Trudeau, proportional representation and a demanding amending formula represented major constraints to any long-term vision. The reforms were thus rather slow and unpredictable, resulting from crises and selective compromises, in accordance with the spirit of the Belgian consociational tradition (Peeters 1994, pp. 197–9).[32] Second, rather than attempting to construct a preponderant pan-Belgian identity, the reforms tended to recognize and institutionalize what Prime Minister Eyskens called the 'facts . . . the specific situations of the country'. In Belgium, the federalization process proved to be the full recognition of the link between territories and sociological characteristics that Natives and Franco-Québécois pursue when they speak of 'self-government' and 'distinct society'. As it was a process of devolution rather than one of integration – the point of departure was a unitary state rather than a multiplicity of separate entities (see Covell 1987, pp. 57–8 and Peeters 1994, pp. 194–5) – such a recognition stood to reason. However, a lack of concern for the building of a federal identity led to an institutionalization of fragmentation. It is revealing that the Belgian federalization process has been described as 'a tentative of conciliation

---

[32] For a criticizm of the lack of transparency and improvised character of such reforms, see Javeau (1989, pp. 150–4).

by *cloisonnement*' (Claeys and Loeb-Mayer 1984; our translation), and still further as a 'de facto separation' (Uyttendaele 1989, p. 13; our translation). After a survey of the four institutional reforms of this process, we shall see more specifically what has been their contribution to identity fragmentation.

In the wake of the regional parties' gains in the 1965 election and of the highly meaningful scission of the Catholic University of Louvain in 1968, the reform of 1970 set the foundations for a complex structure tending towards federation. The complexity can be explained by the fact that Flemings and Walloons polarized over relatively different bases. On one side, the Flemings sought to consolidate their linguistic gains and to get political autonomy in matters closely related to their national identity. On the other side, the Walloons sought to stop their economic decline and to counteract the effects of their minority status. The result was a dual structure. To Flemish satisfaction, the constitution specified the existence of two cultural Communities (French and Flemish), provided both with a legislative body (made up of members from the appropriate linguistic group in the Belgian Parliament), and empowered them with competence over some aspects of 'cultural' (e.g. defence and promotion of language, fine arts, broadcasting) and educational affairs.[33] In these matters, the area of Brussels – in Flemish territory, of bilingual status, and about 80 per cent francophone – thus found itself under a dual jurisdiction. To the satisfaction of the Walloons, three economic Regions were constitutionalized (Flanders, Wallonia and Brussels). However, decisions related to the organization and powers of regional councils were postponed and would have to be passed in accordance with the new majority rules specified in the constitution. These specifications consisted mainly of four guarantees of consociational nature with regards to representation in the Belgian central institutions: (1) the linguistic parity (Flemish–French) in the cabinet (article 99.2); (2) the creation of linguistic groups in both houses of Parliament (article 43); (3) a special majority provision regarding the laws pertaining to cultural and regional matters (they must be passed by a majority vote of the representatives of each of the two linguistic groups in Parliament, and a two-thirds overall majority in each of its two houses); (4) an additional mechanism – the so-called 'alarm bells' – providing parliamentary exceptional procedures when three-quarters of

---

[33] It should be noted that the small German community – less than 1 per cent of the population but territorially concentrated in a small southeastern area acquired from Germany after the First World War– was also constitutionally recognized as a cultural Community. However, the German community had to wait until 1983 to get institutions similar to those of the two other Communities.

the members of a parliamentary linguistic group consider that a decision in a legislative matter not covered by the special majority provision can be harmful to their community (article 54).

With this first reform, a federation was still far from established. Aside from the fact that the establishment of the regional level was delayed, the cultural Communities held no financial autonomy, their legislative councils were composed of members of the Belgian Parliament (double mandate) and they had no executive of their own. A second step towards federation was taken with the 1980 reform. The autonomy of the Communities was then significantly increased by the acquisition of a proper executive, while their powers were expanded to the so-called 'personalized matters'.[34] In addition, the regional structure was finally organized, except for Brussels. The Flemish and Walloon Regions were provided with legislative and executive bodies of their own and acquired complete or partial powers in matters related to territory (e.g. urban planning, environment, housing, employment, energy and aspects of economic policy). The Brussels case remained unsettled, as Wallonia and Flanders were unready to relinquish their competing claims on the capital. Another major element of the second reform was the Parliament's approval of the merging of the Flanders regional council with the Flemish community council. In advocating the commonality of their interests, the Flemings indirectly underlined the divisions among francophones. Finally, the creation of the Court of Arbitration added another piece to the construction of a federation.

One can start to speak of an established federation with the reform of 1988–9. First, the competencies of the regional and community institutions were considerably widened. For instance, the Regions acquired complete jurisdiction over infrastructure, transportation and employment, while the Communities were given new responsibilities over education. In the latter case, this was the main response to the problem of the protection of linguistic minorities in the Fourons and the other so-called *communes à facilités*. Second, in line with their increased powers, the regional and the community institutions acquired a considerable increase in financial autonomy. Third, the Brussels-Capital Region was finally established with its own legislative and executive institutions – with consociational protection mechanisms similar to those in place in the central institutions – and Dutch-speaking, French-speaking and Joint community committees were created for community matters regarding the capital. Finally, the role of the Court of Arbitra-

---

[34] The 'personalized matters' are those closely related to aid to individuals (e.g. health care, family policy, social welfare, the integration of immigrants). However, the social security policy remained an exclusive federal jurisdiction.

tion was widened and tentative cooperation mechanisms between central, community and regional institutions were established.

The most recent reform took place in 1993, making official and more complete the change from a unitary country to a federation. The first article of the 1994 constitution describes Belgium as a 'federal state, composed of Communities and Regions'. In addition to this legal sanction with symbolic value, seven major modifications were achieved. First, several institutions were renamed: central institutions would henceforth be called 'federal', while regional and community executive bodies would be referred to as 'governments'. Second, the conflicting situation of the Brabant province was settled by an administrative separation between the francophone and the Flemish parts of the province. Third, the double mandate was suppressed. The representatives of the Communities and Regions would henceforth be directly elected, such a change increasing considerably the legitimacy and the autonomy of both institutions. Fourth, in line with the abolition of the double mandate, the bicameral system at the federal level was reformed. Fifth, the Communities and Regions were authorized to conclude international treaties in their spheres of jurisdiction and consultation mechanisms were established in order to achieve coherence with the federal foreign policy. With regards to the European Union (EU), 'in line with the Maastricht treaty, regions and communities will represent Belgium in the council when they are competent for the issue concerned' (Fitzmaurice 1996, p. 59). Sixth, the Communities and Regions also acquired limited power with respect to self-organization. Such a power was used to transfer several competencies from the Council of the French-speaking Community to the Regional Council of Wallonia and to the French-speaking Community Committee of Brussels, marking the increasing distance between the francophones of Wallonia and Brussels and the asymmetry with the Flemish merging of Region and Community. Finally, additional powers were devolved to the Regions, including agriculture and scientific research.

In summary, the Belgian federation has currently eight subnational governments: the Flemish Council; the Council of the German-speaking Community; the Regional Council of Wallonia; the Brussels Regional Council; the Council of the French-speaking Community; the Joint Community Committee of Brussels; the French-speaking Community Committee of Brussels; and the Flemish-speaking Community Committee of Brussels.[35] In addition, the federal government retains sub-

---

[35] The nine provinces have only a delegated authority and their relevance is increasingly contested, while the 579 *communes* enjoy a very theoretical form of self-government. On

stantial control in fiscal matters as well as in justice, defence, foreign policy and social security.[36]

An evaluation of the effects of such reforms on identity fragmentation cannot be undertaken without two qualifications. First, the effects of Belgian reforms have been less direct and immediate than those of Canadian identity policies. The Belgian reforms were too complex and technical to induce spontaneous movements of support or opposition. They have contributed to fragmentation through the gradual institutionalization of identity differences and a lack of concern for unity in the new federation. Second, the Belgian federation is still in its infancy. Several of the 1993 modifications did not take place until the 1995 elections. Our evaluation rests on trends that have emerged so far.

In Flanders, in the context of a rising economic power and against the background of an old resentment produced by more than a century of French-language domination, the reforms gave the Flemish identity an opportunity to distance itself a little further from the idea of *belgitude*. The communal and regional powers made it possible to complete the building of a Flemish global society. To be more precise, the so-called 'cultural' powers strengthened the national sentiment. The new structure also served to affirm unity among the Flemings, including the minority in Brussels. So far, this strengthening of Flemish identity has not given rise to a growing support for formal independence – which has remained a rather marginal claim of third parties – but to a decline of intercommunity solidarity, and, more generally, to a growing communitarization of conflicts. The first major challenge to solidarity appeared at the outset of the 1980s, with the Flemish project to regionalize five declining economic sectors concentrated in Wallonia. In 1983, the conflict crystallized in the Flemish refusal to participate in the financing of a restructuring plan for the iron and steel industry in Wallonia. A last minute compromise was reached, but the principle of solidarity and the confidence between communities had been considerably shaken. In 1991, the Overlegcentrum voor Vlaamse Verenigingen (OVV) took a major step towards *cloisonnement*. A private organization forum of the Flemish movement, the OVV not only proposed the regionalization of social security, but it also used a language that was far from inclusive. Its provocative document stated that 'solidarity between individuals of a same people [read the Flemings] must be strictly distinguished and

---

the importance of the geographical configuration of federalism and the advantages of devolving greater powers to the provinces, see Murphy (1995, pp. 95–6).

[36] For a more detailed summary of the four reforms and an analysis of their implications on the institutional make-up of Belgium, see Delpérée (1993), M. Lejeune (1994) and Fitzmaurice (1996).

separated from solidarity between states in an international community (or confederation) [read Europe and Belgium]'. In the opposite scenario, 'there is a threat of serious abuses, as today in Belgium: interpersonal solidarity has been misused in order to transfer huge amounts from one people to the other . . . ' (OVV 1993, p. 65; our translation). On the basis of Paul Van Rompuy's study, the OVV affirmed that '[for] many years, Flemish contributions to social security have been transferred to Wallonia in order to finance Walloon expenditures' (OVV 1993, p. 67; our translation). The OVV concluded that there cannot exist any actual political autonomy or even any coherent policy without the regionalization of social security (OVV 1993, p. 65; our translation). While counterbalanced by subsequent studies (see Van Parijs 1993), the OVV's statistics and conclusions had mobilized public opinion and made the regionalization of social security a prominent demand in Flanders. Theo Hachez argued that the iron and steel and social security issues are not the only ones to have been communitarized on the Flemish side: many issues 'are . . . read with confederal eyes in the north of the country, that is to say, in accordance with a project announced and concerted for Flanders' (Hachez 1995, p. 13), a project generally seen as characteristically more on the right wing on socioeconomic and religious issues. If there is a rise in separatism in Flanders, it is thus primarily in the sense of a growing trend towards *cloisonnement*. Still today, even in the traditional political parties, 'the demand for greater autonomy is increasingly coming to the fore' (Deruette 1994, p. 250)

The Walloon identity has been deeply affected by the institutional reforms as well. In 1970, this identity was primarily socioeconomic and was subordinated to a Belgian sense of allegiance. The pressure of two threats will make it to become more prominent: the hardening of Flemish nationalism of course, but also the hegemony of Brussels' francophones within the institutions of the French Community. On the road to cultural self-assertion, the *Manifeste pour la culture wallonne* has marked a powerful moment. Signed in 1983 by seventy-five key figures in artistic, journalistic and university circles, it reacted mainly to Brussels hegemony. Criticizing the choice of Brussels as the capital of the French Community as well as the marginalization of the Walloon culture within its institutions, the manifesto called for the regionalization of community powers as a requirement for both the development of the Walloon culture and the institutionalization of an equal status with Brussels. Moreover, it proposed to respond to the Flemish position on the iron and steel industry crisis with a project combining socioeconomic and cultural dimensions: with its more leftist leanings, the

Walloon identity was to incorporate a culture conscious of its uniqueness, yet 'tolerant and pluralistic' (Abitbol et al. 1984, pp. 62–3; our
translation). Since 1983, the Walloon regional[37] self-assertion has proceeded on both fronts. On the Flemish front, the 1987 Fourons crisis
and the subsequent electoral success of the Parti Socialiste (PS) have
initiated an increasing use of Walloon regional institutions to identity-
oriented ends (see Tourret 1994, pp. 58–60, 72–3). Beginning in 1991,
the OVV's campaign for the regionalization of social security came to
fuel this new orientation. Since then, Walloon representatives have
regarded the issue of social security as a matter of principle. On the
Wallonia–Brussels front, ten more years of coexistence within the
French Community institutions were sufficient to confirm the gap
between Wallonia and the francophones of Brussels. The 1993 reform
has initiated the institutionalization of this gap, although it is not yet
clear whether it will result in the dissolution of all common structures or
in a new form of association. In sum, the Walloon identity has come to
be more precisely defined and distinguished via intercommunity conflicts and institutional reforms.[38] This Wallonization is a real process of
autonomization and the old political solution of *rattachisme* – Wallonia
uniting with France – has stayed on the margin of the Walloon society.

In Brussels, despite the federalization process, the unitary vision
historically characteristic of the Franco-Bruxellois still seems to have
some hold. In the eyes of many Franco-Bruxellois, the country is far
from the picture proposed by the *Manifeste pour la culture wallonne*.
Home of the EU Commission, capital of Belgium, and bastion of pan-
Belgian nationalism since 1830, Brussels tends to be contemptuous of
Walloon and Flemish identities, which are considered too particularistic.
In the context of European integration, Brussels pan-Belgian nation-
alism has professed moral superiority and has often conceived itself as
the path towards a more universal belonging, in a perspective similar to
Trudeau's. This vision has clashed head-on with the Flemish and
Walloon-Belgian identities.

It is important to note that the federalization process was kept in
isolation from the issue of guest workers and, more generally, from the
question of the immigrants' place in the past, present and future of
Belgium. Such questions have nevertheless had tangible effects on
identity tensions. From the beginning of the 1970s on, particularly in

[37] On the preference of a majority of the Walloon movement members to consider
themselves regionalists rather than nationalists and on their efforts towards establishing
a plural identity, see Destatte (1995, pp. 13–21).

[38] As it stands now, the Walloon identity seems nevertheless more plural than the Flemish
one. However, if the trends towards deep conflicts and reforms persist, the *belgitude*
could find itself more and more marginalized in Wallonia as well.

Brussels, the possibility that most guest workers might be granted citizenship – a proposal receiving rising support among francophones – has generally been perceived as a threat among Flemings. From a Flemish point of view, such a policy would most likely swell the ranks of the francophone population and would make the Flemings still more outnumbered in the capital region. It goes without saying that the Flemish extreme right – firmly established since the beginning of the century and favouring secession – has managed to gain some unexpected ammunition from such a situation, particularly in a context of structural unemployment. Furthermore, the first-generation guest-worker policy has tended to estrange guest workers' children from the 'majority societies'. Born in Belgium and automatically granted citizenship only since 1991 (Soysal 1994, p. 26), these children have often inherited the low and marginal socioeconomic status of their parents and, as a result, have been inclined to show mixed feelings towards Belgium.

Over the last decade, Belgians have been more preoccupied by the necessity to find a balance between unity and diversity, most notably through a debate on 'federal loyalty' surrounding the last two reforms. Many intellectuals focused on the implications of the EU for such an issue. Apart from the classical cosmopolitan point of view, two positions were prominent. First, according to Karel Rimanque, in the context of the new Europe of regions, 'the existence of some *belgitude* is only of secondary importance' (Rimanque 1989, p. 69; our translation). In other words, the nation-state being in decline, the question of Belgian unity has lost most of its relevance. On the opposite side, arguing that the increasing role of regions in the EU will not go without state mediation, Hugues Dumont maintained that the crucial question is political: do citizens desire to have all state mediation performed by regional states? This question implies a choice between various states and the various identities they promote (Dumont 1989, pp. 101–4). It also keeps open the possibility of choosing more than one state and identity. Considering the relatively high level of Euro-scepticism among Flemish nationalists (see Hooghe 1995, pp. 161–3), such a question becomes all the more relevant. This means that the centrifugal forces affecting Belgium are not likely to be less active within the EU. It also means that the European integration does not disqualify the question of Belgian unity, particularly on issues like social security and immigration. Leaving aside the question of the implications of the EU, Francis Delpérée argued that the constitutionalization of 'principles of common life' was the key to 'federal loyalty' (Delpérée 1989, pp. 51–2; our translation). Dumont opposed Delpérée's position by maintaining that 'a federal state is not viable if it cannot rely both on a national sentiment proper at the federal level and an idea of federal law . . . ' (Dumont 1989, p. 108). In 1993, Belgian politicians decided in favour of the constitutional entrenchment of 'federal loyalty' (article 143). In a federation characterized by an increasing political and social *cloisonnement*, such a legal measure seems insufficient, not to say futile. Today, like Canadians, Belgians tend to have fewer and fewer compatible visions of their country. It is unlikely that a constitutional article – even combined with a still considerable affection for the royal family – can reverse or stop such a trend. At the end of the 1993 reform, Prime Minister Jean-Luc Dehaene said that the Belgian federal system 'is the result of a permanent search for a balance between unity and diversity', and that one of its main purposes is to perform the role of a 'shield against separatism' (Dehaene 1993, p. 236; our translation). He also said that there could not be 'federalism without solidarity' (Dehaene 1993, p. 242; our translation). At the time of writing, as additional institutional reforms are in the air, it would be very difficult to argue that Belgian federalism and federation have reached their objectives.

As we mentioned in the previous section, when combined with collective economic success, the exacerbation of feelings of otherness and resentment can seriously threaten intercultural solidarity. Unlike Canada, Belgium has reached an advanced stage in this regard. The iron and steel industry crisis and the increasing will to regionalize social security are only the most visible indicators of the decline of Flemish solidarity towards the Walloon population. There is no doubt that the OVV's document proposed a Flemish strengthening rather than a European extension of primary solidarity.

In addition, despite a lower increase in the political role of the judiciary, intercultural political liberty does not fare better in Belgium than in Canada. The combination of a marked decrease in the powers of the federal government – notably in the area of broadcasting – with a very advanced fragmentation of social institutions – including political parties – [39] and a lack of intergovernmental institutions has considerably damaged the political dimension of citizenship. The Belgian political space has been gradually replaced by a multiplicity of increasingly

---

[39] As Kirk Deschouwer pointed out, the successive scissions of the three main parties along linguistic lines – the Christian Democrats in 1968, the Liberals in 1971 and the Socialists in 1977 – have made Belgium 'the only democratic federation without federal parties'. Voters can no longer participate in federal and intercultural deliberations on the major issues that divide them. In other words, 'they can never choose between the netherlandophone and the francophone propositions. These two visions do not confront each other in the political arena. Voters are limited to a choice between the various degrees of radicalism on each side . . . ' (Deschouwer 1997, pp. 77–8; our translation).

fragmented federate spaces. In such a case, there is not only a decrease in the number of opportunities to act together. The capacity and the very will to act together are also damaged, and this affects intercultural solidarity in the first place.[40] In short, the long-standing rising identity fragmentation and the more recent federal institutional *cloisonnement* have reinforced each other.

Conclusions for a theory of federal citizenship

In our introduction, we wrote that in a multinational and polyethnic state, a federal balance between unity and diversity may be defined as the institutionalization of both the plurality and the asymmetry of allegiances in compatible ways. In the last thirty years, even privileged federations like Canada and Belgium have failed to approach such a balance, even though they have resorted to opposite strategies. In Canada, Trudeau and his supporters have sought to suppress plurality and asymmetry through a process of deterritorialization, personalization and Canadianization of the various ethnocultural and national identities. In Belgium, the reformers have left open the expression of plurality and asymmetry, yet from a perspective of institutional *cloisonnement* which has been conducive to disunity rather than to a pluralization of the various identities. Both avenues have accentuated the fragmentation already in progress and have tended to impoverish citizenship. Considering such findings, a federal balance between unity and diversity seems to be out of range as long as federalism conceives identity questions without paying due attention to their deep historicity and to the relations of power they carry with them.

The disregard for considerations of time and space has been evident with Trudeauist federalism. First, such a federalism has neglected the major effects of sociohistorical variations on perceptions and identities. As it decided to establish bilingualism in Canada – i.e. the traditional solution of French-Canadian nationalists – it did not pay attention to the fact that one hundred years of institutional opposition to French had upset the relative demographic balance of 1867 and had given rise to

---

[40] Gérard Roland, Toon Vandevelde and Philippe Van Parijs shed light on the links between the fragmentation of the political space, the fragmentation of identity and the weakening of intercultural solidarity: 'in Belgium, the electoral system is organized in such a way that francophone and Flemish politicians do not compete with each other but struggle in their respective constituencies, within distinct parties, in order to get the support of essentially separate electorates. The result is, on both sides, a dynamic of outbidding tactics that builds opposite interests, and makes natural the replacement of argumentation within a shared public sphere by negotiation between communities. It thus subjects generous cross-regional solidarity to a permanent threat' (Roland, Vandevelde and Van Parijs 1997, p. 154; our translation).

increasing insecurity among Franco-Québécois. From the 1960s on, Quebec neo-nationalists have tended to see bilingualism as no longer appropriate and feasible. They have redefined Quebec nationalism around the idea of a francophone global society and they have generally considered asymmetry as the sole effective means to favour the development of such a society. As Waddell noted, 'had federal legislation been introduced 30 years earlier, the chances of building a bilingual country would certainly have been considerably greater' (Waddell 1986, p. 105).

Second, the theme of asymmetry offers a good illustration of the Trudeauist disregard for power relations between cultural and linguistic communities. Regarding the individual as their only unit of analysis, Trudeau and his supporters have made languages and cultures strictly individual matters. They thus stripped them of their constitutive context: a territorialized community and a multiplicity of institutions. Here lies the foundation of a conception of federalism that considers provinces as purely juridical and administrative bodies rather than historical political communities being both the source and the effect of sentiments of allegiance. On such sociological grounds, Trudeauists have been unable to conceive that structurally disadvantaged groups could be justified in claiming institutional asymmetry in order to gain a majority territorial status for their language and culture. From a Trudeauist perspective, the need to be a majority illustrates either a lack of confidence that needs to be overcome, or an aspiration for domination that must be suppressed. Unlike Trudeauists, Donald Smiley argued that in a multinational context, equality should be thought of along the lines of Aristotelian prudence: 'treating equals equally and unequals unequally' (Smiley 1992, p. 284). One might contend that Trudeau's own refusal to link particular sociological traits to a specific territory was not grounded on ontological principles, but rather on the practically based conviction that the recognition of a particular territorialized status would necessarily lead to secession. Aside from the inefficiency and unjust character of non-recognition solutions, Michael Oliver (1991, pp. 359–60) and Michael Walzer (1992) brought convincing evidence to show that such a conviction lacks comparative foundations. Many sociological nationalisms have not made secession their first choice and have been far more progressive than Trudeau implied (see Oliver 1991, pp. 359–60), although the language of secession has remained part of their discourse. Trudeau's slippery slope argument testifies to a deep incapacity to live with what Kymlicka has called 'the paradox of federalism'.

The comparative, sociological and historical bases of Belgian federalism are not any less fragile. Although it cannot be denied that Belgian reformers have had to act in the constraining politico-institutional setting of coalition governments, this single factor cannot account for the whole story. As in the Canadian case, the effects of sociohistorical changes have been neglected. For example, in Flanders, the combination of a recent economic prosperity with the resentment caused by more than a century of French-language domination paved the way for a complete identity rupture with francophones. Federal recognition proved to be inevitable, but it should have been combined with a reconstruction of the bonds of political trust among Belgians, the first step towards the building of plural identities. If this type of concern for unity has been mostly absent in the institutional reform process, it is in large part due to the long-standing influence of the consociational tradition in Belgium. According to Arend Lijphart, consociationalism states that in order to maintain political stability, 'it may be desirable to keep transactions among antagonistic subcultures in a divided society – or, similarly, among different nationalities in a multinational state – to a minimum' (Lijphart 1974, p. 84). It thus falls on elites representing each side to reach an agreement on the details of the institutional *cloisonnement*. The consociational approach becomes problematic when applied to global societies or global societies in the making, because it tends to fuel instrumental conceptions of the federation that can be fatal in the case of resentful potentially 'self-sufficient' global societies. In such a context, one must avoid thinking of federation as simply what Dumont called a 'mode of pacification'; it must be supplemented by a 'political project' to ensure a minimal unity (Dumont 1989, p. 108). This means that, contrary to Guy Laforest (1995c) and Michel Seymour (1995), the Belgian model is not likely to put Canada on more stable ground.

These accounts bear important implications for current theoretical debates on citizenship. Although a detailed analysis of contemporary theories of citizenship cannot be undertaken here, it is possible to convey preliminary remarks on some of the dominant theoretical trends. In line with the canons of modern political theory, individualist liberal theories are generally underlain by a creed of the moral superiority of unity. Despite greater theoretical sophistication, such a creed is not very much different from Trudeau's. Trudeau's federalism is based on the premise of the moral superiority of a wider (mono)allegiance embodied in 'universal values'. From such a perspective, federal unity – in this case pan-Canadianism – invariably provides the primary goods of liberal democratic citizenship, while identity plurality and asymmetry is inevitably the source of narrow-mindedness and disunity. Consequently and somewhat paradoxically, any state recognition of cultural diversity must be granted on a uniform individual and pan-state basis; it must be personalized and deterritorialized. The central institutions of a federation are considered morally superior, because they embody a wider allegiance and more universal interests than the institutions of the federate entities. Similarly, many contemporary academic individualist liberal theorists, such as Martha Nussbaum, tend to base their work on a somewhat simple binary opposition: on one side, there are all the various types of national, regional, ethnocultural and linguistic identities, all conducive to disunity; on the other side, there is a cosmopolitan identity embodied in universal liberal values and conducive to unity (see Nussbaum 1996a, p. 4). While replying to her critics that she does not disregard the virtues of identity diversity (Nussbaum 1996b, p. 137), Nussbaum nevertheless maintains her premise by applying a double standard to unity and diversity: on the one hand, she opposes the institutionalization of specific identities because it might threaten the universal liberal values; on the other hand, she never expresses any fear regarding the cultural uniformity and the atomization that might eventually result from the absence of an institutionalization of diversity. She sticks to the paradigm stating that 'the right way for a liberal regime to value diversity . . . entails strong support for a shared public culture that makes the right prior to the good' (Nussbaum 1996b, p. 137). She proposes a strict liberal proceduralism within states and seems to hope to found a world citizenship on a similar basis. However, as exemplified in the Belgian case of the constitution of 1830, the so-called principle of 'liberal neutrality' clearly tends to favour the strongest culture and language. Like Trudeauist federalism, Nussbaum's position not only shows a lack of concern for historical, sociological and comparative considerations, but also a strong normative bias for unity.

Classic nationalist theories are generally based on holistic and particularistic premises antithetical to those of individualist liberal thought. They do not only consider individuals to be unable to transcend their sociohistorical context, but the idea of a plural sense of belonging is seen as incompatible with the exclusive nature of the national sentiment. The Belgian and Canadian examples show that territorial and identity reality is more complex than that and requires something other than the nineteenth century principle of nationality. First, the authoritarian methods of nineteenth-century pan-nationalism can no longer be justified in today's liberal democracies. Second, unitary nationalism implies a large-scale political balkanization that does not match the practical needs or possibilities of today's nations or ethnocultural groups. On the one hand, many small nations and most ethnocultural groups cannot expect to found a viable nation-state of their own or prefer another solution. On the other hand, even in the case of nations willing to secede and having the potential for a viable nation-state, a simple application of the nineteenth-century principle appears very inappropriate. The increasing internal and external migrations of the last decades have affected federate nations and regions to such an extent that the question of recognition – including the option of federal recognition, and even those of secession or partition – is very likely to be raised again within any newly created state.

Radical pluralist theories also defend holistic and particularistic premises, but at the level of a multiplicity of identities (women, gays and lesbians, ethnocultural minorities etc.). This approach is interesting to the extent that it considers that there cannot exist any real equality without the recognition of special status allowing for sociohistorically disadvantaged perspectives to be heard. Iris Marion Young is perfectly right to maintain that '[w]e cannot develop political principles by starting with the assumption of a completely just society, . . . but must begin from within the general historical and social conditions in which we exist' (Young 1989, p. 261). However, radical pluralists often tend to emphasize too strongly the irreducible character of different perspectives, neglecting the unifying potential of a common context and more egalitarian interactions. This particularly contributes to fragmentation in the case of ethnocultural minorities, because they are assumed to be what they rarely are, that is to say, competing global societies.

Finally, civic republicanism is underlain by the creed of the moral superiority of a strictly political allegiance. On the basis of teleological assumptions deeming political participation to be the highest form of *vivre-ensemble*, it defends the idea of a unitary citizenship based on a common political culture. Civic republicans' insistence on the unifying potential of political culture is certainly worth exploring further. However, they also artificially isolate this culture from its sociohistorical context. For them, the common good flows exclusively from belonging to a 'political nation'. Like individualist liberals, they tend to criticize all sociological allegiances without distinction (see notably Beiner 1995, pp. 18–19).

The Belgium–Canada comparison should rather prompt us to explore and develop the idea of a balance between unity and diversity. According to Charles Taylor, 'given the necessity for democratic countries to have a form of unity that gives people the sense of being part of the same moral agent, we must consider that it cannot be a form of unity defined *a priori* by philosophy as being theoretically legitimate or acceptable, but rather one that looks significant to people themselves' (Taylor 1992b, p. 65; our translation). Such a methodological creed implies at least four tasks for citizenship theory: (1) to define more precisely the concepts of unity, diversity and balance; (2) to make an inventory of the respective theoretical virtues and limits they entail; (3) to understand better the evolving nature of identities by studying the exchange processes between various interpretative contexts; (4) to identify empirically the practices and institutions most likely to be conducive to a balance between unity and diversity. In the light of this study, we can already propose that in the area of intercommunity relations, the human capacity for liberty – in the sense of a capacity to extend the limits of our political imagination, of our very sense of possibilities – does not stem from the negation nor from the *cloisonnement* of differences, but more likely from the development of spaces of identity encounters and dialogues.

6   Recognition claims, partisan politics and institutional constraints: Belgium, Spain and Canada in a comparative perspective

François Rocher, Christian Rouillard and André Lecours

Claims for recognition and autonomy have permeated politics in Belgium, Spain and Canada over the last several decades. The transformation in these states' party systems and the debates over their constitutional and institutional arrangements are signs that nationalist movements have been successful in putting their issues on the political agenda. Indeed, the emergence of autonomist or secessionist nationalist parties in Spain and Canada and the split on linguistic lines of the traditional Belgian parties have transformed the political landscape of these societies. These political parties have attempted to rearrange, with varying success, the constitutional and institutional framework. In turn, this framework has shaped their action, posing constraints and offering opportunities. While the action of political parties seeking recognition and autonomy for their communities has introduced an element of instability in the larger societies' political system, the response to their challenge has been instrumental in determining its ultimate consequences.

This chapter addresses two related questions. First, it will show how collective identities in Belgium, Spain and Canada have been institutionalized in partisan politics and how the political parties reflective of these identities have emerged to challenge the constitutional and institutional framework in which they operate. It will also show that these parties may transform a party system in a way that makes it an enduring source of instability. In short, it will shed light on the interactions between the claims of nationalist parties, the overall configuration of party systems and the constitutional and institutional arrangements, for they are at the centre of politics in multinational societies.

Second, this chapter will outline and evaluate the specific constitutional and institutional arrangements that illustrate the formal recognition, or the formal rejection, of the national diversity that characterizes these countries. Particular attention will be devoted to the influence of federalism as an organizing principle, for all three cases have used this model, albeit in different ways, to manage relations between their communities. Canada has been a federal state from its birth in 1867, whereas Belgium evolved from a unitary state to a federal state in the early 1990s. The two countries, profoundly shaped by ethnolinguistic cleavages, have understood and attempted to manage their diversity in very different ways. Spain offers an even more distinctive experience in that it has chosen the path of quasi or semi-federalism. These differences suggest many questions regarding the meaning given, in each case, to the dual principles of integration and respect for diversity. More specifically, it points to questions relating to the nature and degree of political autonomy granted to the different communities as well as to the inevitable tension between, on the one hand, the central state and the larger collective identity and, on the other hand, the presence of regional, community and/or provincial governments and their own collective identity. In sum, this chapter will show how these three multinational societies have attempted to manage tensions between universalism and particularism and evaluate the success of their policies.

Belgium: an eradication of national identity

Political parties and institutions have played a key role in structuring the relationship between the Flemish and French communities in Belgium. The claims of the Flemish movement and the subsequent francophone reaction were institutionalized in the party system through the emergence of nationalist and regionalist parties and, later, with the split of traditional parties upon linguistic lines. The Flemish movement's search for recognition transformed the Belgian party system which, in turn, conditioned the reform of the Belgian state. Both the structure of the party system and the political institutions point to a political system that acknowledges the presence of different communities but remains in a state of constant instability.

The emergence of the Flemish movement is directly connected to the desire of the Flemish community to have its language recognized officially as equal to French. Indeed, the Belgian 1831 constitution was written exclusively by French speakers and contains only one linguistic provision, a declaration of linguistic liberty. This provision constituted a basis for the dominance of the French language, for French was spoken by political elites, nobles and bourgeois, even in Flanders. The Flemish grievances were met by a series of language laws that culminated in the 1898 law on the use of the Flemish language in official documents. This law gave Dutch formal equality with French as an official language.

Other laws covered the use of language in courts (1873 and 1889), in communication between the public and state authorities (1878) and in state-run and private secondary education (1883 and 1910) (McRae 1986, p. 25). The movement then took its linguistic claims further by fighting for the use of Dutch in Flanders.[1] This led to the language laws of the early 1930s that introduced the principle of territorial unilingualism. These laws dealt with the University of Ghent (1930), administration and education (1932), judicial matters (1935) and the armed forces (1938) (McRae 1986, p. 150). The third round of language laws of 1962 and 1963 attempted to close the loopholes of the 1930s laws by providing enforcement mechanisms and, most importantly, by rearranging the linguistic border following the principle of territorial unilingualism. This last strategy necessitated the transfer of communes and the creation of language facilities for minorities in the communes along the border. Only two of these transfers proved problematic and one much more so than the other. Public opinion in the French-speaking communes of Mouscron and Comines was divided but their move from West Flanders to Hainault was generally well-accepted. The transfer of the Voer (or Fourons in French) from Liège to Limburg caused much more of a stir. Ever since, the Voer question has been a sensitive issue in Belgian politics.

The Flemish movement's concerns for the linguistic and cultural future of the Flemish community led to claims for political autonomy. These concerns were brought to Parliament by the Volksunie, a Flemish nationalist political party created in 1954. The Volksunie articulated a bi-communal vision of Belgium and advocated bipartite federalism as an institutional arrangement that would protect the Flemish language and culture. It attained considerable electoral success in the late 1960s and the 1970s as at least twenty of its representatives were elected between 1968 and 1977 (Delwit and De Waele 1996, p. 233). The Volksunie gave birth to another Flemish nationalist party, the Vlaams Blok, that seeks the formation of a linguistically homogeneous Flemish state that would include Brussels. From the negligible force it constituted at its creation in 1977, the Vlaams Blok has become the fourth political party in importance in Flanders behind the Christian Social Party (CVP), the Socialist Party (SP) and the Liberal Party (VLD) (Delwit and De Waele 1996, p. 211).

The Flemish claims for recognition and autonomy provoked strong reactions in the francophone community, for they challenged both an

---

[1] The francophone minority in Flanders, although sociologically prominent, represented in the 1930s approximately only 5 per cent of the population while the Dutch minority in Wallonia was even smaller (around 2 per cent) (McRae, 1986, p. 41).

identity and a state that were associated with French-speakers. These reactions became particularly vigorous in the 1960s with the relative economic decline of Wallonia. Francophones in Wallonia felt that they could not count on the Belgian state to modernize the region's coal and steel industries since they viewed that state as the instrument of the Flemish community. The transformation and strengthening of Wallonia's economy was the main objective of the Walloon nationalist party Rassemblement Wallon (RW) that came into existence in 1967. RW integrated members from four nationalist organizations: the Mouvement Populaire Wallon (MPW), which arose from the Belgian Socialist Party (PSB), the Mouvement Liberal Wallon (MLW), which stemmed from the Liberal Party (PLP), Rénovation Wallonne, which was connected to the Christian Social Party (PSC) and Wallonie Libre (WL), an organization that advocated for Wallonia special ties with France. Besides members of these four organizations, the Rassemblement Wallon included the newly constituted (1965) Parti Wallon (PW) (Vagman 1994, pp. 21–32, 35). In order to achieve this objective, the RW advocated a territorially based federalism. Indeed, the idea of a community-based federalism, that is a federation of the Flemish and the francophone communities, was rejected because Wallonia's economy was radically different from that of Brussels. The RW attained some electoral success in the early and mid 1970s, electing fourteen candidates to the Chamber in 1971 and thirteen in 1974 (McRae 1986, p. 139). It would eventually disappear in the early 1980s as left- and right-wing members felt they could no longer coexist in the same political party.

While the 1960s saw the emergence of nationalist parties in the Flemish community and in Wallonia, it also witnessed the creation, in 1964, of a regionally based party from Brussels, the Front Démocratique des Francophones (FDF). This party emerged as a reaction to the language laws of 1962 and 1963 that froze the linguistic border and engaged in a geographical delimitation of Brussels. French-speaking Brusselers argued that the natural urban expansion of Brussels should not be blocked by a legislative 'iron collar'. The FDF advocated a territorially based federation of three units. It operated in a permanent alliance with the RW from 1968 to 1983 as both parties sought to oppose Flemish prominence and shared a similar vision of Belgium.

The Brussels-based FDF, the Volksunie and the RW voiced different claims and brought to Parliament different visions of Belgium. They shared, however, a common preoccupation with the *question communautaire*. They were so successful in putting their issues on the political agenda of the country that they radically altered the nature of the traditional parties and, by extension, the party system as a whole. As the increase in popularity of the nationalist and regionalist parties had occurred at the expense of the traditional parties representing the liberal, socialist and Christian families, these traditional parties were forced to pay attention to the *question communautaire*. The new salience of communal problems led to the split of the three traditional parties into distinct parties, as the Belgian party system was no longer able to cross-cut linguistic and regional cleavages. The Christian Social Party was the first to split in 1968–9 as a direct result of the University of Louvain (or Leuven) crisis. Louvain, an historically francophone university located in Flanders, sparked an internal quarrel as the Flemish elected representatives of the party pushed for the transfer of all the francophone faculties out of Flanders. The question of Brussels caused the Liberal Party (PLP) to follow the Christian Social Party example between 1970 and 1972, as francophones opposed the limitation of the metropolitan area of Brussels to nineteen communes. The Socialist Party was the last to split in 1978 but had already experienced the formation of two wings following the Louvain crisis and the constitutional negotiations leading to the 1970 reform.

The split of the three traditional parties is a direct consequence of the emergence of nationalist/regionalist parties that sought to improve the position of their respective communities/regions within the Belgian state. As it isolated the linguistic communities from one another, it seriously undermined the stability of the Belgian political system. Indeed, the absence of a national party in Belgium limits the opportunities for a dialogue between communities and lowers the level of mutual understanding. It also creates a situation where national politicians are virtually non-existent, for they are only accountable to members of their linguistic community. This situation is at the heart of the reform of the Belgian state. Indeed, the schism of the traditional families is a defining moment in Belgium's recent political history. It triggered a series of institutional reforms that attempted to acknowledge the existence of Belgium's linguistic communities and provide them with the autonomy necessary to fulfil their specific needs. These reforms, however, sacrificed almost completely the larger Belgian entity.

The St-Michel Accord of 1993 transformed Belgium into a federal state This state reform, which followed the 1970, 1980 and 1988 reforms, produced a new constitutional division of powers between three levels of government: the federal, the communities and the regions. The central government initially exercised all the powers but progressively transferred them to the regions and communities following the reform of 1970 (Brassinne 1989, pp. 295–7). (There are also provinces and municipalities but they are without their own legislative power and remain dependent upon higher levels of government, usually regional councils.) These reforms were the result of a compromise between, on the one hand, Flemish parties concerned with cultural and linguistic issues who advocated a community-based federation, and, on the other hand, the francophone parties preoccupied with Wallonia's economy and Brussels' language situation that supported a territorially based one.

Four types of powers rest with the federal government following this reform: exclusive powers (external relations, defence, police, social security and pensions, health, public services, fiscal and monetary policies); reservation powers at the community level; reservation powers at the regional level; concurrent powers (Fitzmaurice 1996, pp. 121–69). The federal government has the responsibility to foster economic conditions favouring the Economic and Monetary Union. As a result of the residual powers, it also has exclusive competence in sectors that are developing or have yet to develop. The federal reservation power at the community level touches the fields of education, culture and '*matières personnalisables*' which include health and youth policies. At the regional level, they include the environment, civil and military infrastructures, wildlife conservation and the distribution and treatment of water. Concurrent powers are limited to scientific research and export promotion.

Communities are competent to deal, among other things, with identity-related issues. Community governments have exclusive powers in three key sectors: education (including post-secondary education), culture (language, radio and television, public libraries, cultural agencies) and *matières personalisables* (health, hospitals, social assistance, family policies) (Fitzmaurice 1996; Brassinne, 1989). They also have the full range of legislative and administrative tools necessary to exercise their powers. There is, in this constitutional division of power, a formal, and not only symbolic, acknowledgement of Belgium's multinational character. Indeed, institutional reforms in Belgium promoted regional and communal identities at the expense of a Belgian one.

The regional governments represent Wallonia, Flanders and Brussels-Capital. While Wallonia possesses institutions distinct from those of the French community, the institutions of the Flemish region and community have merged. Although the Brussels case is a little more complicated, it is the *de facto*, although not the *de jure*, equal of the other two (Fitzmaurice 1996, pp. 150–2).

The 1993 reform eliminated several (detailed and rigid) national rules concerning the organization and structure of the community and regional governments. It did not, however, change the financing mechanisms established by the 1980 and 1988 reforms. The 1980 reform produced a system whereby regions and communities were financially dependent upon the federal government. The 1988 reform set the rules for transfer payments and looked to increase the fiscal autonomy of the regions and communities. The percentage of federal transfers to each region and community corresponds roughly to the tax money coming out of this region or community. The fiscal means of the communities and the regions are similar. There is no transfer in the name of national solidarity towards the communities but rather a contribution to education that represents in fact a transfer towards the francophone community (Fitzmaurice 1996, p. 159).

The exclusive powers of the communities over education, culture and language are significant for they embody an acknowledgement of the different identities forming the Belgian state. However, the principle of autonomy, which is integral to federalism, has to apply clearly to fiscal resources and public spending. An institutional design as well as a dynamic process, federalism is first and foremost the political project to accommodate within a common state two or more distinctive communities in an ongoing effort to live together and, at the same time, separately. Federalism can only be understood as a difficult compromise between, on the one hand, a single unitary state, one in which the different communities would all be submitted to the homogenizing pressures of the central government, where all the significant policy capacities would rest, and, on the other hand, the respective sovereignty of these different communities and/or that of their member states. By its very nature, federalism is an attempt to find equilibrium between centripetal and centrifugal forces, between the conflicting needs for unity and diversity, for putting together and keeping apart. It rests on the non-hierarchical fragmentation of sovereignty between central and peripheral governments.

In the Belgian case, even if the fiscal autonomy of regions and communities increases in the coming years, in all likelihood the main source of financial revenue for the regional and community governments will remain the federal transfer payments. And this increase in the fiscal autonomy of the regional/community governments is smaller than that of their public spending. When the fiscal transition period ends in 2000, the percentage of the communities/regions' public spending should indeed represent more than 30 per cent of the total public spending.

Two caveats are in order with regard to the hierarchical relationship between the federal and the community or regional governments. First, Belgian federalism is young. It is therefore hard to pass a definite judgement on intergovernmental relations in Belgium or on the fiscal autonomy of regions and communities. The transition from a unitary to a federal state alone represents the beginning of a progressive increase in fiscal autonomy for the regions and communities. Second, tentativeness in the transfer of fiscal autonomy and services is a frequent phenomenon in decentralization efforts that are supposedly inspired by the principles of subsidiarity and efficiency (Rocher and Rouillard 1998; Pollitt 1995). This second factor is compounded by the fiscal and budgetary conditions associated with European integration. The limits imposed by the Maastricht Treaty with regards to deficits slows down the fiscal transfers towards regions and communities. The fiscal restraint entailed by Maastricht leads to a hesitation on the part of the federal government, for it seems to doubt the ability of the regions and communities to avoid deficits. Therefore, it could be argued that, in this respect, European integration constitutes an obstacle towards further decentralization of fiscal resources.

In Belgian federalism,[2] the exclusive powers exercised by the community governments in the sectors of education, language and culture mean that each community can pursue its own cultural development. This rests on the assumption that the federal government will exercise restraint with regards to its reservation power. Because Belgian federalism is only a few years old, it is too early to predict if this will be the case. Nevertheless, since the Belgian state evolved into a federal state in the hope of better managing intercommunity conflicts, and since constitutional reforms in Belgium have over the last thirty years systematically favoured particularism over universalism, it is reasonable to argue that the federal government will, in fact, exercise restraint. In short, not only is the spirit of federalism congruent with such an outcome, so is the historical evolution of centre–periphery relations in Belgium.

This analysis of the new Belgian institutional arrangement reveals that the multinational character of the Belgian state has been formally acknowledged. This recognition, however, has come at the expense of the larger Belgian national identity. These developments were largely the result of major changes in the Belgian party system. Indeed, the emergence of nationalist and regionalist parties followed by the split of

---

[2] We are aware of the formal asymmetry of the institutions. As we have said the Flemish region and community have merged while the Walloon region and francophone community retain distinct institutions.

the three traditional parties on linguistic lines has triggered a search for an institutional architecture that would satisfy Belgium's communities and regions. The current arrangement is not likely to be definitive. The dynamics of the party system create instability in the political system because they reinforce ongoing claims for more autonomy and point towards further constitutional change.

In sum, the main characteristics of Belgian institutional arrangements are as follows:

1. The absence of a formal consecration of a Belgian national identity.
2. The formal political acknowledgement of the multinational character of the Belgian state through the exclusive powers of the communities over language, culture and education.
3. The existence of a hierarchical relationship between the federal government and the governments of the communities and regions.

Spain: an institutionalized hierarchy of identities

Politics in democratic Spain has been shaped to a great extent by Basque and Catalan nationalism. Both the Basque and Catalan nationalist parties have been instrumental in constructing Spain's institutional arrangements. In turn, the system of autonomous communities has structured party politics and, more specifically, nationalist politics in the post-Franco era. It has provided nationalist parties in the Basque Country and Catalonia with different arenas in which to operate and has stimulated the emergence of nationalist parties in other regions. The interaction between the Spanish institutional and constitutional framework and the party systems provides a framework that gives space to Spain's different communities without isolating them from each other or from the larger Spanish entity.

The Basque and Catalan nationalist movements had a defining impact on Spanish politics following Franco's death, because their claims for self-government made it impossible for the Spanish political elite to engage in a transition to democracy while retaining the centralized state model that had characterized Spain since the Civil War. These movements had great legitimacy, because they were among the Franco dictatorship's fiercest adversaries. For Spain, democracy meant that the claims of nationalist movements had to be addressed. The need for quasi-consensus inherent in an enterprise such as the writing of a new constitution gave Basque and Catalan nationalists great leverage in negotiations with the Spanish state. Indeed, they succeeded in having the new constitution recognize the existence of 'nationalities' and 'regions' within the Spanish nation and create autonomous communities that could exercise certain powers.

The negotiations between the first democratically elected Spanish government in more than forty years, headed by Adolfo Suárez of the Unión de Centro Democrático (UCD), and the Basque Nationalist Party (BNP) proved difficult. The BNP was dissatisfied with the proposed constitution because it situated the exercise of the *fueros* only within the framework of the Spanish political system and did not recognize their historical legitimacy independently of the constitution (an idea that would have expressed, according to many Basque nationalists, the right to self-determination for the Basques). It encouraged its followers to abstain in the referendum of December 1978 on the constitution or to cast blank ballots. The nationalist party closely connected with ETA, Herri Batasuna (HB), and the third Basque nationalist party, Euskadiko Ezkerra (EE), urged a No vote mainly because the document did not recognize the right to self-determination for the Basques and did not include Navarre within the Basque Country (Gunther et. al. 1988, pp. 342–3). The constitution was nevertheless approved by a majority of Basque voters although the number of invalid votes in the Basque Country was significantly higher than in the rest of Spain.[3] The Statute of Autonomy that created the Basque autonomous community was adopted via referendum in October 1979 despite the opposition of HB and the dissatisfaction of the BNP (the EE supported the Statute arguing that it represented the first step towards independence) (Gunther et. al. 1988, p. 343; Medrano 1995, p. 146). In Catalonia, where nationalism seeks autonomy rather than independence, the content of the constitution proved satisfying for the two main nationalist parties, Convergència i Unió (CiU) and Esquerra Republicana de Catalunya (ERC), and the Statute of Autonomy was ratified when 88 per cent of those voting supported it in a referendum (Keating 1996a, p. 146).

The Basque and Catalan nationalist parties were at the centre of Spain's institutional reform. Indeed, they transformed the Spanish institutions before making their mark on the party system, as forty years of dictatorship had left them operating in a vacuum. In turn, the new institutional framework quickly shaped the structure of party systems.

In both Catalonia and the Basque Country, nationalist parties have

---

[3] The percentage of invalid votes ranged from 7.5 to 16.3 in the provinces of the Basque Country while the national average was 4.3. The percentage of 'Yes' votes (in favour of the proposed constitution) in the Basque Country ranged from 63.9 to 71.4 of the votes cast while it was of 87.8 in Spain as a whole (Coverdale 1985, p. 241).

enjoyed considerable electoral success. In each Catalan regional election, with the exception of the very first one, the combined seats won by the two nationalist parties (CiU and ERC) surpassed the number of seats won by the national (Spanish) parties. The Catalan party system is dominated by the nationalist party CiU which has won every election held (1980, 1984, 1988 1992 and 1995) while its leader, Jordi Pujol, has been the president of Catalonia since 1980. The more nationalist ERC, which carries a secessionist agenda, has not attained the success of CiU although it has sent between five and fourteen representatives to the Generalitat (Catalan parliament) in the first four elections. In the Basque Country, it is the BNP that has been the dominant party, as it failed to win only one election, that of 1986. That year, the Basque Socialist Party (PSE-PSOE) won a majority of seats because of the fragmentation of the nationalist vote that resulted from a schism within the BNP, leading to the creation of the more nationalist Eusko Alkartasuna (EA). The Basque party system also includes the secessionist HB which has links with the terrorist organization ETA. Although the nationalist vote is more fragmented in the Basque Country than in Catalonia, nationalist parties always win a majority of the seats.

As indicated by the number and success of nationalist parties in the Basque Country and Catalonia, the creation of autonomous communities stimulated nationalist politics in these regions. Perhaps more interesting is that it had a similar effect in regions that historically experienced low levels of nationalist activity.

The Basque nationalist parties PNV, EA and HB, for example, have occupied a significant place within the Navarrese party system, as they put forward the option of the incorporation of Navarre into the Basque Country insisting on the cultural ties between the two regions (many Navarrese of the north speak Basque and feel a kinship with the other Basque provinces) (Donaghy and Newton 1987, p. 102). They had to compete with the (Spanish) national parties as well as with the Navarrese nationalist party UPN. In the Canary Islands, the nationalist coalition CC won the 1995 autonomous elections. Nationalist parties have also appeared in Galicia (Bloque Nacionalista Galego, BNG), Valencia (Uniò Valenciana, UV), Aragón (Partido Aragonés, PAR) and in Andalucía (Partido Socialista de Andalucía, PSA).[4] The case of Andalusia is particularly revealing of the impact of institutions on nationalist activity, as before the transition towards democracy it 'had never laid claim to separate regional identity or articulated mass demands for autonomy' (Gunther et al. 1988, p. 246). Furthermore,

---

[4] The PSA would become the PA (Partido Andalucista) in 1984.

Andalusian representatives forced the Spanish political elite to imagine a third road to autonomy, as Andalusia did not fall into the category of 'historical nationality' associated with the rapid route but did not want to settle for the slow route reserved for all the other regions (Donaghy and Newton 1987, pp. 101–2).

Nationalist parties have also used the national political scene to put forward their claims for increased autonomy and recognition. This is best illustrated by the bargaining that followed the 1996 elections where the Partido Popular (PP) won, but was twenty seats short of an overall majority. As a consequence, the national party most sceptical of the process of devolution towards the autonomous communities and the party that had criticized the Partido Socialista Obrero Español (PSOE) for having been controlled by the CiU since the 1993 elections (the PSOE was sixteen seats shy of an overall majority in these elections) had to seek the support of nationalist parties. It struck deals with the CiU, the PNV and the CC, enhancing the autonomy of the regions and responding to some of the three regions' demands (Balfour 1996, pp. 282–3). Spain's proportional representation system works to the advantage of nationalist parties. It allows even the smaller ones from Catalonia and the Basque Country such as EA, HB and ERC and those from less populated regions or where nationalism is not as strong such as BNG, CC or UV to be represented in Parliament. It also presents these parties with the opportunity to hold the balance of power.

While the position occupied by nationalist parties on the national (Spanish) political scene has kept the system under pressure, it has also allowed the nationalist parties to communicate and cooperate with the Spanish parties and with nationalist parties of other regions. Communication and cooperation also occurs within the Spanish parties, for they have not suffered the fragmentation of their Belgian counterparts and enjoy support, although to different degrees, in every autonomous community. The interaction between party systems and formal institutions in Spain reflects an attempt to tentatively manage the tensions between, on the one hand, the recognition and autonomy of communities, and, on the other, the integrity of the larger Spanish entity.

The Spanish constitutional framework also reflects this tentativeness. The 1978 Constitutional Law creates a quasi-federalism whereby powers are shared between the central government and the governments of the seventeen autonomous communities. The nature and the extent of the powers granted to these governments, the degree of autonomy they enjoy and the way they achieve this autonomy varies from one community to another. The Spanish constitution endorses principles of asymmetry, for it is recognized that the needs and preferences of the different communities will not necessarily be similar (Newton and Donaghy 1997; Maxwell and Spiegel 1994; Pérez-Diaz 1993; Wiarda 1993). The political process of the 1980s, however, saw centralizing forces attempt to homogenize the territorial distribution of power. It also witnessed a reaction by several autonomous communities who claimed for themselves what was awarded to the 'historical nationalities' of Catalonia, Galicia and the Basque Country.

The regionalization process must respect four principles: regional autonomy must not weaken Spanish unity; the process must not affect the ability of the central government to maintain its internal and external stability; the process must increase regional stability through a redistribution of wealth towards the poorest regions; and the central government must ensure that the regional governments have enough fiscal resources to discharge their responsibilities. The first three principles reflect a clear concern for stability. The fourth signals a preoccupation with the extent to which communities can effectively exercise their autonomy.

The powers exercised exclusively by the central government include immigration, currency, trade, external affairs, economic planning and defence. The autonomous communities enjoy exclusive powers with regard to language and cultural matters. The power with regard to language refers only to the regional language, for the 1978 Constitutional Law establishes only one official national language, Castilian. The regional languages, however, can become, in their respective regions, an official language (along with Castilian). Nevertheless, this is consistent with a hierarchical institutionalization of languages and identities. This hierarchy is explicit in section two of the Constitutional Law which introduces a distinction between, on the one hand, the Spanish nation and, on the other hand, the nationalities and regions. Although this article recognizes the right to autonomy for the nationalities and regions, it insists mainly on the indivisibility of the Spanish nation.

The fiscal revenue of the autonomous communities comes from taxes on property, products and activities, charges for public services (ranging from publications to health), surcharges over and above state taxes, a borrowing capacity (short and long term), as well as from investments and industrial, commercial and agricultural services. The autonomous communities also benefit from transfers from the central government and from the European Union.[5]

The Basque Country and Navarre, claiming historical rights, have

---

[5] Regional transfers from the central government can, in turn, be subdivided in the following way: for new services and responsibilities; for autonomous institutions; from the Interregional Compensation Funds; and, finally, a share of the revenues coming

reached special economic agreements with the central government, enabling them to levy and collect all taxes on their respective territory, with the exception of customs duties and taxes on petroleum products and tobacco. Although this arrangement reflects the asymmetrical dimension of the Spanish constitutional framework,[6] the additional fiscal autonomy of the Basque Country and Navarre cannot be exercised without certain controls and limitations coming from the centre, including the need to conform with the general state system of taxation. The two communities have to use the same classification of activities, the same terminology, the same criteria and the same rate of taxation as that of the centre, in both commercial and personal income taxes. These two communities have to give a yearly quota of their fiscal revenues to the central government for the services and powers which the latter still retains and exercises in the two regions (Newton and Donaghy 1997, pp. 137–8). Another significant constraint on fiscal autonomy comes from the obligation for the two communities not to have an overall tax level lower than that of the centre, a provision that is also valid for the other fifteen autonomous communities.

Although the Spanish state has chosen the path of semi-federalism and not that of federalism *per se*, the fiscal and budgetary resources of the communities are a key variable in the effective exercise of autonomy. While their fiscal resources have been increasing on a yearly basis ever since the constitutional reform, the autonomous revenues of communities still make up only a small percentage of their total revenues (with the exceptions of the Basque Country and Navarre). Indeed, the bulk of their revenues consists mainly of regional transfers from the central government. Furthermore, as is the case with the Belgian regions and communities, the public spending of the Spanish autonomous communities is continually rising. In fact, while the communities' public spending was almost non-existent in the early 1980s, it represented 22.69 per cent of Spain's total public spending in 1994, and as much as 34.60 per cent including local public spending (Newton and Donaghy

from the taxes on personal income, inheritance, wealth, transfer of funds, luxury and gambling activities.

[6] This is a dimension of asymmetry that is completely neglected by some authors who strongly argue against this organizing principle (see, for example, Dion 1994). We do not wish to dispute here that the asymmetrical character of Spain may indeed have diminished over time, just as we do not wish to dispute that there seems to be a quasi-consensus on the need to further dimish it in the near future. We simply wish to argue that asymmetry, which was the favoured principle from the start, is still present in Spain's quasi- or semi-federalism. Indeed, as far as the autonomous communities of the Basque Country and Catalonia are concerned, the abandonment of this principle is a potential source of severe tensions with the central government (Newton and Donaghy 1997, pp. 143–4).

1997, p. 126; Maxwell and Spiegel 1994, pp. 73–8; Pérez-Diaz 1993, pp. 210–12). Some scholars have found this to be substantial enough to conclude that Spain has become a model of administrative federalism (Maxwell and Spiegel 1994, p. 77). However, it should be stressed that the Spanish state that preceded the Constitutional Law of 1978, under the Franco regime, was highly centralized/authoritarian, and that the reciprocal negation of the different collective identities, especially in the case of the national (Castilian) identity, was strongly rooted.

The Spanish constitutional and institutional framework is an attempt to strike a balance between the recognition of Spain's communities and the stability of the larger Spanish ensemble. This middle-range position is the result of a struggle between, on the one hand, the centralizing forces that carried over from the Franco regime, and, on the other, the Basque and Catalan nationalist parties. Indeed, these parties are largely responsible for the construction of Spain's quasi-federalism, for they benefited from the legitimacy they gained as a result of their historical opposition to the dictatorship and actively sought recognition for their communities. In turn, the system of autonomous communities created subnational party systems that fostered nationalist activity and shaped the national party system. As was the case for Belgium, the pressures to further decentralize the system are important. In Spain, however, the existence of strong forces defending the integrity of the central state makes the Belgian scenario of extreme fragmentation unlikely.

All in all, the Spanish institutional arrangements can be summarized as follows:

1. Consecration of a national identity, the Spanish one;
2. Formal political recognition of the multinational nature of the state, inasmuch as regional language and culture are under the exclusive jurisdiction of the regional governments (excluding international relations);
3. Explicit hierarchical institutionalization of collective identities, in which only the Spanish identity is recognized as a unified and indivisible nation. The others are defined as nationalities or regions and, to this extent, are viewed as sociopolitical characteristics of the former;
4. Perpetuation of a relationship of tutelage between the central and regional governments, as illustrated by the small fiscal autonomy of the regional governments that rely, for the most part, on the many transfers coming from the centre.

Canada: a crystallization of conflicting identities

The challenge issued by the Québécois nationalist movement to the Canadian state is probably unparalleled in western societies. Quebec was able to further its claim to special status by using Canada's federal system. Indeed, starting in the 1960s, the Parti Libéral du Quebec (PLQ) was able to use the Quebec state to seek autonomy and recognition. The emergence in the 1970s of the sovereigntist Parti Québécois (PQ) increased the pressure on the Canadian state, threatening its very existence. The fragmentation of the federal party system in the 1990s reduced the space available for communication between Canada's linguistic communities. The structure of the Quebec and federal party system and the federal government's inability to meet the province's claims for recognition have combined to make Canada's political system highly unstable.

The Québécois nationalist movement emerged following important changes in Quebec's society (McRoberts 1997b; Latouche 1993; Gagnon and Montcalm 1992; Balthazar 1986). The Quiet Revolution of the 1960s saw the liberal government of Jean Lesage use the state to complement and guide these changes, most notably by attempting to weaken the power of the Catholic Church and to correct the under-representation of francophones in the higher levels of the province's economic structures. In order to perform these tasks, the PLQ argued that the Quebec state needed powers which were exercised by the federal government and proceeded to wrestle them away from it in the name of Quebec's French-speaking community. The Quiet Revolution is also synonymous with Quebec's claims for recognition as a distinct society within Canada. These claims challenged a vision of the Canadian federation resting on the principle of equality of the provinces. In sum, the development of Québécois nationalism was structurally conditioned by Canada's federal system, more specifically by a provincial–federal competition for powers and a battle between alternate visions of Canada.

In the 1960s, some PLQ members, led by René Lévesque, began to argue that in order for Quebec to continue its development, it needed to be a fully sovereign state. Lévesque left the Liberal Party in 1967 and founded the Mouvement souveraineté-association (MSA), and, in 1968, the sovereigntist Parti Québécois (PQ). The PQ sent seven representatives to the National Assembly in the 1970 election (with 23.1 per cent of the vote) and six in the 1973 elections (with 30.2 per cent of the vote). These two elections were significant because the PQ replaced the formerly dominant Union Nationale (a traditional conservative party) as the main alternative to the federalist PLQ. Indeed, the PQ's rise in Quebec's two-party system was a decisive moment for the nationalist movement, for it made it likely that the political party seeking Quebec's independence would win at least one out of two or three elections. In fact, PQ governments were elected in 1976, 1981, 1994 and 1998. The presence of the PQ as one of the two major parties in Quebec's party system also means that the sovereigntist option is unlikely to disappear even when it is unpopular. Indeed, the combination of the PQ's defeat in the 1980 referendum on 'sovereignty-association', its 1985 electoral loss and the apparent resolution of Canada's unity problems with the signing (but not the ratification) of the Meech Lake Accord in 1987 seemed to have dealt a deadly blow to the sovereigntist project. However, it was able to come back with a vengeance when some provincial legislatures failed to ratify the Meech Lake Accord precisely because it continued to dominate the party system.

The death of Meech Lake caused fragmentation in the federal party system, for it prompted a minister of the federal government, Lucien Bouchard, to quit and form a new nationalist party devoted to Quebec's independence, the Bloc Québécois (BQ). For the first time, there was a Québécois nationalist party operating at the federal level. The BQ sent fifty-four representatives to parliament in the 1993 federal elections, as it received 49 per cent of the vote in Quebec. This was enough to make it the official opposition to the Liberal government. These constitutional failures also triggered the rise of the western-based Reform Party which would eventually replace the BQ as official opposition following the 1997 elections. The emergence of nationalist and regionalist parties in the federal party system is an important event, for it further reduces the possibilities for communication between Canada's linguistic communities that a highly competitive provincial–federal relationship had already limited. While institutions and party systems have shaped and sustained nationalist conflicts in Canada,[7] the federal government's failure to accommodate Quebec's claims for recognition is also responsible for the present instability.

The patriation of the Canadian constitution in 1982 represented a

---

[7] Nationalist conflicts in Canada cannot be reduced to the action of the Québécois nationalist movement. The Native peoples of Canada have also posed a serious challenge to the Canadian state in articulating nationalist demands. Native nationalism is, in the early twenty-first century, as fundamental a force in shaping Canadian politics as is Québécois nationalism. Native organizations played a pivotal role in the failure of the Meech Lake Accord which addressed Quebec's concerns but not Natives' concerns. The failure of the Charlettetown Accord, which recognized Natives' right to self-government and proclaimed Native governments to be one of the three orders of governments in Canada, leaves Canada's constitutional problems unsolved.

step backward in terms of the federal government's dealing with Quebec. The patriation did not have Quebec's support, because the PQ government did not approve of an amending formula that did not give the province a veto nor did it approve of the Charter of Rights and Freedoms that gave increased power to judges. Nevertheless, the constitution was patriated. Both the PQ and the PLQ denounced the move. The ensuing constitutional negotiations attempted to specify conditions that would enable the Quebec government to sign the fundamental law of the country.

These negotiations first led to the Meech Lake Accord. This accord met five demands put forward by Quebec Premier Robert Bourassa, one of which was the recognition of Quebec's distinct character. This provision, which would have had little impact on Quebec's autonomy, coexisted with the principle of the equality of the provinces (Rocher and Boismenu 1990). It is the unpopularity of this distinct society clause outside Quebec, along with the complexity of the constitution's amending formula, that caused the failure of Meech Lake. Relatively more ambitious, the Charlottetown Accord sought to address the demands, not only of the Quebec government, but also of different political actors in Canada. While the recognition of the heterogeneous character of Canadian society was present in this accord, it also stressed a multitude of fundamental principles that marginalized the multinational nature of Canada and favoured a centralization of powers (Rocher 1992; Gagnon and Rocher 1992b).

The distinct society clause, whether in Meech Lake or Charlottetown, does not constitute a formal political recognition of the Quebec community as it defines itself, namely as a people or a nation. While the Meech Lake Accord speaks of French-speaking Canadians and English-speaking Canadians, the meaning of the expression 'distinct society' remains unspecified. The Charlottetown Accord defines it as including a French-speaking majority, a unique culture and a civil law tradition (Meech Lake Accord, section 2 (1) (a) and (b); Charlottetown Accord, section 2 (1) (c)). Neither of these two accords declared Quebec an autonomous community, nor did they mention a Québécois people or nation. Furthermore, both of these accords explicitly state that nothing in this provision shall undermine the powers, rights or privileges of the federal and provincial governments (Meech Lake Accord, section 2 (4); Charlottetown Accord, section 2 (3)). In other words, it is explicitly stated that no additional power(s) for the government of Quebec, or any other government, can ever come from the distinct society clause, not even in the area of language. Only the *status quo ante* is really given a formal political recognition. The Charlottetown Accord even insisted, in accordance with this conservative perspective, on the formal equality of the provinces (Charlottetown Accord, section 2 (1) (h)).

In the days following the slim victory of the federalist side in the 1995 referendum on sovereignty, the federal government promised to increase the flexibility of the system and adopted in the House of Commons a resolution recognizing the distinct character of Quebec. The postreferendum climate of confrontation that characterized the relationship between the federal government and the Quebec government, however, was not conducive to respect for that promise. The premiers and provincial legislatures of the other nine provinces adopted a declaration of principle that was to serve as a guide for federal–provincial relations. Stressing a spirit of cooperation, this declaration is especially revealing of the Canadian state's understanding of the many communities it holds and of its hesitant willingness to formally recognize them.

The Calgary Declaration (Dialogue Canada 1997), careful not to revive the polemic still inherent to the distinct society clause, opted for a new formula, that of the 'unique character of Quebec society' (fifth statement). This wording has already proven too little for some, too much for others, and promising, if not satisfactory, for others (Bouchard 1997, A7; Richer 1997, A4; Lévesque 1997, A4; Hébert 1997, A4; Dion and Cornellier 1997, A1, A8). It raises questions about the true extent of this recognition and its inherent logic.

This framework for discussion on Canadian unity is made up of seven major statements of different nature and importance. While some aim at celebrating some Canadian characteristics such as diversity, tolerance, compassion, equality of opportunity (third statement), others state that governments have to work in partnership to better respond to the needs of Canadians (seventh statement). Some others, however, embody a particular vision of the Canadian and Québécois community. The first statement, which reaffirms the principle that Canada is made up of equal citizens, with equal rights, goes beyond a simple will to insert it in the liberal-democratic tradition. It also suggests that Canada is no different than the sum of its citizens, a simple aggregate of individuals.

Particularisms present in the fourth and fifth statements give way to the first statement, for the listing order is neither neutral nor innocent. Therefore, the diversity that is recognized cannot be incongruent with the assumption of the aggregate ensemble. Furthermore, while there is a recognition of the provinces' different characteristics, their equality is once more reaffirmed (second statement). Indeed, particularisms cannot and shall not lead to political claims. It is the aggregate ensemble that is important and not the particular situations or characteristics. In other words, this ensemble celebrates diversity, tolerance, compassion and equality of opportunity (third statement), without formally recognizing anyone.

The vision of Canada made up of equal citizens and equal provinces did not stop the premiers from reaffirming that it is a federation (fifth statement). But federalism seems to be mainly understood as an administrative arrangement in which only the principles of uniformity and homogeneity can guarantee a fair and equal treatment of every citizen. The logic of Canadian federalism is more congruent with a unitary representation of Canada than with the spirit of federalism which combines unity with diversity and seeks to recognize, preserve and promote distinct collective identities within a larger political partnership. The essence of federalism builds on the principles of union and independence. It readily accepts, and even stresses, differentiated treatments and their logical consequence, an asymmetrical distribution of powers. Although this can be understood as the political-administrative illustration of the values of diversity, tolerance, and compassion present in the third statement of the Declaration, it still cannot be reconciled with the value of equality/uniformity present in the second statement.

Particularisms, of course, are not formally negated by the Calgary Declaration. The premiers' framework for discussion does indeed mention the existence of the aboriginal peoples, the English and French languages, and multiculturalism (fourth statement). The Quebec society is nevertheless not conceived in its globality. It does not exist as a collective political entity, autonomous and differentiated. Its unique character is only significant to the extent that it is fundamental for the well-being of Canada (fifth statement). Neither a people, a nation, nor an autonomous political community, Quebec is now only a society with a unique character that contributes to the Canadian well-being. The principles of equality and uniformity of the provinces go against the very possibility of a *projet de société* that would be incongruent with a larger Canadian one. In this respect, the Calgary Declaration takes part in the institutionalized negation of a Québécois collective identity differentiated from the Canadian one. In this respect, it represents a collective thinking pattern that needs to be broken in order to establish the spaces of communication between communities still missing in the Canadian case.

The failure of Canadian political actors to respond to Quebec's claims for recognition and autonomy has kept the Canadian political system highly unstable. Indeed, it is illusory to think that Quebec's claims will fade away, for they are firmly entrenched in the Quebec party system. The fragmentation of the federal party system and the competitive nature of present federal–provincial relations, however, make constitutional reform in Canada a very difficult enterprise.

Beyond a hierarchy of collective identities

The Belgian constitutional reforms have chosen the path of fragmentation at the expense of the preservation and construction of joint spaces where communities can interact. These reforms, which have come at the expense of unity between the two linguistic groups (Karmis and Gagnon 1996). have their origins in the transformation of the Belgian party system in the 1960s and 1970s. This structural reality, along with the new institutional arrangements, led Belgium towards extreme fragmentation. Indeed, if the solution for multinational states is rooted in the recognition of plural identities in a way that avoids a zero-sum game and that facilitates interaction between communities, Belgium fails the test. One can only find the institutionalization of mutual differences and mutual exclusion. In other words, there is an institutionalized territorial glorification of ethnolinguistic cleavages, without a comparable concern for Belgian unity and for the joint spaces through which the linguistic communities can communicate. The Belgian identity cleavage can be understood as horizontal in that it involves two mutually exclusive identities, neither claiming to be the national or pan-Belgian one.

In Canada, this cleavage is vertical, for the Canadian identity attempts to incorporate the other collective identities in a hierarchical fashion, or simply to replace them. This Canadian identity is thought of as the only truly national identity, all others being merely communal or regional identities. As this Canadian identity is strongly embedded in the federal political institutions (Resnick 1994a) and in a rigid federalism (Rocher and Rouillard 1996), it is difficult to make room for distinct and non-hierarchical collective identities. Whereas the mutual recognition of the different communities is a necessary precondition for the construction of the joint spaces so critical to the stability of a multinational society, the Canadian identity seems to feed on the denial, if not the demonization, of the Québécois identity (Rocher 1997).

The institutionalization of this denial appears to be the rule of the last constitutional reforms, attempted or achieved. The patriation of the Canadian constitution that preceded the enactment of the Constitution Act (1982) strongly illustrates this non-recognition of the Québécois identity. Indeed, why would it be necessary to obtain the formal consent of a community that, according to this view, does not even exist (Laforest 1992a)? Multiculturalism policies also take part in this institutionalized non-recognition. These policies, which appear to be progressive and open-minded towards cultural diversity, have stimulated the glorification of the Canadian identity as the only civic one, and favoured a dilution of the Québécois identity in the midst of many other identities, each more folkloric than the next one, but all invariably ethnic (Rocher and Smith 1997; McRoberts 1995b).

In Belgium, since the identity cleavage is horizontal, the joint spaces could theoretically be located within federal political institutions, each community is able to claim kinship within those institutions in an equal but non-exclusive fashion. This could lead, over time, to the joint building of a (pan-)Belgian community, understood as a shared and non-exclusive identity for the Flemish and the Walloon communities without, in contrast with the Canadian experience, trying to replace either identity, whether by negation or demonization. This very possibility seems forbidden in the Canadian case where the Canadian national identity tries to either incorporate the other collective identities in a hierarchical fashion, or simply substitute itself for them. In such cases, further development of the central political institutions can only be accomplished to the detriment of regional/provincial institutions, for the identity dynamic is trapped in a zero-sum game. There is even an additional problem in the Canadian case: as the (pan-)Canadian identity is, to this day, narrowly embedded in the federal political institutions, does the equality of the collective identities entail the non-hierarchy of the federal and Québécois governments? In other words, how is it possible to foster the development of distinct, but non-hierarchical collective identities in a federalism of tutelage consecrated by the Constitution Act (1982), and reaffirmed by the recent federal initiatives and the constitutional reformism of the last two decades? All in all, the Belgian and Canadian cases may be just as similar as they are different, for while the former puts too much emphasis on particularism and the latter on universalism, neither one recognizes, much less encourages, the possibility of non-hierarchical plural identities.

As a possible solution, spaces of identity meetings and dialogues may prove to be more problematic in the Canadian case. The possibility of creating such joint spaces rests on the *previous* mutual recognition of the different communities that would be involved. Only when none of the collective identities is being negated or demonized by the other(s), can the possibility of creating such joint spaces become real. Even though the negation of a collective identity may be more difficult to resolve than its demonization, since the latter does indeed imply a recognition, the difficulty is yet greater if the existence itself of the (pan-)Canadian identity rests in part on the demonization of the Québécois identity.

In Spain, like in Canada, the identity cleavage is vertical, for the collective identities are institutionalized into a hierarchy where only the Spanish one is deemed an indivisible nation, all others being mere nationalities or regions. Yet, contrary to the Canadian case, the Spanish case represents a hesitant but real attempt to balance the recognition of different communities with the preservation of the larger identity. Spain's constitutional and institutional arrangements provide a framework in which different identities are not deemed conflictual but can coexist. In other words, identities are not presented as a zero-sum game. This management strategy has proven far more successful than the assimilationist policies of the Franco dictatorship that stressed complete loyalty to the Spanish identity at the expense of all others (Pérez-Diaz 1993, pp. 204–14; Maxwell and Spiegel 1994, pp. 48–64; Newton and Donaghy 1997, pp. 141–3). Indeed, it seems that regionalization in Spain has strengthened the process of national integration (Pérez-Diaz 1993, pp. 194–214). While an excess of universalism in Canada and particularism in Belgium is threatening the survival of the two states, the compromise reached by Spain appears to have left it in a better position. Indeed, the Spanish case suggests that a state's formal recognition of its multiple collective identities need not destroy the larger identity but can indeed stimulate it and enhance the stability of the system.

The Spanish framework was built in a period of great activity and turmoil. The transition towards democracy gave different actors who had acquired great legitimacy during the dictatorship the opportunity to shape Spain's new institutions. The Spanish case is an important reminder that change and stability are not necessarily antithetical. Indeed, some crises bear elements of stability. In the Canadian case, a productive change necessitates a rupture with the constitutional context produced by the 1982 constitutional reform, for this reform remains an important source of tension between Quebec and the larger Canadian community. Indeed, the present constitutional context, partly shaped by the Constitution Act (1982), inhibits the very possibility of change and makes the search for a solution that does not depart from this framework invariably sterile. Not only does this context shape the means and strategies considered, but it also conditions the ends, objectives and issues of political action (Thelen and Steinmo 1992; Atkinson 1993). The difficulty in breaking away from the present collective thinking pattern is exacerbated by the difficulty in understanding and evaluating proposals for change in a way that is not shaped by the aforementioned thinking pattern. In sum, Canada's constitutional problems can only be solved by a radical departure from the present constitutional framework.

It should be emphasized that, throughout this analysis, the non-hierarchical nature of plural identities in a multinational state such as Belgium, Canada or Spain, refers exclusively to the identity project formally chosen and institutionalized in the constitutional texts, and not the split or shared identity that any citizen may hold at any given time.

This is a fundamental distinction that, far from negating the plural and asymmetrical identities held by most, if not all, citizens in multinational states, really enables these multiple identities to benefit from the same formal recognition and legitimacy. To this extent, the asymmetrical nature of these identities taken at the citizen level goes hand in hand with the non-hierarchical nature of these identities at the institutional level. In fact, it is precisely because these multiple national identities are not institutionalized into a hierarchy in the constitutional texts that it is possible for each citizen to develop and nurture his or her own split or shared identity, his or her own asymmetrical and dynamic combination of plural identities. In other words, the asymmetrical nature of identities at the citizen's level is not problematical at all. If anything, it is the rule. Only the hierarchical institutionalization of the plural identities in the constitutional texts, as well as in the attempted constitutional reforms, is an obstacle to a state's true recognition of its multinational nature.

Conclusion

Far from being a panacea, the last constitutional changes in Belgium and Spain are nonetheless thought to be mostly positive, in that they help to further develop the institutional context necessary to attenuate the tensions inherent to the *status quo ante*. Some scholars do not hesitate to conclude, in the Spanish case, that the process of regionalization has even strengthened the process of national integration, thus suggesting that Spain is no longer trapped in a zero-sum game. Before, every one of the numerous collective identities in Spain excluded all possibilities to hold two or more identities at the same time, each stressing the complete loyalty of its members, each carrying a monopolistic, if not assimilationist component. The absence in the Canadian case of a positive dynamic, similar to that found in the Belgian and Spanish cases, calls for a significant rupture from the present institutional context, hardening since the Constitution Act (1982). Such a rupture necessarily entails a period of crisis. The key element is that some crises bear collective learning, while others do not. The upcoming efforts need to place emphasis on the possibility of collective learning, not on the search, invariably sterile, for a process or solution supposedly consensual or non-conflictual. The difficulty of breaking away from the current collective thinking pattern is exacerbated by the difficulty in understanding, and evaluating a proposal for change in a way other than that shaped by the aforementioned thinking pattern, thus remaining victim of a perennial and invisible vicious circle. Yet changes do happen. But because the institutional context not only shapes and constrains the means chosen and the strategies emphasized, and the ends, the objectives and the issues themselves, the solution can hardly ever come without a period of crisis.

The rupture can only be significant in the Canadian case since, contrary to the Belgian and Spanish cases, the last constitutional change remains an important cause of tensions between the Canadian and the Québécois communities. In other words, not only does the present institutional context, partly shaped by the Constitution Act (1982), inhibit the very possibility of a collective change, but it is also itself a significant part of the problem. In this light, the Belgian and Spanish institutional contexts both favour the rise of a virtuous circle, whereas the Canadian institutional context only allows for the strengthening of a vicious circle.

The distinction to be made between vertical and horizontal identity cleavages helps to explain how and why neither Belgium nor Spain could be a model, albeit a partial one, for Canada. Different problems call for different solutions. Comparative analysis of the three countries makes explicit the distinctive nature of the identity dynamics at play, just as it makes explicit the distinctiveness of the institutionalized contexts in which they respectively unfold. In other words, a *sui generis* case like Canada could only be solved by a *sui generis* solution, one that avoids Belgian particularism, while at the same time going beyond Spain's hierarchical institutionalization of collective identities. While this last solution may prove to be sufficient, at least in the short term, for a country that made its transition towards democracy and became a quasi-federation twenty years ago, it falls short for a country that claims to have been a democracy and a federation for more than 130 years.

7 Ethnoterritorial concurrence in multinational societies: the Spanish *comunidades autónomas*

Luis Moreno

Introduction: conceptual assumptions

Functionalist theories have persistently conveyed the idea that internal territorial differences within nation states would disappear with the extension of liberal democracy and industrial capitalism. As communication of political, economic and cultural matters increased, the peoples of different regions would develop a new common identity, which would transcend their differences (Deutsch 1966).[1] The centre–periphery dichotomy was to decline in importance as society became modernized by means of elite-initiated policies aimed at achieving social standardization (e.g. a common language and citizenship). Likewise, the cultural identities of ethnic groups and minorities would be replaced by a set of class-oriented conflicts, or conflicts among interest groups. Thus, modernization was thought to have brought about an all-embracing nation-state identity rooted in both cultural and civic bases. History, however, has repeatedly falsified such analyses.

At the beginning of the twenty-first century, I think we ought to reconsider both the premises and implications of all-embracing identities, for they are increasingly untenable. While being corroded by the forces of globalization, these identities are also subject to fragmentation, competition and overlap with numerous other senses of belonging. The discontinuity and dislocation of social arrangements allow different identities, particularly those of a territorial nature, to relate to each other in quite an unpredictable manner. In fact, identities are shared to various degrees by individuals and are constantly subject to internaliza-

---

[1] For William Safran, one of the prominent characteristics of American social science in general, and the behaviourist–functionalist school of political science in particular, is its ahistoricist bias. 'History is rejected on two grounds: First . . . as a succession of events that . . . do not lend themselves to comparison and generalization . . . Second . . . because it is associated with pre-modern (primitive) societies' (1987, p. 13). Mainstream Marxists have traditionally taken a functional approach to the analysis of political integration and modernization (cf. Connor 1984).

tion by group members in different ways (Melucci 1989; Giddens 1991; Smith 1991; Greenfeld 1992; Castells 1997).

A considerable problem arises in establishing the boundaries and intensities of the various elements of citizens' self-identification, and in interpreting the causes for political mobilization related to territorial identities. If a strengthening of 'meso-level' identities is noticeable, the consolidation of supranational levels of civic attachment is also important, as evinced most notably by the ongoing process of European integration. This process of convergence in Europe can in fact reconcile supranational, state and local identities which appear to be in conflict.[2]

This chapter deals primarily with the concept of ethnoterritoriality, which refers to a dimension of identity in which conflicts and political mobilization develop and have as their chief social actors those ethnic groups which possess a geographical underpinning. Such a spatial reference is identifiable within the boundaries of a polity, usually one of a compound or multinational composition (Moreno 1988; Rudolph and Thompson 1989; Coakley 1992).

In multinational societies, individuals are tied to several cultural reference groups which might be in competition with each other (Barth 1969). This results in a multiplicity of dynamic and often shared sociopolitical identities, which are not necessarily explicitly expressed. Identity markers are thus malleable and the intensity of their manifestation depends greatly upon contingent circumstances (Anderson 1983; Cohen 1985; Hobsbawm 1990; Brass 1991).

The revival of ethnoterritorial political movements in the western world has coincided with a renewed challenge to the centralist model of the unitary state (Keating 1988, 1996a). In the case of Spain, as in other pluriethnic states, regional devolution and federalization aim to articulate an institutional response to the stimuli of a plural society comprising cultural/ethnic groups with differences of language, history or traditions. This diversity can also be reflected in the party system (Moreno 1997a,b).

Despite its secular ethnic conflicts, Spain is an entity clearly identifiable as having a historical unity. This unity goes beyond the simple aggregation of territories and peoples with no other affinity than their coexistence under the rule of one common monarch or political power.

---

[2] According to Pérez-Agote, the fact that two identities can be referred to a larger entity does not preclude the possible incompatibility of their relationship (1994, p. 311). That would be the case, for example, with exclusive forms of both Basque and Spanish self-identification. However, the subsuming of the those identities under the European confines implies a nexus (even though it is not explicitly sought) of congruence between both exclusive forms of self-identification.

However, the social and cultural cohesion uniting Spain has not eliminated its internal tensions.

Both processes of state formation and nation building in modern Spain explain to a large extent how citizens express their territorial identities and institutional allegiances. During the nineteenth and twentieth centuries, Spanish Liberals and Reformists carried out a large-scale programme of state national uniformity. But the profound attachment of Spaniards to their nationalities and regions remained firm and, in some cases, underwent a cultural revival (e.g. Catalonia *Reinaxença*).

At present, the persistence of a dual identity or compound nationality in Spain reveals the ambivalent nature of its internal ethnoterritorial relations:

Spain . . . is a state for all Spaniards, a nation-state for a large part of the Spanish population, and only a state but not a nation for important minorities. (Linz 1975: 423)

Consequently, Spanish citizens incorporate in variable proportions both local/ethnoterritorial and state/national identities. The degree of internal consent and dissent in decentralized Spain has found in the concept of dual identity a useful methodological tool for sociopolitical interpretations.[3]

Indeed, the quest for self-government by meso-level communities is in full accordance with the variable nature of such duality in citizens' self-identification: the more the primordial ethnoterritorial identity prevails upon the modern state identity, the higher the demands for political autonomy will tend to be. Conversely, the more pronounced the state-national identity is, the less likely it will be for ethnoterritorial conflicts to appear. At the extreme, the complete absence of one of the two elements of dual identity would lead to a sociopolitical fracture in the multinational state, and demands for self-government would probably take the form of full independence. In other words, when citizens in a substate community adopt an exclusive identity, the institutional outcome will tend to reflect this and will also be exclusive.

It has been argued that the accommodation necessary to secure

[3] In all seventeen Spanish *comunidades autónomas* there is a high proportion of citizens who claim some form of dual identity. The question addressed to them in the successive polls is as follows: 'In general, would you say that you feel (1) Only Andalusian, Basque, Catalan, etc.; (2) More Andalusian, Basque, Catalan, etc. than Spanish; (3) As much Andalusian, Basque, Catalan as Spanish; (4) More Spanish than Andalusian, Basque, Catalan, etc.; or (5) Only Spanish?'. In the period October 1990 to June 1995 a degree of duality was expressed by around 70 per cent of the total Spanish population (i.e. categories 2, 3 and 4). Approximately 30 per cent of all Spaniards expressed a single identity ('Only Spanish', or 'Only Andalusian, Basque, Catalan, etc.'). For an analysis of the case of Catalonia see Moreno and Arriba (1996) and Moreno, Arriba and Serrano (1998).

political and institutional stability in multinational societies is almost impossible to achieve. Furthermore, attempts made to achieve such a goal are bound to result in either the break-up of the state or the consolidation of a type of hegemonic authoritarianism to maintain the state's unity (Dahl 1971; Horowitz 1985).[4] Contemporary liberal thinkers have greatly revitalized the debate regarding individual and collective rights. Many of them can be labelled liberal nationalists (Tamir 1993); some have also persuasively argued the case for multiculturalism and the politics of recognition for minorities. However, several of these normative analyses insist upon the unfeasibility of accommodating ethnonational groups within federations, as the case of Quebec and Canada would illustrate.[5]

This chapter upholds the view that ethnoterritorial cooperation and agreement can overcome not only conflicts and divergence within multinational polities, but may also foster a deepening of democracy by means of favouring citizen participation at all levels of institutional life and political decision making.

In the following section a succinct review and interpretation of some of the main developments in Spain's recent history will pave the way for subsequent discussion of the Spanish model of multitiered ethnoterritorial concurrence. The concluding section focuses on the growing role played by those meso-communities in Europe which have been able to make the particular compatible with general. This phenomenon can be labelled as new *cosmopolitan localism*.

Unity and diversity in contemporary Spain

Spain is a multinational state made up of nationalities and regions.[6] Its territorial unity has been put under strain for several reasons, including

---

[4] Robert Dahl's position is in line with the views of Ernest Baker who also regarded political secessionism or authoritarianism as the two viable options in ethnocultural polyarchies. See Connor (1994, p. 124), and Linz (1973, pp. 103–4).

[5] For Will Kymlicka, ethnoterritorial accommodation would not constitute a stable political solution but a previous step to secession (1996b, p. 45). However, subsequent works (notably Kymlicka 1998a) show that it would be a misrepresentation to characterize him as being pessimistic about the viability of multinational federations. Linz's views are that federalism can consolidate liberal democracy in multinational states (1997b). On multiculturalism cf. Kymlicka (1995), Taylor (1992a) and Walzer (1997). On Quebec and the Canadian Federation, cf. Burgess (1990), Gagnon (1993b), and McRoberts (1997a).

[6] 'Nationalities' and 'regions' are the constituent territories of Spain according to the 1978 constitution. It is not easy to distinguish conceptually the term 'nation' from that of 'nationality'. Such a terminological distinction was to a great extent a consequence of the dichotomy between 'nation-state' and 'state of the nationalities' as regards the cases of the Austria–Hungary and Ottoman Empires at the beginning of the twentieth

the centrifugal effect of its ethnoterritorial and linguistic diversity,[7] as well as the tendency of its central state institutions to be either weak or excessively and violently centralized. Moreover, there has traditionally been a lack of congruence between regional political and economic power. This non-congruence[8] has further nourished the centrifugal tendencies evident in recent Spanish history, tendencies that have found expression in a number of armed conflicts.

Centre and periphery in postcolonial Spain

With the Restoration of the monarchy (1876–1923), and the centralizing dictatorship of Primo de Rivera (1923–30) which ensued, a new, centrally led attempt to impose uniformity on the country manifested itself. This effort ended in failure for several reasons.

The establishment of universal male suffrage in 1890 had the notable effect of placing incipient Catalan nationalism, or *Catalanisme*, squarely in the Spanish political scene. The disparity between Catalonia's social structure and that of an impoverished rural Spain was an important factor in the rise of Catalan nationalism (Giner 1980). Differences in socioeconomic composition between Spain's two major cities, Madrid and Barcelona, also became increasingly evident.[9] These elements fuelled a sense of hopelessness amongst members of

century. In broad terms, nationality can be referred to as a minority nation which has acceded to a degree of institutional autonomy or independence within a multinational state and which competes or coexists with a majority nation and/or other ethnoterritorial groups. Cf. Krejcí and Velímsky (1981, pp. 32–43).

[7] Castilian, or Spanish as it is usually referred to elsewhere, is the official language of the Kingdom of Spain. Approximately a quarter the Spanish total population of 40 million is bilingual. Their vernacular languages are also official in their respective territories: Catalan (spoken by 4.2 million in Catalonia; 2.1 million in Valencia; 0.2 million in the Balearic Islands, and 0.05 million in Aragon); Basque (0.7 million in the Basque Country, and 0.05 million in Navarre); Galician (2.3 million). Other official languages, as declared in their regional Statues of Autonomy, are Bable (spoken by 0.4 million in Asturias) and Aranese (0.004 million in Catalonia) (data collected from Sanmartí Roset 1996, p. 67). There are also a number of dialects of the aforementioned languages widely spoken in other regions (Andalusia, Canary Islands, Extremadura, Murcia).

[8] The traditional political and economic non-congruence in Spain has been shown in a permanent rivalry between centre and periphery. This dichotomy has historically translated into two main alternative models of state organization: centralist-authoritarian and federalist-democratic. Cf. Gourevitch (1979) for the types of economic and political non-congruence.

[9] Between 1877 and 1920, the proportion of Madrid workers in the industrial sector grew considerably from 18.4 to 42.5 per cent of the workforce, but remained behind Barcelona in this respect, with 37.1 per cent in 1877 to 54 per cent in 1920. Perhaps it was more significant that the proportion of 'unproductive' middle classes in Madrid, consisting of civil servants, members of the armed forces and domestic staff (23.6 per cent in 1877 and 15.3 per cent in 1920), was greater than that of Barcelona (5.9 per cent in 1877 and 5 per cent in 1920) (data taken from Linz 1967: 209).

the Catalan elite, who put their electoral support behind home-rule parties. The most important of these was the Lliga Catalana (later known as the Lliga Regionalista) which was founded in 1901 and subsequently came to enjoy significant influence under the leadership of Francesc Cambó.

The Basque Nationalist Party, founded by Sabino de Arana Goiri in 1895, was less successful than the Catalanist Lliga in obtaining support across class lines, partly because of its religious emphasis and ethnocentric claims. Early Basque nationalism stressed traditional community values in opposition to bourgeois industrial society, the effects of which included a considerable influx of migrants from the rest of Spain into the Basque Country. A racially based Basque essentialism was the ideological foundation of early Basque nationalism, which combined with a powerful populism and religious exclusivism to produce a discourse quite distinct from that of Catalan nationalism. The latter ideology was more intellectual and less based on 'folklore' from the outset, and has always been less secessionist in character.

Catalan nationalism seems to have provoked greater resistance than Basque nationalism precisely because it offered an alternative view of Spain, something Basque nationalism more frequently turned its back on. Both nationalisms, however, could be seen as political manifestations of a vigorous and prosperous periphery, which contrasted sharply with the often-parasitic centralism of the Spanish state to which it was subordinated.

Regionalism came in different forms in other Spanish territories, reflecting the ethnoterritorial diversity of a plural Spain and, in many cases, inspired by the action of the Catalan and Basque movements. Partly as a consequence of the federal experience of the First Republic (1873), there were clamours for recognition in Galicia, Valencia, Andalusia and Asturias. Chronologically, the appearance of explicit claims for regional autonomy in contemporary Spanish politics occurred in the years around the turn of the nineteenth century.

The Second Republic, the Civil War and the Franco dictatorship

In spite of its short existence, the Second Republic (1931–9) contributed greatly to the resolution of ethnoterritorial conflict in Spain. One of the most notable improvements was the adoption of a regionally sensitive constitution, establishing a state structure somewhere between unitary and federal models. This design conceded statutes of autonomy to

Catalonia,[10] the Basque Country[11] and Galicia.[12] However, the regional autonomy question also played a fundamental part in the political polarization leading up to the Civil War (1936–9). Even within the republican forces the devolution issue created a great deal of turmoil.

Although the autonomist movement was still young, it was spreading throughout Spain by the time the Civil War broke out. With the victory of General Franco's forces, a long period of political centralization ensued, aiming once again to create a uniform Spain.

Two of the great obsessions of the Franco dictatorship (1939–75) were anti-communism and anti-separatism. The 'sacred unity of the homeland' was regarded as an indispensable unifying element and as the very *raison d'être* of General Franco's despotic regime. To a large extent, Francoism justified itself through its ability to suppress and extirpate all forms of home rule,[13] regionalism and substate nationalism. Any form of federalism or wish for autonomy was understood by the Franco regime as 'separatism'.

The Francoist conception of national unity degenerated into an obsessive dogma which brooked no cultural or ethnic variety among the people of Spain. Franco's linguistic and cultural oppression, however, actually ended up stimulating regionalism and peripheral nationalism in Spain. From the 1960s onward, demands for regional autonomy became significantly more intense. During the final years of the regime's existence, the opposition forces developed a programme including the institution of democratic rights and the political decentralization of the Spanish state. In the so-called 'historical nationalities' in particular (Basque Country, Catalonia, and Galicia), the forces opposed to Francoism were able to articulate a political discourse denouncing the absence

---

[10] On 14 April 1931 the Spanish Second Republic was proclaimed. On the same day the Catalan nationalist leader, Francesc Macià, declared the creation of the Republic of Catalonia within the framework of a Spanish confederation. After negotiations with representatives of the central government, the Generalitat was reestablished. The Generalitat is Catalonia's government, of medieval origin.

[11] Three days after the proclamation of the Second Republic, an assembly of Basque mayors gathered by José Antonio Aguirre, leader of the Basque Nationalist Party, claimed their right to autonomy within a Spanish federal republic, by the historic Oak of Guernica. Nevertheless, parliamentary approval of the proposal was thornier than the Catalan statute.

[12] In Galicia, the Organización Regional Gallega Autónoma (ORGA, Autonomous Regional Organization of Galicia), led by Santiago Casares Quiroga, had instigated the drafting of a proposal for autonomy. On 28 June 1936, a referendum was held and around 70 per cent of the Galician electorate voted. The final result was 991,476 votes for and 6,805 against.

[13] With the partial exception of Alava and Navarre. These two *foral* territories were able to keep their fiscal privileges as a 'reward' for the participation of many *Carlistas* from those provinces who joined Franco's forces during the Civil War (Giner and Moreno 1990).

of democracy and the continuous official attacks on their identities. In these communities, democratic and ethnoterritorial claims became inseparable. In this way the ideology of autonomism and political decentralization made its way into Spanish democratic political consciousness.

The 1978 constitution and the decentralization of power

After Franco's death in 1975, the transitional process to democracy began in earnest. If there was general agreement among the democratic parties that decentralization was essential, however, the specific model to be adopted was unclear. A majority wanted home rule for all Spanish nationalities and regions. The constitutional expression of such a strong platform would constitute a major political challenge, for recent Spanish history had witnessed many tragic failures where ethnicity and the territorial sharing of power were concerned.

In the end, the broad political consensus which made the drafting of the 1978 constitution possible also brought with it an element of ambiguity in the territorial organization of Spain. In fact, two different conceptions which had traditionally confronted each other were both given expression in the Spanish *magna carta*: on the one hand, the idea of an indivisible Spanish nation-state, and on the other, the notion that Spain was an ensemble of diverse peoples, historic nationalities and regions. A middle way between these two visions of Spain would thus have to be subsequently negotiated and explicitly recognized in the constitution.

The starting point for this process lay in the provisions of the 1978 constitution itself. In the first instance, this document set the bases for any number of the *comunidades autónomas* to be self-governing, depending on the will expressed by either the inhabitants of each nationality or region, or their political representatives. The constitution also made it possible for the degree of self-government to be wide or restricted, according to the wishes of each nationality or region. Based on these two principles, Conservatives, Centrists, Nationalists, Socialists and Communists ended up hammering out an agreement for the implementation of the federalizing *estado de las autonomías*. The accepted solution took the form of an unwritten pledge to extend the procedures of political dialogue and consociationalism into the future.

This open model of asymmetrical federalization did not, however, specify the ways in which the different spatial entities would ultimately be articulated. Thus, an implicit desire was expressed by the drafters of the 1978 constitution to provide a broad outline of the procedures and degrees of self-government to be pursued by the nationalities and regions, while allowing them a high degree of flexibility concerning their implementation. The formulation of a clear division of powers based upon 'conventional' federal techniques was, however, avoided.

The construction of the *estado de las autonomías* had to follow a 'top-down' process of decentralization. But it should be noted that this way of doing things is just one of the options available in the development of federal systems. The apparent result of this process twenty years later is not much more than a series of federal-type practices amongst several politically competitive units. Even so, the full development of multi-lateral decision making, or the genuinely common exercise of a three-tiered system of governance (at central, regional and local levels simultaneously), remains to be seen.

The decentralization process embodied in the 1978 Spanish constitution has undergone a long period of consolidation. The degree of autonomy for the Spanish nationalities and regions is considerable. This is illustrated by the evolution of the distribution of public expenditure in the three-tiered system of government that is reproduced in table 1:

Table 1 Territorial distribution of public expenditure in Spain (%)

	1981[1]	1984	1987	1990	1992	1997	1999[2]
Central	87.3	75.6	72.6	66.2	63.0	59.5	54
Regional	3.0	12.2	14.6	20.5	23.2	26.9	33
Local	9.7	12.1	12.8	13.3	13.8	13.6	13

[1] Beginning of the process of devolution
[2] Government's estimates
Source: Spanish Ministry of Public Administrations (MAP 1997)

Apart from the Basque and Catalan communities, support for autonomy has been particularly strong in Andalusia and some other regions (the Canary Islands, Galicia and Valencia).[14] It is undeniable that some regions have also been 'encouraged' to seek greater autonomy by their most prominent political parties. In this manner, areas with no self-governing tradition whatsoever have thus suddenly been inspired to claim home-rule rights. This category included communities lacking ethnoterritorial specificity, although some of them claimed to have distinct origins, like Cantabria, La Rioja and even the province of Madrid. In some cases, the decentralization process has also entailed a

---

[14] After fifteen years of decentralization, the Spaniards assessed the process as 'totally positive' (11 per cent), 'more positive than negative' (49 per cent), 'more negative than positive' (21 per cent), and 'totally negative' (10 per cent). The remaining 9 per cent corresponded to 'Don't Knows' (*El País*, 19 November 1995).

splitting of the ethnoterritorial base of certain provinces. One of the consequences of this tendency has been the creation of such hybrids as Castille–La Mancha or Castille and Leon.

The cases of Navarre and the Catalan Countries (*Països Catalans*)[15] exemplify the difficulty of setting clear boundaries in certain regions. Although they include Valencia and the Balearic Islands, for instance, the Catalan Countries are often thought of as a unified whole with a composite identity and as thus deserving political treatment as one unit. This interpretation is popular not just amongst pan-Catalanist parties, but it has even been preferred by the usually more cautious President of the Catalan Government, Jordi Pujol, in his 'federalist' understanding of Spain.[16] For some Basque nationalists, Navarre is similarly seen as an integral part of their country that can never be given up. This has been the claim made by both Herri Batasuna/Euskal Herritarrok, the political branch of the ETA (the Basque terrorist separatists), and the ETA itself. However, it is quite clear that a majority of the people of Navarre believe that the old kingdom should have the right to its own constitution.

As far as popular legitimation is concerned, the decentralization process has now been internalized by most Spaniards. This fact further legitimates continued political decentralization. But although far from over, the decentralization process now arguably needs to adapt to new forms of intergovernmental relations, especially those at the level of institutional collaboration.[17] The articulation of institutional relations involving shared powers and responsibilities lies at the very base of the federal-like ethnoterritorial relations in Spain.

Multiple ethnoterritorial concurrence and the Spanish *comunidades autónomas*

The gradual establishment of the *estado de las autonomías* in Spain has generated a complex set of relations which can be explained in terms of *multiple ethnoterritorial concurrence* (Moreno 1995). This model incorporates in a dynamic manner social, economic and political elements

---

[15] This expression is used by some to denote the Principate of Catalonia, the Kingdom of Valencia and the Balearic Islands. Frequently included is Rosselló (Roussillon), in southern France, where Catalan is spoken.

[16] 'In the specific case of Spain I could conceivably be a federalist, if the federation was based on genuine and authentic nationalities of the state, viz. Euskadi [Basque Country], Galicia, the whole of Castille, and the Catalan Countries (or just Catalonia, if Valencia and the Islands . . . rejected being associated with the Principate)' (Pujol 1980, p. 26).

[17] In 1990 most Spaniards were of the opinion that relations between regional governments and central government should be 'collaborative' (80.7 per cent) and involving shared responsibilities (58.2 per cent) (García Ferrando et al 1994, p. 113).

which are constitutive of the Spanish case of federalization. 'Concurrence' should be understood in this context as the simultaneous occurrence of political events at state and substate levels, within the framework of a multinational society. The term should not simply be thought of as the equivalent of ethnoterritorial 'competition'. In a situation of ethnoterritorial concurrence there are competitive actions between state and substate nationalisms or regionalisms, or between the latter. However, there is no compulsion to eliminate other competing actors. Modern competition, instead, implies the aim of achieving the monopoly by means of eliminating other competitors.[18]

Since the transition to democracy in Spain, agreements and conflicts have taken place in a multiplicity of cases and circumstances. Eventual cooperation and mutual recognition of differences have often been reached between centre and periphery. But these pacts should not be regarded as mechanical outcomes in a lineal political process. Different kinds of innovative solutions have been found to articulate centre–periphery relations. Thus, asymmetry, heterogeneity and plurality remain as chiefly elements of ethnoterritorial concurrence in Spain (Moreno 1997a, b, Requejo 1996).

To further explain the development of the Spanish *comunidades autónomas*, I will use a sequential framework. First, the two 'axioms' of the Spanish context, which are also shared by most decentralized or federal systems, will be outlined: conflicting intergovernmental relations, and the politicization of ethnoterritorial institutions. Second, two 'premises'[19] of the pre-*estado de las autonomías* era will be analysed: the differential fact, and the centralist inertia. Thirdly, I will look at the three pillars or 'principles' upon which the organizational rationale of the 1978 constitution rests, implicitly or explicitly: democratic decentralization, comparative grievance and inter-territorial solidarity. And finally, three 'rules' will be shown to play a most important role in the social and political structuring of the decentralization process in Spain: centrifugal pressure, ethnoterritorial mimesis, and the inductive allocation of powers. These constituent elements, which characterize the model of multiple ethnoterritorial concurrence in Spain, are succinctly reviewed as follows:

---

[18] According to Karl Popper (1976) a situation of concurrence can and ought to be explained as an unintentional consequence (usually unavoidable) of the human actions (conscious and planned) of the competitors. These assume competition as a transitional exercise. Their ultimate 'rational' aim is that of achieving a position of monopoly without further competition.

[19] Axioms, premises, principles and rules should not be regarded as the constituent parts of a philosophical syllogism or as propositions in some logical proof.

(A) The axiom of 'conflicting inter-governmental relations' is associated with the political leanings and partisan affiliations present at all levels of government and other institutions representing territorial interests. Conflict and agreement are present in intergovernmental relations in Spain as in any other federal state. In many respects, these relations also provide a testing ground for Spain's democracy. A climate of permanent political bargaining among local, regional and central governments is bound to remain as the most characteristic feature of the Spanish process of federalization.

Criticism of the degree of dispersion and fragmentation of political life has been voiced in Spain. Some have proposed new forms of centralization as 'solutions' to what is considered to be an unbearable situation. Such criticism comes from those who feel that Spain's stability is threatened by the changing nature of intergovernmental relations and the sense of uncertainty this development implies. But these perceptions are not in tune with Spain's constitutional precepts and their implications, which have thus far fostered a decentralized form of government.

(B) The 'politicization of ethnoterritorial institutions' suggests the desire evident at all three levels of government to maximize their political image and performance. This exercise of meso-governmental patronage is not only carried out for domestic purposes, but also as a means of attracting interest and investment from abroad, given the process of European convergence and the increasing interdependence of the world economy. This accretion of subnational level power is commensurate with the growing capacity of regional elites for negotiation. Their practices are legitimized by the constitutional order and are grounded in the increasing budgetary manoeuvrability of the governments of the *comunidades autónomas*.

In any case, the European vocation of all of the Spanish nationalities and regions and their enthusiasm for further integration is remarkable. In fact, some of the most powerful minority nationalisms in Spain (Basque and Catalan) regard the consolidation of the European Union as highly significant in reducing the powers of central governments and in putting the very idea of the nation-state into retreat. This European outlook is also symptomatic of a general desire to leave behind the long stagnation of the Franco era, during which Spain remained isolated from the process of European integration.

(C) The premise of 'differential fact' refers to a feature, or rather a combination of features, that characterize an ethnic group or community in comparison to others. It is, therefore, a concept deriving much of its meaning from a rather subjective perspective rooted in the ethnicity or ethnic identity of a given people. It seems clear that the mobilization patterns of the 'historical nationalities' have been premised on this 'differential fact' since the earliest stages of the decentralization process in Spain. The idea seems to have particularly resonance in the Basque, Catalan and Galician cases, all notable for their non-Castilian languages, their own cultures, and their specific histories. However, the last two of these elements are also shared by the other *comunidades autónomas*.

Most significantly, the 'differential fact' also manifests itself in the form of powerful nationalist parties and political coalitions in the 'historical nationalities'. This is a key element in the articulation of a popular feeling of being distinct from the rest of the Spanish peoples. Encouraging greater awareness of their own difference has thus become a permanent incentive for many actors in the Basque Country, Catalonia and Galicia to maintain their institutional peculiarities with relation to the other Spanish regions. However, it is worth remembering the sociopolitical mobilization in Andalusia which led to the referendum of 28 February 1980. This expression of popular will allowed Andalusia to achieve the same type of home rule as the 'historical nationalities'. This political development broke the model implicitly accepted by the Basque and Catalan nationalist parties which envisaged only a limited degree of administrative de-concentration for the other Spanish regions. Since then, the premise of the 'differential fact' has been closely linked to the principle of 'comparative grievance' analysed below.

(D) The premise of the 'centralist inertia' is rooted in a long-standing perception that the central administration (erroneously identified with the state as whole[20]) has supremacy over regional and local tiers of governments. This perception is the result not only of a tradition of dictatorial rule, including Franco's dictatorship most recently

---

[20] The very term 'state' is ambiguously employed in the text of the constitution. In some articles (1, 56, 137, and, significantly, in the very title of Title VIII), the intention is for the term to denote the entire organization of the Spanish legal–political system. Thus, the term covers the regional administrations as well as the other agencies and autonomous bodies that make up the state. In other constitutional articles (3.1, 149 and 150), the state is considered to be synonymous with the institutions of the central administration, together with their peripheral administrations, which may on occasions clash with autonomous administrations. The Constitutional Court's judgement of 28 July 1981 clarified the semantic conflict by asserting that the state must be regarded as a composite whole which includes all the institutions of central, regional and local governments.

(1939–75), but also of the Jacobin view imported from France and embraced by Spanish liberals during the nineteenth century.

Thus, at the beginning of the decentralization process a significant number of politicians and state officials disregarded the demands, needs, and expectations of both regional and local administrations. They tried to discredit aspirations for home rule. But the decision of the Constitutional Court against the main provisions of the centralizing *LOAPA* (constitutional law passed in Parliament in 1982 with the support of the two main parties in 1982, but fiercely opposed by the nationalists[21]) was a decisive setback for the attempt to recentralize. Nonetheless, the subsequent tendency towards greater regional autonomy has been hampered by bureaucratic friction and interference, a result of the ingrained centralist mentality which is still widespread among members of the central bodies and institutions in Spain.

(E) Paradoxically, Francoism was the main factor responsible for the development of the principle of 'democratic decentralization'. Under Franco, a unitary concept of Spain was imposed through a defence of Spanish nationalism; this, in turn, was intimately related with the totalitarian ideas and values of some of those who had won the Civil War. Throughout the Franco era, 'Spanish' nationalism had tried to hide the plural reality of Spain. In the eyes of many of those who had lost the war, however, all things 'Spanish' came to be tainted with Franco's cultural genocide, political repression and reinvention of history. As a consequence, many of the democratic forces were suspicious of the 'Spanish' nationalism.

In the early 1970s, the democratic opposition forces to Franco's regime articulated a solid strategy of political action amalgamating the struggle for the recovery of democratic liberties with a desire for greater decentralization of power. Thus the quest for democracy and territorial home rule went hand in hand.

In this sense, the development of peripheral nationalism, regionalism and autonomism can be regarded as an unintended effect of hyper-centralization imposed by Francoism. The rise of regional self-government during the 1970s and 1980s was thus largely due to a desire to

---

[21] After the attempted military coup of 23 February 1981, influential sectors of the centre-right UCD and the socialist PSOE (then government and main opposition parties, respectively) tried to 'harmonize' the decentralization process in the style of German federalism. The mistake was to believe that this could be achieved from the all-encompassing vision of the central state administration. The Constitutional Court annulled most of the provisions of the *LOAPA*, and upheld the principle of regional autonomy. This reinforced the legitimacy of the Court, which was to become a pivotal institution in the consolidation of democracy in Spain.

establish democratic institutions which would bring decision making closer to the people. Since then, the flourishing of democracy and freedom in Spain has been inextricably linked to the protection of decentralized power and the autonomy of Spain's nationalities and regions.

(F) The principle of 'comparative grievance' determines to a large degree the mobilization patterns of the Spanish *comunidades autónomas*. According to this, the right to home rule and the subsequent political mobilization is the result of an ethnoterritorial race in search of equal access to the institutions of self-government. This 'principle' conflicts with the 'premise of the differential fact' claimed by the Basque Country, Catalonia and Galicia. Popular perceptions like those related to the 'comparative grievance' and the 'differential fact' do not translate easily into positive legislation. They reflect social realities which are not necessarily quantifiable in, for example, the degree of fiscal autonomy or the type of home-rule institutions.

In Catalonia, for instance, which is a relatively rich community, perceived fiscal grievances have traditionally manifested themselves in strong arguments supporting political *Catalanisme*. The grievance here is based on the idea that Catalans receive much less from the central administration than their total contribution to the Spanish treasury. This feeling of financial discrimination has been perceived as an obstacle to the further development of Catalonia. More significantly, this perceived unfairness has also often been interpreted as a result of the negligence of an inefficient state apparatus which also fails to promote the growth of other less developed regions in Spain.[22]

Localism in Spain, linked to a strong sense of ethnoterritorial pride, has continued to nourish both expectations and concerns of the *comunidades autónomas*. In particular, it has fuelled formal and informal monitoring efforts by the regions to avoid being discriminated against. None of the Spanish nationalities and regions wants to be left behind.

(G) The principle of 'interterritorial solidarity' is not only a constitu-

---

[22] Curiously, Madrid paid up more in taxes than any other community in 1989. Madrid 'has five million inhabitants, compared with Catalonia's six, but in 1989, the takings for Madrid reached 3.3 billion pesetas, higher than Catalonia's 1.87 billion. In the same year, Andalusia, with seven million inhabitants, paid 0.61 billion, while Valencia, with only four million inhabitants, approached this figure, with 0.54 billion . . . In the collection of all major taxes, the first place corresponds to Madrid, in spite of having one million inhabitants less than Catalonia and a similar income. The difference is striking in the case of the IRPF [personal income tax]: in 1989, 1.01 billion pesetas (Madrid) compared to 0.7 billion (Catalonia)' (Platón 1994, p. 210).

tional precept but also the formal expression of a more prosaic reality: the transfer of financial resources from the wealthier to the poorer regions of Spain. This transfer aims at achieving a common basic level in the provision of social services, so that the standard of living of all Spaniards can be brought to roughly the same level. Furthermore, the 1978 constitution observes that the Spanish state must establish a just and adequate economic balance between the different areas of Spain (article 138).

With the gradual development of the 'home-rule-all-round' process in Spain, nationalities and regions regarded territorial autonomy as providing the means for bringing institutional decision making closer to citizens. *Comunidades autónomas*, particularly the economically poorer territories, also laid emphasis on the constitutional principle of inter-regional solidarity. A financial instrument was created for this purpose, the *Fondo de Compensación Interterritorial* (Interterritorial Compensation Fund), although the aim of redistributing funds has largely been neglected due to the absence of any clear criteria to justify positive discrimination in favour of the poorer *comunidades autónomas*. Differences in management capacity, however, have brought about an incentive for the less-developed regional administrations to catch up with those more advanced in new policy design and provision. A 'demonstration effect' regarding the implementation of policies by the *comunidades autónomas* is noticeable.[23]

(H) The political pressure exerted upon central power by both Basque and Catalan nationalisms contributed decisively in 1978 to a constitutional accommodation, which implicitly recognized the multinational nature of Spanish society. Since then the rule of 'centrifugal pressure' has been repeatedly instrumentalized by the most vigorous ethnoterritorial elites: Basque, Catalan, and Galician nationalists in the first instance, and regionalists in Andalusia, Navarre, Valencia and the Canary Islands at a later stage. In recent times, a similar pattern is observable with respect to other regional parties and formations in Aragon, Cantabria or Extremadura.[24] Note that centrifugal pressure is

[23] An illustration of this is provided by the Family Minimum Income Programme. This was introduced in the Basque Country in March 1998 to combat poverty and situations of social exclusion, and constituted a precedent in the subsequent programmes of minimum income benefits implemented in all seventeen *comunidades autónomas*. Although showing a degree of diversity in policy design and coverage, programmes of 'minimum income' developed by the Spanish 'historical nationalities' and regions aim at combining cash benefits with policies of social insertion (employment promotion and vocational training schemes, primarily).

[24] Among the local parties that have obtained parliamentary representation in Madrid, or in their regional parliaments, the following may be mentioned: Chunta, Coalición

meant to be used not only as a vehicle for negotiation, but also to dissuade certain politicians and civil servants of the central administration from reverting to centralizing tendencies.

The continuous and active presence of representatives of the Catalan and Basque nationalist parties in the Spanish parliament has been crucial. This nationalist input has contributed greatly to the consolidation of an autonomist vision of the state with respect to the political relations of the three levels of government. What is more, the increasing relative power of regional and federated organizations associated with national coalitions and parties has also contributed decisively to the federalization of politics in Spain.[25]

The centrifugal effects of political negotiation on a territorial level in Spain tend to be multiplied by the bilateral relations between central and regional administrations. The practice of bilateralism, combined with comparative grievance, entails major difficulties for the *estado de las autonomías*, given that the seventeen *comunidades autónomas* will be tempted to exert increasing centrifugal pressures of every kind in questions of common interest.[26]

(I) According to the rule of 'ethnoterritorial mimesis', the 'historical nationalities' (Basque Country, Catalonia and Galicia) were the first to aspire to rights and powers comparable to those of the central government such as having their own police force, external signs and ornamental emblems, official visits abroad, exclusive rights established by regional parliaments, public policies in the fields of health, education and social welfare, and so on. Subsequently, a second group of *comunidades autónomas* wanted to imitate 'mimetically' the same powers as the 'historical nationalities' (such as Andalusia in 1981, followed by Valencia and the Canary Islands).[27] Finally, these same communities became

Canaria, Convergencia de Demócratas Navarra, Extremadura Unida, Partido Andalucista, Partido Aragonés, Partido Regionalista de Cantabria, Partido Riojano, Partido Socialista de Mallorca, Partiu Asturianista, Unión Alavesa, Unión Mallorquina, Unión para el Progreso de Cantabria, Unión del Pueblo Leonés, and Unión Valenciana.

[25] The Partido Socialista Obrero Español (PSOE, Socialists and Social Democrats) and Izquierda Unida (IU, Communists, Radical Socialists and Independent Leftists) have an organic federal composition. The Partido Popular (PP, Conservatives and Christian Democrats) has become increasingly regionalized. The crucial importance of the spatial element in Spanish politics has been reinforced by the electoral successes of new regional formations.

[26] Intergovernmental cooperation of considerable political value has been initiated by conferences involving the central government and the *comunidades autónomas*. Even at the level of consultation, these conferences are vital to the articulation of policies discussed, agreed by consensus, or only partially agreed.

[27] Already in 1984, Joan Lerma (former President of the Valencian government) considered that there were not three 'historical nationalities'. He then stated: 'The legal

models for 'latecomer' regions, which have tried to 'imitate' the institutional outlook of the early-rising nationalities and regions.

In line with the concept of ethnoterritorial mimesis, it could be argued that Basque nationalism, especially in its secessionist forms, has gone the furthest in proposing the idea of setting up an independent state for the Basque Country. Given the peculiar confederation of its historical territories, such a state would paradoxically have to be structured very much like plural Spain at present. *Catalanisme*, for its part, wants an independent fiscal system rather like the one operating in the Basque Country, if not simply a greater degree of financial and political autonomy. Galicia would probably follow Catalonia in having more powers transferred from central state institutions. It should be noted, however, that one cannot think of the mimetic process in mechanistic terms. The unfolding of this process will remain closely tied: (a) to the extent to which a majority of citizens of the Basque Country continue to identify themselves, at least partially, as 'Spanish'; and (b) how *Catalanisme* maintains its tradition of being an inclusive nationalism seeking to reform Spain as well as Catalonia. The strength of radical nationalism in Galicia, meanwhile, does not seem to indicate the collapse of a popular desire to belong to Spain as a whole.[28]

(J) The rule of the 'inductive allocation of powers' in the Spanish process of decentralization acknowledges the absence of a clear-cut constitutional division of powers in the three-tier system of government. This rule, which is implicit in the provisions of Title VIII of the 1978 constitution, draws attention to the fact that the Spanish decentralization process has followed an open model of territorial structuring, which only the passing of time has gradually defined and will continue to do.

The 1978 constitution allows for great flexibility of interpretation where the possibility of self-government is concerned. The terms adopted will largely depend on the political will of each nationality or region. Furthermore, the constitutional allocation of specific powers for the *comunidades autónomas*, which does not go so far as to establish a clear and comprehensive division of rights and powers, was the only feasible way to initiate a political decentralization process. It must be

treatment for Catalonia and the Basque Country is the same as that for Galicia, but also for Andalusia, the Canaries and for ourselves [the Valencians]' (*La Vanguardia*, 16 April 1984).

[28] Nationalists in the Basque Country, Catalonia and Galicia have insisted on the idea of a 'shared sovereignty' within the Spanish state. On 16 July 1998 the Declaration of Barcelona was signed by the Basque Partido Nacionalista Vasco, the Catalan Convergència i Unió, and the Galician Bloque Nacionalista Galego. They claimed the establishment of a confederal model of political accommodation in Spain.

remembered that during the transition to democracy this was one of the thorniest issues to reach agreement upon, and therefore required complete consensus.

Once the seventeen *comunidades autónomas* had been established, a further delegation of powers was effected. Its degree of heterogeneity has levelled out over time, although the process is far from over. In contrast to the traditional philosophy upon which other federal systems such as those of Germany, Australia, the USA or Switzerland have been modelled and built, the federalization in Spain can only be regarded as complete once a period of intergovernmental familiarity has elapsed. At the same time, the process of European convergence will exercise considerable influence in the future distribution of regional powers and responsibilities.

Meso-communities and the new cosmopolitan localism in Europe

In Spain, the process of home-rule-all-round has contributed significantly to the extension of a new *cosmopolitan localism*. This phenomenon is reflected in societal interests aimed at both developing a sense of local community and at participating actively in international spheres. There is, thus, a growing congruence between the particular and the general. Note that all Spanish meso-governments have made explicit their European vocation. They all share the desire of a majority of Spaniards to see an EU that would be not only the main economic institutional *locus* in the medium-term future, but whose legitimacy would also provide a foundation upon which to build a future European citizenship.

In Europe, one of the visible effects brought about by financial globalization is the relative obsolescence of the nation-state. The latter has constituted the central arena of the economic life for the past two centuries. Increasingly, however, the nation-state seems to be adopting the role of mere spectator to worldwide virtual financial transactions. The once powerful economic policies established at the national level are now severely restricted by those decisions taken by international trusts, pensions funds and the 'laundered' capital of transnational organized crime. Furthermore, globalization also affects other factors of production, such as the components of industrial goods made in third countries, as well as increasing legions of stateless workers (Strange 1995).

Given this context of internationalization, meso-governments are acquiring a newly found relevance and playing important roles in most aspects of contemporary life. A renewal of community life at the meso-level derives mainly from the synthesis of two main factors: (a) the growing rejection of centralization in unitary states, coupled with a strengthening of supranational politics, and (b) the reinforcement of local identities and societal cultures with a territorial underpinning. This European communitarianism[29] affects not only minority nations (Catalonia, Flanders, Scotland), or new nation-states (Czech Republic, Slovenia), but also regions and metropolitan areas (Brussels region, Greater London, Milan-Lombardy, Paris–Île de France). The latter seem to follow a pattern of recreating those 'medium-size' political communities that flourished in the age prior to the New World discoveries (Italian city-states, the Hanseatic League, principalities). But in contrast with the Renaissance period, there now exists a common institutional tie due to the process of Europeanization.

Meso-governments are no longer dependent on those programmes of rationalization carried out during the nineteenth and twentieth centuries by central bureaucracies and elites. Their own entrepreneurs, social leaders and local intelligentsia have taken up many of the initiatives and roles once reserved for the 'enlightened' actors holding positions of power at the centre of their nation states. Positions of political influence are now more evenly distributed between central, meso-level and local institutions. And the cooption of regional elites to central institutions of government is no longer the sole route available to a 'successful' political career.

In the EU context, the reinforcement of substate territorial identities is deeply associated with powerful material and symbolic referents of the past including culture, history, and territory. Innovative interpretations of these referents have been promoted to seek to overcome the denaturalizing effects of global hypermodernity.[30] However, it is important to point out that the new versions of these old symbols are not based on a reactive parochialism. The very idea of a 'fortress Europe' is not seen as a plausible option for the future. It also appears to be in contradiction with the very cosmopolitan nature of local, national and supranational values in Europe. Immigration from non-EU countries has certainly had a role to play in the renewed strength of xenophobic sentiments in Europe. Nevertheless, immigrants willing to take on the values of civic pluralism and tolerance tend to find no major difficulties integrating

---

[29] This concept is quite distinct from the standard North American interpretation of communitarianism (Etzioni 1993). Many of the incipient communitarian experiences in the United States may be regarded as reactions to specific social cleavages (criminalization of social deviance), as instrumental means of socialization (overcoming suburban constraints), or as alternative lifestyles to dominant values (possessive individualism).

[30] Denaturalizing is used here as meaning the deprivation of the rights of citizenship within an established democratic polity.

themselves into the economic and social life of their first 'port of entry', i.e. local and meso-communities.

According to the influential functionalist school of social sciences, political justice and institutional stability have been regarded as incompatible and unsuitable goals for polyarchies. Attempts to conciliate both goals have been argued to result in the break-up of the state or the consolidation of authoritarianism. The case of multinational Spain offers an example of how multiple identities and political loyalties can be accommodated, thus facilitating ethnoterritorial co-operation and agreement among constituent nationalities and regions. As the case of Spanish *comunidades autónomas* illustrates, multiple concurrence of territorial interests can not only overcome conflicts but can also provide a deepening of democracy by means of bringing political decision-making closer to civil society.[31]

[31] I am thankful for comments and suggestions made on earlier versions of this chapter by Alain Gagnon, John Provart, Daniel Thomas and James Tully.

8 Mutual recognition and the accommodation of national diversity: constitutional justice in Northern Ireland

Shane O'Neill

Northern Ireland is an ethnically and culturally plural political jurisdiction marked by a deep conflict of nationality. Its citizens are divided into two national communities with opposing political aspirations, differing identities and divergent loyalties. Ever since this jurisdiction was brought into existence in 1921 with the partition of Ireland, it has struggled to establish its legitimacy as part of the United Kingdom by failing to gain the allegiance of a large and growing minority of its citizens, namely those who aspire to some form of Irish national unity.[1] At the same time, the unionist majority have maintained that they would face the prospect of political marginalization and cultural exclusion if they were to be forced, as a national minority, into a united Ireland. The dominant tendency within both national traditions has been to deny legitimacy to the aspiration of the other.

This failure of mutual recognition has been the key source of the tension and strife between national communities that has, since the late 1960s, been at the root of a protracted armed conflict. In the absence of a mutually acceptable constitutional settlement to accommodate these conflicting national aspirations, Northern Ireland has been blighted not only by violence but by a chronic instability that has inflicted serious damage on its prospects for economic, social and political development. Hopes that a settlement might be within reach were raised by the 1994 paramilitary cease-fires that have been key elements of a peace process underway since the early 1990s.[2] In May 1998, following the positive endorsement of the Good Friday Agreement given by 71 per cent of all

---

[1] The two main nationalist parties (Social Democratic and Labour Party and Sinn Féin) acquired 39.6 per cent of the vote at the Assembly Election of 25 June 1998. Due to differences in birth rates, and other demographic factors, the percentage of nationalists has consistently been on the rise since partition, such that there is a real possibility of a nationalist majority within little more than a generation (McGarry and O'Leary 1995a, ch. 10).

[2] The IRA suspended its cease-fire of 31 August 1994, from 9 February 1996 until 20 July

voters in Northern Ireland, and by the vast majority of Irish nationalist voters on both sides of the border, there has been renewed hope that legitimate democratic politics might become possible within a just and stable Northern Ireland.[3] We need to assess the extent to which the constitutional settlement envisioned in the Agreement could offer justice, stability and a lasting resolution of this notoriously intractable dispute.

I will begin by setting out the critical perspective that informs the analysis by sketching a normative-theoretical account of constitutional justice that takes cultural diversity seriously (section 1). I will then offer an account of the basic features of the conflict in Northern Ireland before applying this normative framework and defending the view that justice requires a binational form of egalitarianism that suggests a constitutional arrangement based on joint British–Irish sovereignty (section 2). We will then turn to the Agreement itself so as to assess critically its key constitutional elements by establishing how conflicting aspirations are to be accommodated in its provisions for the development of Northern Ireland, and, more generally, of relations between Britain and Ireland (section 3).

I   Constitutional justice and cultural diversity

This analysis is informed by an account of constitutional justice based on a norm of equal citizenship that takes cultural diversity seriously.

No citizen should be alienated from the institutions of state simply because of the fact that some particular social or cultural group affiliation forms an important aspect of that citizen's identity.

To be alienated from the state's institutions is to lack that sense of political agency that we associate with free and equal citizenship. If the state institutions are alien to us then we will experience them as forces of oppression, not as the guarantors of our rights or as channels of collective self-expression. Justice demands that the political constitution should guarantee to all citizens that they will be treated with equal dignity *within their own particular identity-forming contexts*. While each citizen must be included as an equal member of the political community,

---

[3] There have been numerous difficulties with the implementation of the Agreement including two questions that have become interlinked. These relate to the decommissioning of paramilitary weapons and the devolution of power to new institutions of government in Northern Ireland. I will not be analysing implementation controversies such as these here. Regardless of what the immediate future holds, the Agreement represents the twentieth century's greatest achievement in the quest for legitimate government on the island of Ireland.

this should not require members of minority cultures to abandon their distinctiveness, or to deny their particular identities.

It follows, from this normative perspective, that there should be no forced assimilation of cultural minorities, nor should they be coerced into living, Apartheid-style, in separate, isolated enclaves. Both policies, assimilation and separation, grant systematic social and political advantages to members of the dominant culture by forcing members of other cultures to choose between maintaining their distinctive culture and attaining equal membership of the political community. To be forced into making such a choice is *unjust*. Cultural minorities must be accommodated on a basis of equal citizenship in that they should not have to pay a price for preserving their distinctive identities. In societies where there are significant ethnic or national minorities, this may require differential rights with regard to say education or cultural activities, while in other cases it may necessitate special representation rights, or even self-governing autonomy (Kymlicka 1995, ch. 2). As we will see, in the complex case of Northern Ireland, it would seem to require a constitutional framework that can grant equal recognition to two historically antagonistic national communities.

In taking cultural diversity seriously, this account of constitutional justice rejects key features of two significant strands in modern political thought. The first of these strands is that procedural form of liberal theory that derives its constitutional principles from a set of individual rights that purport to be neutral with regard to the ethical commitments of its citizens (Rawls 1972, 1993). The second is that form of communitarianism that gives priority to the collective over the individual by presenting constitutional principles as expressions of the shared values and traditions of particular cultural communities (Sandel 1982, 1996). For communitarian nationalists, the constitution promotes a particular national form of life and expresses a unique national identity. Neither procedural liberalism nor communitarian nationalism can do justice to the reality of cultural diversity since both have at least two contrasting theoretical deficiencies: their accounts of personal identity formation; and their understandings of the ethical basis of constitutionalism. The alternative I advocate here overcomes both sets of deficiencies.

With regard to personal identity-formation, if we want to take the reality of cultural diversity seriously, then we can endorse neither the individualistic conception of the person that is associated with procedural liberalism, nor the essentialism that is associated with communitarian thinking. On the one hand, procedural liberalism abstracts individuals from the context of their ethical ties to particular social groups, including ethnic and national communities (Taylor 1989). In this way it fails to appreciate the extent to which individual identities are situated within a network of group memberships, the structure of which can be a cause of entrenched political conflict. For this reason, the general principles generated by liberal theory often fail to connect with the sources that motivate those political actions that are driven by a struggle for positive recognition of particular identities. The short-comings of such a procedural form of individualistic liberalism are particularly glaring in the context of a deeply divided society like Northern Ireland (McGarry and O'Leary 1995b; O'Neill 1996, pp. 85–8).

On the other hand, communitarianism runs the risk of saddling individuals with a tightly drawn collective identity that limits personal autonomy. While individual identities are embedded within a network of group memberships, it is oppressive to think of cultural character-istics associated with gender, race or nationality as being *essential* to any individual's identity (Appiah 1994). This is oppressive because it lays down in a dogmatic fashion what individuals should take to be the defining features of their identities. Such essentialism fails to reckon with three interrelated factors that are potentially disruptive of collec-tive identities. First, individual identities are formed not only in relation to the structure of group differences but also in personal and intimate relations. These relations may give us some distance from a particular group, thus strengthening our capacity to break away from our traditions of origin. Second, the fact that group memberships intersect one another means that there is always potential to destabilize collective identities by forming cross-cutting political alliances. Such alliances can heighten our sense of having multiple group affiliations and so they work against any tendency to view one collective identity, say our nationality, as being primary or essential to our self-under-standings. Third, the boundaries between social groups are never entirely closed in that certain people will not be easily categorized. These 'others' disrupt the binary thinking, the mentality of 'us and them', associated with essentialism by indicating the historical contin-gency of collective identities. In Northern Ireland these 'others' include those with family affiliations to both traditions, or to neither, and those for whom a cross-cutting collective identity is of greatest significance including, for example, some feminists, or members of the gay and lesbian communities.[4] While group memberships are unavoid-

---

[4] This is not to deny the fact that even politically active feminists in Northern Ireland often seek to be recognized as members of one of the national communities by women from the other tradition (Roulston 1997; Porter 1998). This reflects the fact that many

able features of our identity-forming context, they do not *constitute* the essence of our identities.

We can avoid both liberal individualism and communitarian essentialism by following Iris Young (1990) in seeking to develop a relational conception of social group differences. Social groups, including cultural and national communities, are differentiated by the way in which the members stand in relation to others, particularly with regard to structures of power and privilege (Young 1997, pp. 389–93). Group-based oppression is to be explained with reference to the way in which structures of power assert the superiority of a dominant group by acting as mechanisms of subjugation that serve to disempower other groups. Social structures that privilege one class, sex, race or cultural community, oppress groups whose needs, aspirations or ideals differ from those of the dominant culture. Constitutional structures that serve to alienate a minority national community from the institutions of state are oppressive in just this way. Justice demands that we transform the structure of these group relations so as to bring this oppression to an end.

The concept of a social group is central to this account of justice because our memberships of such groups have important implications for our own individual identities. Group memberships position us socially in ways that precede the exercise of our personal autonomy and this means that we have no choice but to deal with these individual social locations. If a particular group affiliation reflects an important aspect of my personal identity and if that group has been oppressed or underprivileged in some way in relation to others, then my own sense of self-esteem suffers (Honneth 1995, p. 138). Of course, I may simply accept my lot by viewing as fixed the structure of group relations that has been the source of my oppression. Alternatively, I may, in solidarity with other members of the group, assert our group identity. This will involve us in a struggle to achieve a positive recognition of our shared identity as an important aspect of attaining justice for members of the group. It is this dynamic that drives those struggles for recognition associated with socialism, feminism and liberation movements confronting racism, colonialism, homophobia, sectarianism, prejudice against the disabled, and the oppression of cultural and national minorities. But while we may see the assertion of a group identity as necessary to the task of resisting injustice, we should also seek to avoid the restrictions on individual autonomy that are associated with cultural essentialism. The only way we can do that is to create conditions, over the long term at least, that can broaden the scope for personal autonomy

feminists freely acknowledge the political primacy of the national question in this context at present.

by facilitating the disruption of those collective identities that are rigidly constructed.

What this suggests is that a just constitution has to respond to collective struggles against group-based oppression and this may often require the positive recognition of particular group identities, through the affirmation of special rights. But it must also facilitate the disruption of collective identities that place undue restraints on the personal autonomy of individual citizens. The most fruitful way to connect these concerns is to distinguish between the internal cultural diversity within a society, as represented by a wide variety of social groups, and a shared *political* culture that offers a basis for equal citizenship to all individual members of a just political community. While each of us may belong to a variety of different social groups, as citizens we all share equal membership of one political community. The institutions of state should not deny our internal cultural diversity since to do so would be to set in place political structures that privilege the dominant culture in ways that alienate and oppress other social groups. This means that the political culture in which the institutions of state are embedded must be adequately inclusive of all significant groups (Habermas 1998; O'Neill 1997, pp. 169–79).

This distinction between a shared and inclusive political culture and an internal diversity of group-cultures allows us to give a normatively acceptable account of the ethical basis of constitutionalism. It helps us to avoid the problems associated both with the procedural liberal claim that a constitution can be ethically neutral, and the communitarian nationalist view that the constitution must be thought to be expressive of the shared values of one national tradition. The procedural liberal fails to notice that since all constitutions are projects of a particular people, embedded historically in distinctive cultural contexts, none can be ethically neutral. A constitution cannot but affirm the achievements of a particular people in promoting a distinctive political culture. The distinctive ethos of this culture is expressed in the symbols we associate with institutions of the state, be they flags, anthems, emblems or whatever. This is not to say that such a political culture must, as the communitarian nationalist believes, be that of one national community. In a nationally diverse context, such as Northern Ireland, a just constitutional project cannot be thought of in terms of the realization of one nation-state.

Ironically, procedural liberalism and communitarian nationalism share an insensitivity to the possibility of group memberships generating struggles for recognition of particular identities that can challenge the legitimacy of the state (Tully 1995, ch. 3). I have stressed here two key features of a more convincing theory of constitutional justice. First, the theory must grasp the significance of group memberships in providing identity-forming contexts for individuals and in motivating struggles for justice. Secondly, it must affirm the ethical basis of constitutionalism while remaining open to the internal diversity of group cultures by rejecting both ethical neutrality and national purity as inappropriate ideals. The theory will be sensitive to two dimensions of cultural diversity: the internal diversity of group cultures within each state; and the diversity of historically unique political cultures in which particular constitutions are embedded. What this ideal of constitutional justice requires is that a shared political culture should not deny the internal diversity of group-cultures within society. This means that if flags, anthems and emblems are used to express the ethical basis of the constitution, then these should be unifying symbols of an inclusive political culture, not divisive symbols of group-based oppression.

This demand will require a variety of different measures depending on the cultural and historical context. In a relatively homogeneous society, where almost all citizens belong to one national community, this unique political culture may be heavily marked by that national culture but it must make adequate provision for the expression of the cultural distinctiveness of its significant minorities. In a society characterized by mass immigration, the political culture should reflect the multicultural nature of that society by giving due recognition to the cultures of its aboriginal peoples and by respecting cultural differences among its immigrant communities. In a deeply divided society like Northern Ireland, the political culture will have to be inclusive of, and consonant with, two antagonistic national communities as well as being respectful of smaller minority cultures. This normative framework justifies those policies that are required, in specific contexts, to protect individual and group identities by ensuring that each citizen is treated with equal dignity. Citizens should not suffer systematic social and political disadvantages because of the group affiliations that structure their personal identities. If we are not to be punished, and alienated from the institutions of state, because of the ways in which we differ from members of the dominant group culture of our society, then we will need to have grounds to believe ourselves to be equal citizens. We need to feel included as members of a legal community who share a political culture that is expressed in the constitution, the institutions of government and agencies of the state.

From this perspective, we must seek to transform those structures of power that alienate some citizens in granting systematic privileges to one dominant group-culture over others. This kind of group-based oppression is very often the root cause of those political conflicts associated with struggles for recognition, including national conflicts such as that in Northern Ireland. Justice requires that constitutional arrangements should reflect new relations that signify the deconstruction of the hierarchical structure of power that differentiates groups and underpins the antagonism between them. The most secure basis for peace and stability, and the most effective way to resolve conflict, is to establish a constitutional framework expressive of a political culture that is inclusive of all significant social groups. Justice is not ethically neutral: it does not accommodate those who deny internal diversity by obstructing the achievement of an inclusive political culture. Nor can justice reflect national purity in a case where cultural and national minorities demand recognition.

2   The struggle for mutual recognition in Northern Ireland

We can explain the protracted nature of the conflict in Northern Ireland by showing how both of the two broad constitutional options that are of greatest historical significance, the retention of Northern Ireland within the United Kingdom or its incorporation into a united Ireland, inevitably lead to the oppression of one of the national groups by facilitating the domination of the other national culture. What we should learn from the history of this conflict is that, within this context, any constitutional structure that fails to recognize the legitimacy of the differing aspirations, identities and loyalties of the two national communities will be oppressive of one of the national groups. Any such arrangement allows the dominant group to enjoy the powers and privileges associated with the fact that the institutions of the state protect their national aspiration and express their national identity. For the other group, the coercive powers of the state are viewed as alien forces that subjugate and oppress them.

To say that Northern Ireland is exclusively British, or exclusively Irish, is to seek to establish a hierarchical relationship between two groups of citizens: those who identify with the institutions of the state and are thought of as full members of a self-regulating political community; and those who feel alienated from the state and who are basically second-class citizens. The fact of the matter is that it is the large Irish nationalist minority within Northern Ireland that has fallen into the latter category since partition. Unionists may well point out that they would have endured a similar fate had they been forced into a united Ireland as a large national minority in 1921. While there may be plenty of historical evidence that could be used to support this claim, it takes nothing away from the fact that it is the political alienation of Northern nationalists since partition that has fed the conflict.

Historically, the structure of constitutional power has privileged unionists in the sense that they have been able to identify with the institutions of the state while nationalists have been alienated from those institutions. This means that if we are to achieve justice, then the gains involved with respect to the sense of belonging that citizens experience within the political community will be more readily tangible to nationalists than to unionists. The latter will have to give up their *constitutional* privileges relative to the former. It is not surprising therefore that there is greater resistance to change within the unionist community and that the motivation remains strong among many unionists to block any movement that seeks to transform the constitutional *status quo*. The results of the referendum on the Agreement in May 1998 bear this out. The proposals were warmly embraced within the nationalist community. Only 5.6 per cent of Southern voters rejected the Agreement and, while there are no exact figures available, opposition among Northern nationalists was almost certainly at least as low. Exit polls seem to indicate, however, that the accord was accepted by a very small majority of the unionist community (Wilford 1999, p. 300).[5]

While the conflict is best understood as a struggle between competing national communities with incompatible aspirations to self-determination, we should not discount the role of the British and Irish states in helping to create the conditions of conflict (McGarry and O'Leary 1995a, pp. 360–3). Both have some responsibility for the on-going crisis in that neither has managed to convince members of the 'other' national tradition in Northern Ireland that they would, as citizens of that political community, be treated by the state with equal dignity in their own identity-forming contexts. In other words, state-building failures on the part of both the British state, prior to and since 1921, and on the part of the Irish state since 1921, have been significant factors in the conflict (Lustick 1985). Irish nationalists in Northern Ireland continue to feel alienated from the British state, as their fellow nationals in the South had prior to 1921, while unionists still see the Irish state as an alien force

---

[5] We can safely presume that some unionists voted 'No' because of their implacable opposition to the establishment of North/South institutions and to an enhanced role for the Irish Republic in Northern affairs. News reports at the time would seem to indicate, however, that the judgement of many was influenced by the way the Agreement dealt with certain ancillary issues. These include sensitive and emotive matters such as decommissioning, policing and early prisoner release. The inability to forgive past atrocities may have deprived many voters of an opportunity to see beyond violent conflict to a future based on accommodation and mutual respect.

that threatens to envelop them. In this sense it may be illuminating to think of Northern Ireland as an ethnic frontier society, a conflict zone that is affected crucially by the actions of others beyond the frontier, in this case the British and Irish states representing fellow nationals of the key protagonists (Wright 1987).

There are, therefore, important external sources of the conflict that will have to be addressed in any just settlement. This point is overlooked by those whose interpretations focus exclusively on internal differences between the communities without grasping the underlying basis for conflict in the clash of mutually antagonistic nationalities and the way in which the actions of the British and Irish states impact on that relationship.[6] We should not, however, overestimate the significance of these external sources. Whatever the negative contributions of past state-building failures, it is clear that the policies of both British and Irish governments in recent years have been to secure a fair and balanced settlement that would be acceptable to both national communities within Northern Ireland (Arthur 1999). This is why we must, under current conditions, give explanatory primacy to the internal failure of mutual recognition between the two national communities. While partition was imposed on nationalists, the British government has, since the Anglo-Irish Agreement of 1985, sought to cooperate with the Irish government in facilitating an accommodation between the two traditions (Ruane and Todd 1996, pp. 131–9, 295–300). This is made quite explicit in the Downing Street Declaration of 15 December 1993 (McGarry and O'Leary 1995a, pp. 408–23). If the policy is ultimately to be successful, it will have to involve the deconstruction of the hierarchical nature of the group relation between the two communities and that can only be achieved by bringing the politics of internal majoritarianism to a definitive end.

Many interpretations of the conflict have failed to identify the fundamental cause of the continuing antagonism to be the hierarchical nature of the internal group relation between unionists and nationalists. Traditional nationalists have traced the roots of the conflict to the colonial imposition of British rule on the people of Ireland, while traditional unionists have blamed irredentism within the Republic of Ireland for destabilizing Northern Ireland (Whyte 1990, chs. 6–7; McGarry and O'Leary 1995a, part I). These partisan interpretations remain popular within the public imagination and, for this reason they have featured prominently in the rhetoric of many of Northern Ireland's politicians. Both, however, represent failures to recognize the legitimacy of the

---

[6] These internal approaches differ in the emphasis that they give to religious, cultural or economic factors (McGarry and O'Leary 1995a, part II).

differing national aspiration of the 'other' community. Partisan national-ists have failed to recognize that unionists' identification with the British state is genuine and legitimate, while partisan unionists have failed to recognize the legitimacy of the Irish nationalist minority's aspiration to some form of Irish unity. These opposing interpretations render the other community politically invisible in that they assume, strangely enough given the on-going struggle for recognition, that the presence of a large, indigenous minority of citizens with a differing national aspira-tion is of no great significance with regard to the legitimacy of the state. There is no sense, from either perspective, that the rights of self-determination that each community demands for itself should be granted reciprocally to the other national community.

Nor is there any sensitivity in these partisan accounts to the impor-tance that each community attaches to their need for national self-expression in a context where they feel that their own identities are under threat from forces intent on alienating them from the structures of political power. This is why we find scepticism regarding the ideal of 'parity of esteem' among those partisans on both sides who fail to recognize members of the other national community in their difference (Cadogan Group 1996; Rolston 1998). If this ideal, which is affirmed in the Agreement, is taken to mean that members of both communities should be treated with equal dignity in their differing identity-forming contexts, then it would appear to be an important aspect of a just settlement. Individuals should be free to express the cultural and national differences that structure their group affiliations. Scepticism regarding the ideal itself is a reflection of the partisan's inability to acknowledge the fact that the conflict is rooted in a clash of national traditions and in the hierarchical relation between them. Of course we can only afford to 'esteem' those traditions that are compatible with an inclusive political culture. This means that certain exclusivist forms of cultural expression, including the idea that traditional marches can be forced through areas in which they are not welcome, go beyond the limits of toleration (O'Neill 2000).

As should be clear by now, constitutional justice in Northern Ireland has two key requirements from the normative perspective outlined here. The first is the deconstruction of the hierarchical relation between unionists and nationalists as political groups, and the second is the achievement of an inclusive political culture on which institutions that take us beyond this hierarchy could be built. The key is to ensure that members of both national communities feel that they can identify, as equals, with the institutions of the state. If no citizen is to feel alienated from the state then all will need to feel respected within their own identity-forming context. Whether Irish or British, each citizen needs to know himself or herself to be, in every significant way, a free and equal member of the political community. Given the history of this conflict and the size of the minority involved, this would seem to suggest that the institutions of state should be fully binational. They should be both British and Irish and there should be no systematic political or social advantage for those who are members of the majority tradition. An inclusive political culture will be equally respectful of Britishness and Irishness in not privileging one over the other and in not producing one victorious national community and another vanquished one. Binational egalitarianism points us towards joint British–Irish sovereignty as the most just constitutional arrangement.

While we cannot explore such a proposal in any detail, a notable feature of the most compelling model of joint sovereignty available is that it should be thought of as a durable, long-term arrangement, one that will remain in place regardless of which community forms the majority (O'Leary et al. 1993). The idea is that if we are to achieve justice and stability, we need a radical and permanent break from the politics of majoritarianism, something that leaves both groups vulnerable to the contingency of demographics. This may reassure those unionists who are inclined to view this kind of proposal as a stepping stone to a united Ireland. Long-term joint sovereignty provides for greater stability in ensuring that the constitutional position will not change even if demographic trends produce, at some stage in the future, a nationalist majority. Of course, in such a scenario, joint sovereignty would look a lot more attractive to unionists than it has up to now. It is clear that at present most unionists believe that this arrangement asks them to give up far too much, but that would hardly be the case if a united Ireland by consent were to seem like a real possibility (Mitchell 1999, pp. 278–81). The fact is that unionists resist joint sovereignty not because they can convincingly dispute its claim to be just but because they still retain that power of democratic consent that is granted to the majority community simply through weight of numbers. This majoritarian power remains as a key structure in the hierarchical relation between the two national groups and it can only be neutralized, in the long term, if comprehensively egalitarian structures, such as those envisaged in a model of joint sovereignty, can be realized.[7]

One of the virtues of this kind of confederal arrangement is that it

[7] As we will see, this majoritarian power has not been entirely neutralized by the Agreement.

takes us beyond a paralysing obsession with sovereignty thought of in terms of independence and freedom from interference towards a relational conception of sovereignty (Hoffman 1998). The unyielding view of sovereignty as non-interference undermines the possibility of achieving constitutional justice in Northern Ireland (Kearney 1997, p. 24; Anderson 1998, pp. 127–32). In contrast, this binational proposal takes us beyond nationalism while acknowledging the current need for political self-expression of the two national communities. In this sense it is postnationalist without being postnational (Geoghegan 1994). Such an arrangement will underline the ethical uniqueness of the political constitutions of both the United Kingdom and the Republic of Ireland in reflecting more justly the historical struggles and achievements of the particular peoples and nations concerned. The proposed political structures would also reflect the internal ethical diversity of these constitutions. This diversity would be revealed in the asymmetrical relations of England, Scotland (with its own Parliament), Wales (with its own Assembly) and Northern Ireland (where sovereignty would be shared with the Republic of Ireland) to the United Kingdom and in the continuing constitutional differences between the two parts of Ireland.

Since the ethical uniqueness of a political community is expressed through flags, anthems, emblems and so on, a just Northern Ireland will be one in which symbols of both national traditions enjoy equal status, unless they are to be replaced by a set of symbols that are genuinely inclusive. Public buildings should fly both the Union flag and the Irish tricolour until such a time, if ever, that a new flag is accepted by both national traditions. Alternatively no flag should be flown. There are also implications for the celebration of national holidays in that St Patrick's Day should enjoy equal official status as a public holiday as does the July holiday celebrating the defeat of Catholic forces at the Battle of the Boyne in 1690. Wherever there are official national symbols, the honouring of the achievements of particular citizens, the support of representative sports teams, the promotion of the arts, the insignia on coins, the colour of post-boxes and so on, there should be a sensitivity to the binational reality of Northern Irish society. Binational egalitarianism will also have a major impact on policing. Since most nationalists have seen the RUC as a force of alienation, an unreformed force could be neither equally protective nor expressive of both national traditions (McGarry and O'Leary 1999).

Joint sovereignty, as the most egalitarian binational arrangement, recognizes fully the legitimacy of both national aspirations and it resolves the conflict between them by granting them equal constitutional status.[8] Members of both national communities can identify, as free and equal citizens, with the institutions of the state and neither need fear any political transformation leading to their subordination and oppression as a national minority. In this way we might expect such an arrangement to be more rationally acceptable to all concerned than one based on a rigid conception of sovereignty in which they would run a serious risk of ending up as members of an alienated national minority (O'Neill 1996, p. 95–6). These structures would also allow for cultural continuity in making equal citizenship compatible with membership of either national community. But this would involve a critical appropriation of the two national traditions in that only those customs and practices that are compatible with an inclusive, thoroughly binational, political culture can be tolerated. Exclusivist cultural practices that fail to afford equal respect to members of other traditions must be abandoned. Joint sovereignty, therefore, is not ethically neutral since it cannot accommodate all manifestations of culture. Modes of cultural expression that are compatible with mutual recognition must be privileged over those that express the cultural superiority of one tradition over the other.

3   Mutual recognition in the Good Friday Agreement

What did the parties agree to on 10 April 1998?[9] We need to outline briefly the main institutional features of the Agreement before focusing on basic constitutional issues. There were three main institutional strands to the negotiations that were designed to cover the totality of political relationships among the peoples of Britain and Ireland. Strand 1 dealt with internal relations between the two national communities and the setting up of democratic institutions in Northern Ireland. Strand 2 dealt with relations between the two jurisdictions in Ireland

---

[8] For this reason I view the dualism involved here not to be in tension with an 'emancipatory' approach to the conflict but rather to be a requirement of the kind of critical analysis advocated by Ruane and Todd (1996, ch. 11). If emancipation requires a dismantling of the system of relationships that sustain the conflict, then an egalitarian binational constitutional arrangement seems to be a necessary condition of emancipation. It is only when members of both traditions feel reassured that they are recognized as equal citizens, that the potential for other 'non-national' struggles for justice to gather momentum will be greatly enhanced.

[9] Eight political parties joined the two governments in affirming the Agreement. There were three unionist parties (Ulster Unionist Party, Progressive Unionist Party and the Ulster Democratic Party), two nationalist parties (Social Democratic and Labour Party and Sinn Féin) and three cross-community parties (Alliance, Labour and the Women's Coalition) involved. The Democratic Unionist Party led by Ian Paisley and the United Kingdom Unionist Party led by Robert McCartney campaigned vigorously against the entire talks process while these other parties worked their way towards an accommodation. Wilford (1999) gives a detailed description of the terms of the Agreement.

and the setting up of a North/South Ministerial Council. Strand 3 dealt with East/West relations and the setting up of a British–Irish Council and a British–Irish Intergovernmental Conference. The Agreement also included a set of safeguards designed to secure human rights for all on a basis of equality and a set of proposals dealing with economic, social and cultural issues. Finally, the parties grappled with the vexed questions of decommissioning and security, policing and criminal justice, and the early release of paramilitary prisoners.

The various institutional features of the Agreement stand or fall together so that all parties are motivated to seek its full implementation and not only those aspects of it that appeal most to their own constituents. So, crucially, the workings of the Assembly in Northern Ireland and the North/South Ministerial Council are to be mutually interdependent to the extent that the success of each depends on that of the other. So while unionists were initially resistant to the proposals under Strand 2, and nationalists were not very enthusiastic about the proposals under Strand 1, this interlocking binds them together in seeking success for the overall settlement. For this reason, the Irish government was deeply disappointed by the *unilateral* and legally questionable decision of Peter Mandelson to suspend the new institutions in February 2000.

The democratic institutions that were agreed in Strand 1 are basically consociational in form (O'Leary 1999, p. 1630). There is a 108-member Assembly elected by PR(STV) and its key decisions are to be taken on a cross-community basis. A First Minister and a Deputy First Minister who are effectively equal in powers lead a power-sharing Executive Committee. The Assembly jointly elects these quasi-presidential figures into office. The rules make it almost impossible for these offices not to be held by one member from each national community and the Assembly duly elected David Trimble (Ulster Unionist Party) and Séamus Mallon (Social Democratic and Labour Party) on a cross-community basis on 1 July 1998. Seats on the Executive are not in the gift of the First and Deputy First Ministers but rather they are allocated, in accord with the d'Hondt divisor, to parties in proportion to the number of seats they hold in the Assembly. Apart from the power-sharing executive and the rules relating to proportionality, the Agreement is shot through with other key consociational features. These include measures that seek to secure equality for the two national communities without diminishing their cultural autonomy, and a set of minority veto rights (O'Leary 1999, pp. 1638–41).

The Agreement does not focus only on the internal relation between the two national communities. It also addresses the external causes of the conflict by reconstituting relations between the two jurisdictions in

Ireland and between Britain and Ireland. Most significantly the North/ South Ministerial Council (Strand 2) allows for a delegation of powers from both Northern Ireland and the Irish Republic to a set of bodies that can implement their decisions on an all-island basis. There are six North/South bodies that implement agreed policies on a cross-border basis. The Ministerial Council has also agreed on six broad areas of cooperation between government departments and other bodies, North and South. These cover aspects of policy concerning agriculture, education, environment, health, tourism and transport. The Ministerial Council gives Northern nationalists an institutional link to the Irish state and many of them see it as a stepping stone to some form of Irish unity. Unionists regard it as the price to be paid for the Assembly but their hope is that this link, combined with measures to ensure cultural equality within Northern Ireland, will go far enough for most nationalists to see value in the long-term maintenance of the Union.

The British–Irish Council (Strand 3) brings together representatives of both governments, the devolved institutions in Scotland, Wales and Northern Ireland and small neighbouring dependent island territories. They seek to reach agreement with regard to possible cooperation on matters of mutual interest and they may agree common policies. Unlike the relation between the institutions of Strands 1 and 2, there are no equivalent interlocking mechanisms with those of Strand 3. The primary function of the British–Irish Council is to provide an East/West institutional link that may, as we will see, be important should the constitutional status of Northern Ireland change in the future. Another important dimension of this strand is the British–Irish Intergovernmental Conference which allows for an intensification of cooperation between the two governments on various relevant matters including cross-border aspects of questions concerning rights, justice, prisons, policing and so on.

These institutions operate within a constitutional framework that seeks to acknowledge the legitimacy of the competing national aspirations of the two communities while giving priority to a principle of majoritarian consent. The parties recognize the fact that it is a matter of choice for the people of Northern Ireland as to whether they want to remain within the United Kingdom, or become part of a sovereign united Ireland. While it is accepted that a majority in Northern Ireland at present wish to retain the Union, Irish self-determination is also recognized to the extent that the governments will be obliged to bring a united Ireland into being should a majority in both jurisdictions will this in a possible future referendum. We must recall, however, that the institutions set up under Strands 2 and 3 provide important links to the state with which the minority national community in Northern Ireland identifies itself. So while North/South institutions are intended to give nationalists a real political connection with the Irish state, East/West institutions will perform a similar function should unionists find themselves as a minority in a future united, and presumably federal, Ireland.

The Agreement also recognizes the binational nature of Northern Ireland in affirming the right of all its people, both now and in a possible future united Ireland, to hold both Irish and British citizenship. There is also a commitment to promote and facilitate the use of the Irish language within Northern Ireland and an acknowledgement of the sensitivity of the use of symbols and emblems for public purposes. The parties agree that public symbols should promote 'mutual respect rather than division'. But most significantly, the Agreement is binational in insisting that members of both national communities must be treated as equals in their national differences, no matter which of the sovereign governments has jurisdiction in Northern Ireland. It states that governmental power must be exercised

with rigorous impartiality on behalf of all the people in the diversity of their identities and traditions and shall be founded on the principles of full respect for, and equality of, civil, political, social and cultural rights, of freedom from discrimination for all citizens, and of parity of esteem and of just and equal treatment for the identity, ethos and aspiration of both communities. (*Agreement*, Constitutional Issues, 1 (v))

These conditions of equal citizenship are to be realized through the incorporation into Northern Ireland law by the British government of the European Convention on Human Rights and by the establishment of a new Northern Ireland Human Rights Commission. The Commission considers how public bodies are fully to respect 'on the basis of equality of treatment, the identity and ethos of both communities'. There is also a new Equality Commission designed to secure equality of opportunity and freedom from discrimination for all in Northern Ireland. The Irish government is also committed to taking comparable steps in the protection of human rights within its own jurisdiction.

How are we to assess this settlement? By dealing with various relevant political relationships in its three-stranded approach, the Agreement clearly addresses both internal and external sources of conflict. The consociational arrangements within Northern Ireland make cross-community political cooperation possible on a basis of mutual respect. They facilitate democratic, devolved government that empowers all the people of Northern Ireland. The North/South and East/West institutions signify a further distancing from a narrow conception of sovereignty based on non-interference. The Agreement can thus escape the paralysing logic that insists that Northern Ireland is exclusively the sovereign territory of either Britain or Ireland. But it falls short of a thoroughly egalitarian binational political arrangement in which Britain and Ireland would be equally and jointly sovereign. Northern Ireland remains within the United Kingdom for as long as a majority of its citizens so wish. The possibility is, however, left open that majorities in both jurisdictions in Ireland will seek to bring a sovereign united Ireland into being at some point in the future, something which demographic trends certainly cannot rule out. There is therefore a remaining political inequality between the national communities that comes from connecting the question of sovereign jurisdiction to a principle of majoritarian consent. The hope is that this inequality will have very little bite since the minority community, whichever it happens to be, will be protected politically by having institutional links with the other (its preferred) sovereign state, and culturally by having its identity and ethos respected on a basis of equality.

So, is the Agreement a solid basis for constitutional justice in Northern Ireland? The first requirement of justice is the deconstruction of the hierarchical relationship that constitutes unionists and nationalists as social groups. The Agreement certainly makes great strides in achieving the deconstruction of the most pernicious aspects of this hierarchical communal relationship. Nationalists are assured of cultural equality and 'parity of esteem' within Northern Ireland and they have the bonus of being linked in a politically meaningful way to the Irish Republic through the North/South institutions. But the priority given to the consent of a majority internal to Northern Ireland on constitutional matters means that not all the systematic political privileges of the unionist majority have been removed. In this sense, since the United Kingdom and not Ireland is officially sovereign, unionists remain constitutionally dominant to *some* degree. Even if that dominance should not count for much, it has a symbolic importance that may be a source for continuing antagonism, especially at times of communal tension.

Enshrining the principle of consent in this manner means that the Agreement has compromised this demand of justice, and the prospects for stability, to the realities of social power. It legitimizes the will of the majority on fundamental constitutional matters when political majoritarianism has itself been the primary source of the conflict. It also leaves the door open, depending on demographic trends, to a potentially traumatic future consideration of the creation of a united Ireland. Joint sovereignty, by bringing the politics of majoritarianism to a definitive end, avoids these problems and so achieves the deconstruction of hierarchy in a more complete way. Nevertheless, it must be stressed that while the Agreement may fall short of our best assessment as to what justice strictly requires regarding relations between unionists and nationalists, it must also be acknowledged that, within the overall settlement, the power of the majority has been neutralized to a very great extent.

The second requirement of justice is the achievement of a constitutional framework expressive of a political culture that is inclusive of all. The referendum on the Agreement in the North certainly helped to bring a new and inclusive Northern Irish political culture into being. The turnout was high at 81.1 per cent and the fact that 71.12 per cent of voters, including a majority from both national communities, endorsed this historic accommodation was an important sign that a shared and sustained commitment to these novel institutions might just be possible in this new constitutional context. Of course there were those, most though not all of them unionist, who voted against the Agreement because they view any compromise with the other tradition as a defeat or betrayal. They choose to exclude themselves from this emerging political culture of accommodation and their intolerance prevents them from entering into a new relationship of mutual recognition with members of the other national tradition. The hope, of course, is that they will eventually be marginalized and left behind. But this depends on a strengthening of the bonds of solidarity that unite all those who affirm an inclusively binational political culture. They, along with their political representatives and the two governments, must make it clear to the intolerant minority that the political accommodation of national diversity is the only reasonable way forward for Northern Ireland.

I can find no compelling reason to question the idea that the Agreement satisfies fully the requirements of democratic legitimacy, underpinned as it is by the results of the referenda, North and South. Justice, however, is a more stringent test of political arrangements than legitimacy, yet it promises a more fertile grounding for peace and stability. While the political culture expressed in the complex constitutional framework of the Agreement is inclusive, it is not strictly egalitarian. The British national identity remains constitutionally privileged even if every effort is to be made to ensure 'parity of esteem' for both national cultures within Northern Ireland. In spite of the promise of cultural equality, and North/South institutions, the unionist identity has a more immediate consonance with institutions set up in the constitutional context of a devolved United Kingdom. The reverse, of course, would be true in any future united Ireland where the Irish identity would be more immediately consonant with constitutional arrangements.

The gap between parity of esteem and the binational egalitarianism that joint sovereignty would bring might begin to loom rather large if the new institutions cannot deliver on key questions to come with regard to the equal recognition of both cultures. These include efforts to resolve the bitter controversies surrounding contentious marches, particularly at Drumcree, the implementation of the recommendations of the Patten Commission on the future of policing, the use of inclusive symbols, and the celebration of national holidays. It is not easy to see how a thorough-going parity of esteem is to be achieved on all these matters without moving us inexorably in the direction of joint sovereignty. For example, cultural equality would seem to require that the Irish tricolour and the Union flag should have equal status as political symbols. By the time we had realized cultural equality to that extent, it would seem perverse not simply to accept the logical conclusion, that joint British–Irish sovereignty provides the most secure and just basis for long-term political stability in Northern Ireland.

9   Federalist language policies: the cases of Canada and Spain[1]

Pierre Coulombe

Introduction

Language policies serve to regulate the effects of the contact between a majority language and one or more minority languages. Where language constitutes the main marker of communal identity, language policies moderate or, alternatively, intensify intercommunal conflict (McRae 1983, p. 32). While one of their objectives is to ensure peace and order, language laws also have normative grounds. They can be conceptualized as duties fulfilled towards a particular community making moral or historical claims that have currency in a given political context. Understood this way, they are the product of competing claims, individual or collective, to language protection. It is no surprise, then, that a language policy acquires symbolic properties (Rocher and Marcotte 1997, p. 266), for it is a reflection of a state's response to claims of justice and to power struggles among linguistic communities.

In federal states, more than one level of government is usually involved in language matters. This gives rise to a complex language rights regime that combines the policies of two governments whose objectives do not always converge. Federalism implies a delicate balance between unity and diversity, as does a language rights regime that includes a central government policy of one or more official languages statewide alongside a regional government policy that promotes a particular language in its own jurisdiction. A federalist language rights regime in a *multination* state is invested with a symbolism of its own, namely as a recognition of the linguistic identities of the state's constituent nations and of the value of raising some of these languages to official status at the central state level.

One cannot judge the success or failure of federalism in a multination

[1] I would like to thank the following persons for their assistance: Luisa Domenichelli (Università di Roma 'La Sapienza'), Siobhan Harty (University of Wales), Ferran Requejo (Universitat Pompeu Fabra), Diane Roussel, as well as the editors of this volume.

state solely on the basis of its language rights regime, for many other factors are at play. Nevertheless, language policies that fail to achieve the proper balance between unity and diversity, hence that ignore federalist principles, may be perceived as an injustice as well as contributing to the fragmentation of the multination state.

Two cases illustrate this issue: Quebec in Canada and Catalonia in Spain. At the onset, we should remember that there are important differences between the experience of Quebec and that of Catalonia. For example, while Quebec has enjoyed full provincial status within the Canadian federation since 1867, Catalonia has most often suffered persecution by the Spanish state, notably during the years of the Franco regime (1939–75). Even today, the constitutional powers of Quebec surpass those of Catalonia. Moreover, unlike Catalans, whose language is regionally circumscribed, the Québécois have benefited from speaking a prestigious international language. Furthermore, over 80 per cent of Quebec's population has French as a home language whereas Catalonia's population is equally divided between Catalan speakers and Castilian speakers (Rocher and Marcotte 1997, p. 255).

Nevertheless, Quebec and Catalonia share a long history of resistance to linguistic assimilation intertwined with the dynamics of autonomy. Although their respective histories reveal varying degrees of conflicts with the 'centre' and different sociolinguistic circumstances, both the Québécois and the Catalans have forged their sense of political identity as conquered, culturally distinct peoples (Klein 1989, pp. 115, 118). As substate units that claim national distinctiveness, they have secured some degree of autonomy through federalist arrangements: a federal state in Canada since 1867 and a 'state of autonomies' in Spain since 1978. These situations have given rise to state language planning in both countries, each level of government having developed language policies that advance its own vision of nationhood.

In the first section, I raise theoretical issues that underlie the language policies of central and regional governments alike in multination states. This discussion will serve to situate the value of federalist principles in language rights regimes. I then draw from the experiences of Quebec and Catalonia to illustrate the shapes such regimes can take, as well as the deficiencies that can undermine them. There are, of course, other substate units in Spain and Canada that engage in language planning, such as the Basque Country and New Brunswick. The limits of this chapter do not allow me to investigate these other cases here. Examining Catalonia and Quebec can nonetheless inform us on how the co-existence of two language policies in a multination state can be framed as a concrete expression of federalist principles.

Theoretical considerations

Debates about language policy often reveal deeper issues of justice. Rights discourse is central to the conceptual formulation of the requirements of justice, insofar as rights say something about the values we cherish and the duties we hold towards each other in respecting these values. Our duties become, in that sense, duties of justice. The last three centuries saw the list of goods considered most worthy to human well-being extended to include not only goods derived from the value of personal autonomy (choice, dignity etc.), but also goods associated with our communal identity (culture, customs etc.). Thus cultural rights, such as the right to the preservation of one's language, now stand side by side with more traditional individual rights, such as the rights to freedom of expression and to physical integrity. These often take the form of collective or community rights which, even though they irreducibly pertain to human interests, emphasize the situated, rather than solitary, aspect of existence (Coulombe 1995).

The adjudication of the multiple and often conflicting demands made under the rubric of language rights is no small task. The strength of numbers is undoubtedly a relevant factor in the weight accorded to a community's claim. But apart from the *realpolitik* numbers entail, the historical priority of national communities is most often invoked. For example, if a community's political existence was extinguished through conquest or imperialism, its claim to compensatory justice is likely to have cogency. While claims to language protection proceed from universal human rights associated with the good of cultural identity, the force they carry largely depends upon how the claimant's place in history is construed.

Rights discourse is therefore a highly effective conceptual tool communities use in their demands to exercise control over their linguistic destiny. It is powerful because it appeals to those fundamental goods that make life worth living, namely, in this case, cultural identity. Moreover, it calls for state intervention in the market of cultures and languages not only to regulate intercommunal conflict, but also to fulfil a moral obligation, as a matter of justice, towards a particular community.

It would be misleading, however, to associate language rights discourse exclusively with a celebration of linguistic diversity and a policy of multilingualism. Policies of unilingualism can also be grounded in rights. For example, an often legitimate, but nonetheless problematic justification for policies of unilingualism is found in nationalist ideology. Promoting the status of a 'national' language does not always sit well with recognizing a plurality of languages. Since the number of languages spoken in the world is higher than the number of existing states, the belief in 'one nation, one language' has translated into various solutions ranging from policies of assimilation to the creation of separate, linguistically homogeneous states. There is no doubt, in the words of Kenneth McRae, that '[i]n the ideology of nationalism the linguistically homogeneous nation state has acquired a peculiarly magnetic appeal' (McRae 1983, p. 5). Moreover, there is a perverse side to arguments rooted in national entitlements, which usually go like this: 'Because our language is central to our identity, we call upon the state's duty to promote it. But other speech communities cannot make the same claim, for we alone have the status of a nation. Therefore, we have the right to develop a policy of unilingualism.' This kind of discourse is also heard in federal polities. A federated community seeking the respect of linguistic pluralism statewide on grounds of its status as a nation may claim the right to linguistic homogeneity in its own jurisdiction. Here, the community's desire to preserve linguistic diversity at the state level leads to a defence of linguistic homogeneity at the regional level, hence paradoxically meshing uniformity and diversity in a single discourse. Nationalist discourse allows the community to claim at once its right to preserve its national identity vis-à-vis the state at large and its right to deny it to groups within its own borders.

More subtle conduits for uniformity are found within liberal democratic tradition, which tends to be permeated by rights discourse. Democratic theory warns us that allowing diverse cultures and languages to thrive can cause division among the citizenry and thus be an obstacle to the full participation of all in public life. In this view, the assimilation of linguistic minorities should not be seen as a moral offence, but rather as part of a democratization process. The promotion of one common public language responds to the need for social cohesion and integration, especially in a context of high immigration. Here, the argument goes, the community's choice of the majority language as its public language is not derived from any ill intent, nor even from moral or historical considerations, but rather from the risk to the stability of democratic life linguistic laissez-faire poses.

Two elements of liberal tradition, equality and liberty, can also lead to linguistic uniformity, albeit in an indirect manner. The constitutional recognition of a linguistic community can be interpreted as a breach in the equality principle, according to which there should be no first-class and second-class citizens. Denying such official recognition to a particular group becomes a function of the noble endeavour to build an undifferentiated citizenship. Moreover, the value of liberty is sometimes construed as the respect for the free market not only of goods and services, but of cultures as well. Consequently, the state should remain neutral before various linguistic groups in competition, lest it violate 'fundamental' freedoms. In both cases, state intervention to protect weaker linguistic communities is seen as illegitimate. This position, of course, tends to favour dominant languages, which usually prosper in a free-market environment.

Belief in linguistic uniformity is found in nationalist ideology and in particular understandings of the core values of liberal democracy. It merges with the language of rights, thus acquiring force and legitimacy.

Language policy, then, correlates with visions of uniformity or visions of diversity. Both visions are potentially worthy or reprehensible, for there is no general rule from which we can judge *a priori* the value of a given language-planning effort. In a federal polity where language planning falls under more than one jurisdiction, we are likely to observe a complex mix of objectives, some compatible, some not, and a variety of appeals to the values of identity, democracy, equality, liberty, stability, nationhood and so forth.

Each level of government pursues its own objectives, which may correspond to one of the following scenarios. At the regional level, a community makes demands for a portion of sovereignty, in particular sovereignty over those matters crucial to its cultural continuity. It develops a language policy tailored to its circumstances, with provisions that aim at the normalization of its language in various spheres of activity. The territorial model of language planning, whereby individuals entering the community's territory must leave behind any prior claim to language protection, thus becomes attractive. Though the tendency may be for the government to deny special rights for its own minorities, that is not always the case. Nothing in this scenario prevents a regional community from providing a wide range of minority language rights while promoting its own language as the public language.

The rationales behind the central state's involvement in language planning differ in some respects from those of the federated communities. On the central level, the overall objective is to counterbalance the centrifugal forces that tend to further the territorialization of languages and the fragmentation of the state. The central state may recognize one official language statewide, or it can entrench two or more official languages so as to provide guarantees to 'minorities within minorities'. In the latter case, the intent is to ensure the rights of national language groups within autonomous regions are not unduly restricted. Moreover, the recognition of two or more languages at the federal level may serve symbolic purposes insofar as the central state mirrors the various identities of the linguistic communities. Seeing their language receive official status at the central state level gives members of historic communities a sense that their identity is publicly recognized, which in turn can nurture feelings of belonging to the state at large. In addition to meeting these requirements of justice and recognition, a policy of official languages at the federal level may favour political stability to the extent that addressing the problem of minorities and that of recognition contributes to the unity of the state and ensures its self-preservation. Minority protection and symbolic recognition are thus two ways in which centrifugal forces can be countered and conflicts regulated. Still, not unlike the language planning of regional communities, that of the central state partakes in nation-building efforts and may even affirm the priority of one sense of national belonging over another.

It could be argued all of this merely proves that shared sovereignty over language matters is a counterproductive source of tensions. Different policy orientations, each wrapped in the language of rights, inevitably cause friction and a clash of often equally valid claims. One must consider, however, the value of multiple belonging that shared sovereignty over language matters reflects. Federal citizenship is multilayered; dual belonging need not be condemned as unnatural but rather welcomed as an opportunity for citizens to express the many sides of their political identity (Vernon 1988). Federal citizens may belong to two nations and refuse to rank their loyalties. Correspondingly, no level of government alone can claim to speak in their name. But such dual belonging is not free of tensions, especially if the two governments pursue divergent goals. A federalist language rights regime is founded on the acceptance that both of these goals are legitimate, however divergent they might be, for together they affirm the deeper value of multiple belonging.

Whichever way the federation is historically formed, that is, whether it is the product of various communities joining together or the result of the restructuring of a unitary system, it is expected constituent units will work towards the good of the overall collectivity and the central state will respect the plurality of political communities (Lejeune 1994). The joining of intercommunal solidarity with maintenance of multiple identities within a single state is possible only if the desire among communities to seek common goals is nourished and if their respective, authentic identities are both recognized and celebrated by way of proper institutional or constitutional arrangements. To achieve this, a true dialogue between partners, involving negotiations and reciprocal concessions on how to share state sovereignty, is essential. In the case of multination federalism, partners are further required to abandon the pursuit of a single conception of nationhood and to accept instead the coexistence of multiple meanings of national belonging. It is within this normative context that language policies in multination states should be evaluated.

Quebec and Canada

The Canadian experience is telling of the ambivalence that can arise from the coexistence of two language policies in a multination and federal state. Language is the main marker of identity that separates Quebec society from the rest of the country and that divides it from within. Disputes over language are a salient feature of Canadian history. While it is true that in recent years a *modus vivendi* has been reached and demands for a complete overhaul of the language rights regime have rarely been heard, language remains a cause of political tensions and judicial conflicts.

After the conquest of New France in 1760 by the British, different language policies were implemented depending on whether the British authorities wanted to accommodate its French population or not. By the eve of the British North America Act of 1867, which marks the foundation of modern Canada, federalist practices had already emerged despite the unitary form of government imposed by the Union Act of 1840. A limited form of legislative bilingualism had even gained acceptance. These practices laid the foundations for the federal arrangements to be included in the constitution of 1867, which gave provinces powers over their own affairs, notably over education. Guarantees for legislative and judicial bilingualism at the federal level and in Quebec were the only references to language matters as such. These were not very far-reaching, however, and certainly insufficient to defend the interests of francophone minorities left vulnerable to the whims of provincial majorities.

An important change occurred in 1969 with the passage of the Official Languages Act by the federal government of Pierre Trudeau. The law declared English and French the two official languages of Canada and entitled citizens to federal government services in either language. It also led to an increase in the number of francophones in the federal civil service who until then had been underrepresented. In 1982, these language rights were included in a constitutionally-entrenched Charter of Rights and Freedoms. An essential component of this constitutional amendment is that it guarantees the right of official minorities to have their children educated in their mother tongue where their numbers justify it.

One feature of the federal policy is its symmetrical application throughout the country, whereby French-speaking minorities outside

Quebec and the English-speaking minority inside Quebec receive equal constitutional protection. Another noteworthy aspect is that it is modelled on the 'personality' approach to language planning: in principle, individuals carry their language rights from coast to coast with few territorial restrictions.

While the federal government was implementing its policy of official bilingualism in the late 1960s, successive Quebec governments were developing their own language policy. Their overall objective was to improve the status of French within the province so that, as the language spoken by the vast majority, it would have a majority status. It must be noted that before the passing of language laws, English occupied a disproportionate place in Quebec in relation to French, especially in the economic sphere. The cultural division of labour was such that 'capital spoke English and labour spoke French'. Inevitably, the more prestigious English language became the pole of attraction for immigrants settling in Quebec. Today's justifications for these language laws tend to alternate between the need to improve the lot of the French-Canadian majority and the need to integrate immigrants into Quebec society by way of a common, public language.

The first modest attempts in the late 1960s to reverse the inequality between French and English were more persuasive than coercive, and it was not until Quebec's National Assembly enacted the Official Language Act in 1974 that ground rules were laid. French would be the sole official language in Quebec, measures would be introduced to channel the children of immigrants into the French school system, and French would be the language of use in the public sector. In 1977, the Charter of the French Language, known as Bill 101, became the centrepiece of the newly elected sovereigntist government's approach to language planning. It further restricted freedom of choice with regards to the use of French and other languages. For example, immigrants and Canadians alike moving to Quebec were required to send their children to a French school and commercial signs were to be in French only. This law clearly followed the territorial model of language planning.

The language policies of both federal and Quebec governments arose from major changes that occurred in Quebec society after the Second World War, and particularly during the early 1960s. As Quebec underwent a rapid, state-led modernization of its social, economic and political institutions, a strong movement of national affirmation also sought to transform French as a majority language into French as a majority-*status* language. In parallel, the federal government was engaging in its own nation building and, partly in reaction to the rise of Quebec nationalism, was developing its own language policy in the form of pan-Canadian official bilingualism. The language policies of each government are, in that respect, concrete expressions of competing nation-building efforts. One represents a vision of Canada where French-Canadians should find their linguistic identity reflected in public institutions throughout the country. Canadian citizenship should no longer be perceived as antagonistic to membership in francophone society. The other puts forth a vision of Quebec as the true and only home of francophones. Their government should be empowered to make French the only public language in Quebec.

Neither of these two policies in themselves embodies the federal principle. It is rather through their coexistence that unity and diversity are expressed and both visions of nationhood recognized. This is far from being unproblematic.

Some supporters of official bilingualism, for instance, greeted Quebec's language legislation with dismay. That the government of Quebec should respond to an openness to the French fact throughout Canada by restricting the rights of the Anglo-Québécois was, and still is, an abomination in the minds of many. Moreover, Bill 101 is perceived by some as a set of discriminatory practices and limits to freedom of expression masquerading as a collective right and, in that sense, is condemned as illiberal legislation.

Some supporters of Quebec's language law, for their part, view the federal government's policy of official bilingualism as an illegitimate constraint on the province's ability to control language planning (Comité 1996). While demands for institutional bilingualism have always been central to French-Canadian political thought, it is sometimes viewed today as an instrument to obstruct Quebec's endeavours to promote French. The entrenchment of the pillars of official bilingualism in the constitution without the consent of Quebec's National Assembly further undermined its value in the eyes of some Québécois. Because the constitution is no longer considered the product of mutual consent, judicial decisions are deemed to be partial, such as the post-1982 court decisions affecting Bill 101 discussed below (Domenichelli 1998, p. 10). The problem, it can be surmised, stems more from the perceived lack of legitimacy of the deliberative process that produced the Charter language rights than from a negative assessment of the rights themselves.

Critics of the pan-Canadian vision of bilingualism cite three court rulings in particular that confirm the steady erosion of the Charter of the French Language. In 1979, the Supreme Court of Canada ruled that the provisions making French the only official language of legislation and justice violate section 133 of the British North America Act, 1867, which guarantees legislative and judicial bilingualism in Quebec. In

1984, it ruled that the restrictions to English schooling in Quebec violate the Charter of Rights and Freedoms' minority educational rights which guarantee the right of francophones and anglophones who have received their primary education in their language in Canada to have their children receive instruction in that language anywhere in the country. Finally, in 1988, it ruled that the provisions imposing French only on commercial signs violate the sections on freedom of expression and equality rights found in the Canadian Charter of Rights and Freedoms.

These three judicial decisions prompted the government of Quebec to amend the Charter of the French Language. Today, English has recovered its equal status in the legislature and courts; only immigrants, not Canadians from other provinces, are required to send their children to a French school; and while French must appear predominantly on commercial signs, other languages are not forbidden. These constitutional limits to Quebec's control over language policy clearly reveal tension between the two levels of Canada's language rights regime. Nonetheless, public discourse in Quebec increasingly reflects a consensus about the worth of Quebec's language policy, despite the amendments that were made. In fact, it is worth pointing out that Quebec's own judicial order, not only Canada's, had found portions of Bill 101 illegitimate and unconstitutional. Both judicial orders agree on where the Quebec government, or any liberal government for that matter, should draw the line.

As for the principle of a coast-to-coast application of official bilingualism, it is partly challenged by the increasing territorialization of the French–English duality. Quebec's two contiguous provinces, Ontario and New Brunswick, comprise 85 per cent of all francophone minorities outside Quebec (McRoberts 1998, p. 206). Given the strong trend towards greater territorialization of official language communities, the relevance of the pan-Canadian vision is questioned by English-Canadians and Québécois alike, though for different reasons: in English Canada, its relevance is questioned in regions where the francophone population is dwindling, whereas in Quebec it is perceived as a policy that undermines the promotion of French by supporting the English-speaking community of Quebec.

The general point to be made is that, paradoxically, the tensions generated by the coexistence of the two governments' policies hold some value. Federal arrangements allowing Quebec's National Assembly to promote the status of French within its borders while also allowing the Parliament of Canada to promote linguistic duality should not be considered a sign of constitutional failure, but, more positively, as attempts to reach the right balance between diversity and unity.

Catalonia and Spain

The case of Catalonia in Spain also illustrates the challenges involved in reaching the balance between unity and diversity. Since the early eighteenth century, Catalans have been coping with the penetration of Castilian in Catalonia. Castilian became the predominant language used in the public sphere (in literature, culture, education and the media), while Catalan was mostly relegated to the private sphere. Given Castilian's domination in the education system and in the media, and substantial Castilian immigration in the region, Catalan was left in a state of inferiority.

The late nineteenth century and early twentieth century were turbulent years with regards to the status of Catalan. Efforts to revive the language were met by Madrid at times with toleration, at times with repression. In between periods of prohibition, Catalan organizations carried on language corpus and status planning, most notably under the guidance of linguist Pompeu Fabra. The Second Republic (1931) restored the Generalitat de Catalunya (the traditional government of Catalonia suppressed in 1714) which made Catalan and Castilian coofficial languages. The defeat of the republican forces by General Franco in 1939 soon put an end to Catalonia's autonomous status. Catalan was prohibited in the public sphere during forty years of repression and forced assimilation (Bastardas 1987).

The Spanish constitution of 1978, ratified by referendum, recognized the plurality of cultures, languages and institutions in the country. This marked a new beginning for Spain's various nationalities and their relations with the central government. The coexistence of languages is defined in section 3 of the constitution: Castilian remains the only official language of the central state, nationwide, but regional languages may be coofficial in their respective autonomous communities. Moreover, the constitution states that Spain's multilingual heritage is to be the object of special protection, though it is unclear as to what this protection means in concrete terms. The higher constitutional status of Castilian over the languages of autonomous communities is established by the provision that '[a]ll Spaniards have the duty to know it and the right to use it' (Cobarrubias 1989, p. 403). The official character of languages other than Castilian is circumscribed to the activities of the autonomous communities and hence carry no official status in relation to the central institutions such as the Government, Congress, the administration and the courts (Cobarrubias 1989, pp. 402–3; Milian-Massana 1992, p. 563).

The powers Catalonia exercises over its own affairs (for example, language policy) are articulated by the Statute of Autonomy of 1979, which itself rests on the constitutional provisions giving autonomous communities competence in such matters as culture and education. This Statute declares Catalan the national language of Catalonia and affirms its coofficial status with Castilian. What is pertinent here is that the Statute of Autonomy made possible the Language Normalization Laws (1983) designed to promote Catalan in public life. The law clearly states that its purpose is 'to overcome the current situation of linguistic inequality by stimulating the normalization of the use of the Catalan language throughout Catalan territory' (Cobarrubias 1989, p. 415). In other words, the legislation seeks to reverse language shift to Castilian and expand the use of Catalan.

In order to achieve this goal, the law guarantees every person in Catalonia the right to use Catalan orally or in writing in the public sphere, and to use it in their relations with local and autonomous levels of government. The educational system is to be organized in such a way that every pupil by the age of 14 should be bilingual. It also provides for language training for public servants in Catalan and local administrations. In short, the law encourages the penetration of the Catalan language in all spheres where it had previously been excluded or suppressed (Bastardas 1987, pp. 140–7).

An amendment to the Language Normalization Laws, adopted in December 1997, reaffirms the coofficial status of Catalan and Castilian, and maintains Catalan as the fundamental element of the Catalan national character. Moreover, it reinforces the use of the Catalan language in three sectors: Catalan is to be progressively imposed after a few years of schooling, made compulsory in the Catalan public service, and encouraged in local radio and television stations by the establishment of quotas (Rioux 1998). The relevance of pursuing language planning is supported by the census of 1996 that shows progress in the use of Catalan, most notably among the younger segments of society, which can be partly attributed to the provisions of the language policy pertaining to the teaching of Catalan in schools (Company 1998).

The twentieth anniversary of the Spanish constitution, while a momentous occasion, also served to remind Spaniards of its main objective which was to address the conflicts opposing a centralizing, authoritarian Spanish nationalism on one hand and Basque and Catalan nationalisms on the other. The regime of autonomies was precisely designed to end this polarization, recognize the diversity of languages and identities, and create a new division of powers (Solé 1998). These federalist practices remain a major improvement over any previous regime, for they serve to temper the conflict between Spanish and regional nationalisms. In the light of this objective, the Spanish language rights regime can be seen as involving a reciprocal recognition of the value of each level of government's language policy, which in turn restrains nationalistic impulses that might drive policies of unilingualism.

What concerns the central state and Catalonia alike, though from different perspectives, is reaching the right balance between the status of Castilian and that of Catalan, a concern which not only pertains to sociolinguistic forces at play, but also to the more general balance between the Spanish nation seen as an 'indissoluble unit' and the right of nationalities and other regions to autonomy. In Madrid, there is some concern the Language Normalization Laws will unduly disadvantage Castilian speakers. Granting communities such as Catalonia an autonomous status is seen as an historical concession, obviously a radical improvement over the situation that prevailed prior to 1978. But the constitutional framework must, in this view, ensure Castilian remains the common language of all Spaniards despite the status accorded to Catalan. In Barcelona, however, the formal equality between Castilian and Catalan is sometimes considered insufficient to reverse the language shift to Castilian and produce real equality between the two languages, thus the endorsement of greater powers over language planning by the Generalitat. Moreover, the gains made in the normalization of the Catalan language contrast with the need to use Castilian when communicating with the central institutions. The Catalan language is widely used, both in oral communications and in written documents, by institutions under the jurisdiction of the Generalitat, including those of the local administration. However, its use in oral and written communications between the central administration and Catalans in Catalonia itself remains limited.

Conclusion

While it is difficult to compare the language rights regimes of Canada and Spain, given these countries' vastly different historical and sociolinguistic realities, they do share a common challenge with regards to Quebec and Catalonia: the need to respect the linguistic identities of constituent units while nurturing solidarity between them.

Adding to the complexity of this challenge is the underlying issue of recognition. In Canada, the desire to contain centrifugal forces through nation-building policies is sometimes met in Quebec by a desire for recognition. Some Quebec nationalists argue that recognition of Canada's multinational character would provide Quebec with the constitutional space required to promote its national identity – of which the

French language is a key feature – within the Canadian federation. Failure to do so, they argue, only reinforces the desire of the Québécois to secede and form their own 'nation-state' (Gagnon 1996).

Similarly, underlying the challenge of implementing federalist principles in Spain's language policies is the debate over the recognition of historic national identities. The constitution embodies two different visions of Spain: that of a unitary state – with provisions for decentralization – and that of a state which seeks to recognize historic communities. Decentralization alone, nationalists argue, cannot be the guiding principle behind the state of autonomies since it does not offer a symbolic recognition of Catalonia's distinct national identity (Requejo 1998e). Catalonia and other historic communities wish to consolidate their special status within Spain through an asymmetrical distribution of symbolic recognitions and powers among the country's various regions.

The politics of recognition do not take us very far if they only account for the interests of constituent units, without consideration for the unity of the state or solidarity between citizens. Hence mutual recognition is more akin to federalist principles. What I have tried to show is that the language rights regimes of Canada and Spain inform us on the ability of partners in a multination state to follow such federalist principles. In the abstract, the political virtue of a federalist language rights regime is its implied reciprocal recognition of the value of each level of government's language policy. It is a virtue insofar as these language policies are expressions of different, but equally genuine visions of nationhood. Citizens of a nation-state possess a single national identity to which the government caters. Federal citizens of a multination state, conversely, often possess dual national identities to which two governments cater. Multination federalism implies the mutual recognition and celebration of multiple layers of national identities which often compete with each other. Similarly, a federalist language rights regime implies the mutual recognition and celebration of the coexistence of two language policies which may also be in competition. Such a regime's worth is not to be found in either of the policies taken separately; rather, it lies in its capacity to respond to equally valid claims of justice and conceptions of nationhood and to the ever-present danger of fragmentation in a multi-nation state.

The particular form a given federalist language rights regime will take depends on a variety of factors, as the Canadian and Spanish cases illustrate. In essence, it combines a regional policy that addresses the deep-rooted inequalities between national languages and a state-wide policy that addresses broader issues of unity and solidarity. A regime of such mixed objectives undoubtedly sustains tensions, for each pulls in a different direction. The coexistence, however tense, of two policies aiming at meeting these objectives prevents injustices and fragmentations that would result from the neglect of one objective. Such a language rights regime proceeds from constitutional and institutional arrangements allowing all national identities to flourish while preserving the stability and unity of the state.

Michael Burgess

Introduction: strains and tensions in multinational federations

Towards the end of 1787 John Jay defended the new constitution of the United States in the following way:

Providence has been pleased to give this one connected country to one united people – a people descended from the same ancestors, speaking the same language, professing the same religion, attached to the same principles of government, very similar in their manners and customs . . . who . . . have nobly established their general liberty and independence. (Jay No. 2. 1961 [1788], p. 38)

The long search for 'republican remedies' to the evident malaise of the Articles of Confederation led ultimately to federation, social pluralism and constitutionalism. But it is clear from a close analysis of the Federalist Papers that the enduring expression of the principles of constitutionalism which underpinned the new federal political system with such clarity and force were not constructed with a view to reconciling different nationalist demands. The constituent states of the young federation were not inhabited by people of different language, race and culture but by people of the same language, race and culture.

The first case in which the decision to create a modern federal rather than a unitary form of government was determined mainly by the desire successfully to accommodate distinct nationalist differences was the Canadian constitution established by the British North America Act (now the Constitution Act) in 1867. Here the division of the Province of Canada into two quite distinct cultural communities – one mainly English-speaking and the other predominantly French-speaking – along territorial lines was made primarily to resolve the political deadlock that had arisen between them. But it was chiefly at the insistence of French-Canadian political elites that the new Canadian union adopted the peculiarly federal form. They correctly perceived that only in a federal union would their distinct minority culture survive in a sea of anglophones.

Since then the older use of federal principles to unite people living in different political units, who nevertheless shared a common language and culture, has been increasingly complemented by the use of federation to unite people who seek the advantages of membership of a common political unit but differ markedly in descent, language and culture. Multinational federal states survived for over seventy years in the Soviet Union and Yugoslavia, while those in India, Malaysia and (arguably) Nigeria continue to demonstrate the feasibility of using federal principles and structures to reconcile the undoubted benefits that derive from economic and political size with the realities of cultural diversity. Furthermore the tendency towards 'unity in diversity' which inheres in the federal idea remains alive in both Spain and Belgium where novel political, economic and administrative institutions have been installed principally in order to facilitate what Daniel Elazar has called 'self-rule and shared rule' (Elazar 1987, p. 12). And we must not overlook the European Union (EU) where both federal and confederal principles and structures coexist simultaneously in a manner which defies attempts at precise definition.[1]

Canada, then, represents one among many successful multinational federations. Its 134-year history confirms it as one of the most enduring and resilient of modern federations. But Canada remains an experiment. And the dissolution of the Soviet Union and Yugoslavia in 1991 together with the break-up of Czechoslovakia in 1992 remind us that federations are not eternal. The proliferation of federations and federal systems since 1789 has been accompanied by some significant failures. There is no guarantee that the Canadian federation of 1867 vintage will necessarily survive intact into the twenty-first century. Canada today exhibits many serious strains and tensions, the most important of which is Canada–Quebec relations. In this chapter I wish to argue that the current crisis in Canada–Quebec relations is epiphenomenal. In other words it is symptomatic of a more general challenge to the contemporary 'nation-state' in the early twenty-first century. For the purposes of this chapter I intend to explore Canada–Quebec relations from a multidimensional comparative perspective in order to suggest how Canada might seek to accommodate a 'New Quebec' in a 'New Canada'.

The chapter is predicated upon the coexistence of conflict and consensus in Canada–Quebec relations and I will explore briefly the following five separate but interrelated dimensions to this complex relationship: language politics; the 'distinct society'; centre–periphery

---

[1] For a detailed discussion of these concepts, see Forsyth (1981) and Burgess (2000).

relations; asymmetrical federalism; and the structure and process of constitutional reform. Together these dimensions provide an interesting insight into the conceptual, institutional and policy worlds of Canada–Quebec relations. I will conclude with some brief comparative reflections on Canada–Quebec relations and the federal idea.

Five dimensions to Canada–Quebec relations

Language politics

The 1991 Census in Canada revealed that 82.8 per cent of the Quebec population were French-speaking while 10.9 per cent were English-speaking (Gibbins 1994, p. 105). According to Stéphane Dion, the main reason why nationalist feeling has fuelled a powerful secessionist movement in Quebec is the perceived fragility of the French language in North America. In what he calls the 'demolinguistic situation' in Quebec, Dion observed that the emigration of Quebec's anglophone population, together with a lower capacity of the province to attract and keep new immigrants and the spectacular drop in the French speakers' birthrate, decreased Quebec's demographic weight in the whole Canadian population from 29.0 per cent in 1941 to 24.8 per cent in 1986. As a result the share of MPs from Quebec in the House of Commons dropped from 28.0 per cent of the total in 1974 to 25.4 per cent in 1990. In short, 'Quebec is increasingly French, the rest of Canada is increasingly English, and the demographic weight of Quebec is decreasing within the federation' (Dion 1992, p. 89).

What do these statistics suggest about language policy in Canada and what has been its impact upon Canada–Quebec relations? The basic assumptions which guided federal language policy were first established in the early 1960s via the efforts of the Royal Commission on Bilingualism and Biculturalism (known widely as the B&B Commission) whose Report in 1967 presaged the Official Languages Act of 1969. The federal goal was simple: in order for Quebec francophones to see the federal government as 'their' government they had to see Canada as 'their' country. This logic meant strengthening the francophone presence outside Quebec. Federal language policy was therefore designed to recast the image and reality of Canada into that of a bilingual society. The bedrock of this policy was a dualist vision of Canada dominated by English- and French-speaking Canadians. Federal institutions and policies would have a resolutely bilingual face in the conscious attempt to strengthen the 'French fact' outside Quebec. This policy was enthusiastically championed by the Liberal Prime Minister, Pierre Trudeau, whose whole political strategy was driven by his determination to combat Quebec nationalism and separatism.

Dion has claimed that the achievements are 'undeniable' but if the statistics are clear their interpretation is not. For example, francophones represented 12.25 per cent of all employees in federal institutions in 1945 and 26.7 per cent in 1990 (Dion 1992, p. 94). But the number of Canadians over fifteen years old who claimed to be able to converse in French had risen from only 32.3 per cent in 1971 to 32.6 per cent in 1986. And official bilingualism in Canada had increased from 13.4 per cent in 1971 to a mere 16.2 per cent in 1986 (Joy 1992, pp. 11 and 122). In other words the dream of a truly bilingual Canadian society has simply not happened.

In a trenchant critique of Canada's federal language policy, Kenneth McRoberts has already exposed the fallacies which underpinned these assumptions:

They were not the only available bases for a language regime. The Commission made a conscious choice: to apply to the maximum the personality principle. Thus a particular conception of a language regime for Canada, one among several possibilities that might have been proposed . . . became entrenched as the 'official' conception. Apparently the choice was dictated as much by political considerations as by any appreciation of the specific patterns of language use in Canada. The policies the Commission derived from this principle have not accorded well with the linguistic reality of Canada. (McRoberts 1989, p. 142)

The linguistic reality of Canada is that in all of the provinces except Quebec and New Brunswick the official language minorities are both minuscule in numbers and precarious in condition (McRoberts 1989, p. 143). When seeking to regulate the contacts among language communities the state has two basic choices: the territorial principle and the personality principle. According to the territorial principle – which operates in Switzerland and Belgium – language rights vary from one part of the country to another. McRoberts summarized it succinctly:

The rights available to citizens are dependent upon the region in which they reside. Typically, territoriality is combined with unilingualism. Thus different languages enjoy monopolies within different regions. Equality in the status of language lies in the fact that each has at least some area in which it is guaranteed such a monopoly. (McRoberts 1989, p. 143)

Under the personality principle – which operates in South Africa, and, to some extent, in Finland – language rights adhere to individuals and can be exercised wherever they may happen to be in the country. But success depends upon the territorial distribution of the language communities and the proportion of the total population that can speak the official languages. In Finland wherever the Swedish minority accounts for at least 8 per cent of the population of a given commune, public services are provided in the two official languages: Swedish and Finnish. Hence bilingual districts exist but fluctuate according to changes in the population census. As Jean Laponce has observed, the Swedish territorial niche is not secure: first in its being bilingual rather than unilingual and, secondly, in having fluctuating boundaries affected by demography and population mobility (Laponce 1991, p. 178).

Ignoring its own evidence, the Canadian federal government rejected application of the territorial principle to Canada. Despite the fact that the linguistic reality of Canada was much closer to the Swiss and Belgian cases, the federal government patterned its language policies largely on those of Finland. In this context it is easy to understand why Bill 101 – which in 1977 established the Charter of the French Language in Quebec – was construed by many English-speaking Canadians as a blatant violation of both the spirit and the substance of federal language policy. In advocating provincial (territorial) French unilingualism it seemed to be divisive and confrontational. But as both McRoberts and Laponce have remarked, this territorial unilingualism provides a much more secure stronghold for minority language groups than bilingualism. For a minority language group which is also in an economically vulnerable position, formal bilingualism, based upon individual rights, is 'likely to only strengthen the pressures for assimilation to the dominant group' (McRoberts 1989, p. 165).

In summary, two paradoxes can be identified in Canada–Quebec relations as a direct result of federal language policy. First, it 'unintentionally aided Quebec nationalism throughout the 1970s and 1980s by challenging the Quebec government's legislative efforts to protect French in Quebec' (Dion 1992, p. 96). Second the demise of the 'noble dream' has not meant 'the demise of Canada'. On the contrary, the transition of Quebec to a 'preeminently francophone society' has given it a stronger sense of cultural security and economic self-confidence which have led until recently to a new reconciliation to 'the existing political order' (McRoberts 1989, p. 166).

The distinct society

The new reconciliation of Quebec to the Canadian federation as one result of the growing self-confidence that francophone people of Quebec have in their own abilities does not mean that they are now satisfied with the status quo. Indeed the result of the Quebec referendum of October 1995 by which the provincial Parti Québécois (PQ) government sought a mandate to negotiate a new Canada–Quebec partnership strongly suggests otherwise (Crête 1996, pp. 81–92). It merely implies that the basis now exists for a new *modus vivendi* in Canada–Quebec relations. Here we should underline the complexity of francophone public opinion regarding the future of Canada–Quebec relations. It is important to distinguish between the strong support for what Charles Taylor has called 'the politics of recognition' and the weaker support for separation from Canada. In other words, the majority of francophone Quebecers are still receptive to a variety of constitutional reform proposals which in a formal sense would recognise their continuing value to the federation. This recognition by the 'rest of Canada' (known in popular discourse as ROC) would be of immense symbolic significance to francophone Quebec, sending it a positive message of comity, respect and understanding. But, important as this is, it would also extend beyond symbolism. It would give Quebec the necessary constitutional capacity and space more effectively to determine itself within Canada. And, most important, it would be a public acknowledgement and an official endorsement by anglophone Canada that Quebec's aspirations and policy priorities were 'legitimate'. Indeed they would be construed by both ROC and Quebec as being part of what it means to be 'Canadian'.

In the light of events in Canada since the collapse of the Meech Lake Accord in June 1990, the National Referendum of October 1992 and the provincial Quebec Referendum of October 1995, it may seem strange to wish to resurrect the hotly disputed concept of the 'distinct society'.[2] However, recent developments in this regard suggest that it might still be brought back to life as a viable alternative to separation. The evidence of a *Financial Post*–Compas Inc. survey conducted after the September 1994 provincial election in Quebec identified a 'softness' of the sovereigntist vote which suggested that the hard-core separatists were a strong minority but the majority of PQ supporters were willing to change their minds about independence. Indeed 46 per cent of Quebec sovereigntists agreed that they would reject separation if the province was 'acknowledged as a distinct society and received more powers from Ottawa – the so-called Meech Lake option – in a new Canadian constitution'.[3] Since then the federal Liberal government of Jean Chrétien has managed to steer a resolution through Parliament in 1995 formally acknowledging Quebec as a 'distinct society', while the Calgary Declaration of 1997, in which the nine anglophone provincial premiers agreed to recognize Quebec's 'unique character' while reaffirming the equality of the ten provinces, suggests that there may still be some scope

[2] See Burgess (1996).
[3] *The Financial Post*, 1 October 1994, p. 9.

for further negotiations leading ultimately to the formal constitutional entrenchment of the 'distinct society'.

There is no space here to provide a detailed analysis of the evolution and conflicting interpretations of the 'distinct society' but we should note that the first official recognition of this embattled concept was proclaimed as part of the federal government's constitutional proposals entitled 'Shaping Canada's Future Together' which appeared in September 1991. In these proposals it was suggested that 'important elements from the Quebec Act (1774) at the time of Confederation' should be restored so that the French-speaking people of Quebec could reclaim 'the authority to preserve and promote their language and culture within the new federation'. With this aim in mind, it was deemed necessary formally to define the 'distinct society' which would 'include':

(a) a French-speaking majority
(b) a unique culture
(c) a civil law tradition[4]

The decision to define the 'distinct society' was fraught with obvious difficulties. The potential legal, political and ultimately constitutional implications were enormous. Of particular significance was the specific use of the word 'includes' in the definition. The Quebec government was especially concerned about a definition which might have been too restrictive. Since francophone Quebecers have always regarded themselves in practice as being part of a 'distinct society' in Canada, the attempt formally to define it meant stating the obvious. But constitutionalizing the obvious was not as simple and straightforward as it might initially have seemed. After all, to 'include' is also to 'exclude'. There was, then, a natural concern both in Quebec and ROC about how the concept would be defined. In the former, there was the fear of a definition which would be too narrow and confining while in the latter it was anxiety about privileged provincial status in Canada.

The rather weak and prosaic content of the 'distinct society' was carried over into the *Report of the Special Joint Committee on a Renewed Canada* (the Beaudoin–Dobbie Report) which was published in February 1992.[5] And the long journey in quest of legal and constitutional meaning appeared to reach its destination in the Charlottetown *Consensus Report* on the constitution in August 1992. Its popular rejection in

---

[4] *Shaping Canada's Future Together: Proposals* (Ottawa, 1991).
[5] I owe this point of information about the possible scope of the phrase to Professor Ronald L. Watts of the Institute of Intergovernmental Relations, Queen's University, Kingston, Ontario. For its reappearance in the Beaudoin–Dobbie Report of February 1992, see the *Report of the Special Joint Committee on a Renewed Canada* (Ottawa, 1992).

the subsequent National Referendum of October 1992 seemed to spell the end of the 'distinct society' concept as a viable political objective, especially when 55.4 per cent of Quebecers also opposed the Charlotte-town Accord (Burgess 1993, p. 378). However, the concept may still have some relevance and resonance for the future of Canada–Quebec relations for two main reasons. First, it still represents a real alternative *conception* to the new post-Charter Canada of individual rights. Since Quebec's own sense of itself – its collective identity – cannot fit easily into the 'New Canada', the 'distinct society' can be construed in dynamic terms as the means whereby the province can create the space more freely to evolve and to define itself. This is what Christian Dufour meant when he warned that Quebec must avoid prematurely defining 'what it would become later' (Dufour 1990, p. 155).

The second reason for the continuing relevance of the concept to Canada–Quebec relations is power. The 'distinct society' is a power concept which is as closely linked to economic concerns as it is to cultural concerns in Quebec. Today the apparatus of the provincial state is no longer the sole *instrument of* development for Quebec society and economy. The emergence of a self-confident, outward-looking franco-phone bourgeoisie, deriving its power and strength largely from the private sector, has come to represent the 'New Quebec'. Quebec entrepreneurs remain sensitive to any real weakening of the provincial government's powers in Canada but they have come to regard the 'distinct society' as the vehicle of economic expansion. Dufour's notion of the 'distinct society' as 'intrinsically French with an English com-ponent' is therefore something which encompasses the whole pattern of Quebec society. It belongs to Quebec and is congruent with the economic and social realities of Quebec (Dufour 1990, p. 160). Whether or not the result of the Quebec Referendum of 1995 has now effectively rendered the 'distinct society' redundant to the people of Quebec remains a difficult question to answer. It may be that Canada–Quebec relations in the early twenty-first century have reached the point where a new kind of partnership going beyond conventional constitutional reform is required. Much of this depends upon the result of the next provincial election. Meanwhile an Angus Reid opinion poll in December 1997 recorded some surprising results: 86 per cent of those questioned said that they were 'tired of all the talk about referendums and the constitution' while only 36 per cent said they would be in favour of another sovereignty referendum should the PQ be reelected for a second consecutive term of office.[6] This dimension to Canada–Quebec rela-

---

[6] *The Financial Times*, 10 December 1997, p. 3.

tions – the 'distinct society' – is not, however, unique in the contemporary world of multinational federations. Both Malaysia and India are multinational federations where just such an asymmetrical relationship serves successfully to accommodate difference. The politics of recognition in the federal constitution of Malaysia provides a striking example of how this can work. Based upon the original constitution of the Federation of Malaya in 1957, the subsequent Malaysian federal constitution, which included the eleven Malay states and the two Borneo states of Sabah and Sarawak, was introduced in 1963. Since then both Sabah and Sarawak have enjoyed the equivalent of being 'distinct societies' with a relatively wide measure of autonomy within the federation. In India, too, the state of Jammu and Kashmir – one of twenty-six constituent units in the federation – has managed to preserve and promote its distinct cultural identity in the largest liberal democratic federation in the world. Article 370 of the constitution of India (1950) recognized the special status of Jammu and Kashmir, granting it an autonomy in the federation which distinguished it from every other state in the union.[7] These examples should not be exaggerated in their importance, especially given the countervailing centralized features evident in both of these federations, but their very incorporation in the respective constitutions is of more than just symbolic significance. In addition, it should not go unnoticed that the new German *Land* constitution of the Free State of Sachsen – ratified in May 1992 – has formally acknowledged the preservation and development of the 'language, culture and tradition' of the German-Sorben community, thus entrenching this identity in constitutional law.[8]

One conclusion to be drawn from this brief survey of the 'distinct society' in Quebec is that it clearly does not represent a problem which is peculiar to Canada. Indeed its existence in other federations suggests that it may still be a small price to pay for the accommodation of difference.

Centre–periphery relations

Perception is often more important than reality in politics. The reality of Quebec's cultural and economic concerns in Canada is not widely recognized throughout ROC. On the contrary, ROC shares a strong perception of the province as anything but a disadvantaged partner in the

[7] On Malaysia, see Zakaria (1987) and Means (1991). On India, see Hardgrave and Kochanek (1986).

[8] Article 6 (1), *Verfassung des Freistaates Sachsen, vom 27 Mai 1992* (Dresden, 1992). I wish to acknowledge the help of Franz Gress in obtaining this document.

federation. It is widely perceived as having the most dynamic provincial economy in Canada and as being part of the central Canadian economic heartland. And it is precisely this largely anglophone perception of Quebec which continues to nurture the image of the so-called 'spoiled child' of Confederation, always complaining and never satisfied with its lot. Let us look a little closer at this particular perception of Quebec.

It is certainly true for those Canadians who live in the Atlantic and Western provinces that both Ontario and Quebec are tantamount to one dominant economic region, namely, 'Central Canada'. In the introduction to his *Canada and the Burden of Unity*, a classic collection of essays first published in 1977, David Jay Bercuson explained this perception:

The power of Quebec votes and the necessity of the federal government to pay as much heed to Quebec as it does to Ontario reveals the existence of one region – Central Canada – with common characteristics. It is industrialised, populous, part of the St. Lawrence heartland, the holder of an absolute majority of seats in the House of Commons, and the major beneficiary of national economic, cultural and social policies . . . Central Canadian representation at Ottawa forces federal governments to identify with Ontario and Quebec first and foremost . . . The result has been predictable. Federal policies have served the interests of Central Canada. (Bercuson 1977, pp. 2–3)

This attack upon the 'Laurentian thesis' and the 'National Policy' was typical of many of those who wrote from the standpoint of Canada's peripheries and it reflected a particular school of Canadian history epitomized by W. L. Morton who in 1946 identified 'three decisive fields of Canadian historical interpretation: the French survival; the dominance of Ontario; and the subordination of the West' (Morton 1979, p. 44). In short, both Quebec and Ontario have together come to be regarded as the metropolitan economy centred on Toronto and Montreal.

This widespread perception in ROC that Quebec is much stronger in economic terms than it would have us believe is a classic example of the kind of envy, mistrust and suspicion which has come to characterize contemporary Canada–Quebec relations. But the perception of economic strength is hard to square with the challenging political economy analysis of Alain Gagnon and Mary Beth Montcalm whose main thesis is that the overall impact on Quebec of a series of international macroeconomic trends in the 1980s has been economic peripheralization (Gagnon and Montcalm 1990). The impact of 'economic internationalization was largely experienced as economic continentalization' but the increasing integration of Canada's economy with that of the United States was itself only part of an even larger process of economic change. Alongside postwar economic continentalization another significant development has occurred, namely, the westward shift of the American economy. Gagnon and Montcalm point to the core of the North American economy shifting, especially since the 1960s, from the traditional areas of the North-East and Upper Midwest to the South and the West of the United States. In other words, economic internationalization not only integrated the Canadian and American economies but it also led to the restructuring of North American capitalism itself.

One consequence of this economic continentalism has been the marginalization and peripheralization of the Quebec economy. The evidence for this was overwhelming. It was reflected in the consolidation of Toronto and Southern Ontario as the primary focus of financial and industrial activity and in the corresponding decline in Montreal's position as a major Canadian business metropolis. And, according to Gagnon and Montcalm, it was also illustrated by long-term trends in manufacturing in Quebec and in investment patterns which between 1976 and 1982 indicated an annual decline of about 3 per cent compared to an annual increase of about 2.5 per cent in Canada as a whole (Gagnon and Montcalm 1990, p. 6).

The dimension of centre–periphery relations in federations is clearly a highly contestable analytical perspective which yields many different interpretations about economic power resources. Among contemporary federations perhaps Belgium and Germany rank as the most relevant comparative examples, although Spain might also be included as a federation in almost everything but its name. The traditional north–south economic divide in Germany, which in the 1980s had prompted several public discussions about fiscal equalization and constitutional reform, was completely overshadowed in 1990 by German unification and the economic difficulties of integrating five new, extremely poor, eastern *Länder* in the federation. As a result the established economic dominance of Bavaria and Baden-Württemberg has been reinforced in some respects but seriously attenuated in other ways. The overall significance is that they are now just two constituent units in the German national political economy of sixteen constituent *Länder* economies.

Belgium is closer to the Canadian case. The major Flemish–French linguistic cleavage corresponds to a predominantly north–south territorial division of the country and has been recently reinforced by significant economic differences. The economic hegemony of French-speaking Wallonia in nineteenth-century Belgium has been completely reversed since the end of the Second World War. Today the industrial decay of Wallonia in the south stands in stark contrast to the thriving service sector prosperity of Flemish-speaking Flanders in the north which has been the major beneficiary of postwar economic restructuring in Belgium. Contrary to the expectations of many constitutional observers, Belgium succeeded in 1993 in reconstructing itself into a federal state *sui generis*.[9] In Spain the gradual evolution of the seventeen Autonomous Communities toward a reconstituted 'quasi-federal' state of 'imperfect federalism' based upon 'multiple ethnoterritorial concurrence' also highlights the significance of centre–periphery relations (Moreno 1994, pp. 162–93). The political salience of 'peripheral nationalism' and 'contemporary regionalism' have emerged in many cases as 'a consequence of state economic inequality and centre–periphery imbalances' (Moreno 1994, p. 177).

Clearly the centre–periphery approach to the study of federations can be both revealing and misleading. We have to treat it very carefully. It presupposes a basic agreement about precisely where the centre lies in a state and indeed how many so-called 'centres' exist. There may conceivably be more than just one centre. The example of Belgium – where the economic centre currently lies in north-west Flanders – demonstrates that centres move and change, and that public perceptions of centre–periphery relations may be over-simplified. Often they are impressionistic, merely reflecting a narrow view from one particular standpoint within the state. The case of Spain is a useful example of just how complex these relationships can be. The political and cultural resistance of the Basque and Catalan regions – among the strongest manufacturing centres of Spain – interacted in a complex manner with economic grievances arising from Madrid's control over key economic instruments of central government (Agranoff 1994, pp. 61–89).

From this perspective, then, Quebec–ROC relations might be seen in a new light. Quebec certainly has a strong, dynamic provincial economy but, as Gagnon and Montcalm have remarked, it is in many respects not as strong as it looks. This helps to explain why Quebec supported the Free Trade Agreement with the United States in 1989 and subsequently its extension to the North American Free Trade Association (NAFTA) in 1994. In summary, the notion of Quebec as an integral part of the Canadian economic heartland has had an overall divisive impact upon Canada–Quebec relations.

Asymmetrical federalism

In 1965 an article written by Charles Tarlton and entitled 'Symmetry and Asymmetry as Elements of Federalism: A Theoretical Speculation' was published in *The Journal of Politics*. Thirty years later it had acquired an unexpected significance for those scholars who study federalism and

[9] On Belgium, see Witte (1992), Peeters (1994) and Fitzmaurice (1996).

federation (Burgess and Gagnon 1993; De Villiers 1994). Today it has a new conceptual relevance, especially in Canada–Quebec relations where the phrase 'asymmetrical federalism' has already entered the language and discourse of constitutional reform and public policy making.

Tarlton defined the concept of asymmetry as expressing the extent to which component states in a federation do not share in the conditions and concerns common to the federal system as a whole. The ideal asymmetrical federal system would be one 'composed of political units corresponding to differences of interest, character and make-up that exist within the whole society'. The diversities in 'the larger society find political expression through local governments possessed of varying degrees of autonomy and power'. In short, the political institutions and policy processes correspond to 'the real social "federalism" beneath them'. In summary, in the model asymmetrical federal system 'each component unit would have about it a unique feature or set of features which would separate in important ways its interests from those of any other state or the system considered as a whole'. Indeed, clear lines of division would be necessary and jealously guarded insofar as these unique interests were concerned' (Tarlton 1965, p. 869).

It is important to distinguish asymmetrical federalism from the conditions which give rise to it. In other words, the empirical conditions of social diversity – language, religion, class structures, regionalized national economies, demographic characteristics, land-tenure systems, legal identities and cultural/ideological differences – must be distinguished from the constitutional and political relations which grow out of them. Purely factual differences which exist in some form or other in every state are not sufficient to sustain asymmetrical federalism. The socioeconomic conditions must be politically salient. Clearly in Canada–Quebec relations these circumstances are well-established. Let us look a little closer at them.

We have already noted the historical landmarks of Quebec's specificity in Canada. When the Constitution Act established the federal political system in 1867, Quebec entered the new union as a founding people with a firm quest: to preserve and promote their own cultural identity. Accordingly, their educational, linguistic and religious interests were appropriately incorporated in the new constitution, giving it strong asymmetrical features from the outset. This resolute sense of difference was later reaffirmed in 1965 in federal public policy practice with the Quebec Pension Plan, which effectively established a kind of *de facto* asymmetrical federalism in the administrative field, and it was also reflected in the Official Languages Act of 1969 which confirmed the linguistic duality of federal Canada, leaving Quebec as the sole officially unilingual francophone province. The only official bilingual province remains New Brunswick. David Milne has already outlined the various types of asymmetrical relationships that exist in Canada; the legal, constitutional and public policy practices reveal a quite remarkable array of Canadian responses to difference (Milne 1991, pp. 285–307).

The asymmetrical features of Canada briefly outlined above lead us from the empirical to the prescriptive. Today so-called 'asymmetrical federalism' in Canada has acquired a quite strong normative, prescriptive quality which possesses significant theoretical and philosophical implications (see Gagnon, this volume). I have identified three prescriptive elements in this public debate:

a) Charles Taylor's two conceptions of 'rights liberalism', one based upon procedural (individual) liberalism which is inhospitable to difference and the other rooted in substantive (collective) liberalism which recognizes the right to be different and the politics of cultural survival. These two models of liberalism have collided in Canada. Taylor's preference is for an asymmetrical federalism which formally recognizes difference and which he has called 'deep diversity' (see Taylor 1991a, pp. 75–6; also 1991b, 1992a, 1993a).

b) Alan Cairns's 'Two Quebec Asymmetries – the Charter and Jurisdiction'. Construed in terms of three competing equalities – of provinces, of citizens and of two rival national communities – Cairns exposes both the benefits and the costs of adopting asymmetrical federalism in Canada's own Charter of Rights and Freedoms and in the sphere of the division of powers between Ottawa and Quebec, and, indeed, between Quebec and ROC (Cairns 1991, pp. 77–100).

c) David Milne's 'Concurrency with Provincial Paramountcy' (CPP). This prescription is an attempt to break out of the sterile circular 'equality–asymmetry' dilemma. It respects the equality of provinces in a formal sense but makes asymmetry inescapable by providing each province with rights to opt out of national standards or programmes. It does not formalize inequality nor does it grant special status to an individual province. Yet CPP has in principle the real possibility of furnishing Quebec with quite extensive additional jurisdictional powers which could be used to define and express its *de facto* distinctiveness within Canada. According to Milne, it could lead to a 'rather startling practical asymmetry' (Milne 1991, p. 303).

Each of these three aspects of asymmetrical federalism in Canada has significant theoretical and philosophical implications, not least in the field of 'asymmetrical citizenship'. But Canada is not the only federation to have adopted asymmetrical federalism as a means primarily of accommodating difference and buttressing the legitimacy of the state.

Significant asymmetries can also be detected in both federal and non-federal states. Belgium, Germany, the United States, Switzerland, India and Malaysia are federations where these procedures and mechanisms have become part of the political culture. Similarly in Spain and in the new South Africa – which are not federations but states with strong federal elements – there are evolving asymmetrical practices which have been designed to constitutionalize the politics of difference. Even in the United Kingdom, a country which is generally held to be the archetype of unitary government, there are significant asymmetrical 'federal' practices which deviate sharply from the theory of the unitary state (see Burgess 1995).

Asymmetrical federalism, then, has characterized Canada–Quebec relations from the very creation of the federation. And this is one of the strangest paradoxes of Canada–Quebec relations: the historical recognition of Quebec's specificity has never been associated with privileged status until quite recently. It is only in the years since the Constitution Act (1982) that the principle and practice of asymmetrical relations have collided directly with the insistence of ROC upon so-called 'provincial equality'. This is an indication of the size of the gulf which now exists between Quebec and ROC; the constitutional and political environment since the collapse of the Meech Lake Accord in 1990 has not been conducive to a new consensus on the future of Canada–Quebec constitutional relations.

The structure and process of constitutional reform

In many ways it is true to claim that the constitutional crisis of the early 1990s has been outstripped by recent events. The election of the PQ in Quebec in 1994 and its reelection in 1998 – a government committed to separation from Canada – appears to have made further attempts at constitutional reform at least temporarily redundant. There appears to be no middle ground between the constitutional status quo and Quebec separation. Both Quebec and ROC have been taking stock of their political relations since the provincial referendum of 1995. The narrowness of the majority opposed to taking one step further in the direction of separation sent shock waves rippling throughout ROC. But the prolonged polarization of Canada along francophone and anglophone lines in the 1990s shows no sign of abating. Most anglophone publics in ROC are either bored with the long-running constitutional saga or simply refuse to acknowledge francophone concerns, while the francophone majority in Quebec maintains a stalwart defence of their culture as a 'distinct society'. Both parties seem unmoved and immovable.

The Canada–Quebec impasse seems impossible to overcome. An uneasy peace hangs over the public debate about constitutional reform. What, then, is to be done? Certainly Canadians will have to adjust to their new constitutional culture which suggests that future reform cannot be achieved by political elites making deals behind closed doors. This was perhaps the major lesson that Canadian elites learned after the failure of the Meech Lake Accord. There is now a host of new actors – aboriginal peoples, ethnic and linguistic minorities, and women's groups – demanding the right to be at the table of further constitutional negotiations which affect their futures. Whether or not this will enhance the quality of participatory democracy in Canada remains a subject of considerable interest and speculation for political scientists.[10] But what is also of importance in these far-reaching political developments is the impact that they have had upon Quebec's political elites and provincial mass publics. In other words, just as federal Canada's 'process' of constitutional reform has changed so this must not be allowed to overshadow the implications it has had for the provinces. Already in British Columbia and Alberta the determination to utilize provincial referendums to decide future constitutional reform issues and packages suggests more than a short-term reflex reaction to events.

The question of the process and structure of constitutional reform in federations has always aroused considerable passions, fears and anxieties among citizens throughout such unions. This is in the very nature of federations. They are a particular type of state which is founded upon both moral and formal recognition of diversity. Precisely because they are 'federal' states whose original purpose is to structure salient identities and accommodate significant differences, rather than to ignore, suppress and suffocate them, they are subject to a perpetual debate about governance. They are *ipso facto* subject to intensive scrutiny from the variety of publics that they themselves institutionalize. When major constitutional reform is contemplated it is inevitable that a variety of vested interests and organized identities reflecting this 'federality' will mobilize to engage the public debate. And the process of constitutional reform in federations is necessarily a longwinded affair as the multifarious interests and identities jostle for positions and weave in their own competing visions of the future.

In recent years Belgium, Germany and the European Union have each struggled to achieve new constitutional accommodations. Even the

---

[10] For a critique of this subject, see Brooks (1994).

British have moved in this direction with the construction of an elected Welsh Assembly and an elected Scottish Parliament in 1999. The new Labour government is also pledged *inter alia* to pursue House of Lords reform, electoral reform and the administrative reorganization of local government, and in 2000 it fulfilled its pledge for the democratization of the City of London with the mayoral election. And like Canada, Belgium's recent constitutional debate has endured for more than a quarter of a century, culminating in 1993 in a new federation, while even Germany's new federal constitution took four years to be ratified from the moment the Berlin Wall collapsed. In the EU the Single European Act (SEA) of 1987, the Maastricht Treaty on European Union (TEU), ratified in 1993, and the Treaty of Amsterdam (TA), ratified in 1999, each represent incremental steps on the path toward constructing a European constitution. In each of these cases of constitutional reform there are competing interests and divergent visions of the future. The Canadian problem, once again, is not peculiar to Canada.

Nonetheless the constitutional conundrum in Canada is one that is extremely difficult to resolve. Even if it was possible to find some common ground on the diagnosis of the dilemma, there remains the problem of achieving a consensus on the remedy. Alan Cairns has already pinpointed the contradiction between federalism and the Charter of Rights and Freedoms which makes it very difficult to envisage movement in any direction which might enable the practitioners to overcome the current Quebec–ROC impasse:

The contrast of each with the other highlights their distinctive assumptions, as well as the magnitude of the task confronting those who would build bridges between them. They structure the Canadian identity in different ways, and thus in their constitutional coexistence they send contradictory answers to the citizen's query, 'Who am I?' . . . The community message of the Charter contradicts the community message of the amending formula . . . Succinctly, the Charter states what the amending formula denies, that 'federalism is not enough' – that Canadians are more than a federal people. (Cairns 1992, pp. 7–8)

Put simply, Canadians suffer from two competing visions of sovereignty: that invested in the people by the Charter and supported by the courts over and above Parliament and the provinces versus that rooted in the so-called 'equality of the provinces' reaffirmed by the amending formula and derived from parliamentary supremacy.

Conclusion: competing national visions

In this chapter I have tried to examine Canada–Quebec relations according to five distinct but overlapping dimensions in order to furnish the basis for a number of comparative perspectives. The comparative reflections underline the special difficulties that multinational federations in particular face when attempting to come to terms with new strains and tensions within the state which are based upon competing national visions. Often, as in the case of Canada, they are not challenges to the state which are based upon new cleavage structures. Rather, they are threats based upon the revitalization and intensification of old cleavage patterns. But these can be just as dangerous to the integrity of the state, as the examples of Yugoslavia, Czechoslovakia and the Soviet Union amply testify.

This chapter suggests that competing national visions can be successfully accommodated within the constitutional structure of a single state provided that there is a political and constitutional culture which enables citizens to determine themselves both as individual and collective identities. Constitutional reform is constitution building and this means reshaping the state in order to maintain the state. It means making room – finding space – for new (or renewed) organized interests and identities. It means, in short, rethinking the very bases of the legitimacy of the state. In Canada the fundamental polarization of society between predominantly francophone Quebec and overwhelmingly anglophone ROC is not the only important cleavage but it is the most dangerous and divisive one. Only if a bridge, or bridges, can be built between these competing conceptions of political community can Canada–Quebec relations achieve a new *modus vivendi* within the existing federation.

Institutional and policy responses, then, can combine to bridge the impasse but only if the political environment will allow it. If the context of the impasse can be changed it might be possible to change the nature and meaning of the impasse itself. But this would require enormous political imagination and sensitivity. In a particular sense Quebec has nothing new to learn; it is ROC which must be constantly reminded that Canadian history includes a francophone Quebec that remains integral to Canada just as Quebec history includes an anglophone contribution which helped to define what Quebec is today. In Charles Taylor's words, Quebec is 'an entity whose survival and flourishing was one of the main purposes of Canada as a political society'. What has been missing is 'the clear recognition that this was part of our purpose as a federation' (Taylor 1991b, pp. 64–5).

Modes of reconciliation and conflict management

Part III examines the normative and institutional dimensions of modes of reconciliation and conflict management in multinational democracies. In chapter 11, Allen Patten explores two claims made by proponents of the liberal idea of citizenship: (1) that a shared national identity is one of the most important conditions of citizenship (2) that citizens of a state should have a single national identity. Patten's primary concern is whether nation-building projects within multinational societies represent a threat to this liberal ideal of citizenship. Although Patten concludes that nation-building and national-independence projects do contradict the liberal idea of citizenship by conflicting with 'the right to equal recognition of identity in the public sphere', he does point to an alternative way in which the demands of nationalist movements can be accommodated without compromising liberal principles of citizenship. Patten makes the case that a right to equal recognition of identity in the public sphere is one of the entitlements that should be recognized in a liberal theory of citizenship. This principle of equal recognition can conflict with nation-building and national-independence projects because such projects may not provide equal recognition of identity in the public sphere of the new state. From this principle of equal recognition, Patten formulates a new liberal theory of citizenship that is more fitting for the demands of a multinational society than the instrumental nationalist theory of citizenship articulated by classical liberals such as J. S. Mill. This new theory of citizenship, which he labels 'multinational identity', is grounded in a shared commitment to respect for both the civil, political and social rights usually associated with liberal citizenship, and the right to equal recognition in the public sphere.

In chapter 12, 'Nationality in Divided Societies', David Miller examines the liberal objection that the right of self-government for national groups will only promote conflict as the world is so culturally heterogeneous. Miller argues that this objection to self-determination rests on a rather superficial understanding of cultural and ethnic differences. In order to provide a better understanding of demands for self-government, Miller introduces three categories of social division: ethnic cleavages, rival nationalities and nested nationalities. Focusing specifically on the category of nested nationalities, Miller examines how a society can successfully accommodate the demands of a nation through the case of Scotland and the UK. The type of conflict specific to societies with nested nationalities such as the UK is the threat that the dominant group poses to the identity of the minority nation. In the case of Britain, this phenomenon is manifest in the fact that Scots see a clear distinction between Scottish, English and British identities, whereas the English treat the English and British identities as synonymous. As such, Miller proposes that the dominant group recognize the separateness of the nested nationalities, and provide asymmetrical political arrangements for minority nations while continuing to affirm the national identity at the level of the state as a whole.

In chapter 13, 'The Moral Foundation of Asymmetrical Federalism', Alain Gagnon shifts the discussion away from questions about stability in multinational society towards questions of justice. While Gagnon's argument draws on the literatures of political theory and comparative politics, he is quick to warn us against some of the assumptions that each of these literatures makes regarding multinational societies. With respect to comparative politics, Gagnon argues that there is a tendency to assume that societies are homogeneous and individuals from a given political community share the same language, culture and ethnicity. As for political theory, there is a clear bias towards liberalism in the literature which leaves many political theorists unable to account for the issues of deep difference that are inherent to multinational societies. Gagnon compares three normative justifications of asymmetrical federalism (a communitarian, a refined classical liberal and one based on the principle of deliberative democracy) and concludes that the demand for and opposition to asymmetrical federalism is not merely a justification for a power grab, but rather it is grounded in fundamentally different conceptions of the good. Normative arguments in favour of asymmetrical federalism answer claims that the fundamental good in a society is democratic citizenship. In particular, advocates of asymmetrical federalism for Canada (especially those influenced by communitarianism and deliberative democracy) argue that asymmetrical federalism reinforces the country's democratic system by encouraging public participation in the decision-making process, accommodating differences between political communities and buttressing the democratic legitimacy of the federal state. On the other hand, supporters of the territorial vision of federalism (typically classical liberals) maintain that traditional notions of national citizenship may be undermined. Through an examination of the history of relations between the government of Quebec and the government of Canada, Gagnon concludes that contrary to the assumptions of liberals, opposition to minority rights has led to unstable political situations in several multinational federal settings, and that – again contrary to liberal tenets – the call made for asymmetrical federalism by most Québécois has not yet led to a large disaffection for the Rest of Canada.

In the concluding chapter, Richard Simeon and Daniel-Patrick Conway provide an overview of the themes of this volume by answering the question: 'How effective is federalism as an institutional framework for managing conflicts between ethnic groups?' Locating federalism as a middle ground between secession and assimilation, Simeon and Patrick-Conway are interested in determining under what conditions federalism is a stable solution to ethnic conflict and when federalism is merely a stage on the road to either independence or centralization. The authors focus on Canada, Belgium, Spain and the United Kingdom, as they are all multinational federations with ethnic groups that are territorially concentrated. Because there are so many varieties of federalism, and so many different cultural situations in which a federal system could be implemented, Simeon and Conway refrain from making broad generalizations about the effectiveness of federalism in multinational societies. As a result of their survey of different federal systems, the authors conclude that the compartmentalized federalism of Canada's system of government is more likely to enhance conflict than the interdependent federalism of countries such as Germany. Furthermore, Simeon and Conway conclude that federalism alone is not enough to avoid conflict in multinational societies. They argue that federalism must be complemented with societal and institutional processes that promote overarching identities and values for the whole society that parallel the identities and values of specific ethnic groups. Electoral systems can also affect ethnic relations by exaggerating linguistic and regional differences and providing politicians with incentives to use exclusionary electoral strategies. Finally, Simeon and Conway argue that Charters of Rights can provide overarching common values for a society and offer protection for 'minorities within minorities', thereby avoiding calls for 'partition' by subnational groups.

11   Liberal citizenship in multinational societies[1]

Alan Patten

1   Instrumental nationalism

One point of consensus emerging from the liberal–communitarian debate is that the success of free institutions depends crucially on the degree to which citizens are animated by certain dispositions and solidarities (Sandel 1984; Taylor 1989; Dworkin 1989; Macedo 1990; Galston 1991; Rawls 1993; Kymlicka and Norman 1994). Although liberals affirm and celebrate the rights of individuals to form, pursue and revise their own ends and life-plans, they cannot be indifferent to whether those individuals recognize and internalize certain obligations, responsibilities and virtues. For free institutions to operate successfully, citizens need, for instance, to exercise self-restraint and toleration. Citizens must also exemplify the virtue of 'reasonableness': they must show a willingness to settle political disagreements by appeal to reasons that are acceptable to others rather than through recourse to coercion (Macedo 1990; Rawls 1993; Kymlicka and Norman 1994). Free institutions depend, in addition, on the willingness of citizens to accept certain burdens and sacrifices for the sake of the common good. They must be willing to vote, to maintain a minimal degree of knowledge about current events, and to speak out and demonstrate against injustice. They must even be prepared, in extreme circumstances, to risk their lives to preserve the institutions of their freedom.[2]

These points are now widely recognized by liberals and communitarians alike. Much less agreement has been forthcoming about what

---

[1] Earlier versions of this chapter were delivered at the Department of Sociology, McGill University, the North Hatley, Quebec Conference on 'Liberal Justice and Political Stability in Multinational Societies', the Université de Montréal Conference on 'Nationality, Citizenship, and Solidarity', the University of Exeter Political Theory Workshop, and the Nuffield College Political Theory Workshop. Many thanks to the participants in all of these events for their comments and criticisms. Thanks also to FCAR and SSHRC for research funding helping me to complete this chapter.
[2] For a fuller account of the 'liberal virtues', see Macedo (1990), Galston (1991) and Kymlicka and Norman (1994).

conditions must be in place for the different motivations and solidarities required in a successful liberal polity to be generated and sustained. This issue is of great theoretical and practical concern for liberals. It is of theoretical concern because liberals may need to abandon some of their commitments in order to accommodate the need to foster and sustain the required citizen dispositions. Critics of some strands of liberal thought have argued, for instance, that recognizing the importance of citizen dispositions would require liberals to rethink their understanding of liberty and to jettison the doctrines of neutrality and the primacy of rights (Sandel 1984; Taylor 1989; Skinner 1986 and 1992).[3] The problem of how to generate and sustain the motivations and solidarities presupposed by a free society is of great practical concern to liberals because few, if any, modern societies approach anything like the full liberal ideal of a free and just society. A better understanding of how effective citizen dispositions are developed and maintained may help efforts to approach that ideal.

My aim in this chapter is to explore, in the context of the liberal idea of citizenship, one influential account of the conditions that must be in place for strong and reliable citizen dispositions to be generated and sustained. The account I have in mind makes two central claims. The first is that a shared national identity is one of the most important of these conditions. The second claim draws on the first: given the importance of a shared national identity, efforts should be made politically to ensure that the citizens of the state share a single national identity. This can be engineered either through a nation-building project – an attempt to diffuse and consolidate a single national identity on the territory of the state – or a national-independence project – an attempt by a group bound by a single national identity but forming part of a multinational state to obtain its own state.

An early formulation of this instrumental case for nationalism can be found, for instance, in Rousseau's essay *The Government of Poland*. Rousseau argues that, in order to preserve their liberties against threats from Russia, the Poles need to be 'formed *nationally*, by distinctive legislation' (Rousseau [1782] 1972, p. 11; emphasis in original). 'Give a different bent to the passions of the Poles', he advises:

in doing so, you will shape their minds and hearts in a national pattern that will set them apart from other peoples, that will keep them from being absorbed by other peoples, or finding contentment among them, or allying themselves with them. (p. 12)

---

[3] For a response to some of these arguments, see Patten (1996).

Rousseau suggests that this nation-building project should be pursued in a number of ways. The state should attempt to 'maintain or revive . . . ancient customs and introduce new ones that will also be purely Polish' and it should encourage the 'creation of games, festivities, and ceremonials' of a Polish character (p. 14). Public officials should wear distinctively Polish clothing (p. 14), and an education system, staffed by Polish rather than foreign teachers, should be used to 'shape the souls of the citizens in a national pattern' (pp. 19–20). He goes so far as to suggest that the Polish people be imbued with 'an instinctive distaste for mingling with the peoples of other countries' (p. 14).

Whereas Rousseau's essay is one of the most important early statements of the instrumental case for nation-building, John Stuart Mill's chapter on nationality in *Considerations on Representative Government* offers an influential formulation of the instrumental argument for national independence movements (Mill [1861] 1991, ch. 16). The presence of two or more nationalities within the state, he argues, leads to 'mutual antipathies', fear of injuries from the other groups, and a situation in which 'none feel that they can rely on the others for fidelity in a joint resistance' (p. 429). Mill voices a particular worry about the behaviour of the military in multinational societies:

soldiers to whose feelings half or three-fourths of the subjects of the same government are foreigners, will have no more scruple in mowing them down, and no more desire to ask the reason why, than they would have in doing the same thing against declared enemies. (p. 429)

On the basis of these and other considerations, Mill concludes that 'free institutions are next to impossible in a country made up of different nationalities' and thus that 'it is in general a necessary condition of free institutions, that the boundaries of government should coincide in the main with those of nationalities' (pp. 428, 430).

At first glance, it is not at all clear what liberals should make of arguments of this kind.[4] Although many postwar liberals were extremely hostile to nationalism, they are also committed to the ideal of a free society. If willing the end entails willing the necessary means, then one view would be that liberals have no choice but to endorse the instrumental argument in favour of nation-building and/or national-independence projects (assuming its empirical assumptions are correct). This does not, of course, imply that liberals must endorse all real-world cases of nationalism, since some nationalisms are manifestly not instrumental to the maintenance of free institutions. But it might require that they recognize that some relatively benign form of nation-

---

[4] More recent statements of the instrumental nationalist argument can be found in Miller (1995, pp. 90–7, 139–40), and Barry (1989).

alism is an essential prerequisite for realizing liberal values (Taylor 1989, p. 175).

As I see it, instrumental nationalism raises two important questions, which I want to focus on in the remainder of this chapter. The first is whether, from the point of view of the liberal idea of citizenship, there are any costs imposed by nation-building and national-independence projects. And the second is whether, if there are such costs, the liberal idea of citizenship has the resources to offer a different account of the conditions under which essential citizen dispositions can be generated and sustained – one which could undermine the appeal of nation-building and national independence. My argument will be that the answer to both questions is 'yes'. Nation-building and national-independence projects typically do offend the liberal idea of citizenship in at least one way: they conflict with what I shall call 'the right to equal recognition of identity in the public sphere'. Fortunately, however, there is no necessary contradiction within the liberal idea of citizenship, because there is an alternative account of the conditions under which essential citizen dispositions are generated and sustained which does not call for nation building and national independence. Sometimes the full ideal of liberal citizenship will be unattainable and nation building and national independence will be an acceptable second best for instrumental reasons. But, if my arguments are correct, we should not think that instrumental nationalism has succeeded at reconciling liberalism with nationalism.

2   Liberal citizenship

A theory of citizenship can be thought of as an attempt to answer at least three distinct questions. The first might be called the *membership question*. Who is to be given the status of citizen? Are all adults residing on the territory of the state to be regarded as citizens or only some subset of them? If it is only a subset, then on what basis is the subset to be defined? The second question can be called the *entitlement question*. What rights and entitlements are conferred on an individual in virtue of having the status of citizen? If I am a citizen, what does this entitle me to in the way of non-interference, or positive support, from my fellow citizens, either directly or provided through the medium of the state? The third question can be termed the *social expectation question*. What responsibilities, dispositions and identities are expected of a person in virtue of having the status of citizen? If I am a citizen, what dispositions am I expected to develop and exercise and what identity or identities, if any, should I share with my fellow citizens? In short, the first question concerns who is to be considered a full member of the community, the second concerns what one can expect to 'get' in virtue of being a full member, and the third concerns what the community expects of one as a full member.[5]

A persuasive theory of citizenship is one which gives plausible answers to each of these questions, taken one by one, and which can show that the three answers given are mutually compatible and supporting. Debates about citizenship have often focused on just one of these questions. For example, T. H. Marshall's famous mid-century essay, 'Citizenship and Social Class', is usually associated with the entitlement question: he wanted to argue that the status of citizenship implied not just civil and political rights but also social rights (Marshall 1965). Sometimes, however, debates about citizenship have addressed all three questions at once and have been concerned with the coherence and mutual compatibility of the three answers. For instance, the eighteenth-, nineteenth- and early-twentieth-century debates about the suffrage centred on the question of whether one could consistently answer the three questions in the following way. To the membership question, the answer was that virtually all adults should have the status of full citizen. To the entitlement question, the answer was that this status entails a set of political rights, including the right to vote in parliamentary elections. And to the social expectation question, the answer was that someone who has the right to vote is expected to display political virtues such as independence, sound judgement, impartiality and public-spiritedness. Conservative critics of extending the suffrage argued that these three answers are mutually incompatible: the people to whom it was contemplated giving the vote, they thought, could not be expected to display the required virtues.

A *liberal* theory of citizenship gives answers that are informed by liberal values to each of the three questions and gives some account of how the three answers cohere together which makes reference to the operation of liberal social and political institutions. I will assume, without really exploring the issue, that a liberal response to the membership question would give to virtually all minimally competent adults residing on the territory of the state for some minimal length of time the opportunity to be citizens or full members of the community. The assumption here is that any attempt to justify denying citizenship to

---

[5] Strictly speaking, a theory of citizenship, as I am characterizing it, would need to be complemented by a theory of residency, a theory of permanent residency, and so on. Each of these kinds of status raise questions of membership, entitlement and social expectation, that parallel the questions posed by a theory of citizenship.

significant categories of residents on liberal grounds is almost certainly bound to fail.

I will also take it that answering the membership question in this way implies that there will be cultural diversity amongst the class of people who are considered citizens. This diversity can take a number of different forms of relevance to this paper. The most straightforward case is one in which different citizens of the community have different national identities. A distinct case is one where some citizens have a plurality of national identities. And a third case is where some (but not all) citizens have no strong sense of national identity at all but primarily define their identities in other ways (religion, locality, occupation, etc.). The fact of cultural diversity – in one of these different senses – seems to hold empirically for enough interesting real-world cases that we are safe in assuming it given the liberal answer to the membership question. In any event, the instrumental argument for nation building and national independence – which is the focus of this paper – *presupposes* a baseline cultural diversity amongst citizens and thus it will be useful to grant this assumption in order to explore the argument's compatibility with liberal citizenship.

The main problem in spelling out the liberal idea of citizenship is to answer the entitlement and social expectation questions, given the context of a plurality of national identities amongst the citizen body. In what follows, I first examine how a liberal theory of citizenship would handle the entitlement question in this context and then what it would have to say about the social expectation question.

3   Equal recognition in the public sphere

I take it that T. H. Marshall's trio of civil, political and social rights, in some form or other, will be central to any recognizably liberal account of the rights and entitlements accorded to citizens (Marshall 1965). These rights will work to constrain nation-building and national-independence projects in various ways. For instance, one way to accelerate a nation-building process might be to restrict the freedoms of speech or association of cultural minorities, but I assume that on a liberal view of citizenship this would not be allowed. It seems unlikely, however, that nation-building and national-independence projects would be completely ruled out by respect for the civil, political and social rights that are standardly associated with liberal citizenship. Consider, for instance, Rousseau's recommendation that public officials wear the traditional national costume in order to help promote the formation of a distinctive national identity. It is not clear that any civil, political and social rights – as these are normally understood – would be violated by such a policy.

There would be a more fundamental tension between liberal citizenship and nationalism, however, if it could be shown that liberalism is committed to what I shall call a 'right to equal recognition of identity in the public sphere'. Let me explain what I mean by this right and then advance some considerations for why it belongs in an account of liberal citizenship.

In recent years political theorists have become increasingly sensitive to the ways in which constructions of the public sphere can unequally advantage different people (Young 1990, chs 4 and 6; Tamir 1993, ch. 2; Kymlicka 1995, ch. 6, section 1; Spinner 1994, ch. 4). A standard example is the designation by the state and major institutions of civil society of certain dates on the calendar as public holidays and days of rest (Kymlicka 1995, pp. 114–15; cf. Bader 1997 and Carens 1997). In most western countries, the choice of these days reflects the identity and practices of the historic Christian majority. Christmas, Easter and Sundays are all accorded a special status which is not enjoyed by the important dates on the calendars of other religions. This way of constructing the public sphere gives Christians advantages which are not enjoyed by others.

One advantage is that the choice of these particular holidays and days of rest can be taken as a form of public *affirmation* of the value of the Christian way of life and identity that is not enjoyed by other religions. A second is that the choice of these particular days *accommodates* the practices associated with Christianity in a way that is not true for other religions. Whereas the calendar is arranged in such a way that most people are not working, and are not at school, at times when major Christian rituals and celebrations take place, it can be more difficult to fit the practices of other religions into the standard western work- and school-week. Finally, as a consequence of the first two advantages enjoyed by Christians, they enjoy a third advantage as well: the choice of holidays and days of rest associated with Christianity *promotes* the maintenance and reproduction of the Christian community from generation to generation. Because of the public affirmation, and the accommodation of the practices, existing members are encouraged to remain within the community and it is relatively more attractive for new members to join.[6]

There are numerous other examples of how the construction of the public sphere can unequally advantage people with different identities, ways of life and tastes. The formal (or informal) decision to use exclusively some particular language in the public sphere has important

[6] Taylor (1992a) emphasizes the importance to some cultural groups of reproducing their community from generation to generation.

consequences for the affirmation, accommodation and promotion of various linguistic communities. In the sphere of education, decisions about curriculum content can unequally advantage different groups and individuals in a similar way, and the same is true of decisions about media and broadcasting, the choice of state symbols, the wording of official documents, the selection of appointed officials, and so on. In all of these contexts, the way in which the public sphere is constructed can represent a significant advantage or disadvantage to different people according to their identity, tastes, cultural affiliations, and so forth.

These examples help to illustrate how different individuals can be unequally advantaged with respect to the recognition of their identities in the public sphere. But what could it mean to posit a *right* to *equal* recognition of one's identity in the public sphere? Let me focus on the terms 'right' and 'equal' which, I think, raise the most important issues.

To say that there is a 'right' to equality in the public sphere is to say that there is a consideration, or reason-for-action, usually relating to the right-holder's interests and well-being, that 'preempts' or 'replaces' certain other kinds of considerations and reasons-for-action that voters, policy makers, legislators, judges and so on, might otherwise have appealed to (Raz 1986, ch. 7). For instance, one kind of consideration that would be preempted by a right to equality in the public sphere is the will of the majority. The mere fact that the majority would like only their own identity to be affirmed, accommodated, and promoted in the public sphere, and cast their vote accordingly, would be defeated by such a right.

It is important to note, however, that, although asserting a right to equal recognition in the public sphere means that certain reasons and considerations standardly appealed to in politics will be preempted, it does not imply that *all* possible reasons and considerations are pre-empted. Some considerations might override the right to equal recognition in the public sphere. It may be practically very difficult, or even impossible, to affirm, accommodate, and promote more than some fixed number of identities on some given issue.[7] It seems possible to have two

---

[7] If it is impossible to accommodate more than some fixed number of identities, then is it sensible to talk of a 'right' at all? Kai Neilson has suggested to me that it is not, arguing that talking of a 'right' in this context violates the principle that 'ought implies can'. A problem with this objection, however, is that 'right' need not imply 'ought'. It is possible to think of examples where a choice must be made between two conflicting rights-claims (say because it is impossible to be in two different places at the same time). It would violate the 'ought implies can' principle to say that both rights-claims ought to be met, but it does not violate that principle to use the language of rights to describe both claims – indeed, this is why we might feel it necessary to offer apologies, excuses, and so on, to the rights-claimant whose claim is not met. If a public sphere (say the European Union) has all the public languages it can possibly contain, and then a new language group

official languages in the public sphere, for instance, but to have many more than this may be practically unfeasible, or prohibitively expensive, in certain contexts. Other considerations which could conceivably override the right to equal recognition in the public sphere include: a Millian concern with preventing harm to others; a perfectionist concern for discouraging 'bad' or worthless identities; the goal of cultural preservation; and the need to maintain the bases for social solidarity. I will take up this final kind of consideration in the last section of the chapter when I return to the question of citizen dispositions and solidarities.

The question of what constitutes 'equal' affirmation, accommodation and promotion of one's identity is more difficult to handle. It seems fairly clear to me, for instance, that a public television system which failed to provide any religiously or ethnically based programming, but catered only to the preferences and identity of the majority, would not be offering equal recognition in the public sphere. But does equality require that the same number of hours of programming be devoted to each different identity in the community or only a number of hours of programming that is proportionate with the number of people who have that particular identity?[8] Another problem is that the requirements of affirmation, accommodation, and promotion could potentially conflict with one another. Consider the example of immigration and Quebec. Equal affirmation of the anglophone identity in Quebec might require a target of accepting a proportion of anglophone immigrants that is commensurate with the anglophone share of the population. But if there is a tendency for immigrants who are initially classified as neither anglophone nor francophone to assimilate into the anglophone community upon arrival, then equal accommodation and promotion of the francophone and anglophone identities in Quebec might call for a higher rate of francophone immigration.

For the purposes of this chapter, I will assume that our intuitions about what constitutes 'equality' in different cases will at least allow us to identify serious inequalities, even if finely tuned discriminations are more controversial. One point that should be emphasized, however, is that equal recognition in the public sphere need not imply that there is any positive level of affirmation, accommodation or promotion at all. If the state is going to get into the business of affirming, accommodating and promoting certain kinds of leisure activity, for instance, then it

comes along demanding inclusion of its language in the public sphere, then I do think it is appropriate to use the language of rights to describe the group's claim, even if we think those claims ought not to be accommodated.

8 For discussion of a case raising similar issues – public funding for men's and women's sports – see Young (1990, p. 178).

should probably strive to do so for a variety of different activities that reflect the different tastes, preferences and so on of different citizens. But there is no particular reason implied by the right to equal recognition in the public sphere why the state, or any other institution of the public sphere, needs to get into the leisure activity business at all.

Indeed, in some contexts there will be very compelling reasons to think that it would be preferable for the state (and other major institutions of the public sphere) to avoid recognizing any identities at all where this is an alternative open to it. For one thing, it will always be difficult to be confident that *all* of the different identities seeking recognition are in fact being granted that recognition: avoiding recognition altogether, where this is an option, avoids the problem of creating insiders and outsiders.[9] Another reason why it might be best to avoid recognition of identity altogether arises out of the observation that identity groups are almost always internally heterogeneous. The danger is that any particular attempt to recognize some identity will involve specific ideas and narratives relating to what somebody with that identity is like – ideas and narratives that may, in fact, not be shared by everyone belonging to the identity group. Referring to gay and African-American identities in contemporary America, for instance, K. Anthony Appiah worries that 'the politics of recognition requires that one's skin colour, one's sexual body, should be acknowledged politically in ways that make it hard for those who want to treat their skin and their sexual body as personal dimensions of the self' (Appiah 1994, p. 163). On the other hand, there will always be contexts in which the state and other institutions of the public sphere cannot help but recognize at least one identity or there is compelling reason for it to do so: this is likely to be the case for decisions about school curricula, public broadcasting, state symbols, language and, as I will argue in the next section, political boundaries. It is in these contexts, where universal non-recognition is not really an option, that the right to equal recognition in the public sphere becomes most salient.

Having given some idea of what is meant by the 'right to equal recognition in the public sphere', it is now time to ask what place, if any, this right has in the liberal idea of citizenship. Some will doubt that the right in question has special importance in liberal citizenship. Liberals should, of course, oppose any principle allowing majorities to enact legislation actively seeking to suppress minority identities where that legislation involves violations of standard liberal rights and freedoms. But why should they endorse a right to equal recognition of

---

[9] Thanks to Marc Stears for pressing me on this.

identity that could be claimed even when standard liberal rights and freedoms are being respected? Turning the question around, why should it not be permissible for the majority to legislate the construction of the public sphere according to its own identity commitments and not those of minorities? Take the example of language. Is it really correct to say that an attempt to establish the language of the majority as the only official language of the community would violate the rights of linguistic minorities?

What is needed, in effect, is some positive reason – allied with liberal principles – for thinking that recognition of identity is the kind of consideration that preempts other possible considerations, such as the preferences of the majority. I have already indicated three ways in which recognition of identity is advantageous to a bearer of that identity: it can work as a public *affirmation* of the value of that identity; it can help *accommodate* the practices and modes of living associated with that identity; and it can help to *promote* the survival of a community of people bearing that identity (which may be a cherished goal of a bearer of the identity). But of course merely showing that X is advantageous to some agent, even very advantageous, is not on its own sufficient to establish that the agent has a right to X. Some further argument is still needed.

Let us start with a case where a liberal's intuitions would be pretty clear. A group of five people are unexpectedly given a cake and are wondering how to divide it. One person proposes that the cake be divided into five equal pieces. Another, however, proposes that the cake be divided according to a majoritarian principle: any division of the cake that is acceptable to three or more people will be considered legitimate. There is no consensus amongst the group about which of the distributive principles should be followed and a vote is called for. Three of the five vote for the majoritarian principle and then proceed to vote for a division of the cake in which they each are given one-third of the cake and the other two get nothing. Most liberals, I assume, would regard this as a classic instance of majoritarian tyranny in which the equality rights of the two minority members (the two who get nothing) are violated. In this specific example, at least, the liberal intuition is that each individual's interest in having an equal share preempts the majority's desire to monopolize the cake for itself. The intuition itself might be defended in a number of different ways. A utilitarian liberal, for instance, might appeal to the principle of diminishing marginal utility to defend the priority accorded to equality in this kind of case, and a contractualist liberal might appeal to the maximin principle.

Can liberal intuitions about this kind of case provide a basis for including the right to equal recognition of identity in the public sphere as part of the liberal idea of citizenship? At first glance, the cases look very different. The example just outlined involves a one-off division of an exogenously given good that can be divided up into more or less equal shares and distributed to the members of the relevant community who consume it individually. Debates about the character of the public sphere – its language, boundaries, symbols and so on – look very different: decisions relating in some way or other to the character of the public sphere are constantly being made; they often involve generating particular goods (e.g. providing some government service in a particular language) rather than distributing them; it will frequently be the case that the good, once generated, cannot be divided up into equal shares and distributed to different people; and the goods in question are often non-rival, in the sense that their enjoyment by one person does not diminish their availability for enjoyment by others.

With a closer look, however, it is hard to see why any of these differences between the two kinds of cases should be relevant. Consider a different example. Instead of an exogenously given cake, the good to be allocated is programming on a public broadcasting television station, and the allocation is to be made on an annual basis. Here the goods in question are to be generated (rather than distributed from some exogenously given source), once generated they cannot in any sense be further distributed, and they are non-rivalrous. Despite these differences, I assume that a liberal's intuitions would still be very similar to those concerning the cake case: it would, for instance, violate the rights of an opera-loving minority of two for some sports-loving coalition of three persons to push through a scheme in which nothing but sports was shown on the station. The fact that a new decision about programming is to be made each year might make the majoritarian scheme less objectionable, if those in the minority can be confident that, in any given year, everyone has the same probability of being in the majority coalition. But, if the minority believes that tastes are relatively stable from year to year, and will continue to provide a salient point around which majority coalitions can mobilize, then it is hard to see how the fact that the decision is repeated every year makes the majoritarian scheme any less objectionable.

The general principle underlying these judgements about the cake and programming cases is something like the following: when a good can be allocated (generated, distributed) in such a way that all enjoy (or have access to) a more-or-less equal amount of it, then it would violate the equality rights of the minority for some majority to push through a scheme in which it alone enjoyed the good simply because that is what its members would most prefer. The claim that the liberal idea of

N. P.

citizenship should incorporate a right to equal recognition in the public sphere is an application of this principle. The claim is that any reason-for-action that might follow from the mere fact that the majority would prefer that only its identity be recognized in the public sphere is preempted by the interest that minority identity groups have in the recognition of their identity in the public sphere as well.

The argument I have just been making shows, I think, that a minority identity group's interest in the equal recognition of its identity preempts one potential public policy justification – namely, an appeal to the preferences and will of the majority. But is this enough to establish that there is a 'right' to equal recognition of identity? After all, there may be countless other public policy justifications that might be appealed to in support of a relatively homogeneous public sphere. If it is enough, then it might seem that I am using the term 'right' in a sense that is much too weak to be of great interest. Two kinds of responses are needed to this sort of objection. The first is simply to observe that there are people – including contemporary political philosophers writing on nationalism – who believe that the preference of the majority is sometimes sufficient to justify constructions of the public sphere according to the majority's identity alone.[10] The argument I have been making is a challenge to this view. The second kind of response is more ambitious. It would involve showing that a minority identity group's interest in recognition preempts other kinds of considerations as well that might otherwise have been appealed to in favour of greater homogeneity. Although I will not attempt to prove it here, I think that an argument of this kind might plausibly be developed for certain kinds of considerations. If the minority's interest in equal recognition is sufficient to preempt the preferences of the majority, then, for instance, it is presumably also sufficient to preempt appeals to the (somewhat) greater expense that might be involved in a heterogeneous public sphere.

4   Nationalism and the public sphere

I have been arguing that a right to equal recognition of identity in the public sphere is one of the entitlements that should be recognized in a liberal theory of citizenship. The importance of this right will depend, in part, on the extent to which a pluralistic public sphere can generate various effective citizen dispositions and solidarities. If it were true that only a homogeneous public sphere could be relied upon to generate

---

[10] See, for instance, the discussion of language in Carens (1995b, pp. 58–60, 66), and the discussion of secession in Nielson (1998, p. 266).

these dispositions and solidarities, then this might be a compelling reason to suspend the right to equal recognition in the public sphere in particular contexts. Before examining this issue, however, it is important to ask what the implications of the right to equal recognition in the public sphere are for nation-building and national-independence projects. Earlier, it was noted that the civil, political and social rights standardly associated with liberal citizenship seem to constrain, but not rule out, the pursuit of these nationalist projects. Does the inclusion in the liberal idea of citizenship of a right to equal recognition in the public sphere give us cause to revise this view of the relationship between liberalism and nationalism?

The reason to think that it might is that both nation-building and national-independence projects typically involve quite fundamental reconstructions of the public sphere. These changes do not necessarily introduce inequalities in the public sphere, but they may do so. Where they do, they can conflict with the right to equal recognition in the public sphere and, to that extent, with the liberal idea of citizenship.

The possibility of such a conflict is perhaps most apparent with nation-building projects. Such projects involve, for instance, modifications to the education curriculum, the introduction of a single language of business in major institutions of the public sphere, regulation of the media and broadcasting, the manipulation of state symbols, the wording of official documents and pronouncements, and so on, with the aim of diffusing and consolidating a single national identity on the territory of the state. It is conceivable that certain measures of these kinds would not, in some contexts, conflict with the affirmation, accommodation and promotion of other identities in the community. The nation-building project might aim to forge a unified national identity 'on top of' the existing cultural and national identities rather than to replace them. To a considerable extent the scope for superimposing such an identity on top of other identities in this way will depend on the precise character of the various existing identities: how open they are to complementary identities, how much importance they attach to specific social and political institutions, and so forth.

It is not hard to imagine situations, however, in which nation-building policies do generate inequalities in the public sphere. Consider, for instance, an attempt to introduce a 'national' curriculum into the schools which reflects the practices, perspectives and narratives of the ascendant national group but not those of various national minorities. Or consider the policy of adopting a single language of the public sphere in a linguistically heterogeneous community. These policies, like many others, clearly conflict with the right to equal recognition in the public sphere: they more fully affirm, accommodate, and promote some identities and ways of life in the community than others.

It might seem less clear how the right to equal recognition in the public sphere can conflict with a national-independence project – the attempt by some distinct national group to achieve its own sovereign state. It is tempting to hold the view that, so long as the new nation-state respects the usual political, civil and social rights cherished by liberals, and so long as it respects, where possible, the right to equal recognition in the public sphere, then there could be nothing objectionable about a national-independence project from the standpoint of the liberal idea of citizenship.

This view ignores, however, the important connection between national identity and political institutions and boundaries (cf. Miller 1995, ch. 2). It is typically a constitutive part of a person's national identity to identify with a particular territory as the 'homeland' of the national group and with a particular set of institutions connected with that territory as the locus of the group's public, political life. The way in which meaningful political boundaries are drawn, and the kinds of functions and responsibilities that are assigned to institutions corresponding to those boundaries, can thus affirm, accommodate and promote different identities to different degrees.

Before concluding that there is a potential conflict between national-independence projects and the right to equal recognition in the public sphere, however, it is necessary to have some idea of what 'equality' could mean with respect to boundary drawing. For it might be thought that the drawing of political boundaries is one of those areas in which the construction of a pluralistic public sphere is impossible – that, as far as boundaries are concerned, it is only possible to affirm, accommodate and promote a single identity.

A moment's reflection shows this view to be badly mistaken, however. It assumes the extreme case of an entirely unitary state when, in fact, many multinational states incorporate federal structures and other arrangements for regional self-government by culturally distinctive groups. Where federal or other similar arrangements are in place, a rough equality in the public sphere can be achieved between different national identities. Some will find their identity expressed in the territory and institutions of the larger, 'federal' structure, and others will identify with a subunit of that structure (and, of course, many people will identify with both). Provided that significant functions and responsibilities are assigned to each level, a kind of rough equality in the affirmation, accommodation and promotion of different national identities is worked out. Consider, for instance, the devolution arrangements introduced in Scotland in 1999. These arrangements promote equality in the public sphere between those whose identity is primarily Scottish and those whose identity is primarily British. Whereas the creation of uniquely Scottish institutions, including a Scottish parliament, gives public expression to the Scottish identity, retaining certain powers and responsibilities in London gives a public, political life to the British identity.[11]

A national-independence project clashes with the right to equality in the public sphere when two conditions hold. First, there must be a plurality of different national identities on the territory for which independence is being sought. And second, there must be federal, or other similar, arrangements in place which give roughly equal affirmation, accommodation and promotion of these different identities, or such arrangements must be a viable alternative to the project.[12]

5   Liberalism and citizen dispositions

So far I have been arguing for two main propositions: (1) that the liberal idea of citizenship should embrace a right to equal recognition in the public sphere; and (2) that this right can conflict with nation-building and national-independence projects. It is now time to confront the suspicion that the pluralistic public sphere I have been defending will be

---

[11] On the Scottish case see Miller (1995, pp. 117–18): Miller defends limited self-government for Scotland but argues that 'Complete independence for Catalonia or Scotland would violate that part of the identity of both these peoples which seeks to participate in the self-determination of the larger nation.' Miller makes a similar argument for the case of Quebec: 'Assume that a constitutional settlement can finally be reached in Canada which (as the present constitution does) gives considerable self-determination to the people of Quebec . . . while at the same time the continued overarching authority of the Canadian government gives expression to the identities of those inhabitants who think of themselves as Canadians rather than as Québécois. Such a settlement may represent the best fulfilment of the principle of nationality, whereas outright secession would realize it for one group but deny it to the other' (p. 117). There is a tension in Miller's work between these statements, which express a preference for multinational states in certain contexts, and his argument elsewhere (pp. 90–7 and 139–40) that 'nationality alone' can provide the trust and solidarity required for social justice.

[12] It is worth observing that the federal-style arrangements most in tune with the right to equality in the public sphere may well be asymmetrical. If a distinctive minority national identity is mainly concentrated in one region of a state, then equality in the affirmation, accommodation, and promotion of the minority and majority identities may be encouraged by introducing and strengthening social and political institutions specifically for that region. The same egalitarian considerations would not necessarily require that similar regional institutions be introduced elsewhere in the country if existing institutions of the state already cater to the majority national identity which predominates there. For application of these considerations to the Canada/Quebec case, see the important discussion in Kymlicka (1998a).

incompatible with the generation of effective citizen dispositions.[13] As we saw at the start of the chapter, Rousseau, Mill and other instrumental nationalists claim that a single, shared national identity is a necessary background condition for the generation of effective citizen dispositions required to support ·many of the rights and entitlements cherished by liberals. Does the liberal idea of citizenship contain the resources to explain how effective citizen dispositions might be generated even in a community containing a plurality of different national identities?

In attempting to respond to this challenge, let me proceed by simply laying out a form of identity that seems both compatible with the liberal idea of citizenship and potentially able to provide the background conditions required for the generation of effective citizen dispositions. I will then try to respond to several serious objections to this proposal. The proposal starts from the simple thought that a *national* identity is only one kind of identity that people can share. Other forms of identity can encourage the attachments, facilitate the communication and trust, and actualize the solidarities that instrumental nationalists associate with national identity. People who do not share a national identity might, for example, share a religious identity, and certain attachments and solidarities might be generated between them on this basis. I do not of course mean to suggest that liberals would have multinational states construct a shared identity around one of the existing, established religions. This option is foreclosed by the multifaith character of most modern societies. The important point is that various forms of non-national identity are already realized around us and seem capable of generating dispositions and solidarities of the relevant kind.

The common identity that seems most appropriate for the citizens of a liberal, multinational state is one grounded in a shared commitment to the genuinely multinational state – that is to say, to the state which respects, not only the civil, political and social rights standardly associated with liberal citizenship, but also the right to equal recognition in the public sphere. Let us call this a *multinational identity*. A multinational identity would involve a commitment to the ideal of making a social order in which different national groups have different objects of identification and different modes of belonging but share a willingness to live together under arrangements which reflect and endorse the pluralistic character of their society. It would involve, in other words, a shared commitment to the ideal which Charles Taylor has termed 'deep diversity' (Taylor 1993a; cf. Habermas 1992 and Kymlicka 1996a).

I can foresee at least three important objections to the suggestion that

---

[13] Miller (1995, pp. 139–40), voices this suspicion about Iris Marion Young's 'radical multiculturalism'.

a multinational identity can help to reconcile a liberal commitment to equality in the public sphere with the need to generate effective citizen dispositions. The first objection is that the proposed 'multinational' identity is not culturally 'concrete' or 'thick' enough to reliably generate the required citizen dispositions.[14] Sharing a 'multinational' identity looks a lot like merely sharing values, and this, as Wayne Norman has convincingly argued, is unlikely to be sufficient to generate certain dispositions (Norman 1995). The response to this objection, however, would be to question whether an identity really does need to be defined in a culturally thick or concrete manner, so long as the people sharing the identity do not *merely* share values but also conceive of themselves as a 'we', engaged in certain common projects and purposes. It can be argued that an American identity defined in terms of the Declaration of Independence and other similar documents, or the phenomenon of 'Charter patriotism' in Canada, are good examples of strong but culturally thin identities. The important point is that it is possible for a community to have concrete objects of shared identification that do not seem culturally thick.

A second objection is that what I am terming a 'multinational identity' is really just a fancy term for a particular form of national identity. To use some popular terminology, it describes a national identity that is defined in 'civic' rather than 'ethnic' terms. Thus, I have not after all challenged the claim that a shared national identity is needed to generate effective citizen dispositions. Instead, I have merely offered a *refinement* of that claim – one which further specifies the exact character of the national identity having the desired instrumental properties.

Which forms of identity get called 'national' is, of course, partly a matter of stipulation. If critics really want to insist that the form of identity I have been defining is 'national' rather than 'multinational', then I am not convinced it is so important to disagree with them. What would be important to notice about this view is that, if an identity having the features described above is possible (whether we call it a 'civic national identity' or a 'multinational identity'), then instrumental nationalists can no longer argue that it is *necessary* to abandon equality in the public sphere through nation-building or national-independence projects. A form of identity (however we label it) would be possible which could provide the necessary background for the generation of effective citizen dispositions without upsetting equality in the public sphere.

Having said this, there are good reasons to call the proposed form of

[14] Thanks to Geneviève Nootens for suggesting this objection.

identity a 'multinational' rather than a 'national' identity. For it is often thought that national identities, as opposed to other forms of identity, have certain specific characteristics. For instance, it has been suggested that people sharing a national identity: (a) share an identification with a particular territory that represents the 'homeland' of their group; (b) share an identification with particular institutions and practices as representing the public, political expression of their identity; and (c) share the belief (perhaps wrongly) that they have in common certain objective cultural characteristics. If a 'national identity' is taken to involve these specific features, then what I am calling a 'multinational identity' is not just a particular form of national identity but represents a distinct kind of identity that people might share. People animated by multinational identity need not think of the same territory as constituting their 'homeland', they can think of different institutions and practices as representing the public, political expression of their identities, and they can think of themselves as having very different objective cultural characteristics.

The third important objection needing consideration is that the appeal to a 'multinational identity' is simply wishful thinking. It looks like a *deus ex machina* wheeled in at the last moment to stabilize a situation that is in fact inherently conflictual. Merely pointing out the *possibility* of a multinational identity hardly seems likely to help solve conflicts in places like Belgium or Northern Ireland, let alone somewhere like Bosnia.

A dose of reality is always a useful antidote to overly abstract philosophical discussions of pressing real-world issues like nationalism. But for three different reasons I want to insist on the importance of articulating an ideal of a multinational identity.[15] The first is that it is important for the language and rhetoric we use to describe solutions to different problems that we be able to distinguish the ideal from a compromise or a 'second best'. In some contexts it is unfortunately true that the absence of certain effective dispositions means that the least unattractive option is to override some right or appease some injustice. The Dayton Accord on Bosnia was justified in roughly these terms by some people. We do not, however, conclude from the Bosnian case that the principle of non-aggression, say, cannot be considered part of the

---

[15] There is a fourth reason as well that is relevant in certain contexts: the 'national-independence' and 'nation-building' solutions may also be wishful thinking. Think how destabilizing national-independence and nation-building projects are in the Northern Irish context, for instance. The creation of a multinational identity (grounded in the principles of the Good Friday Agreement) looks like the most realistic long-term solution to the conflict in Northern Ireland, if, indeed, there is any realistic long-term solution at all.

liberal idea of citizenship. Rather, we are more likely to view this as a case in which the absence of certain liberal dispositions in a portion of the population means that the liberal idea of citizenship is not fully realizable. Likewise, if a 'multinational' identity is available in some contexts but not in others, then rather than questioning whether equality in the public sphere is indeed part of the liberal idea of citizenship, we may want to say the full liberal ideal of citizenship is simply not attainable in certain contexts. Without a full articulation of the ideal, however, we would not even know when we are appeasing and when liberal citizenship is being realized.

A second reason for articulating the concept of a multinational identity is that it may help us to understand something about multi-nation communities – be they cities, provinces or states – which do work tolerably well. If we assume from the start that only a shared national identity can generate the dispositions and solidarities needed for the success of a just and free social order, then we may lose an important category for understanding our political experience. It is arguable, for instance, that the Canadian identity shared by many in Quebec is of the multinational rather than the national form. Many Quebecers identify with Canada as a context in which the different founding nations can each be accommodated and respected, and their disillusionment with Canada reflects, in part at least, a sense that this multinational vision of Canada is not shared by Canadians outside of Quebec.

Finally, even where a multinational identity has not been reliably established, the ideal of such an identity can still help to guide decisions about how to construct the public sphere. Politicians and public officials frequently assume that they have a responsibility to engage in nation building – that they should seek to diffuse and consolidate a single national identity on the territory of their state. The idea of a multi-national identity offers an alternative to this assumption: rather than using decisions about the construction of the public sphere to build up a single shared national identity, politicians and public officials might try instead to diffuse and consolidate a shared multinational identity: an identity defined by the project of making a society in which different national groups resolve to live together without abandoning their na-tional differences. If the arguments of this chapter have been correct, then this would be a contribution not only to social solidarity but to the realization of the liberal idea of citizenship.

Nationality in divided societies[1]

David Miller

Introduction

When people like myself defend the principle of national self-determination – the principle that where a body of people form a national community, they should be allowed to control their own affairs through institutions of self-government – they run into a barrage of objections from liberals. One objection, very much in the spirit of Pope's famous couplet, 'For forms of government let fools contest / Whate'er is best administer'd is best', says that what matters is good government, not self-government. More specifically, what matters is that governments should respect the liberties and rights of their subjects and pursue enlightened policies generally; who does the governing, whether compatriot or foreigner, is of no intrinsic importance. A second objection points to the external costs of national self-determination. Political communities which are empowered through self-government to pursue the interests of their members will do so at the expense of outsiders. Their policies will be based on narrow notions of national interest, and are likely to harm the freedom and well-being of the vulnerable and destitute the world over. In place of national government we should have world government, or at least a strong international regime of some kind.

These are objections of principle to national self-determination, one stemming from classical liberalism, the other from a more modern

[1] Earlier versions of this chapter were presented to audiences at the University of Newcastle, the University of Edinburgh and Arizona State University; it was also presented to the Conference 'In Search of Justice and Stability: A Comparative and Theoretical Analysis of Canada, Belgium, Spain and the United Kingdom' organized by the Research group on Multinational States, McGill University, March 1998 and to a panel on 'Liberalism and Nationalism' at the American Political Science Association Annual Conference, Boston, September 1998. I should like to thank all those who spoke at these meetings for their helpful comments, and especially Alain Gagnon and Dominique Arel for their written suggestions.

cosmopolitan liberalism. They will not be my concern here.[2] Instead I want to try to respond to a third kind of liberal objection, which runs along the following lines. 'Considered in the abstract, the idea of national self-determination is quite appealing. It is evident that people's autonomy and well-being are promoted when they are able collectively to determine the future shape of their society. If all the world were like Iceland – a culturally homogeneous political community inhabiting a well-defined territory to which no other community has any claims – the principle of self-determination would be perfectly valid. But unfortunately the Icelandic case is quite exceptional. Almost everywhere else we find territories inhabited by a kaleidoscope of groups with competing cultural identities, stemming either from long-standing historic rivalries, or from more recent patterns of immigration. Existing states are almost without exception multicultural, and in these circumstances applying the principle of national self-determination will mean one of two things. Either it will mean allowing the dominant group in any place to impose its cultural values on dissenting minorities in the name of national self-determination. Or it will justify minority groups in their struggle for autonomy, a struggle which in the nature of things is liable to turn violent. In short, the political geography of the contemporary world more closely resembles Bosnia than it does Iceland, and in that context the only sane response to nationalist aspirations is to try to damp them down as quickly as possible.'

This objection is certainly a powerful one, drawing as it does on the very underlying values that are used to support the principle of nationality itself. So how should defenders of the principle respond to it? I am going to suggest that we must scrutinize the idea of a cultural kaleidoscope more carefully, and draw distinctions between different ways in which political communities may be culturally divided. I will not deny that there are cases in which the nationality principle runs into trouble. But I shall argue that in many others it can guide us towards political arrangements that meet the cultural demands of more than one group. The mere fact of cultural pluralism does not undermine the principle; everything depends on the character of the pluralism.

For this purpose I want to distinguish between three types of social division that may be found inside a political community; ethnic cleavages, rival nationalities and nested nationalities.[3] I present these

---

[2] My general defence of national self-determination can be found in Miller (1995, esp. ch. 3).

[3] Will Kymlicka (1995, esp. ch. 2), has underlined the importance of distinguishing between ethnic groups and national minorities if we wish to develop a political theory of multiculturalism. I depart from his position first by distinguishing between two kinds of national minorities, as indicated in the text, and second by placing less emphasis on the

as ideal types, recognizing that in the real world there will be many mixed or intermediate cases – cases, that is, in which either different types of division are juxtaposed in the same state, or the divisions that exist seem to fall somewhere between my pure types.[4] I believe, however, that we need to begin with a relatively simple typology, in order to see that the principle of nationality has quite different implications in the three pure cases. That is, it matters a lot, normatively speaking, whether the cultural pluralism we are looking at is generated by ethnic cleavages, rival nationalities or nested nationalities. Once we know what the principle entails in each of these simple cases, we can begin to think about the messier instances of cultural heterogeneity that we find in actual contemporary states. In this chapter I am going to focus on the case of nested nationalities, partly because I've tried to address the other two cases elsewhere,[5] but mainly because this case hasn't been much discussed in the existing literature on nationalism. The example I shall chiefly use is Scotland and England and their relationship to Britain as a whole. But first I need to explain my threefold distinction properly.

Ethnic cleavages, rival nationalities and nested nationalities

A state is ethnically divided, but not multinational, when it contains two or more distinct ethnic groups each of which is nonetheless able to participate in a common national identity. So what is an ethnic group? It is a set of people with a distinct set of cultural values and a shared language, who recognize their cultural kinship with one another, and engage in practices that set them apart from outsiders: they intermarry,

---

immigrant status of ethnic groups. Although immigration is a major source of ethnic pluralism, it is not the only source, and my own account of ethnicity does not treat it as a defining feature. In part, this may reflect a contrast between North American and European perspectives.

[4] I am also not sure that my categorization is exhaustive. If we consider the position of aboriginal groups such as native Americans or Australian aborigines, then as Kymlicka has emphasized it is wrong to treat them simply as ethnic groups, but on the other hand they do not fit easily into either of my categories of national minority. Their social and political structure is not sufficiently developed for them to constitute integral nations rivalling the dominant national groups in the states to which they belong; but because of the way in which they were incorporated historically into nation-states, it is also difficult for their identities to nest comfortably within the overarching national identity. (The reasons why they cannot be treated as nested nationalities will become clearer as we proceed.) Perhaps then we should treat aboriginal groups as a fourth category when discussing the implications of the principle of nationality.

[5] I have looked at responses to ethnic pluralism in Miller 1999, and at different ways of responding to the demands made by rival national groups in Miller 1998c.

forms clubs and associations, attend churches, synagogues and mosques etc. The group may often embrace the myth that they form an extended family in the biological sense, although in reality ethnic identities are usually to a greater or lesser extent a matter of choice. For present purposes there is no need to delve deeply into the difficult question of how precisely ethnicity should be understood and how far it should be seen as a freely acquired and malleable source of personal identity. What needs underlining are two features that ethnicity characteristically lacks. The first is that ethnicity is not an intrinsically political identity, meaning that ethnic groups as such do not aim or aspire to become self-governing political communities. Of course ethnic groups will want to control their own churches, social clubs, trade unions, and so forth. They will also very often want political representation in the shape of elected politicians willing to promote their interests and concerns in government. And they may demand symbolic recognition in the sense that national institutions should acknowledge the group's culture in one way or another (as Muslims in Britain argued that the Millennium Dome should house not only exhibits connected with Christianity but others linked to Islam). But this is very different from aiming for political autonomy as an independent unit. This is connected with the second feature, namely that ethnic identity involves no particular territorial claims. There is no territory which the group claims as its own – indeed ethnic groups tend to migrate from place to place as they rise or fall in the social scale. There may well be a homeland which the group sees as its place of origin, and members may be concerned that the ancestral homeland keeps its political integrity, but this does not and cannot translate into a demand for territorial control in the state of residence. Thus Italians in the US will care about the fate of Italy, Ukrainians in Canada about Ukraine, Jews in Britain about Israel, but this is clearly very different from aspiring to control all or part of the US or Canada or Britain itself.

It follows that in principle a society divided along ethnic lines can have a common national identity and enjoy national self-determination in a relatively straightforward manner. Although ethnic identities may give rise to political demands, they are essentially cultural identities whose field of expression is civil society, and they can be combined with overarching national identities: to use the examples I just gave, Italian-Americans will standardly think of themselves as ethnically Italian but as having American nationality, and similarly for the other two cases. Of course many practical difficulties may intervene: ethnic rivalries may make cooperation within the state difficult, the national identity may include cultural elements that some ethnic groups find unacceptable, and the nation may find itself at war, literally or metaphorically, with the homeland of one of its constituent groups – Japanese ethnics in America, for example, are still feeling the repercussions of the Second World War. But the principle remains clear, that in societies with ethnic cleavages national identity should be forged or remade in such a way that all groups can take part in a collective project of self-determination.

This reveals a fairly sharp contrast with my second case, that of states inhabited by rival national groups. Here we find groups with mutually exclusive national identities each seeking to control all or part of the territory of the state. There are various possible configurations here: the groups in question can be territorially concentrated or territorially dispersed, they may or may not identify with national groups in neighbouring states, and their conflicting claims may extend across the whole of the state's territory or be confined to specific disputed areas. To mention some examples, Jews and Palestinians in Israel are two free-standing groups who make significantly overlapping claims to the territory of that state; Serbs and Croats in Bosnia are groups identifying with adjoining nationalities with conflicting claims to control parts of Bosnian territory; Catholics and Protestants in Northern Ireland illustrate the case where the two communities are intermingled and make rival claims to the whole of the territory in question. The detailed configurations differ, but the kind of division involved makes it virtually inevitable that the relationship between the groups should be an antagonistic one. This is because rival territorial claims in the present will stem from a history of conflict in which one group has moved into territory previously held by the other, or in which patterns of political control have varied historically, at one time the As governing one tract of territory, at another time the Bs governing a different tract, and so forth. So part of what it means to belong to group A is that one defines oneself in opposition to (and typically regards with some contempt) members of B, and it is this fact, along with the dispute over territorial control, that prevents an overarching national identity emerging across the various national groups. There is no Israeli national identity over and above a Jewish or Palestinian identity, no Bosnian national identity over and above a Serb, Croat or Muslim identity, etc.[6] (Members of the rival communities may of course recognize that *de facto* they share a common citizenship, but this is not the same as conceiving of themselves as

---

[6] A recent television report from Bosnia showed a reporter standing in a classroom of small children (the education system is now a divided one). He asked 'How many of you think of yourselves as Bosnians?' No hands went up. 'How many of you think of yourselves as Serbs?' Every hand went up.

united in one community with a shared history, similar aims and values, etc.)

These are hard cases for the principle of nationality, which is not to say that the principle has no guidance to offer. When faced with rival nationalities within an existing state, achieving the best approximation to full national self-determination will depend on how the communities are configured. In some instances the best solution may be to permit one national community to secede, in others to redraw borders so that more people fall under the aegis of a neighbouring state, in yet others to engineer an elaborate constitutional settlement which preserves a balance of power between the rival communities for the time being, and which may with the passage of time lead to the emergence of a genuinely shared identity. But I don't want here to discuss these options at any length (see Miller 1998c for a fuller discussion). I am more interested in showing how the cases just described differ from those in my third category, which I call nested nationalities.

We find nested nationalities when two or more territorially based communities exist within the framework of a single nation, so that members of each community typically have a split identity. They think of themselves as belonging both to the smaller community and to the larger one, and they do not experience this as schizophrenic, because their two identities fit together reasonably well.[7] Among the contemporary states that fall into this category, I will argue, are Belgium, Britain, Canada, Spain and Switzerland. These are states whose citizens mostly share an overarching national identity – as Belgians, Britons, Canadians etc. – while also identifying with, and displaying loyalty to, subcommunities within the larger nation – Flanders and Wallonia, Scotland and Wales, Quebec, Catalonia and so forth.[8] Two points need to be

---

[7] The idea that people can sustain social and political identities at different levels without significant internal conflict is now fairly familiar. Anthony Smith spoke of 'concentric loyalties' (1981, p. 164), and this idea was taken up and applied in an illuminating way to the Scottish case in Smout (1994). Two further points are worth noting. If we use the metaphor of concentric circles of identity, this is only to indicate the wider or narrower spatial range of the various identities that a person may bear (Smout starts with the family and ends with supranational groupings); it is not to say anything about the relative *importance* of these identities. Moreover in some cases we should think not just in terms of concentric circles but also of overlapping circles, where people identify to some degree with neighbouring communities as well with more inclusive ones. (A Scottish Catholic living in Glasgow may feel some affinity with Irishmen across the water as well as with Scotland, Britain, Europe etc.) I am grateful to Zenon Bankowski for emphasizing this latter point.

[8] For evidence supporting my claim that national identities in these states typically exhibit such a duality, see, for Belgium, McRae (1986, esp. ch. 3), and Maddens, Beerten and Billiet (1998); for Canada, Webber (1994, esp. ch. 6), and McRoberts (1997a, esp. ch. 10); for Spain, Keating (1996a, ch. 5) and Medrano (1995, esp. ch. 11); for Switzerland, McRae (1983, esp. ch. 3), and Steinberg (1996, esp. ch. 7).

made immediately about the states in question. First, we cannot say that every citizen is the bearer of two neatly nested political identities. Instead we find, typically, that some citizens identify exclusively with the larger unit, some exclusively with the smaller unit, and many more identify in varying degrees with both. Thus if we take the inhabitants of Catalonia as a putative example of a nested nationality, and ask how they identify themselves vis-à-vis Spain as a whole, we find that 'Equally Spanish and Catalan' is the most popular self-description, followed by 'More Catalan than Spanish', with smaller numbers claiming exclusively Catalan and exclusively Spanish identities (Keating 1996a, p. 130). The second is that we can divide states with nested nationalities into those in which one community is preponderant, and those in which two or more have roughly equal weight – Britain, Spain and Canada being examples of the first, Belgium and Switzerland of the second. In the second case, we may expect to find members of each nested community displaying a dual identity – thinking of themselves as both Walloon and Belgian, for instance. In the first case, however, we may expect to find an asymmetry. Whereas people who belong to one of the minor nationalities will typically endorse a dual identity, those belonging to the numerically dominant group are likely to identify themselves nationally only with the inclusive unit. Thus English people will typically regard themselves simply as British, Canadians outside Quebec simply as Canadians, and the Castilian-speaking majority in Spain simply as Spanish. (They may in addition have regional or provincial identities, but these are not regarded as forms of nationality in the way that Scottish, Québécois or Catalan identities are.) As we shall see, this asymmetry creates political problems in the states in question.

In describing these political communities with nested nationalities, I have deliberately side-stepped a terminological question that usually carries with it major political ramifications: shall we call the larger community a nation and the subgroups something else – national minorities, for instance – or shall we say that Catalonia, Wallonia and Scotland are nations, in which case what term shall we use to describe Spain, Belgium and Britain? The label matters because of the power of the idea of national self-determination. Once it is conceded that a territorial community genuinely constitutes a nation, we seem already to have shown that there is good reason for the community in question to be granted political autonomy.

But in fact neither answer is correct as it stands. Both exhibit the fallacy of thinking that nations are like natural species. Just as one can be either a cat or a dog, but not a bit of each, so, it is assumed, one has either to be a Catalan or a Spaniard as far as national identity is concerned, but not both. But this is surely a mistake.[9] One can be both Catalan and Spanish (indeed as we have seen many people in Catalonia describe themselves in precisely this way), perhaps emphasizing different aspects of the double identity in different contexts or for different purposes. In that case there is no right answer to the question 'Which is really the nation, Catalonia or Spain?' The question is badly put, and we need to find terminology that is less misleading. We could use the terminology that I favour and describe the Catalans and the Scots as nested nationalities;[10] or if this does not go far enough to appease nationalist sensibilities we could call them nations-within-a-nation. The important point is that whatever terminology we use should convey the idea that national identity can exist at more than one level.

Another error that should be avoided here is that of describing the larger political community simply as a multinational state, with the implication that its source of unity consists entirely in allegiance to a common set of political institutions. What is being suggested, in other words, is that genuine nationhood is confined to the Scots, the Catalans and the other smaller communities, whereas Britain and Spain are at best examples of a kind of civic nationalism, which does not imply a common history, language, culture, etc. but merely recognition of the authority of a constitutional or political framework. Now I do not in fact think that the idea of civic nationalism is a helpful one, except perhaps as a way of marking one end of a spectrum (with ethnic nationalism at the other end) to bring out qualitative differences between different kinds of nationalism. But whether or not there are any real cases that approximate to 'civic nationalism' (the US is probably the most likely candidate – but as I have argued elsewhere (Miller 1995, p. 141), even American national identity contains historical and cultural elements that are hard to interpret as purely civic), it seems clear that examples I am discussing do not belong in this category. Belgian, British, Canadian, Spanish and Swiss nationality all come heavily freighted with cultural and historical associations; by no stretch of the imagination could these

[9] The idea that one must belong exclusively to a single nation is linked to the idea that national loyalty must take precedence over all other ethical demands to which one may be subject. Clearly, if one's supreme duty is to act as the interests of one's nation require, it makes no sense to suppose that one might belong simultaneously to two nations. But the ethical doctrine is untenable, and once that is abandoned, it is not difficult to think of a person balancing her or his loyalties to a larger and to a smaller country, particularly where, as I shall try to show in the Anglo-Scottish case, the two identities dovetail reasonably well.

[10] There are historical precedents for using 'nationality' to identify the smaller community and 'nation' to identify the inclusive community: this terminology is used in, for instance, the Spanish constitution of 1978 which prepared the way for regional autonomy for Catalonia and the Basque Country.

national identities be regarded as purely civic. So 'multinational state' is a misleading way of describing states whose internal divisions place them in my third category; it is much more appropriate as a description of category two, states made up of rival nationalities, where the state itself is either an instrument in the hands of one nation, as in the case of Israel, or the arena where the rival nations jostle for advantage, as for example with Yugoslavia before its break-up, or many African states today.

From a normative perspective, states with nested nationalities can be seen as falling somewhere in between my categories one and two. Because the component nationalities have most of the properties of independent nations, including a territorial homeland, their claims must be treated quite differently from the claims of ethnic groups; the Scots in Britain have a claim to self-determination which Muslims, say, in Britain do not, and this is on grounds of principle, not merely the practical obstacles to granting self-determination to the latter group. But equally their claims are significantly different from those of nations in category two (rival nationality) states, because they have to be harmonized with the claims of the larger community. So full independence or secession from the existing state are not appropriate solutions. To see why, we need to look more closely at how nested nationalities are created – about the background against which split-level national identities can emerge.

The English, the Scots and British national identity

The most obvious factor, looking at the cases I have cited, is that the nations in question have coexisted for a long period in a single political unit, while at the same time each component part has kept its distinct cultural features: in particular, language has served as the main carrier of cultural difference in each case other than Britain. In the British case, language has been less important as a dividing factor, particularly if we are thinking about the English and the Scots, but other features – the fact that Scotland has had its own separate legal system, education system and religious institutions throughout the period of political union – have helped to offset this. However the recipe for successfully nested nations involves more than just political integration plus cultural difference. Taking the Anglo-Scottish relationship as my example, and oversimplifying greatly what is a long and complex story, I shall suggest three other factors that have contributed to the formation of a single, but pluriform, nation in Britain. These factors are cultural overlap, mutual economic advantage and an interwoven history.

In referring to overlapping cultures, I am expressing the thought that

English and Scottish cultures, although having distinct features overall, are sufficiently convergent that participants in each can readily understand the other, there is a good deal of mutual borrowing, individuals can relocate themselves fairly readily from one to the other, and so forth. I believe this holds with regard to the political cultures of the two peoples and also culture in the wider sense of literary, artistic, philosophical etc. traditions.

Speaking very generally and somewhat anachronistically, we can say that these are both liberal cultures in which ideas of religious freedom, personal independence and resistance to absolute monarchy have been paramount. The fact that the Scottish Reformation took place within a couple of decades of its English counterpart is a significant starting point. It meant that in the period following the Union of the Crowns in 1603 political argument in the two countries ran on roughly parallel tracks, with debates about the relationship between church and state, royal prerogative v. the supremacy of parliament, and so forth. Political alliances formed naturally across the border, for instance between English Puritans and Scottish Presbyterians.[11] In both countries rival national histories were constructed in an effort to show that each author's preferred political programme had ancient antecedents – English narratives about Anglo-Saxon liberty and the Norman yoke were paralleled north of the border by competing stories about the relationship between Scottish monarchs and the nobility, going back as far as the legendary King Fergus in 330 BC (see Kidd 1993, ch. 3) Although the *dramatis personae* were different, the range of messages the stories were used to convey was much the same in both cases.

The convergence in political culture was not so great that the Union of Parliaments in 1707, which brought the British state proper into existence, can be presented as a voluntary agreement on both sides. Although the Scottish parliament approved the Articles of Union, there was much dissent outside, and many ballads were written lamenting the loss of Scottish independence. Nevertheless there were good reasons internal to Scottish political culture for approving the Union, and some of these were expressed in the debates of the time, for instance by parliamentarians such as Seafield, Paterson and Seton who pointed out that the liberties of the Scots, and especially their religious liberty, could

---

[11] The religious background to the Act of Union is highlighted in Dicey and Rait (1920). They point out, for instance, that the King James Bible, published in 1611, 'was read, and has been constantly read by every English and Scottish Protestant sufficiently educated to read any book . . . The religious, the moral, the social, and the political effects of such a Bible hardly admit of exaggeration. It made Englishmen and Scotsmen ultimately speak, read, and write one and the same language, and it linked together the religious ideas of all British Protestants' (p. 333).

best be secured by the creation of a strong common parliament, and a unified state able to repel common enemies (by implication the Catholic powers of Europe). Alongside this there ran a clear appreciation of the advantages to the Scottish economy of free trade with England.[12]

It was in the century following the Union, however, that cultural convergence accelerated, allowing us to speak of a British national identity emerging over and above English and Scottish identities. This is particularly evident in the work of the leading figures of the Scottish Enlightenment, who not only saw themselves as writing for a general British audience, but contributed significantly to the transformation of English political culture through their reworking of Whig ideology. It has often been suggested that this required these writers to turn their backs on their Scottishness. Evidence for this of a somewhat trivial kind can be seen in their attempts to weed out distinctively Scottish verbal expressions from their writing, but more seriously in their repudiation of the Scottish historical past, which is regarded as distinctly murky by comparison to England's. (When Hume discusses Scottish affairs in his *History of England,* for example, there are frequent passing references to the disorderly character and political backwardness of Scotland by comparison with its southern neighbour. At one point he considers the charge against Edward I that he ordered the annals of Scottish history to be destroyed in order to remove the basis for claims to Scottish independence. However, says Hume, 'it is not probable, that a nation, so rude and unpolished, should be possessed of any history, which deserves much to be regretted' (Hume [1754–62] 1983, vol. II, p. 113)). Yet it is possible to interpret the achievement of these writers in a different way: their aim was to present the British constitutional settlement of 1689 as the best example available of a liberal regime, enshrining religious toleration, the liberties of subjects, parliamentary supremacy, and so forth, and one therefore which the Scots, given their past history, should be glad to be part of, but without crediting the English specifically with a natural genius for liberty. As Kidd has put it 'Hume and other Scottish writers aimed to educate the English to appreciate their liberties by replacing their vulgar exceptionalism with a pan-European historical perspective' (Kidd 1993, p. 211).

There was of course a rival political culture manifested in Jacobitism that presented a very different view of Scottish history. Here the martial glories and liberty of the past were contrasted with the fettering imposed by the Union. But Jacobitism was condemned to be either reactionary or nostalgic, and its appeal to Lowland Scots in particular was therefore

---

[12] See Scott (1979), and also Pryde (1950) which includes the text of the Treaty of Union.

rather limited. In the longer run, when Jacobitism as a political force was exhausted, the Stuarts, and especially the romantic figure of Bonnie Prince Charlie, could be rehabilitated as symbols of Scotland's colourful past by those whose political principles remained liberal and Unionist. This, it has often been pointed out, was the particular achievement of Sir Walter Scott, whose fictional reworking of Jacobite history combined a sympathetic portrayal of the participants themselves as Scottish patriots with a clear message that their cause was a doomed one and that the future of Scotland lay in a modernizing Britain.[13]

Broadly speaking this cultural pattern has been passed down to the present: my claim is not that English and Scottish cultures are identical, which would be patently absurd, but that there is a great deal of convergence, in political culture especially, and also that writers, philosophers, artists and others have been able to move easily between the two audiences. This is especially relevant in the light of Gellner's thesis that the rise of exclusive forms of nationalism in nineteenth-century Europe is to be explained by the barriers to social mobility facing educated members of outlying cultures within modernizing states.[14] In the case of the Scots, linguistic and cultural overlap meant that access to the wider cultural marketplace provided by Britain was easily available, and many Scots chose to take advantage of it.[15] This is the first factor making a dual-level Anglo-British or Scottish–British identity feasible.

The second factor is mutual economic advantage, the fact that both communities have benefited from the continuing existence of the Union. I am not suggesting here that we should treat national identities as epiphenomena of economic forces. Nevertheless it is clear that one factor that fuels nationalist sentiment in divided societies is a sense that you are being exploited by the other group or groups.

In the present case both English and Scots were culturally well-equipped to take advantage of the large market created by the Union and the liberal economic regime of eighteenth-century Britain. To the extent that Weber was right about the origins of the spirit of capitalism, the Calvinist ethos prevalent in Scotland should have provided a particularly good basis for economic take-off.[16] Scotland's failure to

---

[13] For the historical trajectory of Jacobitism, see Pittock (1991).

[14] Gellner (1983, esp. ch. 5). For a much more elaborate account along these general lines of why Scottish nationalism failed to develop in a way parallel to that of other peripheral European nations, see Nairn (1977).

[15] To take one example: Allan Ramsay, arguably the most accomplished portrait painter Scotland has produced, based himself in London while continuing from time to time to undertake commissions in Edinburgh. He was appointed Painter-in-Ordinary to George III in 1760. His well-known portrait of Hume, now hanging in the Scottish National Portrait Gallery, was almost certainly painted in London.

[16] See the detailed analysis in Marshall (1992).

develop prior to Union is usually attributed to lack of investment capital and difficulties in gaining access to English and European markets. This was reversed following the Union, and particularly in the second half of the eighteenth century, when Scottish economic growth actually out-stripped England's in certain respects, for instance in overseas trade. England meanwhile benefited from having a larger market in which to sell its manufactured goods, and from the influx of Scottish talent, engineers, architects and so forth.

With the passage of time the pattern of Scotland's economic develop-ment has come to mirror that of Britain as a whole: as David McCrone has shown, if one looks at indicators such as industrial structure or the percentages of people in different occupational groups, Scotland's posi-tion is close to the average for Britain as a whole, and in some cases significantly closer than that of particular English regions such as the North West (McCrone 1992, esp. ch. 3). So although living standards in Scotland have never caught up with those in the southern part of England, the claim that both parties to the Union have benefited from it economically seems to me irrefutable. In the recent period there has also of course been the particular benefit to the Scottish side that because of the way in which the formulae for government expenditure are defined, Scots receive on average something like £1.15 per head for every £1 per head spent on public services in England. (I do not mean to give the impression that this is necessarily unfair, because to a considerable extent it reflects the different conditions that prevail in Scotland, but it does underline the continuing economic advantage to Scots of re-maining in the Union, an advantage which has continued since the Parliament was established.[17])

The third element contributing to the formation of a common British nationality over and above English and Scottish ones is what I have called an interwoven history. This is not just a matter of the two peoples being locked together in the same state for several centuries, nor is it simply a question of the two peoples having impacted on one another's development, for this would also be true of rival nationalities, my second category of cases. What I am pointing to instead is active collaboration between members of both nations in determining the course of political change, and so in defining the historic identity of the whole. In the period following the Union Scots quickly grasped the opportunities open to them to participate in British political life, to the extent of provoking an English backlash in the later part of the eighteenth

---

[17] The reasons for the disproportion are explained in McLean (1998). McLean also examines nationalist claims about the offsetting effects of tax revenues from North Sea Oil.

century, when, as Linda Colley has reminded us, John Wilkes and his followers railed against the political influence of Scotsmen, who were not only suspected of harbouring tyrannical tendencies – the legacy of Jacobitism – but of grabbing the best posts in government and administration (Colley 1992, ch. 3). As the empire expanded through the nineteenth century, the interweaving increased. It has often been pointed out that the Scots played a disproportionate role in imperial government, in the armed forces which stabilized it, and in settling and colonizing the imperial lands – Canada is the outstanding example. To the extent that British national identity was shaped by the imperial experience, by the sense of mission that underlay it and the victories and defeats that inevitably accompanied it, the English and Scots are bound together in a community of memory.[18]

It is sometimes suggested that if the empire played a central role in the consolidation of a common British identity, that identity must have begun to fade as the empire shrank, or in other words that the historical interweaving I have described no longer exists in a postimperial Britain. There is no question that the retreat from empire, along with other factors, has seriously disrupted British national identity.[19] But it is wrong to suggest that the influences that originally created and shaped a national identity must continue to operate indefinitely if the identity is to survive. Once formed, such identities have remarkable staying power, in part because of the multiple functions – both personal and political – that they perform for the people who adopt them. Moreover even without the empire as their springboard Scots continue to play a prominent role in British domestic politics. At the time of writing in 1998, four of the most senior government posts (apart from the Scottish Secretary himself) – Chancellor of the Exchequer, Foreign Secretary, Defence Secretary and Lord Chancellor – are all held by Scots, and it is only because of the tragically premature death of John Smith that we do not now have a Scottish Prime Minister. In that sense the interwoven history I have briefly described continues apace.

How should nested national identities be expressed politically?

The purpose of this historical cameo has been to point to the conditions that lead naturally to the emergence of a split-level national identity in

---

[18] To take one example of many, when Wolfe defeated Montcalm on the Plains of Abraham, his left wing was commanded by Brigadier James Murray, a Scottish officer who went on to be Governor of Quebec and eventually of Canada as a whole.

[19] I have explored this in Miller (1995, ch. 6).

societies divided in the way that Britain is divided. My claim is not that such identities are cast in aspic and must persist indefinitely into the future: that would be absurd, and at odds with the historical evidence about the emergence of a British identity that I have just been drawing on. It is rather that the wider identity cannot be seen as detrimental to, or as artificially imposed upon, members of the subnations. On the contrary, enthusiasm for the larger identity has usually been greatest among members of the smaller nations: the Scots have been keener to describe themselves as Britons than the English have (even Robert Burns was sometimes happy to wear this badge[20]). And here we must confront one of the major difficulties facing nationally divided societies in which one component nation, because of its relative size, has played a dominant role: members of that dominant nation find it harder to distinguish between the two levels of identity. Nearly all Scots have a clear sense of how British identity differs from both Scottish and English identities, but on the English side there is often confusion: most Englishmen would find it hard to explain what it means to be English as opposed to being British. As I suggested earlier, it is even doubtful that there is such a thing as an English *national* identity in the proper sense: there is a cultural identity that finds expression in certain distinctive tastes and styles of life, but if we look for the hallmarks of national identity such as political culture and shared history, we would be hard put to find anything that is distinctively English as opposed to British.

This asymmetry causes difficulties. Given that nationality depends upon mutual recognition, one could say that the source of the problem with British national identity lies with the English, who fail to understand the differences between themselves and the other nationalities as national differences: the Scots are just English people with a different accent, quaint but appealing costume and a folk culture. Scottish people rightly resent this obliviousness. The proper response is to create a political structure that explicitly recognizes the nature of the difference between the two communities. The reason for creating a devolved parliament in Edinburgh with constitutionally defined autonomous powers is not merely that it allows Scottish people some degree of control over their own cultural and social institutions, but that it gives

---

[20] Here is one stanza from Burns that seems unlikely to be recited at Scottish National Party conventions (the SNP is strongly pro-European in outlook):
　　Be Brtain still to Britain true,
　　Amang oursels united;
　　For never but by British hands
　　Must British wrongs be righted.
　　　　　　　　　('The Dumfries Volunteers', from Kinsley 1971, p. 604)
For more on Burns see Smout 1989.

expression to one-half of the dual national identity I have been describing. Its importance is symbolic as much as material. For that reason the question 'If Scotland gets a parliament, why doesn't England or why don't the English regions?' seems to me misplaced. Given the characteristic way in which English and British identities are blurred in the minds of the English, there is no distinct English national identity that demands political recognition. If there is a good case to be made out for regional assemblies in England, this would rest either on practical considerations having to do with the efficient delivery of public services, or on the general democratic argument that decisions should be made as near as possible to the people affected by them, not on any analogy with the Scottish or Welsh cases.

The same phenomenon can be observed in the Canadian and Spanish cases, where one cultural group dominates the other nested nationalities. It has often been pointed out that English Canadians outside Quebec largely think of themselves as Canadians-who-happen-to-speak-English, rather than as a distinct national group within Canada (see, for instance, Webber 1994, pp. 208–11, and Kymlicka 1998d, pp. 29–41), and this in turn makes it hard for them to regard the Québécois as a nation and not simply as French-speaking Canadians. In Spain, the Castilian-speaking majority have regional identities (to Andalusia, Navarre, Valencia, and so forth), but unlike the Catalans and Basques their national identity is unambiguously Spanish. It is sometimes suggested that things would become easier if the dominant group began to think of themselves as a separate nation.[21] This proposal seems artificial, however, given that the institutions and history of the dominant group are largely identical with those of the nation as a whole. It is more plausible to ask of the dominant group that it should recognize the separateness of the nested nationalities, and give practical expression to this recognition in the shape of asymmetrical political arrangements (parliaments for Scotland, Wales, the Basque Country and Catalonia, distinct society status for Quebec) while continuing to affirm its national identity at the level of the state as a whole.

At the same time, the analysis I have given of nationality in divided societies tells against the break-up of those societies into separate states. Where people have nested national identities, their higher-level identities also demand recognition through institutions of political self-determination. But what if one community begins to demand the opposite? What if a majority of Scots come to favour Scottish independence? Two issues arise here. The first is that we cannot treat a demand for

---

[21] This suggestion has been made in the Canadian context by Philip Resnick (1994a) and in the British context by Bernard Crick (1991).

independence (for instance a majority vote in that direction in a referendum) as decisive evidence that Scottish identity has become detached from British. The demand has to be interpreted: it might, for instance, be motivated largely by perceived economic advantage, or by indignation at some slight delivered by the English people or their representatives. But even if we treat the vote as an expression of political identity, it is still possible that the majority verdict is on this occasion wrong. The vote expresses a judgement: it says, in effect, 'the way that we now understand ourselves as a people requires that we should form a separate state'.[22] Just as we might say of an individual who tries not merely to reinterpret but to jettison the identity he has been brought up to have that he probably doesn't understand himself, we can say that for Scots to renounce their higher-level British identity would in one way be to fail to understand who they are, what makes them the people they are today.

In reply to this it might be said that such an interpretation seems to trap people in their own past: their inherited identities are being made to take precedence over their current sense of who they are. I agree that national identities are always in flux, and that independence votes by nested nations have to be treated as evidence that their identities are being reshaped in opposition to the larger nation of which they have up to now formed a subunit. If such votes are repeated, and if the majorities are substantial, then the evidence for this conclusion becomes strong. But I still want to insist that what is at stake is essentially a judgement about which political arrangement best expresses the complex set of national and other political identities that most people in contemporary democracies possess, and that such judgements are not self-validating.

However this argument might not seem decisive by itself. To use a somewhat misleading analogy, we think individual people should be free to divorce even when doing so is a mistake in the sense that they're giving up a valuable relationship for something that is less valuable. So the fact that the Scots would be denying an important part of their identity in opting for independence might not seem a conclusive reason for denying their wish. But there is also a second consideration. The

---

[22] In one sense it is true that nations are constituted by the will of their members. But this proposition needs careful analysis. Nations indeed only exist because the people who make them up continue to affirm their wish to remain associated (this is the truth in Renan's famous description of the nation as 'a daily plebiscite'). But the affirmation is grounded in beliefs about the shared history and shared cultural characteristics that make it appropriate for the people in question to live in association, and this second aspect of nationhood is equally important. As with all beliefs, these may be true, false, exaggerated, distorted, etc. Someone who says 'the Scots should separate from the UK: they have nothing in common with the English' is supporting his demand with an unwarranted assertion.

British people taken together have established a valid claim to control the whole territory of Britain, and this claim would be infringed by a unilateral secession. Claims to exercise territorial authority arise when people sharing a common national identity form a political community, and occupy territory over a substantial period of history.[23] Thus the English too now have a stake in Scottish lands, a stake that arises from the process that I described earlier, namely the emergence of a common national identity from overlapping cultures, mutually advantageous economic cooperation and an interwoven history. Unless and until there arises some kind of radical discontinuity such that these historical factors cease to affect contemporary political identities, the English majority have a right to resist unilateral secession, and for the reasons I have given they would be justified in doing so.[24]

The truth of this argument is sometimes obscured in contemporary political debate by the popularity of the doctrine that political boundaries should be decided by majority vote, so that if the inhabitants of any particular territory vote for independence in a referendum, that territory should be granted independence forthwith. The British government may appear to have signalled its assent to this doctrine when it said that it had no inherent interest in the territory of Northern Ireland, so that if at some future point there should be a majority in that territory favouring union with Ireland, their wish should be granted. It may have been necessary to say this to get the peace process under way, but the doctrine itself is wrong. It might seem to follow naturally from liberal and/or democratic principles, but in fact it doesn't. If we try to settle boundaries by appeal to liberal principles of consent alone, then we end up potentially with an infinite regress with each individual person claiming sovereignty over the piece of territory he or she happens to be standing on.[25] Equally, majority voting as a way of implementing democratic principles applies only once the boundaries of the relevant constituency have been determined. A majority vote cannot be used to fix these boundaries, since the outcome of such a vote will itself depend on who is included in and who excluded from the electorate that takes

---

[23] I have argued this at greater length in Miller (1998c, section 2).

[24] I do not mean that they would be justified in using every means at their disposal to resist a secessionist movement in Scotland; in particular I do not think that physical force should be used. One reason is that the use of force to preserve the unity of a nation-state is likely to be self-defeating: the experience of being subjected to physical coercion will destroy the sense of common national identity that allows us to speak of an overarching nation in the first place. In general, the means used to defend territorial claims have to be proportionate to the importance of those claims.

[25] The regress can be stopped, but only by introducing further stipulations that make the outcome of applying the consent principle essentially arbitrary See my critique of the consent theory of secession in Miller (1995, ch. 3, section 3).

the initial vote. Because of this indeterminacy, it is tempting to use existing administrative boundaries to define the public among whom an independence vote will be held. But this is defensible only if these boundaries already enclose a political community with common interests and a shared identity.[26] We cannot, therefore, escape making qualitative judgements about national identities, and how far smaller group identities can nest comfortably within them. Only when it is established that the people living in region R do indeed constitute a separate nationality with a strong claim to self-determination, can a referendum in R then serve as a procedural device to legitimate their secession from existing state S.[27]

Nationalists of all kinds need to be true to their core belief, that where a group of people form a community with a common national identity, it is of very great importance that they should be able to exercise political self-determination. But this must apply universally and to identity at all levels. So where a political community includes nested nationalities, each layer of identity must be given proper recognition. That is the reason for seeking a constitutional settlement which devolves appropriate powers to the subnations, but it also reveals why majority voting alone cannot decide what is the appropriate structure of authority: a unilateral English vote to annul Scottish devolution ought to be given no more weight than a unilateral Scottish vote for independence. It is tempting for subnation nationalists to believe that by repeatedly demanding referendums on independence they will one day get the answer that they want, but in yielding to this temptation they abandon the principles that make nationalism an ethically appealing creed in the first place.

Conclusion

To return from this argument about the use and abuse of referendums to the general theme of my chapter, I have proposed that if we want to apply the principle of nationality to culturally divided societies, we must draw some qualitative distinctions: specifically between ethnic divisions, rival nationalities and nested nationalities. Politically speaking, these cannot be treated in the same way: a political arrangement that might work for an ethnically plural state won't work for one inhabited by rival

[26] For further discussion of the limitations of using existing administrative boundaries to define the territory in which a secessionist vote will be held, see Moore (1997 and 1998).

[27] For a fuller discussion of the conditions under which secession is ethically justifiable, see Miller (1998c, sections 2–3).

nationalities. I have been exploring particularly the phenomenon of nested nationalities, and trying to show how genuinely split-level national identities may arise, and how best to respond to their existence. Whether the factors that I cited to explain the emergence of a common British identity among the English and the Scots apply also in the case of Belgium, Canada, Spain, Switzerland and other societies with nested national identities remains to be seen. Cultural overlap may be less evident in linguistically divided societies; an interwoven history may be easier to achieve where the overarching nation-state emerged from a compact between its component nationalities rather than from a conquest; and so on. Such historical differences will determine how comfortable it is for present-day citizens in these societies to embrace split-level identities. My aim has simply been to explain how nested national identities are possible at all, and to draw some practical implications for the idea of national self-determination.

13   The moral foundations of asymmetrical federalism: a normative exploration of the case of Quebec and Canada[1]

Alain-G. Gagnon

This chapter is not so much about stability as it is about justice. Several authors have proposed over the years to elaborate workable political arrangements to maintain political stability in plural societies, but too few have explored the need for justice. It is argued here that the objectives sought by political elites should never be limited to stability, as we are reminded too frequently by the poor fate of peoples in less democratic settings.

In this chapter, I intend to concentrate my attention on the notion of justice as it applies to highly democratic federal countries. To avoid being sidetracked I will concentrate on federal countries, that is political entities that are sociologically diverse.[2] Consequently, I will not be discussing the case of territorial or mononational federations due to their homogeneity.

Two literatures will be brought together to understand plural (federal) societies: comparative politics and political theory. Two caveats are in order. First, from a comparative politics perspective, there is a well-known tendency to stress homogeneity and assume that the citizens from a given polis share the same views, speak the same language, and are coming from the same ancestors (McRae 1979). This prevailing view has led many comparativists to equate homogeneity with political stability. A good illustration of this view is the work of Alvin Rabushka and Kenneth A. Shepsle. They believe that a 'stable democracy (cannot) be maintained in the face of cultural diversity' (Rabushka and Shepsle 1971, p. 462), and that it would be wrong to think otherwise. However, a significant body of literature developed during the seventies and eighties

---

[1] I wish to thank students of my graduate seminar on Quebec politics at McGill, among which Fredrick Appel, Can Erk, Sarah Fortin, Charles Gibbs, Raffaele Iacovino, Dimitrios Karmis, Damion Stodola and Luc Turgeon, with whom I have exchanged on this theme over the years.
[2] In the literature on comparative federalism, the first author to identity the importance of this factor was William S. Livingston (see Livingston 1952).

around the notion of consociational democracy – which refers to a political arrangement based on a grand coalition, segmental autonomy, proportional representation and minority veto – to find ways to accommodate diversity and political stability. Most influential here are the works of Arend Lijphart (1968a, 1982) and Kenneth McRae (1983, 1986).

From a political theory perspective, there is a clear bias in favour of liberal individualism in the Western world. The most noted spokesperson for this position is Chandran Kukathas who points to three central tenets about liberalism: (a) 'liberal theory is *individualist* in asserting or assuming the moral primacy of the person against claims of any social collectivity'; (b) 'it is *egalitarian* because it confers on all such individuals the same moral status and denies the relevance to legal or political order of differences in moral worth' and (c) 'it is universalist because it affirms the moral unity of the human species' neglecting the role of other cultural expressions (Kukathas [1992] 1995, p. 231).[3] Several authors have taken exception with this conventional interpretation during the last decade as a mounting literature is questioning the above hypotheses. Among the most prominent of these authors let me mention John Gray (1989), Will Kymlicka (1995), James Tully (1995), and Iris Marion Young (1990). All of these authors are questioning the capacity of liberalism to take into account issues of deep difference and are proposing to reinterpret the conventional tenets of liberalism short of which it would impossible to understand fully the world in which we are presently evolving.

Current-day politics, especially as it pertains to the cases of democratic federal societies, is challenging several assumptions prevailing in both dominant comparative politics and political theory with respect to homogeneity and individualism. The expressions of group loyalty as well as the cultural assertion of political communities in federal societies reveal the extent to which individualism and homogeneity have been incapable at understanding modern political phenomena.

The ability of federal systems to accommodate differences within states and between nations is under scrutiny around the world, but especially in advanced liberal democracies.

One important direction for the study of comparative federalism is the path offered by asymmetrical federalism. Indeed, one of the central themes of the Research Committee on Comparative Federalism and Federation has been a close examination of asymmetrical federalism, with a view to better manage political conflicts in democratic federal

---

[3] The influence of John Rawls' *A Theory of Justice* (Rawls 1971) on Kukathas is clear here.

countries. Most work in this area has concentrated on the institutional aspects of implementing asymmetry in federal systems (see, for instance, Watts 1996, pp. 57–63 and De Villiers 1994).

To date, little discussion has taken place on the values and ideologies – the 'human passions' for Montesquieu – inherent in asymmetrical federalism. While material and structural interests remain essential to an understanding of the forces at play in constitutional politics, a great part of political deliberation can be attributed to varying assumptions about what is good or valuable in a society. The study of this aspect – which I call the normative dimension – is often reduced to a second level of importance.

In this chapter, I will explore some avenues for the comparison of normative arguments used in Quebec and in Canada, but that can as easily apply to the cases of Catalonia and Spain or Wallonia and Belgium, to uphold various images of asymmetrical federalism, and I will attempt an exploratory mapping of these value structures. I hope to show that the demand for and opposition to asymmetrical federalism is not merely pragmatic – in the sense of justifying a power grab, or preventing outright secession – but rather it is normative in that it embodies different conceptions of the good.

Three normative explanations for asymmetrical federalism are explored. First, the communitarian conception of the good that is grounded on the notion that people are not acting as individuals first; in other words, individuals are the product of their own political community. It is suggested that states ought to be organized to protect community, and in plural states this clearly requires asymmetrical organizations. In the case of Quebec, the justification for asymmetry is that it allows for the better protection of a community defined by language and culture. Asymmetrical federalism is associated here with the importance of groups as providers of culture. In other words, Quebec being the primary provider of culture for Quebecers, it deserves more power than a political unit which is simply a subdivision of a larger cultural unit. This communitarian justification for asymmetry clearly involves the politics of recognition and rejects, for instance, the uniform application of the pan-Canadian Charter of Rights and Freedoms.

A second normative justification for asymmetry purports a refinement of the classical liberal idea of equality among citizens. Considering that a non-territorial federalism means individual member states can legislate differently and that citizens of the same country can receive distinct services and treatments as regards subjects of provincial jurisdiction, asymmetrical federalism simply accentuates such an understanding. In such a context, the notion of citizenship is further refined through a support in favour of an equitable treatment (rather than equal treatment) between communities, and by extension between individuals. The concern here is for equality of outcome rather than for identical treatment.[4]

A third normative justification is not the protection of distinct cultures as such but the need to secure the conditions of an enlarged democratic setting. The idea is that conditions that sustain a common public debate through time must be found. Such a deliberative democracy is best accomplished within well-circumscribed cultural communities, the modern expression of Montesquieu's small republics. Again, asymmetrical federalism is perceived as providing the appropriate response for the full accomplishment of a plural democratic federal setting.

Each of these three categories contains normative justifications for asymmetrical federalism that value different ends – different conceptions of the good life – that are specific to each society. There is a need to examine the notion of asymmetry and see how it can better serve the purposes of modern federal polities. But first, a distinction is in order with respect to the concepts of mononational and multinational federal societies, only the latter group constitutes the principal focus of this chapter.

Clarifying the concepts

Too often students of federalism do not take the time to define the concepts they work with, and simply assume that those are already understood, so why bother. This leads to profound misconceptions of what is under examination. Students of federalism have been disproportionately influenced by its American embodiment, comparing other types as exceptions to the rule. So, the dominant image of federalism in comparative politics has been to define it in territorial terms, making the United States the main referent. But what of Belgium, Canada, Switzerland and, more recently, the federalization of Spain? Those federal societies do not fit the territorial model. Expectedly mononational federations have tended to be more stable in part due to the fact that their citizens have a sense of sharing much more ensconced than is normally the case in multinational federations, Switzerland being the exception.

Juan Linz makes an interesting point when referring to democratic federal countries as he clearly differentiates between federal states for

---

[4] A similar dichotomy is drawn by Kenneth McRae in his interpretation of the Meech Lake proposal (see McRae 1992).

which the principal objective is to bring together political units that were apart into a single body politics (essentially the territorial *qua* mononational definition) and federal states for which the main objective is to hold together political units of different language groups, religious communities, cultural groups or national components (essentially the multinational definition). Cases identifiable with mononational federalism include Australia, Austria after 1918, Germany after 1821, and the United States, whereas cases closer to multinational federalism are Belgium, Canada, India, Spain, and I would add Switzerland, although Linz considers the latter as a member of a state-nation since its citizens identify first with the whole federation (Linz 1997c, pp. 13–20).

Mononational cases are not particularly useful for our purposes since they are not traversed by cultural pluralism and rarely refer to the notion of asymmetrical federalism which is viewed as an oddity in liberal democratic settings. References to asymmetrical federalism in mononational cases are normally limited to the size of member states, their relative economies, their respective political influence, and the like, and they tend to deal with issues of degree more than of kind. In the case of multinational federal countries, the issues at stake are of a very different nature since they focus on competing definitions of the good life *per se*.

Pointing to the American case, Ferran Requejo asserts rightly that,

If we remain within the orbit of American federalism, the answer to the question about the possibilities of regulating democratic citizenship in [multinational] societies is basically a negative one . . . It is fundamentally a 'territorial' model, and one that is governed by homogenizing interpretations of the democratic concept of 'popular sovereignty' – which avoids the basic question, unanswered in democratic theory, about who the people are, and who decides who they are – as well as ideas about equality of citizenship and equality between the federated units. (Requejo 1997, p. 21)

The issues of equality of citizenship and equality of the federated entities are particularly useful when studying the notion of asymmetrical federalism. There are many forms of asymmetry but the ones that are most consequential for political communities are political and constitutional asymmetries. Differences of size, population and wealth of federal members play a role in the exercise of powers, but what matters most is the sharing of authority in a federation.

An asymmetrical federal structure implies the constitutionally entrenched federal character of a state, measured by the division of powers between central and regional governments or by the composition of central decision-making institutions, whose member states have dissimilar relationships to the central government, its jurisdiction, institutions, or laws (King 1982). By its insistence upon constitutional entrenchment, this definition excludes *de facto*[5] asymmetrical arrangements in which asymmetry may result from differing populations, cultures, economic activities or political choices. In this text, I concentrate on asymmetrical federalism denoted by the fluctuating division of jurisdictions between member states, to the exclusion of supranational expressions of federalism.

In the Canadian context, asymmetrical arrangements between the provinces and the central government have been a continuing feature due to different purposes and strengths of the states constituting the evolving federation. With the emergence of the Quiet Revolution of the 1960s, accompanied by the profound change of political ideologies that occurred in Quebec during that time, demands for the constitutional recognition of this member state as a province *pas comme les autres* started to augment significantly. The first official recognition of this aspiration coming from Ottawa since the beginning of the Quiet Revolution was contained in the Laurendeau–Dunton Commission report, in which the cultural duality of the Canadian state was clearly defined as a fundamental constitutive principle.

However, demands for the asymmetrical decentralization of powers to the Quebec government have often been viewed by Canadians outside of Quebec as a potential threat to the continuation of the federation, and have rendered the claim for 'asymmetrical federalism' a controversial project. A dominant impression of asymmetrical federalism by Canadians outside of Quebec (COQ) holds that demands for recognition of a 'special status' for the province within the Canadian federation amounts to a strategic manoeuvre on the part of the Quebec political elite to gain more power. Let me point out however that the existence of *de facto* asymmetry within the Canadian federation, in terms of administrative arrangements as well as geo-demographic traits, has often been noted (Milne 1991) and has, at times, led to justifications for *de jure* asymmetry. There has been some support in favour of asymmetry over the years. As a noted example, one of the conclusions of the 1991 report of the Citizen's Forum on Canada's Future, the consultation process that led to the Charlottetown Accord, specified that

Given that provinces have entered confederation on different terms and operate under different provisions, we believe that special arrangements in provinces based on special needs are a fundamental principle of Canadian federalism. This principle would apply where needed to all provinces. (Citizens' Forum, p. 124)

---

[5] For a further analysis of *de facto* and *de jure* allocations of powers see Gagnon and Garcea (1988); for the application of this distinction to the case of Spain, see Requejo (1996).

The authors of the Report continued by stating that Canadians should seek equality 'in the face of specific needs', with the result that 'Quebec should have the freedom and means to be itself – a unique society with its own distinctive place in a renewed Canadian family' (Citizens' Forum, p. 124).

In contrast, the role of asymmetrical federalism has been extolled as a diluent of 'secession-potential'. In this connection it is worthwhile noting that Reginald Whitaker has identified a phenomenon in which the popularity of asymmetrical federalism declined as the threat of Quebec sovereignty diminished (Whitaker 1993, pp. 107–14).

Although pragmatic views of asymmetrical federalism such as those outlined above may themselves contain a normative dimension, they are different from the broad categories of values and ideologies outlined in the introduction because they do not directly address the question: what is good for a given society? Responses such as administrative efficiency, convenience or national unity for its own sake pale in the light of the response provided by normative considerations. I will now examine the first of these categories, the communitarian principle.

Forging communities

The first normative justification that has been evoked to encourage the adoption of asymmetrical federalism derives from the importance of communities in social life. In response to the question 'what is a fundamental good in our society?' the normative values contained within this category answer: 'our community, culture, identity and heritage'.

All individuals, it is argued, are fundamentally social beings who require a cultural baggage, such as a collection of symbols or a vibrant language that can be used in all aspects of social relations, in order to secure a sense of belonging and identity. Social life necessitates the flourishing of the culture of a political community, which should be protected and promoted by the state to ensure its long-term continuation. Espousing this view, it is inevitable that one should desire, as well as demand, that a government in assuming leadership on behalf of a political community be vested with the powers necessary to implement corresponding policy measures.

The defence of community originates in Greek philosophy and was reflected in the organic, corporate thought of the Middle Ages. Later, in the seventeenth and eighteenth centuries, European thinkers such as Johann Althusius and Montesquieu renewed this tradition in response to the absolutist notions of sovereignty that were being used to justify centralized monarchical powers. At the time of the American Federal convention of 1787, the decentralized structure incorporated in the Articles of Confederation was defended by those who idealized the social organization of small communities, and who aimed to create a political organization for the colonies that corresponded to the ideal of the small, pastoral republic. Although these anti-federalists lost their quest for state sovereignty, many authors have suggested that their opinions nonetheless shaped the federal structure that was finally adopted (Ketcham 1986, pp. 16–17).

In Canada, the federal structure incorporated into the British North America Act of 1867 was lauded, especially by the political leaders and clergy of Quebec, as a safeguard of the religion, language, educational and legal institutions of the new province. Studying that period, Samuel V. LaSelva reminds us that at the time, 'The Canadian tension relates not to liberty but to identity and to the relation (or clash) between local identities and national identity . . . Canada was to be a nation in which multiple loyalties and multiple identities flourished' (LaSelva 1995, pp. 38 and 41).

This understanding of Canadian federalism, based on multiple identities, has had many supporters throughout the country since its inception though it has been undermined from time to time by Canadian unitarists. In the early twentieth century, the autonomists led by Ontario's Premier Oliver Mowat, took up the fight against the imposition of 'national, uniform standards on culturally, religiously, and linguistically distinct provinces' (Vipond 1995, p. 102).

For advocates of constitutional 'special status' for Quebec, the breaking of the impartiality of federalism on the issue of community is a wholly positive development. It is argued that Quebec should be constitutionally recognized as a nation because this reflects a fundamental reality of the Canadian federation: the patterns of allegiances and identity in Quebec *are* different from those of the Rest of Canada. The distinct society notion can be viewed in a highly symbolic fashion, and its effects on the development of a sense of a political community are highly significant.

A more concrete argument for asymmetrical federalism, however, resides in the identification of a public good in Quebec that is foreign to the other member states of the federation: the protection and promotion of the French language and culture in North America. Indeed, Quebec is the sole jurisdiction in North America in which French speakers have a majority status. Therefore, it is argued, the Quebec government ought to be vested with responsibilities that extend beyond those of other provinces, such as upholding the interests of a Quebec nation, French-speaking minorities outside of Quebec, and *la francophonie* in North America.[6]

For the late Fernand Dumont, the issue amounted to one of the necessary role of the state to defend the nations on a given territory. He asserted that 'If it falls on the state to promote the equality of citizens and the distribution of wealth, this responsibility concerns in particular the maintenance and flourishing of national communities' (Dumont 1995, p. 55).

Arguments of asymmetrical policies designed to protect or, for this matter, promote Quebec's culture can also be based on historical continuity. It is argued that there is a collective good in the preservation of languages, traditions, institutions and symbols of previous generations, and the members of a political community such as Quebec, Catalonia or Wales should act not only as inheritors but as trustees of their respective cultures and political legacies.

The Spanish constitution of 1978 recognizes the importance of maintaining such a continuity, making it a point of solidarity. In its preamble, it stipulates that the constitution ought to 'protect all Spaniards and peoples of Spain in the exercise of human rights, of their cultures and traditions and of their languages and institutions'. The constitution also confirms in article 33 that 'The wealth of the different language variations of Spain is a cultural heritage which shall be object of special respect and protection.'

In Canada, James Tully is assuredly the scholar who has made the most significant contribution to the study of constitutional politics based on the discourse of historical continuity. For Tully, a federal relationship between governments can be equated to the relations between individuals. As individuals possess a culture of rights, duties and responsibilities, governments also relate to their counterparts in a relationship that is based on conventions. These conventions, which for Tully form the crux of the federal spirit of common constitutionalism, are three in number: the convention of mutual recognition, the convention of continuity and the convention of consent (Tully 1995, pp. 116–39).

According to Tully, the division of powers between the federal and provincial governments specified in the British North America Act were constructed under the guise of the first two conventions: the recognition of the cultures of the original member states of Confederation and the continuity of those cultures in the new constitutional framework. In the

---

[6] The Tremblay Report, commissioned by the Quebec government in 1953, was the first to articulate fully the role of the Quebec government with respect to those responsibilities. Cf. Kwavnick (1973, p. 211).

case of Quebec, the culture of Lower Canada was recognized, preserved and continued in its Civil law, property traditions, and French language, customs and religion. For Tully, respect for the three conventions of federalism can lead to further claims in favour of asymmetry in a federation when powers falling under the jurisdiction of member states are centralized.[7]

The decision on the part of the central government (along with the nine anglophone provinces) to break the three conventions of common constitutionalism in 1981 undermined *overarching loyalties*, to use Arend Lijphart's concept, between Quebec and the Rest of Canada. It also undermined federal trust, or what Germans call the *Bundestreue*, since the practice of constitutional politics requiring the support of Quebec for fundamental constitutional changes was brought to a stop.[8]

Our first category of normative justification for asymmetrical federalism has concentrated on the importance of social groups as providers of culture. But what of individuals? This is the theme to which I will turn in the next section.

Addressing inequalities

A second category of values underlying the defence of asymmetrical federalism can be found in the expression of equality between people.

The relation of asymmetrical federalism to the concepts of liberty, equality and justice is riddled with complicated and controversial normative interpretations about the trilogy of groups, individuals and the state. The aspects that emerge most often from this debate involve issues surrounding the meaning of citizenship and the nature of equal treatment of individuals. Most often, detractors of asymmetrical federalism are of the view that it leads to unbalanced and unfair practices, and that it inevitably creates second-class status for citizens who do not see themselves as being part of a given political community.

In the Canadian context, Alan Cairns suggests, for example, that an asymmetrical application of the Canadian Charter of Rights and Freedoms leads to an asymmetrical citizenship (Cairns 1991, p. 88). That view is also based on a normative model which stresses a common set of

---

[7] In the case of the 1982 repatriation of the constitution from Britain, Tully makes the point that the three conventions have been broken.

[8] For a useful discussion of the subject, refer to Bertus de Villiers (1995) and Kymlicka and Raviot (1997). The latter article is an essay based on a series of papers presented during a conference on the theme of 'Identities, Participation, and Common Life in Federal States' which was held at Laval University and the University of British Columbia, 30 September–2 October 1996.

values and rights, enshrined in the constitution, a single sovereign people and a superseding nationality.

I argue here that in adopting an alternative normative discourse based on the view of Canada as a collection of distinct political communities, it is also possible to maintain an understanding of Canadian citizenship in which all Canadians are considered equals. From that standpoint there is no tension between citizenship and allegiance towards a federal political community. Richard Vernon has argued that citizens in truly federal states are 'federal citizens' in that their loyalties may be divided between orders of government, each sovereign within their spheres of jurisdiction. Citing Proudhon, Vernon suggests that 'to the extent that the *federal principle* leaves open the question of priority, permitting individuals to balance one attachment against the other, it permits more scope' (Vernon 1988, p. 10).

Various conceptions of citizenship coexist within multinational federal democratic regimes and they ought to be supported, I would argue, as long as they are subject to the liberal requirement for the general equality of citizens within individual member states.

Federalism, especially multinational federalism, assumes that citizens of a member state can be subject to different laws. More to the point, Reginald Whitaker argues that '[m]odern federalism is an institutionalization of the formal limitation of the national majority will as the legitimate ground for legislation. Any functioning federal system denies by its very processes that the national majority is the efficient expression of the sovereignty of the people' (Whitaker 1992, p. 167). This difficulty has largely been resolved in federalist theory as students of federalism have accepted the legitimacy of divided sovereignty in a federation.

Asymmetrical federalism follows the same path as federalism in the reconceptualization of citizen equality from the model of a unitary (or uniform) state in which all are treated identically under the law, but pursues the course a little further. It does so by accepting the belief that dissimilarity in jurisdiction as well as laws is appropriate for individual member states of a federation.

As such, asymmetrical federalism has been retained as a means by which the concept of equality can be broadened from a restrictive interpretation of equal treatment to the more subtle ones of equality of opportunity, or the global equality between nations. Programmes such as affirmative action, which are designed to ensure greater equity by eliminating traditional obstacles to equality for discriminated and disadvantaged groups, are justified through an understanding that socioeconomic historical patterns have an impact on the equality of individuals.

For James Tully, the distinctions within equality can be summarized as identical versus equitable treatment. He suggests that the practice of legal monism correlates with the former concept whereas that of legal pluralism is related to the latter (Tully 1992). Similarly, procedural liberalism is the hallmark of the first, while communitarian liberalism acts as the model for the second. Asymmetrical federalism is quite often cited as an instrument of equity rather than strict equality, and a tool of communitarian rather than procedural liberalism. In this way, the equality of individuals and nations in a federation should be considered in the light of their particular needs and historical developments, not in terms of their identical relation with other individuals or member states in a federation.

Recently, several works on Canadian and Spanish politics, for example, have stressed the place of equality and equity in the debate on asymmetrical federalism. In *Canada: Reclaiming the Middle Ground*, Donald Lenihan, Gordon Robertson and Roger Tassé have argued that Canada must come to terms with differing conceptions of procedural and communitarian liberalism within federal states.[9] Political questions such as what separates individual from collective (as well as group rights), and how they should be evaluated, contain a sociocultural dimension which must be considered in relation to the descriptive reality of various cultural contexts.

While classical liberalism imposes formal equality on all citizens, Lenihan and his colleagues argue that, it fails to account for unequal consequences of policy measures on diverse regions, and for this matter on diverse nations. The quest for equality of treatment should not preclude the goal of equality of outcome. The issue has accentuated pertinence when it is argued that the equality of the member states of a multinational federation must be maintained in spite of different socio-economico-cultural backdrops. They write,

The claim that provincial equality implies same treatment is open to the same kind of objection raised against a formal approach to the equality of persons. Those who argue this way seem to confuse the (sound) claim that the federal government should treat the interests of all provinces with equal concern and respect with (unsound) claim that all provinces should be treated the same. This ignores the fact that provinces (like individuals) sometimes have special needs or may be burdened by circumstances. (Lenihan et al., p. 184)

The issue of equality of outcome becomes more complex when one considers the nature of the laws or rights that are used to determine

---

[9] For the need to further differentiate between collective and group rights, see Ferran Requejo (1997, p. 2); for a viewpoint that Canada's Supreme Court judges at times take into account group rights in rendering their decisions, see Eisenberg (1994).

equality. The distinction between individual and group rights has its roots in antiquity, but remains highly relevant to this topic. Several authors have suggested that the Quebec–Canada, and for this matter Catalonia–Spain tensions stem from differing views of rights. Where English Canada is more familiar with individual rights, it is argued that Quebecers intend to use group rights to further individual rights.

André Burelle makes the argument that Canada's present political quandary stems from the inability of the Canadian state to recognize the different values shaping Quebec society. That author defines this competing value structure as the *droit à la différence* of the Québécois people. He invites both Quebecers and Canadians outside of Quebec to come half way toward each other. Those who insist that Quebec's differing value structure be upheld must be willing to accept, he asserts, the necessity for the preservation of a social and economic union within Canada, in which the central government will exercise a major role. In turn, those who support the individual-rights only option must recognize and be willing to provide the Quebec state the necessary tools with which to assert its right to difference (Burelle 1995, p. 105).[10]

Among these tools, the Canadian Charter should not be imposed on a pan-Canadian level without first respecting the country's differing conventions and cultures, according to Tully (1994a, pp. 157–78) – a sentiment echoed by many Quebec political scientists. One of the most outspoken on this issue is Guy Laforest, who has charged that former Prime Minister Pierre Elliott Trudeau used the Canadian Charter as an overt instrument of a 'typically English-Canadian nationalism' in an attempt to shape and invent the Canadian nation without paying attention to the existence of a Quebec nation. Considering the power of the Prime Minister to unilaterally appoint judges not only to the Canadian Supreme Court but to the provincial Superior and Appeal Courts as well, Laforest makes the point that 'through the judicialization of the political system, the Charter works against Canada's federal nature, for the judicial power reflects the federal reality of our country most poorly' (Laforest 1995b, pp. 133–5, 191). To improve matters, one can imagine a political solution that would require an asymmetrical application of the Canadian Charter of Rights and Freedoms, so that the distinctness of both Quebec and aboriginal communities is not placed under the tutelage of the homogenizing tendency of its application.

So far, I have argued that normative arguments defending asymmetrical federalism in multinational federal democratic states can be traced to general principles related to community and equality. The third and

---

[10] For a series of pertinent proposals to accommodate both Quebecers and Canadians, see Gibbins and Laforest (1998).

final category appears to me the most important of all: upholding democratic institutions.

Deepening democratic principles

In response to the question: 'what is a fundamental good in a given society?', normative arguments in favour of asymmetrical federalism answer: democratic citizenship. In particular, it is argued in Canada that asymmetrical federalism reinforces the country's democratic system by encouraging public participation in the decision-making process, accommodating differences between political communities and buttressing the democratic legitimacy of the federal state. In return, supporters of the territorial vision of federalism maintain that traditional notions of national citizenship may be undermined.

A normative argument for the federal principle suggests that federalism maximizes the public participation of individuals in the democratic life of their society. In connection with this point, Jeff Spinner points out that,

The liberal state should work toward ensuring that all of its citizens are fluent in the public language . . . Deny ethnic children of the dominant language and they will undoubtedly retain many aspects of the ethnic culture – and remain economically subordinate. Allophones in Quebec who want to preserve all of the elements of their culture by preventing their children from learning French well and encouraging them to remain fluent in their native language are condemning their children to lives of obstructed economic opportunities. (Spinner 1994, p. 154).

In this view, citizens are most interested and knowledgeable about issues that relate most directly to their particular political community, region or locality. They are most likely to understand local problems and hold elected officials more accountable for their actions. Provincial or state administrations thus provide the government that is the most responsive and accountable to the population, while the central government is responsible for policies of joint interest.

This argument for federalism may be traced back to the Baron of Montesquieu, among others. Several passages of Montesquieu's *De l'esprit des lois* are devoted to the value of small republics in protecting the liberty of citizens. Monstesquieu recognized that individuals act not only as unique entities but as members of a cultural group, society, people, or nation. The culture of a people – which he calls a general spirit – can flow from 'climate, religion, laws, the maxims of government, examples of past things, mores and manners' (Montesquieu [1849] 1989, part III, book xix, ch. 4). Nowadays, we refer to identity toward a political community. This general spirit guides the civic action life of individuals; likewise, in the political realm, one can identify 'public goods' based on this general spirit. Montesquieu argues that the laws governing individuals should be shaped in the spirit of the relative culture of the people and should work toward the achievement of the public goods that are specific to that community (Montesquieu 1989, part I, book viii, ch. 16).

For Montesquieu, a citizen of a small republic feels a greater allegiance to that state than he or she would to a larger state, and therefore popular sovereignty is more widely protected. However, Montesquieu's writings reveal that he was also concerned with the advantages of union for small states. According to Montesquieu, large monarchies were more able to defend their territory and to pursue international relations than small republics, although they represented a compromise of liberty for authority. Montesquieu found a solution to this perpetual dichotomy of the competing values of liberty and authority in the federal system of government.

A similar theory can be found in the writings of the nineteenth-century French theorist, Pierre Joseph Proudhon, who wrote that local or small governments were always more likely to act as a bulwark against abusive power than larger governments. Highly centralized bureaucracies, necessary to regulate certain elements of social life, also erode the liberty of citizens by distancing popular sovereignty. The federal principle could be viewed as a balance between the competing concepts of authority and liberty – what the central government offers of the former, the regional government offers of the latter (Proudhon 1979, pp. 43–9).

The desire to protect liberty by ensuring local sovereignty, as articulated by Montesquieu and Proudhon, is integrally linked to the concept of political community, and leads to justifications for asymmetrical federalism. For Jeremy Webber, all political communities are structured on a common language which has served to frame public debate, and thereby to build a general consensus of objectives and allegiances within the community. Public debate and participation occur in one language only, that of the political community. He argues that, 'When Canadians follow a public debate, they are usually following the version that occurs in their public language. When they care about the outcome of that debate, they do so in terms of relating to the discussion they know' (Webber 1994, p. 204).[11] In short, languages may cross political communities, but the reverse does not hold.

---

[11] This observation makes it particularly difficult to believe that a real dialogue can take place between uniformist Canadians and asymmetrist Quebecers.

The language each community knows applies also when interpreting a given constitution in a multinational federal setting. While studying the Spanish case, Ferran Requejo makes the point that contrary to the prevailing view that the state is neutral in liberal democratic societies in practice the reality is much different. He asserts that,

Apart from recognizing the rights of citizenship, liberal institutions introduce a whole range of hegemonic linguistic and cultural traits into the public sphere in order to create a homogeneous 'national' identity 'from above' . . . [Liberal democratic rights and rules] have never been 'neutral' as far as individual identities are concerned, because those rights and rules include a whole range of implicit *particularist* cultural values (such as language, reconstruction of history, 'common' traditions, etc.) which are beyond than mere procedural and universalist issues. (Requejo 1997, pp. 7–8)

The lack of neutrality rendered through the expression of dominant rights and rules in multinational federal states underlines once more the importance to value the implementation of asymmetrical federalism. The contribution of Charles Taylor is particularly relevant here. For Taylor, the challenge of several multinational states is to recognize deep diversity.

To build a country for everyone, Canada would have to allow for second-level 'deep' diversity, where a plurality of ways of belonging would also be acknowledged and accepted. Someone of say, Italian extraction in Toronto, or Ukrainian extraction in Edmonton, might indeed feel Canadian as a bearer of individual rights in a multicultural mosaic. His or her belonging would not 'pass through' some other community, although the ethnic identity might be important to him or her in various ways. But this person might nevertheless accept that a Québécois, or a Cree, or a Déné, might belong in a very different way, that they were Canadian through being members of their national communities. (Taylor 1991a, pp. 75–6)

Taylor advances the idea that Canadian society is influenced by a 'participatory model', as opposed to the strict rights-bearing model paradigm that characterizes the United States. It is essential, Taylor argues, that citizens hold respect for the public institutions that determine the rules of social and political life, that they possess a personal stake in the commonly defined good life, and that members of a plurinational community have a shared identity. The heterogeneity of Canada leads Taylor to conclude that 'we do not have and cannot develop a single national identity' (Taylor 1993a, p. 100) primarily due to the distinctiveness of Quebec. This leads that author to call for substantial decentralization of the Canadian federation, and where the jurisdictional needs and priorities of the English-Canadian provinces do not correspond to those of Quebec, that asymmetrical federalism should be fully instigated. Taylor's argument clearly falls under the democratic category because his main concern lies with political participation which, in turn, determines cultural identity.

Placed in federal theory, the writings of Webber, Taylor and Requejo reveal that these authors, like those who propound respectively an asymmetrical solution for Canada[12] and Spain, adopt a view of the federal state as 'community of communities', in which member states act as the primary political expressions of popular will.

An additional point about asymmetrical federalism concerning normative principles which fall into the democratic category involves the issue of legitimacy. Here legitimacy in a federal society is a function of the attitudes and patterns of allegiance of the population. Thomas Hueglin suggests that 'Federal legitimacy depends primarily on whether the premises of federalism as ideology are fulfilled, i.e. whether federations do indeed contribute to the promotion of freedom by making government more responsive to the popular will' (Hueglin 1987, p. 35).

The present federal system in Canada is suffering from a lack of legitimacy in Quebec, and this situation has been heightened since the patriation of the constitution in 1982. In connection with this, an important point is made by Janet Ajzenstat: 'What changed is that the 1982 act is no mere program of the federal government, but part of the constitution, the supreme law of the country' (Ajzenstat 1995, p. 127).

Ajzenstat correctly asserts that the decision to patriate the constitution severely undermined the legitimacy of the Canadian federal system among Quebecers. For her, the legitimacy in crisis is due to the fact that, as of 1982, the principles prevailing in a liberal democratic setting have been seriously weakened.

Procedural liberalism was said not to tolerate a prior idea of the good in politics – the constitution, the system of government should be neutral with respect to ideology and political interest. The constitution is the rule book for the game of politics. The fact that it does not prefer one way of life, one political ideology or program, is what enables parties to come and go in office, secures respect for political opposition, and enables marginal groups to bid for influence. The procedural constitution is supposed to be above politics, immune to political manipulation, in order to make politics possible. (Ajzenstat 1995, p. 127)

All of that has been pushed aside with the 1982 patriation. Politics is

---

[12] Some authors in English Canada have suggested that as a resolution to difficulty for asymmetry posed by the equality of the provinces doctrine, Quebec should be removed from the category of province altogether, see Alan Cairns (1991, p. 89). Others have noted that Quebec, in concert with other member states, could gain significant new powers that are appropriate to their needs by enshrining the concept of concurrency with provincial paramountcy, see Milne (1991, p. 302). Normatively, Quebec would be recognized as a separate political community in the first proposal, while in the second, the member state would be considered one component of a single albeit decentralized Canadian community.

no longer possible, short of judicial litigation, between the nations that gave birth to the Canadian experience. Nowadays, we find ourselves in a situation where groups (women, environmentalists, gays, ethnic and religious goups, etc.,) are making claims with the main purpose of improving their lot; the idea of a neutral constitution has gone by the wayside. As a result, justice in Canada is rendered according to one's political strength and is no longer based on the unwritten principles that gave birth to the original compact which led to the establishment of the Canadian federation.[13]

Conclusion

Neglecting the moral foundations of federalism is unproblematic so long as the practice of federalism is accepted. (LaSelva 1996, p. 171)

We have seen that the philosophical statements and ideological positions of upholding multinational democratic federal polities can be divided into three general principles: the democratic principle which seeks responsive government, widespread political participation and heightened sensitivity toward citizenship; the communitarian principle which aims to maintain culture to ensure historical continuity and equity; the liberal principle which speaks a language of equality and liberty. In this chapter, I have suggested that the normative judgements found within these principles act as crucial underpinnings of asymmetrical federalism.

Federalism and especially asymmetrical federalism is a process of offering a variety of options to cope with multinational states. To the extent that the federal principle can establish itself as a flexible and dynamic force, creative variation from the traditional structure of federations, such as asymmetrical federalism, offers a powerful tool of accommodation[14] in democratic multinational countries.

As I mentioned at the outset, this chapter stresses fundamental issues facing Canada, and similar multinational federal settings, among those are the quest for justice, equity and equality. Asymmetrical federalism is proposed as a political solution to changing political conditions, and is also intended as a model of empowerment (Gagnon 1993a and Smith 1995b, p. 16).

[13] According to Ajzenstat, in the Canadian context, 'the quarrel is not really about the requirements that will satisfy justice. It is about what justice *is*. To be treated justly now means being first in a constitutional pecking order, and each group advances the definition of justice – that is, the scheme of ranking – that gives it pre-eminence.' See Ajzenstat (1995, p. 132).

[14] Will Kymlicka made the point that 'What is clear . . . is that if there is a viable way to promote a sense of solidarity and common purpose in a multinational state, it will involve accommodating, rather than subordinating, national identities' (Kymlicka 1995, p. 189).

In sum, what we know about the Canadian federal system is that tampering with the federal spirit on the part of the central government has led to a situation of real political instability.[15] It now remains to be seen, with the herein proposed asymmetrical federalism, to what extent stability can be restored. In this chapter, we have also seen that the opposition to minority rights, contrary to what is predicted by classical liberals, has led to unstable political situations in several multinational federal settings. In the Canadian case, it is worth mentioning that the call made by most Quebecers in favour of asymmetrical federalism has not, contrary to liberal orthodoxy, led to a large disaffection for the Rest of Canada.[16]

In closing, if Quebec is to remain in a political partnership with the Rest of Canada in the twenty-first century, it is clear that the option of ignoring the concept of asymmetrical federalism simply does not exist.

---

[15] Looking at the emerging federal state in Belgium, Francis Delpérée reminds us that 'La forme la plus élémentaire de la loyauté fédérale, c'est, en effet, le respect de la constitution fédérale. C'est le respect de la règle de jeu' (Delpérée 1995, p. 133).

[16] As attest the results of a CROP poll done for *L'Actualité* and TVA in 1992 – see 'Le Canada dans la peau', in *L'Actualité* (July 1992), pp. 21–30, 34–6.

Richard Simeon and Daniel-Patrick Conway

Introduction

In a special issue of *The Annals of the American Academy of Political and Social Science* entitled 'Ethnic Conflict in the World Today', Martin Heisler argued that 'the peaceful and effective management of conflict between ethnic groups involves the building of rules and institutions for coexistence in a single society, state and economy' (Heisler 1977). The question we address in this chapter is: How effective is federalism as an institutional framework for managing these kinds of conflict? In particular, when, and under what conditions, does federalism constitute a stable, enduring solution, rather than a transitional phase on the way either towards secession or centralization? Is it inevitable that federal solutions are unstable? Are some models of federalism more likely to succeed than others and if so, under what conditions?

We will look at one long-standing democratic federal system, Canada, and three newly emerging federal or quasi-federal systems, Belgium, Spain and Scotland. All are multinational federations, rather than what Juan Linz calls mononational federations, such as Germany or Australia (Linz 1997b). We will also focus on managing conflict among groups that are territorially concentrated. Federalism itself is not a plausible solution when minorities are spread widely throughout the majority population, although Elkins (1995) has shown that many federalist devices can be used even in these cases.

Federalism is only one way of managing or accommodating diversity. It occupies a middle ground on a continuum running from separation or independence for each group at one pole, and complete assimilation or the submergence of difference at the other. It seeks to maintain the unity of the larger state, while giving recognition and empowerment to minorities. It is predicated both on devolving autonomy to the minorities, and on recognizing and protecting them in the larger society and polity. Multinational federal states are, as Linz put it, 'an effort to hold together within the state those who are thought to be separate nations,

338

and who therefore find an unitary state unacceptable' (1997b, p. 27). Federalism is certainly not the only option for mediating such conflicts. It is one answer to the challenge posed by McGarry and O'Leary: how to 'establish whether multi-ethnic states can be stabilized in ways which are compatible with liberal democratic values and institutions' (McGarry and O'Leary 1993, p. 4).

Views on the relation of federalism to the management of ethnic conflict vary considerably. For example, Diamond and Plattner (1994) argue that 'ethnic conflict – particularly ethnopolitical threats to the central state – can often be mediated through a judicious implementation of federalism and constitutional guarantees for the protection of individual collective (minority) rights'. Others, such as Maynes (1993), contend that 'specialists in ethnic conflict are wary of federal solutions because they tend to promote secession. Both are right. Given the widely varying models of federalism, and the differences in the societal conditions in which federalism may be implemented, it is virtually impossible to make broad generalizations about the effectiveness of federalism in multinational societies. Rather we must see its effects as contingent. We can only explore whether and how institutions 'matter' by exploring the interaction between them and the societies in which they are embedded. Any assessment of its utility will depend on the individual circumstances of each case.

Additionally, federalism is never the whole answer: it is only one of several institutional devices through which the twin goals of successful conflict regulation in multinational societies can be achieved. These goals are: first, to ensure that each of the national groups within the state feels that it has sufficient autonomy to guarantee its integrity and survival; and, second, to ensure that there will be sufficient accommodation between them that unrestrained conflict is avoided, common goals can be achieved and a common political space maintained by carefully crafted political and civil arrangements (Linz 1997a, p. 413).

The logic of federalism

The logic in support of federalism is simple: conflict will be reduced by a measure of disengagement, of separation. Harmony will be increased in a system in which territorially concentrated minorities are able to exercise autonomy or self-determination on matters crucial to their identity and continued existence, without the fear of being overridden or vetoed by the majority group. Similarly, a federal system will limit the ability of the majority to impose its will on the minorities. Hence they will be reconciled to the system – realizing both the advantages of autonomy and the benefits – economic, social and otherwise – of participation in a larger political entity. Thus, 'In a federal system, a national state majority cannot prevail over a minority that happens to constitute a majority in one of the local communities that is constitutionally privileged' (Dahl, in Linz 1997b). Federalism provides protection against domination by the majority, an opportunity for self-fulfillment and self-development for the minority, through institutions that it controls, while maintaining the ability of both groups to pursue common goals.

But another line of argument suggests that federalism is Janus-faced. It asserts that federalism can perpetuate and intensify the very conflicts it is designed to manage. This is because they are institutionalized and entrenched in the very design of the political system. Federalism empowers minority elites who are likely to have a vested interest in sustaining and perhaps exacerbating the conflict. At the extreme, federalism can provide the institutional tools and resources for nation building; a base that can make a move towards secession plausible and viable in the future (Dion 1992). As we will see, this 'slippery slope' argument is one that has been prominent in debates in several of our countries.

So the question is: which analysis is right? Or, more specifically, under what conditions is federalism more likely to constitute a stable accommodation within a divided society; and under what conditions will it be more likely to prove ineffective and unstable, leading to dissolution or secession?

Difficulties in making generalizations

There are enormous difficulties about making any sort of generalization about federal systems. First, with respect to democratic, multinational federations, such as we are considering here, there is a very small number of cases, each with widely varying history and circumstances.

Second, the causal arrows run both ways. On the one hand federalism is a response to, and is shaped by, the underlying divisions; on the other, federalism can powerfully influence societal divisions and the ways in which they are mobilized and expressed. It privileges some, and undercuts others (Cairns 1976).

Third, there is the question of what do we mean by 'success' in managing conflict? Avoidance of violence, chaos and stalemate are criteria that all sides can accept. But beyond that, success or failure depends on the perspective one brings. Minorities are likely to judge 'success' primarily by the extent to which federalism maximizes their group's freedom and autonomy. Majorities are likely to judge it in terms of whether it limits their freedom of action. Minorities are likely to judge it a failure if autonomy is decreased or aspirations for greater autonomy are not met. Majorities are likely to see failure in the loss of power to those minorities, or if they see them as receiving special privileges. Secession may be the ultimate success for at least some members of national groups in the federation; for many members of the majority, it is the essential failure. However, if it comes to secession, it is interesting to ask whether that is more likely to be occur in a peaceful and orderly way when it occurs under a federal system. Perhaps so, because partial institutional disengagement has already taken place. The newly independent state already has a government.

Yet another difficulty in generalizing about the effectiveness of federalism in managing ethnonational conflicts is that federal institutions themselves vary so much. There is no single model: federations differ along a great many dimensions, and each is in some sense *sui generis*. There are as many adjectives attached to the term federalism as there are federal countries, hence William Riker's famous observation that federalism does not exist; and no generalizations can be made about it (1975). This suggests that an exploration of our question requires two levels of analysis. We can ask whether federalism makes a difference as a generic system of governance; or we can look at variations within federations to assess whether some federal designs may be more effective than others.

Federations also vary in their underlying political dynamics. Perhaps most important here is what we call building or disbuilding; or what Linz calls 'bringing together' or 'holding together' (1997b, p. 12), to which could be added 'coming apart'. Carl Friedrich (1968) describes federalism not as a single static form of government, but as a process. If so, we need to ask in what direction the process is going. Is it a matter of previously separate units coming together for whatever reason? The best recent example of this, perhaps, is the European Union. Or is the dynamic one in which previously unitary or relatively centralized regimes are coming apart, with powers devolving to provincial units at an accelerating rate, with no logical stopping place short of secession? Once either dynamic has become established, it will be very difficult to reverse. Finally, the effects of federal institutions will be greatly affected by their interaction with other aspects of the institutional structure such as the electoral system and the design of legislatures and executives. Especially pertinent are the mechanisms of intrastate federalism, or representation of states and provinces at the centre. The key issue here is whether national institutions serve to ensure full participation of the minorities in national as well as regional politics, and the extent to which they bind federal and provincial governments into relationships of trust and mutual dependence. With these observations in mind, let us examine some cases.

Canada

Canada is one of the world's oldest, and historically most stable federations. Viewed over the long term since its inception in 1867, most observers would consider it highly successful in providing the institutional basis for managing the relationship between French- and English-speaking Canadians, and among the diverse Canadian regions. In recent years, however, this sanguine assessment has been called into question. Since the 1960s Quebec identity has increasingly taken the form of a Quebec-centred nationalism. In 1976, the Parti Québécois came to power in Quebec. Its goal was 'sovereignty-association' – an independent, sovereign Quebec that would continue to maintain economic links with the remaining Canada. In 1980, it called a referendum, seeking a mandate to negotiate 'sovereignty-association', which was defeated. There followed extensive constitutional negotiations aimed at finding a new accommodation between Quebec and the Rest of Canada. (See Russell 1993 for the narrative of these events.)

In 1982, substantial amendments were made to the constitution. Most notable were the adoption of a detailed Charter of Rights and Freedoms, and a new amending formula. However, Quebec was not a party to this agreement. Both federalists and sovereigntists in Quebec argued that the Constitution Act, 1982, not only failed to respond to Quebec demands for greater autonomy in the federal system, but actually weakened its position (Banting and Simeon 1983a). Quebec appealed to the Supreme Court of Canada, arguing that history and convention had established that no substantial constitutional amendment could be made without the consent of Quebec. The court rejected this argument.

In 1987, with a federalist government in power in Quebec, and a federal government with strong support among Quebec nationalists, all eleven federal and provincial governments agreed on the 'Meech Lake Accord.' It was designed to respond to Quebec's traditional demands, by adding to the constitution a clause recognizing Quebec as a Distinct Society within Canada, placing some limits on the power of the federal government to intervene in provincial jurisdiction through its use of the 'spending power', guaranteeing Quebec representation on the Supreme Court of Canada, and recognizing some Quebec jurisdiction over immigration. However, during the three years that the amending process allotted for ratification in the federal and provincial legislatures, mass opposition to the Accord developed outside Quebec. Two provinces failed to ratify the Accord, and it failed. This episode demonstrated a profound difference in perceptions of the nature and purpose of the Canadian federation. For most Quebecers it is seen as a partnership of two equal peoples, for most non-Quebecers, it is seen as a partnership of 30 million individual citizens, and of ten equal provinces.

In 1991–2, there was yet another attempt to find accommodation. In this round, negotiators sought to respond to criticizms of the Meech Lake process. There would be far more attention to public consultation, and a broadening of the constitutional agenda to address issues of importance to Canadians outside Quebec – the rights of aboriginal peoples, the concerns of smaller provinces, especially in the west, for greater representation in the national government, and others. The result was yet another intergovernmental agreement, the Charlottetown Accord. It was defeated in referenda held simultaneously in Quebec and the other nine provinces in October 1992.

These successive failures helped to reelect a Parti Québécois government in Quebec in 1994. In October 1995 it held another referendum, calling for 'sovereignty with partnership,' with the implication that after a 'yes' vote Quebec would move to secession, with or without the agreement of the Rest of Canada. This referendum was defeated but by the slimmest of margins – less than one per cent. Clearly the future of the Canadian federation remained in the balance. No longer could federalism be seen as a stable solution. The earlier Confederation bargain had eroded; and no agreement was possible on a new one.

While efforts to reform the federation continue – largely outside the constitutional arena – attention has increasingly turned to debate about the rules that might govern secession and the subsequent relationship between Quebec and the Canada that remained. Seeking clarification on this matter, the federal government submitted a reference to the Supreme Court of Canada, seeking its opinion on whether Quebec has a right to secede unilaterally, in either Canadian or international law. The Court (1998) said there was no such right, but that if a clear majority of Quebecers, answering a clear question, voted for sovereignty then the rest of Canada would have a constitutional obligation to negotiate with Quebec. Both sides would have to respect the fundamental constitutional principles of democracy, the rule of law, federalism and respect for minorities. In the meantime, Quebec public opinion remains closely divided between some form of renewed federalism giving greater recognition to Quebec, and sovereignty with continued economic and political ties to Canada; both the status quo, and outright independence remain minority views. Surveys also show that the majority of Quebecers, sovereigntists and federalists alike, continue to hold dual identities, as Quebecers first, but also as Canadians.

Since the institutions of federalism have remained unchanged throughout this period, federalism by itself cannot explain the growth of Quebec nationalism, and the increased tension. Its roots lie in the economic and social changes – urbanization, industrialization, secularization – that took place in Quebec throughout much of the last century, culminating in the modernizing 'Quiet revolution' of the 1960s. These developments rendered obsolete the 'confederation bargain' embodied in the Constitution Act, 1867. Broadly speaking, that bargain assured Quebec significant autonomy in linguistic, social and cultural affairs, but left the economy and national political elites largely in the hands of English-Canadians. Modernization meant two things. First, English and French speakers would now compete more directly on the economic terrain. Second, traditional Quebec ideology, dominated by a conservative Catholicism, had been hostile to the state. Hence, it did not look to the Quebec state as the instrument of cultural survival. In federal–provincial affairs, Quebec governments frequently resisted federal intrusions (especially in the postwar development of the welfare state), but made few claims for additional powers. By the 1960s, however, a liberal, secular Quebec now embraced the provincial state, arguing the need to be 'maîtres chez nous', and for additional powers. In addition French-Canadian identity shifted from the cultural 'French-Canadian', to the political 'Québécois'. Interestingly, this dynamic of Quebec nation building developed simultaneously with diminishing economic disparities between French and English Canadians, with federal policies to strengthen bilingualism across the country, and with a strong Quebec presence in the federal government, including Prime Ministers from Quebec for all but a few brief periods since 1968.

Broad societal changes in the rest of Canada also contributed to greater conflict. In particular, the mobilization of different divisions, such as aboriginal rights and gender, challenged a politics preoccupied with managing linguistic conflict, and placed other issues on the federal and constitutional agenda. Second, the increasing cultural diversity of 'English Canada' rendered the image of a Canada predicated on the 'partnership of two founding peoples' less persuasive. This idea was increasingly challenged by the idea of the equality of individual citizens (strongly reinforced by the adoption of the Charter of Rights and Freedoms in 1982) and the equality of ten provinces (Stark 1992). Both concepts challenged the idea of distinctive or special status for Quebec.

Moreover, the process of democratization rendered the traditional pattern of elite accommodation less and less legitimate. By the 1980s, two of the central prerequisites for successful elite accommodation had broken down: first, many of the Quebec elites were no longer committed to maintain the system; and, second, citizens were increasingly unwilling to defer to elites. In both the Meech Lake and Charlottetown cases, unanimous agreements between federal and provincial governments were overturned by mobilization from below.

Federalism, however, was deeply implicated in all these changes, and did much to shape how they played out. First, federalism meant that when a more secular, state-oriented nationalism emerged it had a fully developed provincial state at its disposal. Successive governments elected after 1960 then used this provincial state aggressively to promote Quebec nation building, across a wide variety of fields. Especially in the 1960s it was also able to achieve (by non-constitutional means) significant increases in its autonomy and share of financial resources. Indeed, as Dion points out, it could be argued that Quebec had become perhaps the most powerful subnational government in the world (1992). In that sense, it would be only a small step to move to independence itself.

Federalism also meant that issues of jurisdiction, fiscal federalism, and the constitution were negotiated as a form of elite accommodation in the intergovernmental arena. The central participants were executives of federal and provincial governments engaged in 'federal-provincial diplomacy'. Hence the interests of governments were central to the policy-making process. Moreover, as Quebec sought greater autonomy and engaged in nation building, there was a tendency for other provinces to emulate Quebec, engaging in their own 'province-building' exercises, and increasingly challenging federal power.

More generally, it could be argued that the Canadian model of 'divided federalism' is especially likely to provoke a competitive rather than cooperative, or, as Niou and Ordeshook (1997) put it, 'bargaining' rather than 'integrative' pattern of relationships among groups. By 'divided federalism' I mean a regime in which there are few institutional links between levels of government; each is its own self-contained system. In formal terms, powers are divided into watertight compartments. Each level has its own independent financial base. An ineffective, federally appointed Senate means that there is no effective representation of regions and provinces within the national government (Simeon 1998).

These effects of the institutional design are powerfully reinforced by the interaction of federalism and the Westminster system of parliamentary government, with its concentration of power in the executive. The first-past-the-post electoral system helps produce a highly regionalized party system, and makes it possible for governments to rule with weak representation from important regions. The concentration of power in the cabinet, combined with strict party discipline, undermines the ability of MPs to speak for their province.

Combining the federal design and parliamentary government gives intergovernmental relations much of the tone of international relations. With little mobility between governments, the interests and power of political elites are heavily wrapped up in the status and power of their own government. There has recently been important progress towards a more collaborative form of federalism, but this must overcome the institutional logic of divided federalism. Moreover, Quebec has remained largely outside that process, reinforcing dualism in practice if not constitutionally (Simeon and Cameron 2000).

Finally, the Canadian debate poses two remaining questions. First, in the debate about 'distinct society', 'special status', and 'asymmetrical federalism' two broad positions have been in contention. Both involve clear predictions about the consequences of institutional design. On one side is the view most closely associated with former Prime Minister Trudeau. It argues that conceding special powers simply sets up a dynamic of the 'slippery slope' whose end point can only be secession. This is because Quebec elites have a strong incentive to demand further and further concessions, and because inexorably the ties that bind Quebecers to the national government and polity will be cut, as their ties to the provincial state increase. Hence the strategy to limit autonomy, and instead to seek ways to further enhance the presence of Quebecers in Ottawa (Trudeau 1998; for critiques of this position, see Laforest 1995b and McRoberts 1997a).

Proponents of 'distinct society' make the opposite prediction. If greater autonomy is *not* conceded the consequence will be secession, and sooner rather than later. Quebecers will believe that their national identity cannot be accommodated within Canada, hence they will decide to go it alone. This profound dispute remains unresolved. We cannot know for certain whether the recognition of Quebec as a distinct society in the Meech Lake Accord would have provided a logical stopping point, or instead have laid the grounds for further steps towards eventual secession. If it had passed, would there have been the referendum of 1995, and would it have come so close to passing?

Second, the Canadian experience raises the question of whether it is desirable, or possible, to write down the accommodation between language groups in formal constitutional language. To do so requires clear agreement on symbolically divisive issues such as identity, recognition, equality and power. The reality of such differences is what makes constitutional reform a priority; but that same reality prevents agreement. An alternative view suggests that such questions may be better left to constitutional silences, 'abeyances', gaps and ambiguities (Thomas 1997; Lazar 1998). But once the constitutional genie is out of the bottle, it is hard to replace.

Belgium

Founded in 1830 as a unitary constitutional monarchy, four stages of devolution, in 1970, 1980, 1988 and 1993, have turned Belgium into a highly complex federal state. Belgian federalism is made up of institutions 'that are among the most complex found anywhere in the world. They reflect the long history of intricate maneuvering and elaborate compromise that has characterized Belgium's "language problem"' (Murphy 1995, p. 73). There is no certainty that the recent parade of constitutional revisions, each more decentralist that its predecessor, has come to an end. Alaluf puts the problem succinctly. The two nationalist movements (Flemish and Walloon) 'are not minority nationalities seeking greater autonomy or independence, but social movements struggling for control of the state itself' (Alaluf 1993, p. 74).

The history of ethnolinguistic conflict in Belgium is complex. As Lisbet Hooghe explains, 'There are three major games, each with a limited number of parties involved: Flemish nationalism versus the francophones on cultural identity, Walloon nationalism versus Flanders and Brussels on socio-economic grievances, and (francophone) Brussels versus the rest of the country on center-periphery matters' (Hooghe 1993, p. 48).

Regional identity was not a salient issue in Belgium's founding. After seceding from the Netherlands, Belgian politics became divided along Catholic versus liberal lines, not nationalist lines. Nationalist movements are a more recent phenomenon (Hooghe 1993, p. 45). Flemish nationalism developed over the issue of language. While the constitution of 1831 had guaranteed linguistic liberty, in reality, the francophone elite dominated public administration (Kurzer 1997, p. 35). Long resenting the exclusive use of French in public life, a small group of Flemish intellectuals sought to gain recognition of the Flemish language. In 1919, the Flemish nationalist Frontpartij was formed (Deschouwer 1991). The 1950s and 1960s saw an increase in Flemish demands, demands which also gained an economic focus. Walloon nationalism on the other hand, developed partly to counter what Walloons saw as excessive Flemish demands (Murphy 1995, p. 80) but more importantly, in reaction to increasing industrial decline in Wallonia after 1945. Postwar economic development has been heavily concentrated in Flanders, while French-speaking Wallonia has stagnated (Kurzer 1997, p. 40). Indeed the first serious challenge (albeit short-lived), to Belgian unitarism came from the Walloon movement (Hooghe 1993).

The peculiar situation of Brussels has compounded the linguistic conflict. Despite its geographical position just north of the language line (Murphy 1995, p. 80), the francophone population grew rapidly by dint of the city's function as the bureaucratic capital. By 1910 French speakers were in the majority. Some of these were Walloon émigrés but many were Flemish. 'Hence, Brussels was neither a Walloon city from the standpoint of ancestry nor a Flemish city from the standpoint of language' (Murphy 1995, p. 80). Indeed, there are interesting parallels between the roles of Brussels and Montreal in Canada. Many attempts have been made to resolve Belgium's linguistic tensions. A series of language laws in the 1920s and the 1930s first tried to address these problems through the 'territorial division of Belgium as a state divided into two main language regions, Flanders and Wallonia, and a capital city combining elements of both' (Murphy 1995, p. 81). However centrifugal forces continued to erode the crosscutting cleavages that had characterized Belgian consociationalism. This was most apparent in the division of the Belgian party system along linguistic lines. As Covell explains, 'first Social Christians, then Liberals, and finally Socialists divided into separate Dutch and French-speaking wings, each seeking votes on only one side of the language frontier and recombining only for the purposes of government formation' (Covell 1986, p. 264).

By the end of the 1960s, devolution as a way to resolve escalating conflict was fully on the agenda.

The first set of constitutional reforms, in 1970, recognized the existence of different territorial and cultural entities and their rights to autonomy, while simultaneously trying to preserve a unitary Belgian state. These amendments were two-tracked, 'regionalization on the one hand and acknowledgement of regionalist (or nationalist) aspirations in state-level institutions on the other' (Hooghe 1993, p. 55). The changes officially recognized four linguistic regions with territorial jurisdiction over a number of social and economic matters (Walloon, Flemish, German and a bilingual Brussels Region) and three cultural communities with jurisdiction over cultural and personal affairs (Dutch, French and German speaking) (Kurzer 1997, p. 36). Both the regions and the cultural communities were to be run by separate institutions with their own executive and civil services. However, 'the powers of the cultural and regional councils were narrowly circumscribed . . . and fiscal allocations from the national government were small' (Murphy 1995, p. 85). Institutional changes at the centre involved the consociational devices of parity of Dutch and French speakers in government, certain majority requirements for the passing of language and constitutional revisions, and an 'alarm bell procedure' whereby any proposed legislation would be referred to the national cabinet if three-quarters of one language group deemed it harmful to community relations (Hooghe 1993, p. 55).

In the reforms of 1980, regional and community legislation gained the same legal status as national laws. The cultural councils were converted into community councils and given new powers in healthcare, tourism, broadcasting, scientific research and social assistance (Murphy 1995, p. 85). The authority of the regional councils was also expanded. However, the tools to manage monetary and fiscal policy remained firmly entrenched at the national level. The new model aimed at creating exclusive instead of concurrent competencies in order to reduce the possibility of conflict. But several factors combined to frustrate effective policy making and exacerbate conflict. The community councils continued to consist of members of the national parliament instead of being chosen by direct election. The financial arrangements did little to encourage financial responsibility (Hooghe 1993, p. 57). Policy areas were seldom allocated as a coherent whole to one level. And the complex relationships of two regions and three communities frustrated effective policy-making and inhibited regional autonomy. The reforms of the 1980s thus failed to establish a workable compromise between local autonomy and central authority. The 1988 reforms were a victory for federalists. They transferred a large proportion of state power away from the centre to the regional and community councils and their executives. The reforms 'attempted to strike a new balance between centrifugal and centripetal tensions by opting for federalization' (Hooghe 1993, p. 57). New powers over education were handed over to the community level and the regions were given control over infrastructure, public transportation, employment, and the use and conservation of natural resources. The federal government maintained its hold over the general legislative and fiscal framework, but the exclusive competencies were made more explicit than they had been in 1980 and the budgets of the regional and community institutions were significantly expanded. Regional institutions were created for Brussels.

Finally, the 1993 Saint Michael's Accords brought about the full federalization of Belgium (Witte 1992). The amended constitution proclaims that Belgium is no longer a 'national state' but a 'federal state, composed of communities and Regions', each of which would henceforth have its own government and prime minister (Downs 1996, p. 169). The most important change was the transfer of all residual powers to the regional and community governments. Education and cultural affairs, foreign commerce, agricultural affairs and environmental planning, have all been decentralized (Downs 1996, p. 169) and regional governments have been given treaty-making rights with foreign governments (Murphy 1995, p. 88). The federal level maintains responsibilities for justice, defence, social security and the Belgian economic and monetary union (Van Houten 1998, p. 12). The new constitution has also authorized direct elections to the Flemish and Walloon parliaments, and the Senate's role has been redefined to mediate between the federation's constituent institutions. No longer could politicians sit in both regional and central governments (Downs 1996, p. 170). Thus Belgium has been transformed into a federal system. But has it reached a stable equilibrium, or will the dynamic of disbuilding continue? On the one hand, the new 'federal' Belgium appears to be reasonably stable. The constitutional revisions were achieved peacefully and so far there has been little serious consideration of constitutional reform beyond the Saint Michael's Accords. The reforms facilitated elite accommodation when interaction was inescapable (Hooghe 1993, p. 64). Consociational practices remain entrenched at the national level. The cabinet consists of seven francophone and seven Dutch-speaking ministers and the secretaries of state. In order to amend legislation concerning the organization of the state, a majority in each language group as well as a two-thirds majority is required.

Brussels is a model of compromise as a 'bilingual territory, with political guarantees for the Dutch-speaking minority, and a region with a slightly lesser status and competencies than the Flemish and Walloon region' (Van Houten 1998). The Brussels executive consists of a president and two francophone and two Dutch-speaking ministers who are elected by the regional council which is itself linguistically divided in proportion to votes cast. There are special protection mechanisms should minority interests be threatened. Ironically, Brussels is also a stabilizing element in that it ties Flanders and Wallonia together. Flanders chose Brussels as its regional capital and refuses to surrender it, while Wallonia continues to try to strengthen its links to the francophone population and Brussels' economic resources (Van Houten 1998). These considerations suggest that Murphy may be correct in his estimation that 'Belgium is probably not on the brink of a Czecho-slovak-style breakup' (Murphy 1995, p. 89).

On the other hand, while Belgian federalism provides institutions designed to encourage cooperation, these same institutions can actually help to disbuild it. Federal institutions have 'strengthened both the self-sufficiency of the linguistic groups or their elites and have enabled them to exploit the centre' (Hooghe 1993, p. 64). A good example of this is the Belgian Senate. While some members of the Senate are appointed by the communities, the Senate is no longer 'a genuine "federal" chamber of parliament' (Van Houten 1998, p. 16). Regions are therefore free to push for increased autonomy since there is no impetus to defend or take account of federal decisions. The abolition of the dual mandate of members of parliament makes elite cooperation even more unlikely, especially if we bear in mind that all political parties in Belgium are regional and only run candidates in their own region. 'This means that all politicians, federal and regional, are accountable to the same (regional) electorate, and that the voters are no longer able to choose between Flemish, Walloon or "Belgian" positions' (Van Houten 1998, p. 16).

Language, economics and Brussels are still the major potential stumbling blocks. Federalism has not resolved these issues. In fact it has exacerbated them by structuring so many interests in terms of opposition between French-speaking Wallonia and Dutch-speaking Flanders. Controversies over the drawing of the language line continue, while the regions themselves (with the exception of Brussels) have become linguistically homogeneous. As in Canada, the dynamics of the system encourage interregional competition and limit the development of cross-cutting cleavages.

Flanders continues to demand more autonomy in order to exploit its economic advantage. As Guy Verhofstadt, senator of the VLD, the liberal party in Flanders, explains, 'an autonomy without control and authority on revenues is not an autonomy, simply because it denies control of the most important instrument at the disposal of politics, namely taxes. As long as the decision-making including large parts of social policy will not be assigned to the regions, I believe that the Belgian communitary issue will go on smoldering' (1996).

Public opinion also suggests that Belgium has failed to find a stable solution. Significant proportions among both language groups support proposals for separation. Economic disparities heighten the tension: the Flemish seek greater fiscal autonomy to minimize sharing their wealth with the Walloons; the latter, lagging economically, seek greater sharing from the centre. Revived discussions on European federalism and greater powers for the European Parliament have been used by Belgian subnational elites to press for their own increased autonomy (Kurzer 1997, p. 35).

Finally, the tortured compromises have produced a complex federalism that is proving confusing to the electorate. An opinion poll in the Brussels-based daily *Le Soir* found that 49 per cent of voters believed that in the new federal system 'the diverse levels of power have become too complex' to the extent that citizens 'no longer know who is responsible for what'. Overall, 'federalism may have been achieved, but cleaning up the corruption and relieving the underlying social ills that breed support for separatist and anti-democratic political forces will not allow Belgium's federalists much time to rest on their laurels' (Downs 1996, p. 174). Thus Belgium is in a period of disbuilding, and Belgians too have been unable to constitute themselves as a 'sovereign people'. Federalism has been a necessary response to fissiparous tendencies, but it has not been able to stem them. Rather, it has created a dynamic of disintegration that seems to feed on itself, and there are few rewards or incentives to those who would reverse the drift. There is no guarantee that the increasingly decentralist constitutional amendments have come to a final stopping place.

Spain

The post-Franco creation of the federalist *estado de las autonomías* (State of Autonomies) appears to have been highly successful in mitigating cultural-linguistic conflicts. 'Spain has transformed itself from a highly centralized dictatorship into something akin to a multiparty federal democracy' (Heller 1998, p. 1). Its central features are a conscious attempt to reinforce the unity of Spain while accepting the existence of distinct nationalities within it. While Spain is not formally constituted as a federal state, a leading socialist politician, Jodi Solè Tura, argues that 'what is important is not the name but the thing. The crucial issue is that Spain ends up working as a federal state' (quoted in Guibernau 1995, p. 250).

Linguistic diversity and competing national loyalties have long been a staple of Spanish history. Conflict between the Castilian centre and culturally distinct regions – especially the 'historic nationalities of Catalonia, the Basque country and Galicia – was one of the major causes of the Civil War and the subsequent demise of the Second Republic' (Gunther et al. 1988, p. 242).

Emerging victorious from the civil war, Franco made concerted efforts to repress cultural and linguistic diversity and regional loyalty, eliminating what he believed to be direct challenges to his vision of Spain as 'complete, with a single language, Castilian, and a single personality, Spanish' (Gunther et al. 1988, p. 242). Basques and Catalans were the prime targets of such repression. In both regions, public use of the regional language was banned. Cultural associations were outlawed. Even names were Castilianized and, in the Basque country, inscriptions in Euskera were removed everywhere from public buildings to tombstones. But as Davydd Greenwood notes, Franco's repression 'probably did more for the creation and maintenance of modern Basque identity than any other concerted action by the Basques themselves could have' (Greenwood 1985, p. 211). Franco's centralism created a powerful association between regionalism and democracy on the one hand, and national unity and repression on the other. Hence the transformation of the Spanish state after 1976 was based on the twin pillars of parliamentary democracy and regional autonomy (Clark 1992, p. 225).

The constitution of 1978 was negotiated by a parliamentary commission that represented all national and regional parties. Seeking to reflect the dual goals of maintaining the unity of the Spanish state, while recognizing the regionalist aspirations of its constituent parts, article 2 declares that 'The Constitution is based on the indissoluble unity of the Spanish nation, the common and indivisible homeland of all Spaniards, and recognizes and guarantees the right to autonomy of the nationalities and regions which make it up and solidarity among all of them.' (Spanish Constitution) Article 3 confirms Castilian as the official tongue but recognizes that local languages would be official in autonomous communities and article 4 states that the national and local flags should fly together at official occasions and on public buildings. The devolution of power to the regions involved a form of asymmetrical federalism (Agranoff 1993; Guibernau 1995). The constitution therefore made varying degrees of autonomy possible, 'for the degree of self-government to be wide or restricted according to the wishes of the nationalities and regions' (Moreno, in this volume). This strength was also its weakness. The exact powers that would be granted to the regions were left deliberately vague, although certain guidelines were provided. These included housing, agriculture, town and country planning, sport, tourism, health services and social services. Madrid would retain control of key powers such as foreign affairs, external trade, shipping and aviation, the justice system and defence. Other issues such as education were not specifically assigned.

In order to achieve home rule, a provincial council first had to decide that it wanted its province to become an autonomous community, or join with others to become one. In the regions that had won autonomy in the Second Republic (the Basque Country, Catalonia and Galicia), the procedure was relatively simple. Once a statute had been agreed to by the local assembly and by Madrid, it could be ratified by a simple majority in a referendum (Keating 1993, p. 218). For the other communities, two routes were available, one offering more power, but more difficult to achieve (article 151), the other simpler, but devolving less authority (article 143). However, an interesting demonstration effect took hold, and most regions opted for the more demanding test. As Hooper explains, it became 'a sort of regional virility test . . . for local politicians, the pressure to demonstrate their loyalty to, and faith in, their region, by supporting home rule under article 151 was immense' (Hooper 1995, p. 45).

The powers of the regional administrations were also asymmetrical. 'The Basques and Catalans, for example, got their own police forces, whereas the Galicians and Andalusians did not. The statutes of home rule passed for Valencia and the Canary Islands were different, both from each other and from other "slow track" Autonomous Communities' (Hooper 1995, 428–9). Financial arrangements varied as well. In the Basque Country and Navarre moreover, a traditional arrangement was reestablished whereby the regional authorities collected the taxes and handed sums over to the central government to compensate for the services provided by Madrid. In the rest of Spain, this procedure was reversed, Madrid collected the taxes and gave regional administrations what they estimated they would need (Hooper 1995, p. 429).

An important step in the evolution towards federalism occurred in 1980, when the Cortes adopted the Institutional Law for the Harmonization for the Autonomy Process, or LOAPA. Its central purpose was to ensure that state law should prevail in any conflict between state and regional competencies, even those that had been delegated to a region in its statute of autonomy. Nationalists, especially in the Basque Country and Catalonia, argued that LOAPA was an attempt to limit the scope of their statutes and appealed to the constitutional court. The court ruled that the constitution's support for equal rights to all citizens and groups did not entail institutional uniformity, and struck down several of LOAPA's key provisions (Keating 1993, p. 220), including those clauses which guaranteed state law supremacy over regional law. Asymmetry, or 'variable geometry', however, continued to be controversial, and a negotiated agreement in 1992 further narrowed the gap in powers between the regions (Hooper 1995, pp. 430–1).

Spain's transition to regional devolution and federalism appears to have been highly successful. Few Spaniards wish to return to a unitary state (Keating 1993, p. 220). The constitution seems to have found the right balance between the encouragement of regionalism and the maintenance of a 'Spanish' identity.

However, the real success of Spain's '*estado de las autonomías* may lie in what has *not* happened rather than what has' (Hooper 1995, p. 435). While there have been countless disputes and constitutional litigation between the centre and the regions, the overall unity of the Spanish nation is not in question. The major conflicts are now not between the centre and the regions, but between richer and poorer regions. Outright separation is not on the agenda, except for small minority groups. This has been largely due to the moderation of the elites and regional leaders and, to an extent, the successful formation of nested nationalities. 'With neither state nor minority nationalism making exclusive claims, dual identities are more acceptable' (Keating 1993, p. 225). 'The nationalities question no longer threatens to tear Spain apart' (Keating 1993, p. 224).

Nevertheless, it is likely that the autonomous communities will continue to bargain for more powers. This is especially true for Basque and Catalan nationalists who continue to seek recognition of the 'historic nationalities,' and do not see themselves as simply two communities among seventeen regions. Hooper adds that 'demanding concessions from the central government has become a way of life, a raison d'être, for the moderate nationalists who are under constant pressure from overtly separatist movements' (1995, p. 435). Many Catalonians – by no means all of them fervent nationalists – talk as if a confederal solution, in which everything but foreign affairs, trade negotiations and defence would be handled by the Generalitat, was somehow inevitable.

As we have seen, the constitution is a vague document – obviously deliberately so. It created numerous grey areas where it was unclear whether power ought to be exercised by Madrid or by one or more of the regional administrations. This helps ensure the intergovernmental tug of war will continue, but at the same time provides a flexibility that can avoid constitutional crisis. Constitutional silences and ambiguities have been part of the Spanish solution.

Federalism is clearly a critical element in Spain's success. But it is also supported by the fact that regional parties have been bound into national government. According to Heller, 'since the 1993 elections, which brought an end to eleven years of single-party (socialist) majorities, their participation in coalition politics has been a distinguishing feature of Spanish politics. This participation not only has gained them substantial benefits for their regions but has also enabled minority governments in Madrid to cleave to their programs much more closely than might be expected' (1998, p. 1).

Meditating on the consequences of *de facto* federalism for Spain, two observers of devolution in Britain conclude: 'Spain's rolling programme of asymmetrical devolution has not resulted in the chaotic scenarios predicted by opponents of devolution, nor has the process led to greater demands for independence in the historic nations.' Devolution 'may not have reached a steady state, but it has led to an accommodation between the centre and the regions . . . This is no mean accomplishment in a country that once fought a civil war over this issue' (Hazell and O'Leary 1999, p. 26).

Scotland

In 1999, the people of Scotland elected the first Scottish parliament since 1707. New parliamentary assemblies were elected in Wales and in Northern Ireland. While it is highly premature to describe the United Kingdom as a federation, devolution is 'likely to transform the nature of the UK as a multinational state' (Hazell and O'Leary 1999, p. 21). The Scotland Act 1998 gives the new parliament the right to legislate on all but a number of matters reserved for Westminster – foreign and defence policy, security, immigration, fiscal and monetary policy, market regulation and social security. Northern Ireland will have similar powers along with innovative procedures to ensure equality between its main religious groups. Wales will have more limited powers. This is a major transformation of what was once thought of as the classic unitary state.

Precisely the same debate has occurred in Britain with respect to Scottish devolution as has occurred in Canada with respect to recognition of Quebec as a distinct society. Is devolution the first step towards eventual independence; or is it a means of ensuring that the Scots will remain securely part of the British Union?

Like Canadian supporters of asymmetrical federalism, Britain's Labour government believes that the creation of an autonomous Scottish parliament is necessary to forestall the growth of irresistible pressure for full Scottish independence. Donald Dewar, Labour's former secretary of state for Scotland, insisted that 'Scotland will remain firmly part of the United Kingdom' (Foreword to Scotland Bill). The White paper, *Scotland's Parliament* (1997, para. 3.1) makes the case: 'The Union will be strengthened by recognizing the claims of Scotland, Wales, and the regions with strong identities of their own. The Government's devolution proposals, by meeting these aspirations, will not only safeguard but also enhance the Union.'

Others however, see 'federal' solutions as the first step on a slippery slope to regional independence. For the Conservative opposition, Scottish devolution represents the first step towards the breakup of Britain, a 'fast track to separation'. As the former Prime Minister John Major put it, devolution would 'eventually lead to the break-up of the United Kingdom' (1997). It would be, as another opponent puts it, 'a motorway without exit to an independent state' (Dalywell, in Hazell 1999, p. 23).

Perhaps ironically, and certainly with different motivations, the Scottish National Party (SNP) agrees. For them it is also a first step on a long road towards independence. It asserted that if it had won the first election, it would have proposed a referendum seeking a mandate to secede.

While Scotland has always maintained some degree of independence from Britain, retaining control over its legal and education systems, its own state church and a distinctive Scottish Office in Edinburgh, it has not had an independent parliament for over three hundred years. Over most of this period, Scotland and England became tightly integrated economically and culturally. Scots played leading roles in British industrialism, in the building of the empire and in British political life. Political cleavages revolved more around Britain's distinctions of class than around considerations of nationality. There was thus little incentive or opportunity for the emergence of a distinct Scottish nationalism based on demands for greater autonomy and self-government. It was relatively easy to sustain 'nested nationalities' (Miller 1998b). Nationalist parties had little impact before the 1960s.

Just as in Quebec, however, Scottish nationalism grew in the period after 1960. Dion (1992) suggests that nationalist movements grow out of a combination of 'grievance' and 'opportunity'. In the Scottish case, the grievance came from the declining economic fortunes of the 1970s that 'deepened the pattern of uneven development in regional and national terms within Britain, in which England prospered . . . compared with Scotland and Wales' (Krieger 1993, p. 90). Grievance also stemmed from a sense that the Scots, who voted overwhelmingly for the Labour Party, were frozen out of power during the Conservative regimes of Margaret Thatcher and John Major at Westminster. The opportunity was provided first by the sense that North Sea oil might provide the key to Scottish economic development; second, by the presence of the European Union, which provided a potential counterweight to the dominance of Westminster; and third, by the rise and success of ethnonationalist movements elsewhere.

Michael Burgess has convincingly demonstrated that federalist ideas have a long history in British political thought and practice (Burgess 1995). But while the concept of federalism had often been proffered as a solution to Irish nationalist separatism, British governments have consistently resisted federalism, insisting on Westminster's sovereignty as absolute and indivisible. For traditionally centralist British (especially Conservative) governments, the arguments against devolution have always been clear – it would herald the break-up of the United Kingdom.

Nevertheless, growing support for the Scottish National Party (SNP) and Plaid Cymru (Welsh nationalist party) led the Conservatives in 1968 to support the idea of a Scottish Assembly. Then Labour set up the Royal Commission on the constitution (1969–73) (Kellas 1983 p. 151). The Kilbrandon Commission recommended legislative and executive devolution to Scotland and Wales with a minority wanting advisory Regional Councils for England. A second upsurge of nationalist voting in 1974 pushed the Labour government into accepting the report and recommending Assemblies for Scotland and Wales (Kellas, 1983, p. 152).

In 1978, as a result of a pact between Labour and the Liberals, referenda on devolution were held in both Scotland and Wales. Passage required not only a majority of votes cast, but also support from 40 per cent of the whole electorate. As a result both referenda were defeated. Subsequent Conservative governments quashed any further debate on devolution.

However, detailed proposals were developed in a Scottish Constitutional Convention in 1989, and the Labour Party endorsed the idea. When it came to power in 1997 it wasted little time, quickly preparing White Papers, and holding a referendum in September 1997. In the referendum 74.3 per cent were in favour of a Scottish Parliament (45 per cent of the total electorate) and 63.5 per cent were in favor of tax-raising powers.

The devolution now in place sets up a unicameral Scottish Parliament with competencies over economic development, transport, health, local government, schools, housing, law, environment, agriculture, sports and the arts. The central government retains control over constitutional issues, foreign policy, defence, security, employment and social security economic and monetary systems, trade and transport safety. Scotland will be able to vary the income tax by 3 pence up or down and will be able to change the form of local council tax, but the bulk of Scotland's revenues will be provided by a block grant out of general UK taxation. Structurally, there is a Westminster-style Scottish Executive headed by a First Minister who will recommend the appointment of other ministers.

Members of the Scottish Parliament (MSPs) are elected by two systems, 73 members by first past the post in constituencies, 56 by proportional representation. There are eight additional MSPs from each of the European Union constituencies. These innovations, along with others in Northern Ireland and Wales, illustrate another advantage of federalism: the ability to experiment in different jurisdictions.

Unresolved is an issue that has also been raised in Canadian debates.

Should MPs from Scotland in Westminster be permitted to vote on legislation that will not apply to Scotland? This issue, known as the West Lothian question, was settled to a degree in 1978 through a parliamentary rule that if an English bill were passed with the support of Scottish MPs, then there would have to be an additional vote from which they would abstain.

As Britain has moved to a quasi-federalist regime, it faces the same question as does Spain. Has it found a formula to reconcile nationalist aspirations with the concern for national unity in a quasi-federal system? The government asserts that 'Scotland will remain firmly part of the United Kingdom.' Tony Blair argues that 'The sovereignty of the United Kingdom parliament will remain undiminished' (MacWhirter, *Scotsman* 25 July 97). The White Paper echoes this sentiment, stating that the 'UK parliament is, and will remain, sovereign in all matters' – a classic reaffirmation of the unitary state. However, it continues 'as part of the Government's resolve to modernize the British constitution, Westminster will be choosing to exercise that sovereignty by devolving legislative responsibilities to a Scottish parliament without in any way diminishing its own powers'.

The reality is that this is a fundamental constitutional change. The dynamics it will create are difficult to anticipate. One possibility is that of disbuilding. This suggests that the combination of an elected legislature, with real powers, and control over the bureaucratic apparatus of the Scottish Office, will lead to a demand for ever greater powers. Scottish nationalists now have an institutional vehicle through which they can advance the cause for independence, and force confrontations with Westminster. While the SNP narrowly lost the first Scottish election, it is likely that at some point it will come to power, and use this power to push for a referendum on independence. As Alex Salmond, leader of the SNP notes (1998), 'The events of last September were a beginning, not an end – a process rather than an event.' Non-SNP governments, like federalist governments in Quebec, will be forced by electoral calculations to emphasize autonomy.

This is the pessimistic view: federalism, and asymmetry, as the slippery slope to ending the Union. The alternative view suggests that devolution will indeed strengthen the Union. It ensures the Scots a sense of identity, of political recognition, and autonomy, while permitting them to remain as full participants in the larger system, in which they have played such a major role. The question becomes whether the groups that Canadians call the 'soft nationalists' will find devolution as now enacted a satisfactory end point, or only a taste of things to come. As Hazell and O'Leary conclude: 'Devolution could either strengthen or weaken or simply change the overall government of the UK . . . Left to themselves the forces are centrifugal . . . It will require some imaginative reengineering of the centre, and a spirit of trust and generosity on both sides, to make the devolution work' (1999, p. 45).

Institutional change creates other dynamics as well. Most interesting is whether Britain moves towards a more fully developed federal system, in which England, or regions within England, also develop a sense of identity and a desire for more autonomy. Again, the parallel with Spain is instructive. Hazell and O'Leary suggest the likelihood of a 'rolling devolution'. 'Scotland, Wales and Northern Ireland will set the pace; interest in the English regions will pick up as the bandwagon starts to roll' (1999, p. 41). There will be a high degree of asymmetry.

Summary

These four cases all tell somewhat different stories. Federalism in Canada has proven to be an enduring and flexible model for accommodating Canadian linguistic and regional diversity, but its continuing capacity to do so remains in doubt. In Belgium, the move to federalism is part of a disbuilding dynamic, and seems far from a stable outcome. Spain's asymmetrical federalism, by contrast, seems to have been remarkably successful in reconciling nation and region. Which of these two paths Scotland and Britain follow remains unknown.

Thus, the stability that federalism creates may be only temporary; it can easily become a 'framework for further demands' and may not constitute 'a stable, durable solution' (Linz 1997b, p. 30). In all these divided societies, federalism is a dynamic fluid process.

Conditions under which federalism is likely to prove successful

This discussion raises the question: are there conditions under which federalism is likely to be more or less successful in the management of ethnocultural conflict?

First, does the design of the federal system itself matter – in terms of how powers are distributed, the strength of intrastate mechanisms and the mechanisms of intergovernmental relations? As argued above, I think it probably does. (See also Meadwell 1998.) The separated or divided Canadian model, with its watertight, compartmentalized mode of dividing powers, a Senate that represents neither citizens nor governments of the constituent units, and a form of intergovernmental relations that consists of diplomatic interactions among executives as if they

were international actors seems less able to establish a stable accommodation. It does provide Quebec with a high degree of autonomy, but
does not offset the integration of Quebecers into the federal system. The
logic of watertight compartments – as distinct from concurrent powers –
is a recipe for a zero-sum approach to overlapping responsibilities, and a
politics of fighting for turf. Executive-dominated intergovernmental
relations reinforce this tendency, focusing conflicts on the strategic goals
of premiers and prime ministers, and undercutting more cooperative
'functional' cooperation at lower levels. At least in recent years, the logic
of Canadian intergovernmental relations has suggested a move towards
a confederal model. In addition, the decentralized and divided model of
Canadian federalism – making Quebec, in Dion's terms, the most
powerful subnational government in the world – equips Quebec with the
tools and resources that make a move towards secession both plausible
and viable (1992).

This contrasts sharply with the German model of federalism which
emphasizes interdependence, partnership, cooperation and consensus
(Simeon 1998). Under such conditions, the two orders of government
are much more tightly bound. Secession or confederalism thus becomes
less likely. One should not exaggerate this argument however. Germany
is not a multinational federation. It is possible that if the German *Länder*
did represent strong ethnic or linguistic populations, the interdependen-
cies and resulting need for cooperation would generate conflict and
paralysis.

This suggests that 'federalism is not enough' (Cairns 1995). By
themselves, federal institutions are no guarantee of either success or
failure. They need to be reinforced by other factors, both societal and
institutional. Given that federalism is a process of 'building out' it needs
to be balanced by a process of 'building in'. In other words, the success
of federalism depends, to a large extent, on the 'integrative counter-
weights' to the process.

At the societal level it seems clear that in addition to strong national
or community loyalties and identities, federalism can only survive if
these are paralleled by significant elements of shared or overarching
identities and values. Federalism is predicated on the existence of
'nested identities' (see Smith 1995a), the ability to maintain dual
loyalties, a sense of simultaneous difference and of commonality. Miller
argues that nested nationalities 'think of themselves as belonging both to
the smaller community and to the larger one, and they do not experience
this as schizophrenic, because their two identities fit together reasonably
well (Miller 1998b). Once this symbiosis erodes, then federalism is
indeed likely to give way to secession. Such feelings of common interest

and mutual respect are critical conditions for the success of federalism, whether expressed as the *vouloir vivre ensemble* in Canada or Belgium, *Ubuntu* in South Africa, or *Bundestreue* in Germany.

The values of both the minority and the majority are important here. For the minority group it is a question of whether they retain some identity and loyalty to the larger entity. For the majority, the willingness to temper the commitment to simple majority rule and to accept the institutionalization of difference are critical. Majoritarianism, Lijphart says, is both undemocratic and dangerous in heterogeneous societies (1977, p. 3). Nordlinger (1972) goes further, arguing that the majority must be prepared to make the major concessions. (These observations are highly relevant to the current Canadian debate, where there is on the one hand the growth of sovereigntist sentiment, and on the other a declining willingness outside Quebec to make concessions, or to temper concepts like majoritarianism, and the equality of citizens and provinces with the recognition of Quebec as a 'distinct society').

Institutions may affect whether such dual values and loyalties are sustained. Mutually advantageous economic linkages, and the presence of other divisions in the society that cross-cut or overlap the ethnic/ linguistic divide are also required.

Even more important, is the evolution of civil society, below the level of institutions and constitutional debate. Institutions cannot keep a country together if there is no other social cohesion. Hence it is critical to assess the dynamic of societal networks and their associational linkages. Is there a trend towards increasingly separated societies in which intragroup dynamics dominate? Are groups that once were able to bridge across groups finding accommodation more difficult, and are they dividing themselves into the social equivalents of confederalism, 'sovereignty-association' or secession? If so, the capacity of federal institutions to manage accommodation at the political level will dramatically decline. More research on this dimension of social capital in divided societies is greatly needed. Again, we need to consider the causal arrows here: does fragmentation or division at the institutional level drive division at the societal level; or does disengagement at the societal level precede political-institutional change?

Institutional factors other than federalism are also likely to affect the capacity to manage ethnic conflict. We have already mentioned the importance of intrastate elements in central institutions, especially but not limited to second chambers. Electoral systems are also important, primarily because of the extent to which they can distort or exaggerate regional and linguistic differences or create incentives for exclusionary rather than inclusive electoral strategies. Executive dominance and simple majoritarianism in the parliamentary institutions of each level of government also shapes the conflict. The effect of Canada's institutional makeup is to structure the relationship between French-speaking and English-speaking Canadians as a Quebec–Canada relationship, as a partnership between two powerful, centralized governments, each of which mutes or excludes minority political views. Thus they sharpen and polarize the debate. Additionally, the existence of nine other provinces, endowed with the same powers as Quebec, has other effects. Other provinces and regions have an incentive to emulate Quebec, and assert their own status as 'distinct societies'. It should come as little surprise therefore, that they powerfully support arguments for the 'equality of the provinces' model, as distinct from the 'partnership of two nations' model.

Party systems exist at the boundary between institutions and societies. If federalism is to be a device for integration and accommodation, then it needs to be supported by integrative party systems. This includes both the existence of at least some parties able to attain cross-regional and national support as well as linkages between the party systems that exist at central and regional levels. In Canada of course, we have seen long periods when the major national parties have been unable to win support in one or more major regions; and in recent years explicitly regional and 'national' parties (the Reform and the Bloc Québécois) have grown stronger. In addition, especially in Quebec there are sharp differences between provincial and central party systems, and even between parties of the same name but at different levels. Indeed, the political incentives facing federalist leaders at the central level (to win Canada-wide support) and at the provincial level (to combat the sovereigntists) virtually guarantees conflict between them. In Spain, the role played by regional parties in national coalitions is an important factor. In Belgium the virtually total linguistic division among the political parties removes an important vehicle for integration. Again, there is the dilemma: integrative parties are needed to bridge the ethnolinguistic divide; but that divide (along with regional cleavages) means that integrative parties will face major hurdles, especially in divided federal systems.

A final institutional factor is the existence of Charters of Rights. They can help provide overarching common values and can provide assurance to the 'minorities within the minorities', thus helping reconcile them to the power that a decentralized federation gives to the minority national group. The boundaries of ethnicity seldom coincide perfectly with the political boundaries of states. Without guarantees for their status, the options for these 'minorities within the minority' become far less attractive – either 'ethnic cleansing' to bring political and cultural boundaries into line, or 'partition'.

Thus, federalism is not the only institutional factor affecting how ethnonational politics are played out; and the effects of federalism depend greatly on the role of federalism within the larger institutional and social structure. As well, in all the cases studied here, the international environment – the EU for Belgium, Spain and Scotland; North American economic integration for Canada – will continue to have an important influence on the relations between national and subnational governments.

Conclusions

For the reasons stated at the outset, there can be no firm conclusions about the effectiveness of federalism for the management of the kinds of conflicts discussed above. Nevertheless, short of repression, the territorial sharing of power that federalism represents seems essential in any formula for managing geographically concentrated ethnolinguistic divisions within a state. Federalism does not guarantee 'success', but it is hard to see any form of successful accommodation of multiple nations within a single state that does not include federalism. In addition, we generally agree with Linz that 'Federalism, rather than self-determination and independence, is a more constructive, less conflictual, and often a more democratic solution, although it will never fully eliminate the tensions in multi-national societies' (1997b, p. 15). It does not prevent or eliminate these conflicts, but it can make them more manageable (p. 41). 'It is not a universal panacea, but it can provide a positive response to one of the great problems of our time' (p. 45).

We must recognize, however, that federalism is often not a stable solution. By providing resources and institutional levers to nationalist elites, it can produce a dynamic of 'disbuilding,' in which demands for increased powers can lead to further calls for autonomy, the only logical stopping place for which is secession. It may well be that once such a dynamic is established, a kind of 'path dependency' develops which is very hard to reverse. Canada is perhaps a contemporary example. The most important question to arise from this analysis is to think of ways to better understand the conditions under which federalism is likely to constitute a stable outcome, and the factors which undermine a previously established settlement. In Canada, for example, the federation existed for 100 years before a serious secessionist challenge arose.

Federal outcomes will be most stable when the autonomy, self-determination and powers that they confer on the minority groups are counterbalanced by other forces – shared values, an integrative party system, sense of mutual commitment, responsive central government – factors that bind the groups together. Elazar defines federalism as a combination of 'self-rule' and 'shared rule' (1987). Successful accommodation, as James Coleman (1992) notes, requires elements of both.

In addition, while it is true that federalism is often not a stable solution, we cannot assume that the alternatives – either the attempt to maintain a centralized status quo, or secession – are any more so. On the one hand, failure to respond to devolutionist pressures in Belgium, Spain, or even Scotland was probably not sustainable. On the other hand, while 'velvet divorces' are not impossible (and may be facilitated by the prior existence of federalism), secession entails its own enormous risks and uncertainties, and is exceedingly difficult to accomplish, especially in societies where the linguistic and territorial lines do not fully coincide. So while federalism may not be a stable outcome, it is not clear it is any *less stable* than alternatives (McGarry and O'Leary 1993, p. 12). It is worth at least two cheers.

References

Abbott, Philip (1996). 'What's New in the Federalist Papers?', *Political Research Quarterly* 49.3: 525–45.

Abitbol, Maurice et al. (1984). 'Manifeste pour la culture wallonne', *La Revue Nouvelle*, January, pp. 62–4.

Achten, Dirk (1998). 'L'effet tardif d'un peu de fermeté flamande', *Le Soir*, 12 February.

Acton, Lord (1996) [1862]. 'Nationality', in Gopal Balakrishnan (ed.), *Mapping the Nation*. New York, pp. 17–38.

Agranoff, Robert (1993). 'Intergovernmental Politics and Policy: Federal Arrangements in Spain', *Regional Politics and Society* 3: 1–28.

Agranoff, Robert (1995). 'Asymmetrical and Symmetrical Federalism in Spain', in Bertus de Villiers (ed.), *Evaluating Federal Systems*. Cape Town/Dordrecht: Juta & Co/Martinus Nijhoff Publishers, pp. 61–89.

Agreement Reached in the Multiparty Negotiations (1998). Belfast: The Stationery Office.

Ajzenstat, Janet (1995). 'Decline of Procedural Liberalism: the Slippery Slope to Secession', in Joseph H. Carens (ed.), *Is Quebec Nationalism Just? Perspectives from Anglophone Canada*. Montreal and Kingston: McGill-Queen's University Press, pp. 120–36.

Alaluf, Mateo (1993). 'Belgium', in Joel Krieger (ed.), *The Oxford Companion to Politics of the World*. New York: Oxford University Press, pp. 73–6.

Aldecoa Luzarraga, Francisco (1999). 'Towards Plurinational Diplomacy in the Context of the Deepening and Widening of the European Union (1985–2005)', in A. Aldecoa and Michael Keating (eds.), *Paradiplomacy: the International Relations of Sub-state Governments*. London: Frank Cass, pp. 82–94.

Alfred, Taiaiake G. (1998). *Peace, Power, Righteousness: an Indigenous Manifesto*. Toronto: Oxford University Press Canada.

Almond, Gabriel (1956). 'Comparative Political Systems', *Journal of Politics* 18: 391–409. Reprinted in Almond (1970). *Political Development: Essays in Heuristic Theory*. Boston, ch. 1.

Amin, Ash and Nigel Thrift (eds.) (1994). *Globalization, Institutions, and Regional Development in Europe*. Oxford: Oxford University Press.

Anderson, Benedict (1983). *Imagined Communities: Reflections on the Origins and Spread of Nationalism*. London: Verso.

Anderson, James (1995). 'Arrested Federalization? Europe, Britain, Ireland', in

Graham Smith (ed.), *Federalism: The Multi-Ethnic Challenge*. London: Longman.

Anderson, James (1998). 'Rethinking National Problems in a Transnational Context', in David Miller (ed.), *Rethinking Northern Ireland*. London: Longman, pp. 125–45.

Anderssen, Erin and Edward Greenspon (1998). 'Federal Apology Fails to Mollify Native Leaders', *The Globe and Mail*, 8 January, p. A4.

Appiah, K. Anthony (1994). 'Identity, Authenticity, Survival: Multicultural Societies and Social Reproduction', in Amy Gutmann (ed.), *Multiculturalism and the 'Politics of Recognition'*. Princeton: Princeton University Press, pp. 149–63.

Arendt, Hannah (1977). *Between Past and Future*. Harmondsworth: Penguin Books.

Arendt, Hannah (1998). *The Human Condition*, 2nd edn. Chicago: University of Chicago Press.

Arthur, P. (1999). 'Anglo-Irish Relations and Constitutional Policy', in Paul Mitchell and Rick Wilford (eds.), *Politics in Northern Ireland*. Boulder, CO: Westview Press, pp. 242–64.

Atkinson, Michael M. (1993). *Governing Canada. Institutions and Public Policy*. Toronto: Harcourt Brace Jovanovitch.

Azaña, Manuel (1977) [1932]. *Defensa de la autonomía de Cataluña*. Barcelona: Undarius.

Bader, Veit (1997). 'The Cultural Conditions of Transnational Citizenship: On the Interpenetration of Political and Ethnic Cultures', *Political Theory* 25: 771–813.

Badie, Bertrand (1992). 'Comparative Analysis and Historical Sociology', *International Social Science Journal*, August, pp. 319–27.

Badie, Bertrand (1995). *La fin des territoires. Essai sur le désordre international et sur l'utilité sociale du respect*. Paris: Fayard.

Baker, Judith (ed.) (1994). *Group Rights*. Toronto: University of Toronto Press.

Balfour, A. J. (1912). *Aspects of Home Rule*. London: Routledge.

Balfour, Sebastian (1996). '"Bitter Victory, Sweet Defeat": the March 1996 General Elections and the New Government in Spain', in *Government and Opposition* 31.3: 275–87.

Balme, Richard (1996). 'Pourquoi le gouvernement change-t-il d'échelle', in Richard Balme (ed.), *Les politiques du néo-régionalisme*. Paris: Economica, pp. 11–39.

Balthazar, Louis (1986). *Bilan du nationalisme québécois*. Montreal: L'Hexagone.

Banting, Keith and Richard Simeon (eds.) (1983a). *And No One Cheered: Federalism, Democracy and the Constitution Act*. Toronto: Methuen.

Banting, Keith and Richard Simeon (eds.) (1983b). *Redesigning the State: the Politics of Constitutional Change in Industrial Nations*. Toronto: University of Toronto Press.

Barry, Brian (1989). *Democracy, Power and Justice: Essays in Political Theory*. Oxford: Oxford University Press, pp. 100–5. Originally published as 'Political Accommodation and Consociational Democracy', *British Journal of Political Science* 5 (1975): 477–505.

Barth, Fredrik (ed.) (1969). *Ethnic Groups and Boundaries: the Social Organization of Cultural Difference*. Boston: Little, Brown.

Bartlett, Robert (1993). *The Making of Europe. Conquest, Colonization and Cultural Change 950–1350*. London: BCA.

Bastardas Boada, Albert (1987). 'L'aménagement linguistique en Catalogne au xxe siècle', in Jacques Maurais (ed.), *Politique et aménagement linguistiques*. Quebec: Conseil de la langue française, pp. 123–58.

Bauch, Hubert (1998). 'Anglos Resent Curbs: Poll', *The Gazette*, 29 May.

Bauer, Otto (1996) [1907]. 'The Nation', in Gopa Balakrishnan (ed.), *Mapping the Nation*. London: Verso, 39–77.

Beaufays, Jean (1988). 'Belgium: a Dualist Political System?', *Publius* 18: 63–73.

Beiner, Ronald (1995). 'Why Citizenship Constitutes a Theoretical Problem in the Last Decade of the Twentieth Century', in Ronald Beiner (ed.), *Theorizing Citizenship*. Albany: State University of New York Press, pp. 1–28.

Bellamy, Richard (1999). *Liberalism and Pluralism: Towards a Politics of Compromise*. London: Routledge.

Bellamy, Richard and Dario Castiglione (1997). 'Constitutionalism and Democracy: Political Theory and the American Constitution', *British Journal of Political Science* 27: 595–618.

Bercuson, David Jay (1977). *Canada and the Burden of Unity*. Toronto: Macmillan of Canada.

Bergeron, Josée (1997). 'Les frontières matérielles et imaginées de l'Etat-providence: les politiques familiales en France, au Canada et au Québec de 1945 à 1993'. PhD thesis, Carleton University.

Bicamerale (1997). Commissione Parlamentare per le Riforme Costituzionali (1997). *Progetto di legge constituzionale*. Rome: Camera dei Deputati, no. 3931, Senato della Repubblica, no. 2583, 30 June 1997.

Bickerton, James, Alain-G. Gagnon and Patrick Smith (1999). *Ties that Bind: Parties and Voters in Canada*. Toronto: Oxford University Press.

Biorcio, Roberto (1997). *La Padania promessa*. Milan: Il Saggiatore.

Bissoondath, Neil (1994). *Selling Illusions: the Cult of Multiculturalism in Canada*. Toronto: Penguin.

BNG-PNV-CiU (1998). *Declaración de Barcelona*. Bloque Nacionalista Galego, Partido Nacionalista Vasco, Convergència i Unió.

Boismenu, Gérard (1996). 'Perspectives on Quebec–Canada Relations in the 1990s: Is the Reconciliation of Ethnicity, Nationality and Citizenship Possible?', *Canadian Review of Studies on Nationalism* 23.1–2: 99–109.

Borloo, Jean-Pierre (1996). 'La révolte des magistrats francophones bruxellois', *Le Soir*, 15 November.

Borrows, John (2000). 'Questioning Canada's Title to Land: Aboriginal Peoples and the Rule of Law', *Speaking Truth to Power: Talk about Treaties*. Vancouver, BC: The Law Commission of Canada and The British Columbia Treaty Comission (2 March), unpublished.

Bouchard, Lucien (1997). 'Calgary nous rapetisse, nous comprime et nous réduit', in *Le Devoir*, 17 September, A7.

Brand, Jack, James Mitchell and Paula Surridge (1994). 'Social Constituency and Ideological Profile', *Political Studies* 42: 616–29.

Brass, Paul (1991). *Ethnicity and Nationalism. Theory and Comparison*. New Delhi: Sage.

Brassinne, Jacques (1989). *Les nouvelles institutions politiques de la Belgique*. Brussels: Dossier du CRISP, no. 30.

Braudel, Fernand. (1986). *L'Identité de la France*. Paris: Arthaud-Flammarion.

Breton, Raymond (1986). 'Multiculturalism and Canadian Nation-Building', in Alan Cairns and Cynthia Williams (eds.), *The Politics of Gender, Ethnicity and Language in Canada*. Ottawa: Supply and Services Canada, pp. 27–66.

Breton, Raymond (1988). 'From Ethnic to Civic Nationalism: English Canada and Quebec', *Ethnic & Racial Studies* 11: 85–102.

Breuilly, John (1994). *Nationalism and the State*, 2nd edn. Chicago: University of Chicago Press.

Breuilly, John (1995). 'The Sources of Nationalist Ideology', in Anthony D. Smith and John Hutchinson (eds.), *Nationalism*. Oxford: Oxford University Press, pp. 103–13.

Brooks, Stephen (1994). 'Consent and Constitutional Change in Canada', *Journal of Commonwealth and Comparative Politics* 32.3: 279–99.

Brown, Alice, David McCrone and Lindsay Paterson (1996). *Politics and Society in Scotland*. London: Macmillan.

Brown-John, Lloyd (ed.) (1988). *Centralizing and Decentralizing Trends in Federal States*. Lanham: University Press of America.

Brubaker, Rogers (1992). *Citizenship and Nationhood in France and Germany*. Cambridge, MA: Harvard University Press.

Buchanan, Allen (1991). *Secession: the Morality of Political Divorce from Fort Sumter to Lithuania and Quebec*. Boulder, CO: Westview Press.

Bullman, U. (ed.) (1994). *Die Politik der dritten Ebene. Regionen im Europa der Union*. Baden-Baden: Nomos.

Burelle, André (1995). *Le mal canadien: essai de diagnostic et esquisse d'une thérapie*. Montreal: Fides.

Burg, Steven L. (1996). *War or Peace? Nationalism, Democracy, and American Foreign Policy in Post-Communist Europe*. New York: New York University Press.

Burgess, Michael (1989). *Federalism and European Union: Political Ideas, Influences and Strategies in the European Community, 1972–87*. London: Routledge.

Burgess, Michael (ed.) (1990). *Canadian Federalism: Past, Present and Future*. Leicester: Leicester University Press.

Burgess, Michael (1993). 'Constitutional Reform in Canada and the 1992 Referendum', *Parliamentary Affairs* 46.3: 363–79.

Burgess, Michael (1995). *The British Tradition of Federalism*. Leicester: Leicester University Press.

Burgess, Michael. (1996). 'Ethnicity, Nationalism and Identity in Canada–Quebec Relations: the Case of Quebec's Distinct Society', *Journal of Commonwealth & Comparative Politics* 34.2: 46–64.

Burgess, Michael and Alain G. Gagnon (eds.) (1993). *Comparative Federalism and Federation: Competing Traditions and Future Directions*. London: Harvester Wheatsheaf.

Cadogan Group (1996). *Square Circles: Round Tables and the Path to Peace in Northern Ireland*. Belfast: The Cadogan Group.

Cairns, Alan (1977). 'The Governments and Societies of Canadian Federalism', *Canadian Journal of Political Science* 10: 695–725.

Cairns, Alan (1991). 'Constitutional Change and the Three Equalities', in Ronald L. Watts and Douglas M. Brown (eds.), *Options for a New Canada*. Toronto: University of Toronto Press, pp. 77–100.

Cairns, Alan (1992). *Charter Versus Federalism: the Dilemmas of Constitutional Reform*. London: McGill-Queen's University Press.

Cairns, Alan C. (1995). 'Constitutional Government and the Two Faces of Ethnicity: Federalism is Not Enough', in Karen Knop et al. (eds.), *Rethinking Federalism: Citizens, Markets, and Governments in a Changing World*. Vancouver: UBC Press, pp. 15–39.

Cairns, Alan C. (1997). 'Constitutional Reform: the God that Failed', in David. M. Hayne (ed.), *Can Canada Survive? Under What Terms and Conditions?*. Toronto: University of Toronto Press, pp. 47–66.

Cameron, David and Richard Simeon (forthcoming). 'Intergovernmental Relations and Democratic Citizenship', in B. Guy Peters and Donald Savoie (eds.), *Governance in the Twenty-First Century: Revitalizing Public Service*. Montreal: McGill-Queen's University Press.

Camilleri, Joseph and John Falk (1992). *End of Sovereignty? The Politics of a Shrinking and Fragmenting World*. Aldershot: Edward Elgar.

Campbell, Gordon (1998). 'We Should All Get to Vote on Nisga'a Agreement', *Times Colonist* 6 August, p. A12 and *Vancouver Sun* 11 August, p. A11.

Canada. Royal Commission on Aboriginal Peoples (1995). *Canada's Fiduciary Obligation to Aboriginal Peoples in the Context of Accession to Sovereignty by Quebec*, 2 vols. Ottawa: Minister of Supply and Services Canada.

Canada. Royal Commission on Aboriginal Peoples (1996). *Report of the Royal Commission on Aboriginal Peoples*, 5 vols. Ottawa: Minister of Supply and Services Canada.

Cardus, Salvador, Jordi Berrio, Lluis Bonet, Enric Saperas, Josep Gifreu and Isidor Mari (1991). *La politica cultural europea: una aproximación desde Cataluña al problema de las identidades culturales*. Madrid: Fundación Encuentro.

Carens, Joseph H. (ed.) (1995a). *Is Quebec Nationalism Just? Perspectives from anglophone Canada*. Montreal and Kingston: McGill-Queen's University Press.

Carens, Joseph H. (1995b). 'Immigration, Political Community, and the Transformation of Identity: Quebec's Immigration Politics in Critical Perspective', in Joseph H. Carens (ed.), *Is Quebec Nationalism Just?* Montreal and Kingston: McGill-Queen's University Press, pp. 20–81.

Carens, Joseph H. (1997). 'Two Conceptions of Fairness: a Response to Veit Bader', *Political Theory* 25.6: 814–20.

Carens, Joseph (2000). *Culture, Citizenship and Community: a Contextual Exploration of Justice*. Oxford: Oxford University Press.

Castells, Manuel (1997). *The Information Age: Economy, Society and Culture*, vol. 2: *The Power of Identity*. Oxford: Blackwell.

Citizens' Forum on Canada's Future (1991). *Citizens' Forum on Canada's Future: Report to the People and Government of Canada*. Ottawa: Canadian Government Publishing Center.

Claeys, Paul H. and Nicole Loeb-Mayer (1984). 'Le "para-fédéralisme" belge: une tentative de conciliation par le cloisonnement', *Revue internationale de science politique* 5: 473–90.

Clark, Robert P. (1992). 'Territorial Devolution as a Strategy to Resolve Ethnic Conflict: Basque's Self-Government in Spain's Autonomous Community System', in Anthony Messina, Luis Fraga, Laurie Rhodebeck and Frederick Wright (eds.), *Ethnic and Racial Minorities in Advanced Industrial Democracies*. New York and London: Greenwood Press.

Coakley, John (1992). 'Conclusion: Nationalist Movements and Society in Contemporary Western Europe', in John Coakley (ed.), *The Social Origins of Nationalist Movements*. London: Sage Publications, pp. 212–30.

Coakley, John (1993). 'Introduction: the Territorial Management of Ethnic Conflict', *Federal and Regional Studies* 3: 1–22.

Cobarrubias, Juan (1989). 'The Protection of Linguistic Minorities in the Autonomous Communities of Spain', in Paul Pupier and José Woehrling (eds.), *Langue et droit: actes du Premier Congrès de l'Institut international de droit linguistique comparé*. Montreal: Wilson et Lafleur, pp. 399–434.

Cohen, Anthony (1985). *The Symbolic Construction of Community*. London: Tavistock Publications.

Coleman, James S. (1992). 'Democracy in Permanently Divided Systems', *American Behavioral Scientist* 35: 363–75.

Colley, Linda (1992). *Britons. Forging the Nation 1707–1837*. London: Pimlico.

Collinge, Michael (1987). 'Le sentiment d'appartenance: une identité fluctuante', *Cahiers du CACEF* 130: 7–23.

Columberg, Dumeni (1998). 'La situation de la population francophone vivant dans la périphérie bruxelloise', Projet de rapport, *Commission des questions juridiques et des droits de l'homme*, Conseil de l'Europe. Available on *Le Soir*'s website: www.lesoir.com.

Comité interministériel sur la situation de la langue française (1996). *Le français langue commune. Enjeu de la société québécoise*. Quebec: Direction des communications du ministère de la culture et des communications.

Company, Enric (1998). 'Tres de cada cuatro habitantes de Cataluña saben hablar catalán y dos lo escriben', *El País*, 16 April, p. 1.

Connolly, William (1983). *The Terms of Political Discourse*, 2nd edn. Oxford: Martin Robertson.

Connolly, William (1999). *Why I Am Not a Secularist*. Minneapolis: University of Minnesota Press.

Connor, Walker (1978). 'A Nation Is a Nation Is a State, Is an Ethnic Group, Is a . . . ', *Ethnic and Racial Studies* 1.4: 379–88.

Connor, Walker (1984). *The National Question in Marxist-Leninist Theory and Strategy*. Princeton: Princeton University Press.

Connor, Walker (1994). *Ethnonationalism: the Quest for Understanding*. Princeton: NJ: Princeton University Press.

Conversi, Daniele (1997). *The Basques, the Catalans and Spain. Alternative Routes to Nationalist Mobilization*. London: Hurst.

Cook, Curtis (ed.) (1994). *Constitutional Predicament: Canada After the Referendum of 1992*. Montreal: McGill-Queen's University Press.

Cook, Curtis and J. D. Lindau (eds.) (2000). *Aboriginal Rights and Self-Government*. Montreal: McGill-Queen's University Press.

Coulombe, Pierre (1995). *Language Rights in French-Canada*. New York: P. Lang.

Courchene, Thomas (1995). *Celebrating Flexibility: an Intepretative Essay on the Evolution of Canadian Federalism.* C. D. Howe Institute Benefactors Lecture 1995. Montreal: C. D. Howe Institute.

Covell, Maureen (1986). 'Regionalization and Economic Crisis in Belgium', *Canadian Journal of Political Science* 19: 261–81.

Covell, Maureen (1987). 'Federalization and Federalism: Belgium and Canada', in Herman Bakvis and William Chandler (eds.), *Federalism and the Role of the State.* Toronto: University of Toronto Press, pp. 57–81.

Coverdale, John F. (1985), 'Regional Nationalism and the Elections in the Basque Country', in Howard R. Penniman and Eusebio M. Mujal-Leon (eds.), *Spain at the Polls, 1977, 1979, 1982: a Study of the National Elections.* Durham, NC: Duke University Press, pp. 226–50.

Crête, Jean (1996). 'The Quebec 1995 Constitutional Referendum', *Regional and Federal Studies: an International Journal* 6.3: 81–92.

Crick, Bernard (1991). 'The English and the British', in Bernard Crick (ed.), *National Identities: the Constitution of the United Kingdom.* Oxford: Blackwell, pp. 90–104.

CSA (1988), 'A Claim of Right for Scotland', in O. Dudley Edwards (ed.), *A Claim of Right for Scotland.* Edinburgh: Polygon.

Dahl, Robert (1971). *Polyarchy, Participation and Opposition.* New Haven, Conn: Yale University Press

Dahrendorf, R. (1994). 'The Changing Quality of Citizenship', in Bart van Steenbergen (ed.), *The Condition of Citizenship.* London: Sage, pp. 10–19.

Dahrendorf, R. (1995). 'Preserving Prosperity', *New Statesmen and Society,* 13/29 December.

De La Granja Sainz, J. L. (1995). *El nacionalismo vasco: un siglo de historia.* Madrid: Tecnos.

De Schryver, Reginald (1981). 'The Belgian Revolution and the Emergence of Belgium's Biculturalism', in Arend Lijphart (ed.), *Conflict and Coexistence in Belgium: the Dynamics of a Culturally Divided Society.* Berkeley: Institute of International Studies, University of California, pp. 13–33.

De Villiers, Bertus (ed.) (1994). *Evaluating Federal Systems.* Cape Town/Dordrecht: Juta & Co./Martinus Nijhoff Publishers.

De Villiers, Bertus (1995). *Bundestreue: the Soul of an Intergovernmental Partnership.* Johannesburg: Konrad Adenauer Stiftung, Occasional papers.

De Wachter, Wilfrid (1987). 'Changes in a Particratie: the Belgian Party System from 1944 to 1986', in Hans Daalder (ed.), *Party Systems in Denmark, Austria, Switzerland and the Netherlands.* New York: F. Pinter, pp. 285–363.

De Wachter, Wilfrid. (1996). 'La Belgique d'aujourd'hui comme société politique', in Alain Dieckhoff (ed.), *Belgique: la force de désunion.* Paris: Editions Complexe.

De Winter, Lieven and André-Paul Frognier (1997). 'L'évolution des identités politiques territoriales en Belgique durant la période 1975–1995', in Serge Jaumain (ed.), *La réforme de l'Etat . . . et après?* Brussels: Presses de l'Université de Bruxelles, pp. 161–76.

Dehaene, Jean-Luc (1993). 'Discours de clôture', in Francis Delpérée (ed.), *La constitution fédérale du 5 mai 1993.* Brussels: Bruylant, pp. 235–42.

Delpérée, Francis (1989). 'Y a-t-il un Etat belge?', in Hugues Dumont et al.

(eds.), *Belgitude et crise de l'Etat belge*. Brussels: Facultés universitaires Saint-Louis, pp. 49–53.

Delpérée, Francis (ed.) (1993). *La constitution fédérale du 5 mai 1993*. Brussels: Bruylant.

Delpérée, Francis (1995). 'Le fédéralisme sauvera-t-il la nation belge?' in Jacques Rupnick (ed.), *Le déchirement des nations*. Paris: Éditions du Seuil, pp. 123–37.

Delwit, Pascal and Jean-Michel De Waele (eds.) (1996). *Les partis politiques en Belgique*. Brussels: Editions de l'Université de Bruxelles.

Deprez, Kas and Persoons, Kas (1984). 'On the Ethnolinguistic Identity of Flemish High School Students in Brussels', *Journal of Language and Social Psychology* 3: 273–96.

Deruette, Serge (1994). 'Belgium', *European Journal of Political Research* 26: 247–54.

Deschouwer, Kris (1991). 'Small Parties in a Small Country: the Belgian Case', in Ferdinand Muller Rommel and Geoffrey Pridham (eds.), *Small Parties in Western Europe*. London: Sage, pp. 135–51.

Deschouwer, Kris (1997). 'Une fédération sans fédérations de partis', in Serge Jaumain (ed.), *La réforme de l'État . . . et après? L'impact des débats institutionnels en Belgique et au Canada*. Brussels: Editions de l'Université de Bruxelles, pp. 77–83.

Destatte, Philippe (1995). 'Ce nationalisme wallon', in Philippe Destatte et al. (eds.), *Nationalisme et postnationalisme*. Namur: Presses universitaires de Namur, pp. 13–21.

Deutsch, Karl (1966). *Nationalism and Social Communication*, 2nd edn. Cambridge, MA: MIT Press.

Dewar, Donald (1998). 'Secretary of State's Parliamentary Statement', in *The Scotland Bill*, London: House of Commons Library.

Dialogue Canada (1997). 'Calgary Declaration', http://www.uni.ca/calgary.html

Diamond, Larry and Marc F. Plattner (1994). *Nationalism, Ethnic Conflict and Democracy*. Baltimore and London: Johns Hopkins University Press.

Dicey, Albert V. (1912). *A Leap in the Dark: a Criticism of the Principles of Home Rule as Illustrated by the Bill of 1893*, 3rd edn. London: John Murray.

Dicey, Albert V. and Rait, Robert S. (1920). *Thoughts on the Union between England and Scotland*. London: Macmillan.

Dion, Jean and Manon Cornellier (1997). 'Chrétien durcit le ton', *Le Devoir*, 25 September, pp. A1 and A8.

Dion, Stéphane (1991). 'Le nationalisme dans la convergence culturelle: le Québec contemporain et le paradoxe de Tocqueville', in Raymond Hudon and Réjean Pelletier (eds.), *L'engagement intellectuel: mélanges en l'honneur de Léon Dion*. Sainte-Foy: Presses de l'Université de Laval, pp. 291–311.

Dion, Stéphane (1992). 'Explaining Quebec Nationalism', in R. Kent Weaver (ed.), *The Collapse of Canada?* Washington DC: Brooking Institution, pp. 77–121.

Dion, Stéphane (1994). 'Le fédéralisme fortement asymétrique: improbable et indésirable', in F. Leslie Seidle (ed.), *Seeking a New Canadian Partnership: Asymmetrical and Confederal Options*. Montreal: Institute for Research on Public Policy, pp. 133–52.

D'Oliveira, Hans Ulrich (1994). 'European Citizenship: Its Meaning, Its Potential', in R. Dehousse (ed.), *Europe after Maastricht: an Ever Closer Union?* Munich: Law Books in Europe, pp. 126–48.

Domenichelli, Luisa (1998). 'Canada et Belgique: comparaison entre deux stratégies linguistiques', paper presented at the international conference *Politique et stratégie linguistique au Canada: bilan et perspectives*, Avignon, 3–5 June.

Donaghy, Peter J. and Michael T. Newton (1987). *Spain: a Guide to Political and Economic Institutions*. Cambridge: Cambridge University Press.

Downs, William M. (1996). 'Federalism Achieved: the Belgian Elections of May 1995', *West European Politics* 19.1: 168–75.

Dubuisson, Martine (1998a). 'Débat sur la circulaire flamande interprétant les facilités linguistiques', *Le Soir*, 2 March.

Dubuisson, Martine (1998b). 'Sondage: les Flamands face à la circulaire Peeters', *Le Soir*, 16 March.

Dubuisson, Martine (1998c). 'Deschouwer: la Flandre ne veut plus d'une influence francophone', *Le Soir*, 16 March.

Dubuisson, Martine (1998d). 'Les Flamands allègent le rapport Columberg', *Le Soir*, 26 September.

Dufour, Christian (1990). *A Canadian Challenge*. Halifax, Nova Scotia: Institute for Research on Public Policy.

Dumont, Fernand (1995). *Raisons communes*. Montreal: Boréal.

Dumont, Hugues (1989). 'Etat, Nation et constitution: de la théorie du droit publique aux conditions de viabilité de l'Etat Belge', in Hugues Dumont et al. (eds.), *Belgitude et crise de l'Etat belge*. Brussels: Facultés universitaires Saint-Louis, pp. 73–124.

Dunford, Mick and Kafkalas, Grigoris (1992). 'The global-local interplay, corporate geographies and spatial development strategies in Europe', in Mick Dunford and Grigoris Kafkalas (eds), *Cities and Regions in the New Europe*. London: Belhaven, pp. 3–38.

Dworkin, Ronald (1989). 'Liberal Community', *California Law Review* 77.3: 479–504.

Economist (1999). 'Scotsmen, Welshmen and Englishmen', 1 May, p. 15.

Eisenberg, Avigail (1994). 'The Politics of Individual and Group Difference in Canadian Jurisprudence', *Canadian Journal of Political Science* 27: 3–21.

Elazar, Daniel (1987). *Exploring Federalism*. Tuscaloosa: University of Alabama Press.

Elazar, Daniel (1991). *Federal Systems of the World*. Harlow: Longman.

Elkins, David J. (1995). *Beyond Sovereignty: Territory and Political Economy in the Twenty-First Century*. Toronto: University of Toronto Press.

Etzioni, Amitai (1993). *The Spirit of Community. Rights, Responsibilities, and the Communitarian Agenda*. New York: Crown Publishers.

Everson, Michael and Ulrich Preuss (1995). 'Concepts, Foundations, and Limits of European Citizenship', *Diskussionspapier* 2/95. Bremen: Zentrum für Europäische Rechtspolitik.

Ferguson, Adam (1767). *An Essay on the History of Civil Society*, reprinted 1966. Edinburgh: Edinburgh University Press.

Fitzmaurice, John (1996). *The Politics of Belgium: a Unique Federalism*. Boulder, CO: Westview Press.

Forsyth, Murray (1981). *Unions of States: the Theory and Practice of Confederation.* Leicester: Leicester University Press.

Forsyth, Murray (1994). 'Towards the Reconciliation of Nationalism and Liberalism', in Guy Laforest and Douglas Brown (eds.), *Integration and Fragmentation: The Paradox of the Late 20th Century.* Kingston: Institute of Intergovernmental Relations, pp. 7–23.

Fossas, Enric (1995). 'Autonomia y asimetría', *Informe Pi i Sunyer sobre Comunidades Autónomas.* Barcelona, pp. 890–907.

Foucault, Michel (1982). 'The Subject and Power', in Hubert Dreyfus and Paul Rabinow (eds.), *Michel Foucault: Beyond Structuralism and Hermeneutics,* Chicago: University of Chicago Press, pp. 211–27.

Foucault, Michel (1984). 'Polemics, Politics, and Problematizations: an Interview', in Paul Rabinow (ed.), *The Foucault Reader.* New York: Pantheon, pp. 381–90.

Foundation Europe of the Cultures (1996). *Towards a Europe of the Cultures. Target 2002.* Brussels: Foundation Europe of the Cultures.

Friedrich, Carl (1968). *Trends of Federalism in Theory and Practice.* New York: Praeger.

Furnivall, John Sydenham (1948). *Colonial Policy and Practice.* Cambridge: Cambridge University Press.

Gagnon, Alain-G. (1993a). 'The Political Uses of Federalism', in Michael Burgess and Alain-G. Gagnon (eds.), *Comparative Federalism and Federation: Competing Traditions and Future Directions.* Toronto and London: University of Toronto Press, pp. 15–44.

Gagnon, Alain-G. (ed.) (1993b). *Quebec: State and Society.* Scarborough, Ont.: Nelson Canada.

Gagnon, Alain-G. (1996). 'De l'Etat-nation à l'Etat multinational: le Québec et le Canada face au défi de la modernité', *Cahiers du Programme d'études sur le Québec.* Montreal: Programme d'études sur le Québec, Université McGill.

Gagnon, Alain-G. and Joseph Garcea (1988). 'Quebec and the Pursuit of Special Status', in R. D. Olling and M. W. Westmacott (eds.), *Perspectives on Canadian Federalism.* Scarborough, Ont.: Prentice-Hall Canada, pp. 304–25.

Gagnon, Alain-G. and Mary Beth Montcalm (1989). *Quebec: Beyond the Quiet Revolution.* Scarborough, Ont.: Nelson Canada.

Gagnon, Alain-G. and Mery Beth Montcalm (1992). *Québec: au-delà de la Révolution tranquille.* Montréal: VLB Éditeur.

Gagnon, Alain-G. and François Rocher (1992a). 'Faire l'histoire au lieu de la subir', in Alain-G. Gagnon and François Rocher (ed.), *Répliques aux détracteurs de la souveraineté du Québec.* Montreal: VLB Éditeur.

Gagnon, Alain-G and François Rocher (1992b). 'Multilateral Agreement: the Betrayal of the Federal Spirit', in Douglas M. Brown and Robert Young (eds.), *Canada: the State of the Federation 1992.* Kingston: Institute of Intergovernmental Relations, pp. 117–27.

Gallie, W. B. (1956). 'Essentially contested concepts', *Proceedings of the Aristotelian Society* 56: 167–98.

Galston, William (1991). *Liberal Purposes: Goods, Virtues, and Duties in the Liberal State.* Cambridge: Cambridge University Press.

García Ferrando, Manuel, Eduardo López-Aranguren and Miguel Beltrán (1994). *La Conciencia Nacional y Regional en las España de las Autonomías.* Madrid: Centro de Investigaciones Sociologicas.

Gellner, Ernest (1983). *Nations and Nationalism.* Oxford: Blackwell.

Genesee, Fred and Naomi E. Holobow (1989). 'Change and Stability in Intergroup Perceptions', *Journal of Language and Social Psychology* 8: 17–38.

Geoghegan, Vincent (1994). 'Socialism, National Identities and Post-nationalist Citizenship', *Irish Political Studies* 9: 61–80.

Gibbins, Roger (1994). *Conflict and Unity: an Introduction to Canadian Political Life.* Scarborough, Ont.: Nelson Canada.

Gibbins, Roger and Sonia Arrison (1995). *Western Visions: Perspectives on the West in Canada.* Peterborough, Ont.: Broadview Press.

Gibbins, Roger and Guy Laforest (1998) (eds.). *Beyond the Impasse.* Montreal: Institute for Research on Public Policy.

Giddens, Anthony (1991). *Modernity and Self-Identity: Self and Society in the Late Modern Age.* Cambridge: Polity Press.

Gilmour, David (1985). *The Transformation of Spain: from Franco to the Constitutional Monarchy.* London: Quartet Books.

Giner, Salvador (1980). 'The Social Structure of Catalonia', *The Anglo-Catalan Society Occasional Publications,* University of Sheffield.

Giner, Salvador (1984). 'Ethnic Nationalism, Centre and Periphery in Spain', in Christopher Abel and Nissa Torrents (eds.), *Spain: Conditional Democracy.* London: Croom Helm, pp. 78–99.

Giner, Salvador and Luis Moreno (1990). 'Centro y periferia: la dimensión étnica de la sociedad española', in Salvador Giner (ed.), *España.* Madrid: Sociedad y Política, pp. 169–97.

Gladstone, W. E. (1886). 'Speech Presenting Government of Ireland Bill', Hansard CCCIV: 1036–139.

Gourevitch, Peter (1979). 'The Re-emergence of "Peripheral Nationalisms": Some Comparative Speculations of the Spatial Distributions of Political Leadership and Economic Growth', *Comparative Studies in Sociology and History* 21: 303–22.

Government of Canada (1998). 'To Aboriginal Canadians: "Our profound regret"', *The Globe and Mail,* 8 January, p. A19.

Government of Canada, Government of British Columbia and the Nisga'a Nation (1998). *Nisga'a Final Agreement.* Victoria: British Columbia Ministry of Aboriginal Affairs.

Govier, Trudy (1998). *Socrates' Children: Thinking and Knowing in the Western Tradition.* Peterborough, Ont.: Broadview Press.

Grand Council of The Crees (Eeyou Astchee) (1998). *Never Without Consent: James Bay Crees' Stand Against Forcible Inclusion into an Independent Quebec.* Toronto: ECW Press.

Gray, John (1989). *Liberalisms: Essays in Political Philosophy.* London: Routledge.

Greenfeld, Liah (1992). *Nationalism. Five Roads to Modernity.* Cambridge, MA: Harvard University Press.

Greenwood, Davyd (1985). 'Castilians, Basques and Andalusians: an Historical Comparison of Nationalism', in Paul Brass (ed.), *Ethnic Groups and the State.* London: Croom Helm, pp. 202–27.

Greschner, Donna (1998). 'The Quebec Secession Reference: Goodbye to Part V?' *Constitutional Forum Constitutionel* 10.1 (Fall): 19–25.

Guibernau, Montserrat (1995). 'Spain a Federation in the Making?' in Graham Smith (ed.), *Federalism: The Multiethnic Challenge*. London: Longman, pp. 239–54.

Gunther, Richard, Giacomo Sani and Goldie Shabad (1988). *Spain after Franco: the Making of a Competitive Party System*. Berkeley: University of California Press.

Habermas, Jürgen (1992). 'Citizenship and National Identity: Some Reflections on the Future of Europe', *Praxis International* 12: 1–19.

Habermas, Jürgen (1998). 'Struggles for Recognition in Constitutional States', in Ciaran Cronin and Pablo De Greiff (eds.), *The Inclusion of the Other: Studies in Political Theory*. Cambridge, MA: MIT Press, pp. 203–36.

Hachez, Théo (1995). 'La fausse barbe de la Belgique confédérale', *La revue nouvelle*, April, pp. 10–13.

Hardgrave Jr, Richard L. and Stanley A. Kochanek (1986). *India: Government and Politics in a Developing Nation*. New York.

Harris, Cole (ed.) (1998–1999). *BC Studies* 120 (Winter).

Harty, Siobhan (1998). 'The Nation as a Communal Good: a Nationalist Response to the Liberal View of Community', paper presented at the 56th Annual Meeting of the Midwest Political Science Association, Chicago, 23–25 April.

Hawkes, David and Bradford Morse (1991). 'Alternative Methods for Aboriginal Participation in Process of Constitutionnal Reform', in Ronald L. Watts and Douglas M. Brown (eds.), *Options for a New Canada*. Toronto: University of Toronto Press, pp. 163–87.

Hazell, Robert (ed.) (1999). *Constitutional Futures: a History of the Next Ten Years*. Oxford: Oxford University Press.

Hazell, Robert and Brendan O'Leary (1999). 'A Rolling Programme of Devolution: Slippery Slope or Safeguard of the Union?' in Robert Hazell (ed.), *Constitutional Futures: a History of the Next Ten Years*. Oxford: Oxford University Press.

Hébert, Chantal (1995). 'Même à Ottawa le bilinguisme en arrache', *La Presse*, 26 April, p. B1.

Hébert, Michel (1997). 'Calgary n'est pas une coquille vide insiste Daniel Johnson', *Le Devoir*, 25 September, A4.

Heisler, Martin (1977). 'Ethnic Conflict in the World Today', *Annals of the American Academy of Political and Social Science* 433: 1–140.

Held, David (1995). *Democracy and the New Global Order*. Cambridge: Polity Press.

Heller, William B. (1998). 'In Lieu of a Center: Regional Parties and National Politics in Spain's *Estado de las Autonomias*', paper presented to the American Political Science Association, Boston.

Herrero de Miñon, Miguel (1998). *Derechos Históricos y Constitución*. Madrid: Tauros.

Hobsbawm, Eric. (1990). *Nations and Nationalism since 1780: Programme, Myth and Reality*. Cambridge: Cambridge University Press.

Hobsbawm, Eric. (1992). 'Nationalism. Whose Fault-Line Is it Anyway?', *Anthropology Today*, February 1992.

Hoffman, John (1998). *Sovereignty*. Buckingham: Open University Press.
Honneth, Axel (1995). *The Struggle for Recognition*, trans. Joel Anderson. Cambridge: Polity Press.
Hooghe, Liesbet (1991). *A Leap in the Dark: Nationalist Conflict and Federal Reform in Belgium*. Ithaca: Cornell University Press.
Hooghe, Liesbet (1993). 'Belgium: From Regionalism to Federalism', *Regional Politics and Society* 3: 44–67.
Hooghe, Liesbet (1995). 'Belgian Federalism and the European Community', in Barry Jones and Michael Keating (eds.), *The European Union and the Regions*. Oxford: Clarendon Press, pp. 135–65.
Hooghe, Liesbet (ed.) (1996). *Cohesion Policy and European Integration. Building Multi-Level Governance*. Oxford: Clarendon Press.
Hooper, John (1995). *The New Spaniards*. London: Penguin Books.
Horowitz, Donald (1985). *Ethnic Groups in Conflict*. Berkeley: University of California Press.
Hueglin, Thomas (1987). 'Legitimacy, Democracy and Federalism', in Herman Bakvis and William Chandler (eds.), *Federalism and the Role of the State*. Toronto: University of Toronto Press, pp. 32–54.
Huizinga, Johan (1950). *Homo Ludens: a Study of the Play Element in Culture*. Boston: Beacon Press.
Hume, David (1983) [1754–1762]. *The History of England*. Indianapolis: Liberty Classics.
Huntington, Samuel P. (1996). *The Clash of Civilizations and the Remaking of World Order*. New York: Simon & Schuster.
Huyse, Luc (1981). 'Political Conflict in Bicultural Belgium', in Arend Lijphart (ed.), *Conflict and Coexistence in Belgium: the Dynamics of a Culturally Divided Society*. Berkeley: Institute of International Studies, University of California, pp. 107–26.
IEA (1995). *Uniformidad o diversidad de las Comunidades Autónomas*. Barcelona: Institut d'Estudis Autonòmics.
Jauregui, Gurutz (1996). *Entre la tragedia y la esperanza: Vasconia ante el nuevo milenio*, 2nd edn. Barcelona: Ariel.
Jauregui, Gurutz (1997). *Los nacionalismos minoritarios en la Unión Europea*. Barcelona: Ariel.
Javeau, Claude (1989). 'De la belgitude à l'éclatement du pays', in Hugues Dumont et al. (eds.), *Belgitude et crise de l'Etat belge*. Brussels: Facultés universitaires Saint-Louis, pp. 147–55.
Jedwab, Jack (1996). *English Fact in Montreal*. Montreal: Les Editions Images.
Jedwab, Jack (1997). 'Numbers Game. New Census Will Help Measure True Impact of Bill 101', *The Gazette*, 30 August.
Jeffery, Charlie and Peter Savigear (eds.)(1991). *German Federalism Today*. Leicester: Leicester University Press.
Jenson, Jane (1995). 'Citizenship Claims: Roots to Representation in a Federal System', in Karen Knop et al. (eds.), *Rethinking Federalism: Citizens, Markets and Governments in a Changing World*. Vancouver: University of British Columbia Press, pp. 99–118.
Joffe, Paul (1999). 'Quebec Secession and Aboriginal Peoples: Important

Signals from the Supreme Court', in David Schneiderman (ed.), *The Quebec Decision*. Toronto: James Lorimer and Company, pp. 137–42.

Jones, Barry and Michael Keating (eds.) (1995). *The European Union and the Regions*. Oxford: Clarendon Press.

Joy, Richard (1992). *Canada's Official Languages: the Progress of Bilingualism*. Toronto: University of Toronto Press.

Karmis, Dimitrios (1993). 'Cultures autochtones et libéralisme au Canada', *Canadian Journal of Political Science/Revue canadienne de science politique* 26: 69–96.

Karmis, Dimitrios (1994). 'Interpréter l'identité québecoise', in Alain-G. Gagnon (ed.), *Québec: état et société*. Montreal: Quebec Amérique, pp. 305–27.

Karmis, Dimitrios and Alain.-G. Gagnon (1996). 'Fédéralisme et identités collectives au Canada et en Belgique: des itinéraires différents, une fragmentation similaire', *Revue canadienne de science politique* 29.3: 435–69.

Katz, Ellis and G. Alan Tarr (eds.) (1996). *Federalism and Rights*. Lanham, MD: Rowman & Littlefield.

Kearney, Richard (1997). *Postnationalist Ireland: Politics, Culture, Philosophy*. London: Routledge.

Keating, Michael (1988). *State and Regional Nationalism. Territorial Politics and the European State*. London: Harvester-Wheatsheaf.

Keating, Michael (1992). 'Regional Autonomy in the Changing State Order: a Framework of Analysis', *Regional Politics and Policy* 2.3: 45–61.

Keating, Michael (1993). 'Spain: Peripheral Nationalism and State Response', in John McGarry and Brendan O'Leary (eds.), *The Politics of Ethnic Conflict Resolution*. London and New York: Routledge, pp. 204–25.

Keating, Michael (1995). 'Les régions constituent-elles un niveau de gouvernement en Europe?' Colloquium, *Les Régions en Europe*, Rennes, September 1995.

Keating, Michael (1996a). *Nations against the State: the New Politics of Nationalism in Quebec, Catalonia and Scotland*. London: Macmillan.

Keating, Michael (1996b). 'Scotland in the UK: a Dissolving Union?' *Nationalism and Ethnic Politics* 2.2: 232–57.

Keating, Michael (1998a). *The New Regionalism in Western Europe. Territorial Restructuring and Political Change*. Aldershot: Edward Elgar.

Keating, Michael (1998b). 'Le gouvernement asymétrique: principes et problèmes', *Politique et Sociétés* 17.3: 93–111.

Keating, Michael (forthcoming). 'Nations without States: the Accommodation of Nationalism in the New State Order', in Michael Keating and John McGarry (eds.), *Minority Nationalism in the New State Order*.

Keating, Michael and David Bleiman (1979). *Labour and Scottish Nationalism*. London: Macmillan.

Kellas, James (1983). 'The Politics of Constitution-Making: the Experience of the United Kingdom', in Keith Banting and Richard Simeon (eds.), *Redesigning the State*. Toronto: University of Toronto Press, pp. 146–55.

Kerremans, Bart (1997). 'The Flemish Identity: Nascent or Existent?' *Res Publica* 39.2: pp. 303–14.

Ketcham, Ralph (ed.) (1986). *The Anti-Federalist Papers and the Constitutional Convention Debates*. New York: Penguin.

Kidd, Colin (1993). *Subverting Scotland's Past: Scottish Whig Historians and the creation of an Anglo-British Identity, 1689–c. 1830*. Cambridge: Cambridge University Press.

King, Preston T. (1982). *Federalism and Federation*. Baltimore: Johns Hopkins University Press.

Kinsley, James (ed.) (1971). *Burns: Poems and Songs*. Oxford: Oxford University Press.

Klein, Juan-Luis (1989). 'Etat et territoire au Québec et en Catalogne: introduction à une étude comparative', in Gilles Sénécal (ed.), *Territoires et minorités de l'Amérique française au lac Meech*. Montreal: Association canadienne-française pour l'avancement des sciences, pp. 114–22.

Knop, Karen, Sylvia Ostry, Richard Simeon and Katherine Swinton (eds.) (1995). *Rethinking Federalism: Citizens, Markets and Government in a Changing World*. Vancouver: UBC Press.

Kohn, Hans (1967) [1944]. *The Idea of Nationalism: a Study in Its Origin and Background*, 2nd edn. New York: Macmillan.

Krejcí, Jaroslav and Vítezslav Velímsky (1981). *Ethnic and Political Nations in Europe*. London: St Martin's Press.

Kukathas, Chandran. (1995) [1992]. 'Are There Any Cultural Rights', *Political Theory* 20: 105–139, reprinted in Will Kymlicka (ed.), *The Rights of Minority Cultures*. New York, Oxford University Press, pp. 228–56.

Kurzer, Paulette (1997). 'Decline or Preservation of Executive Capacity? Political and Economic Integration Revisited', *Journal of Common Market Studies* 35. 1: 31–56.

Kwavnick, David (ed.) (1973). *The Tremblay Report*. Toronto: McClelland and Stewart.

Kymlicka, Will (1989). *Liberalism, Community and Culture*. Oxford: Oxford University Press.

Kymlicka, Will (1993). 'Misunderstanding Nationalism', *Dissent*, Winter: 130–7.

Kymlicka, Will (1995). *Multicultural Citizenship: a Liberal Theory of Minority Rights*. Oxford: Clarendon Press.

Kymlicka, Will (1996a). 'Social Unity in a Liberal State', *Social Philosophy and Policy* 13.1: 106–36.

Kymlicka, Will (1996b). 'Federalismo, nacionalismo y multiculturalismo', *Revista internacional de filosofía política* 7: 20–54.

Kymlicka, Will (1998a). *Finding our Way: Rethinking Ethnocultural Relations in Canada*. Toronto, Oxford: Oxford University Press.

Kymlicka, Will (1998b). 'Is Federalism a Viable Alternative to Secession?' in Percy B. Lehning (ed.), *Theories of Secession*. London: Routledge, pp. 111–50.

Kymlicka, Will (1998c). 'Le fédéralisme multinational au Canada: un partenariat à repenser', in Guy Laforest and Roger Gibbins (eds.), *Sortir de l'impasse: les voies de la réconciliation*. Montreal: Institut de recherche en politiques publiques, pp. 15–54.

Kymlicka, Will (1998d). 'Multinational Federalism in Canada: Rethinking the Partnership', in Roger Gibbins and Guy Laforest (eds.), *Beyond the Impasse:*

Towards Reconciliation. Montreal: Institute for Research on Public Policy, pp. 15–50.

Kymlicka, Will and Wayne Norman (1994). 'The Return of the Citizen', *Ethics* 104: 352–81.

Kymlicka, Will and Wayne Norman (eds.) (2000). *Citizenship in Diverse Societies*. Oxford: Oxford University Press.

Kymlicka, Will and J.-R. Raviot (1997). 'Vie commune: aspects internationaux des fédéralismes', *Etudes internationales* 28: 779–843.

Laden, Anthony (2001). *Reasonably Radical: Deliberative Liberalism and the Politics of Identity*. Ithaca: Cornell University Press.

Laforest, Guy (1992a). *Trudeau et la fin d'un rêve canadien*. Sillery, Quebec: Septentrion.

Laforest, Guy (1992b). 'La Charte canadienne des droits et libertés au Québec: nationaliste, injuste et illégitime', in François Rocher (ed.), *Bilan québécois du fédéralisme candien*. Montreal: VLB Editeur, pp. 124–51.

Laforest, Guy (1995a). *De l'urgence*. Montreal: Boréal.

Laforest, Guy (1995b). *Trudeau and the End of a Canadian Dream*. Montreal: McGill-Queen's University Press.

Laforest, Guy (1995c). 'Esprit de géométrie et esprit de finesse', *Le Devoir*, 24 February p. A10.

Laforest, Guy (1998). 'Standing in the Shoes of the Other Partners in the Canadian Union', in Roger Gibbins and Guy Laforest (eds.), *Beyond the Impasse: Toward Reconciliation*. Montreal: Institute for Research on Public Policy, pp. 51–79.

Laitin, David (1987). 'South Africa: Violence, Myths, and Democratic Reform', *World Politics* 39: 258–79.

Laitin, David (1989). 'Linguistic Revival: Politics and Culture in Catalonia', *Comparative Studies in Society and History* 31: 297–317.

Laitin, David (1992). 'Language Normalization in Estonia and Catalonia', *Journal of Baltic Studies* 23: 149–66.

Lambert, Wallace E. et al. (1960). 'Evaluational Reaction to Spoken Languages', *Journal of Abnormal and Social Psychology* 60: 44–51.

Langlois, Simon (1991a). 'Le choc de deux sociétés globales', in Louis Balthazar, Guy Laforest and Vincent Lemieux (eds.), *Le Québec et la restructuration du Canada, 1980–1992: enjeux et perspectives*. Sillery, Quebec: Editions du Septentrion, pp. 95–108.

Langlois, Simon (1991b). 'Une société distincte à reconnaître et une identité collective à consolider', Commission sur l'avenir politique et constitutionnel du Quebec (Bélanger-Campeau Commission), *Document de travail 4*, pp. 569–95. Quebec: La Commission.

Laponce, Jean (1991). 'Reducing the Tensions Resulting From Language Contacts: Personal or Territorial Solutions?' in David Schneiderman (ed.), *Language and the State: the Law and Politics of Identity*. Cowansville, Quebec: Editions Yvon Blais, pp. 173–79.

LaSelva, Samuel (1993). 'Re-imagining Confederation: Moving Beyond the Trudeau-Lévesque Debate', *Canadian Journal of Political Science/Revue canadienne de science politique* 26: 699–720.

LaSelva, Samuel (1996). *The Moral Foundations of Canadian Federalism: Para-*

doxes, Achievements, and Tragedies of Nationhood. Montreal: McGill-Queen's University Press.

Latouche, Daniel (1993), '"Quebec, see Under Canada": Quebec Nationalism in the New Global Age', in Alain-G. Gagnon (ed.), *Quebec: State and Society*. Scarborough, Ont.: Nelson Canada, 40–64.

Lazar, Harvey (ed.) (1998). *Canada: The State of the Federation 1997: Non-Constitutional Renewal*. Kingston: Institute of Intergovernmental Relations, Queen's University.

Lejeune, Marc (1994). *Introduction au droit et aux institutions de la Belgique fédérale (sur la base de la nouvelle Constitution coordonnée)*. Brussels: La Charte.

Lejeune, Yves (1994). 'Le droit fédéral belge des relations internationales', *Revue générale de droit international public* 98: 577–628.

Lemieux, Vincent (1996). 'L'analyse politique de la décentralisation', *Canadian Journal of Political Science/Revue canadienne de science politique* 29. 4: 661–80.

Lenihan, Donald, Gordon Robertson and Roger Tassé (1994). *Canada: Reclaiming the Middle Ground*. Montreal: Institute for Research on Public Policy.

Lévesque, Lia (1997). 'Johnson demande l'aide du CPQ', *Le Devoir*, 23 September A4.

Levine, Marc (1990). *The Reconquest of Montreal*. Philadelphia: Temple University Press.

Lijphart, Arend (1968a). *The Politics of Accommodation: Pluralism and Democracy in the Netherlands*. Berkeley: University of California Press.

Lijphart, Arend (1968b). 'Typologies of Democratic Systems', *Comparative Political Studies* 1: 3–44.

Lijphart, Arend (1969). 'Consociational Democracy', *World Politics* 21: 107–25.

Lijphart, Arend (1974). 'Consociational Democracy', in Kenneth McRae (ed.), *Consociational Democracy: Political Accommodation in Segmented Societies*. Ottawa: McClelland and Stewart, pp. 70–89.

Lijphart, Arend (1977). *Democracy in Plural Societies: A Comparative Exploration*. New Haven: Yale University Press.

Lijphart, Arend (1982). 'Consociation: the Model and Its Application in Divided Societies', in Desmond Rea (ed.), *Political Co-Operation in Divided Societies*. Dublin: Gill and Macmillan, pp. 166–86.

Linz, Juan (1967). 'The Party System of Spain: Past and Future', in Seymour Martin Lipset and Stein Rokkan (eds.), *Party Systems and Voter Alignments: Cross-National Perspectives*. New York: Free Press, pp. 197–282.

Linz, Juan (1973). 'Early State-Building and the Late Peripheral Nationalisms against the State: the Case of Spain', in S. N. Eisenstadt and Stein Rokkan (eds.), *Building States and Nations: Models, Analyses and Data across Three Worlds*. Beverly Hills: Sage, pp. 32–116.

Linz, Juan (1975). 'Politics in a Multi-Lingual Society with a Dominant World Language: the case of Spain', in Jean-Guy Savard and Richard Vigneault (eds.), Les états multilingues: problèmes et solutions. Quebec: Presses de l'Université Laval, pp. 367–444.

Linz, Juan (1997a). 'Some Thoughts on the Victory and Future of Democracy', in Axel Hadenius (ed.), *Democracy's Victory and Crisis*. New York: Cambridge University Press, pp. 404–26.

Linz, Juan (1997b). 'Democracy, Multinationalism and Federalism', paper presented at the International Political Science Association Conference (August), Seoul.

Linz, Juan (1997c). *Democracy, Multinationalism and Federalism (Working Paper No. 103)*. Madrid: Centro de Estudios Avanzados en Ciencias Sociales, Instituto Juan March.

Livingston, W. S. (1952). 'A Note on the Nature of Federalism', *Political Science Quarterly* 27: 81–95.

Lode, Wils (1996a). *Histoire des nations belges*. Ottignies: Quorum.

Lode, Wils (1996b). 'Mouvements linguistiques, nouvelles nations?' in Alain Dieckhoff (ed.), *Belgique: la force de désunion*. Paris: Editions Complexe.

Lustick, Ian S. (1979). 'Stability in Deeply Divided Societies: Consociationalism versus Control', *World Politics* 31: 325–44.

Lustick, Ian S. (1985). *State Building Failure in British Ireland and French Algeria*. Berkeley: Institute of International Studies.

Mabille, Xavier (1986). *Histoire politique de la Belgique*. Brussels: CRISP.

MacCormick, Neil (1996). 'Liberalism, Nationalism and the Post-Sovereign State', *Political Studies* 44: 553–67.

Macedo, Steven (1990). *Liberal Virtues*. Oxford: Oxford University Press.

Maclure, Jocelyn (2000). *Récits identitaires: le Québec à l'épreuve du pluralisme*. Montreal: Québec-Amérique.

MacWhirter, Iain (1997). 'Westminster Effectively Stripped of Sovereignty', *The Electronic Scotsman* (http://www.alba.org.uk).

Maddens, Bart, Roeland Beerten and Jaak Billiet (1998). 'The National Consciousness of the Flemings and the Walloons: an Empirical Investigation', in K. Deprez and L. Vos (eds.), *Nationalism in Belgium: Shifting Identities, 1780–1995*. Basingstoke: Macmillan, pp. 198–208.

Majone, Giandomenico (1995). *Unity in Diversity, Competition with Cooperation: Europe's Past as its Future*. Florence: European University Institute, mimeo.

Major, John (1992). 'Foreword by the Prime Minister', in Secretary of State for Scotland, *Scotland and the Union*. Edinburgh: HMSO.

MAP (1997). *Estudio sobre reparto del gasto público en 1997 entre los distintos niveles de administración*. Madrid: Ministerio de Administraciones Públicas.

Marshall, Gordon (1992). *Presbyteries and Profits: Calvinism and the Development of Capitalism in Scotland, 1560–1707*. Edinburgh: Edinburgh University Press.

Marshall, T. H. (1965). *Citizenship and Social Class*. Cambridge: Cambridge University Press.

Martiniello, Marco (ed.) (1995). *Migration, Citizenship and Ethno-National Identities in the European Union*. Aldershot: Avebury.

Maxwell, Kenneth and Steven Spiegel (1994). *The New Spain: From Isolation to Influence*. New York: Council on Foreign Relations Press.

Maynes, Charles William (1993). 'Containing Ethnic Conflict', *Foreign Policy* 90: 3–21.

McCrone, David (1992). *Understanding Scotland: the Sociology of a Stateless Nation*. London: Routledge.

McGarry, John and Brendan O'Leary (eds.) (1993). *The Politics of Ethnic Conflict Regulation*. New York and London: Routledge.

McGarry, John and Brendan O'Leary (1995a). *Explaining Northern Ireland.* Oxford: Blackwell.

McGarry, John and Brendan O'Leary (1995b). 'Five Fallacies: Northern Ireland and the Liabilities of Liberalism', *Ethnic and Racial Studies* 18: 837–61.

McGarry, John and Brendan O'Leary (1999). *Policing Northern Ireland: Proposals for a New Start.* Belfast: Blackstaff.

McKay, David (1997). 'On the Origins of Political Unions: The European Case', *Journal of Theoretical Politics* 9.3: 279–96.

McLean, Iain (1998). 'The Semi-Detached Election: Scotland', in Anthony King (ed.), *New Labour Triumphs: Britain at the Polls.* Chatham, NJ: Chatham House Publishers, pp. 145–75.

McRae, Kenneth (1979). 'The Plural Society and the Western Political Tradition', *Canadian Journal of Political Science* 12: 675–88.

McRae, Kenneth (1983). *Conflict and Compromise in Multilingual Societies: Switzerland.* Waterloo: Wilfrid Laurier University Press.

McRae, Kenneth (1986). *Conflict and Compromise in Multilingual Societies: Belgium.* Waterloo: Wilfrid Laurier University Press.

McRae, Kenneth (1992). 'The Meech Lake Impasse in Theoretical Perspective', in Alain-G. Gagnon and A. Brian Tanguay (eds.), *Democracy With Justice: Essays in Honour of Khayyam Zev Paltiel.* Ottawa: Carleton University Press, pp. 140–53.

McRoberts, Kenneth (1989). 'Making Canada Bilingual: Illusions and Delusions of Federal Language Policy', in David P. Shugarman and Reg Whitaker (eds.), *Federalism and Political Community: Essays in Honour of Donald Smiley.* Peterborough, Ont.: Broadview Press, pp. 141–71.

McRoberts, Kenneth (1993). 'English-Canadian Perceptions of Québec', in Alain-G. Gagnon, (ed.), *Quebec: State and Society.* Scarborough, Ont.: Nelson, pp. 116–29.

McRoberts, Kenneth (1995a). 'In Search of Canada "Beyond Quebec"', in Kenneth McRoberts (ed.), *Beyond Quebec: Taking Stock of English Canada.* Montreal: McGill-Queen's University Press, pp. 5–28.

McRoberts, Kenneth (1995b). 'Living with Dualism and Multiculturalism', in François Rocher and Miriam Smith (eds.), *New Trends in Canadian Federalism.* Peterborough, Ont.: Broadview Press, 109–132.

McRoberts, Kenneth (1997a). *Misconceiving Canada: the Struggle for National Unity.* Toronto: Oxford University Press.

McRoberts, Kenneth (1997b). *Quebec: Social Change and Political Crisis.* Toronto: McClelland and Stewart.

McRoberts, Kenneth (1998). 'Les minorités linguistiques dans un partenariat Canada-Québec', in Guy Laforest and Roger Gibbins (eds.), *Sortir de l'impasse: les voies de la réconciliation.* Montreal: Institut de recherche en politiques publiques, pp. 203–34.

Meadwell, Hudson (1998). 'Nations, States and Unions: Institutional Design and State Breaking', paper presented to the American Political Science Association, Boston.

Means, Gordon Paul (1991). *Malaysian Politics: the Second Generation.* Singapore: Oxford University Press.

Medrano, Juan (1995). *Divided Nations: Class, Politics, and Nationalism in the*

Basque Country and Catalonia. Ithaca and London: Cornell University Press.

Melucci, Alberto (1989). *Nomads of the Present*. London: Hutchinson Radius.

Michel, Bernard (1995). *Nations et nationalismes en Europe centrale*. Paris: Aubier.

Michelmann, Hans and Panayotis Soldatos (1990). *Federalism and International Relations*. Oxford: Clarendon Press.

Milian-Massana, Antoni (1992). 'Droits linguistiques et droits fondamentaux en Espagne', *Revue générale de droit* 23.4: 561–82.

Mill, John Stuart (1991). 'Considerations on Representative Government', in *On Liberty and other Essays*. Oxford: Oxford University Press.

Mill, John Stuart (1995) [1860]. 'Considerations on Representative Government', in Omar Dahbour and Micheline R. Ishay (eds.), *The Nationalism Reader*. Atlantic Highlands, NJ: Humanities Press, pp. 98–107.

Miller, David (1995). *On Nationality*. Oxford: Clarendon Press.

Miller, David (ed.) (1998a). *Rethinking Northern Ireland*. London: Longman.

Miller, David (1998b). 'Nationality in Divided Societies', paper presented to the American Political Science Association, Boston.

Miller, David (1998b). 'Secession and the Principle of Nationality', in Jocelyne Couture, Kai Nielsen and Michel Seymour (eds.), *Rethinking Nationalism*. Calgary: University of Calgary Press, pp. 261–82 and in Margaret Moore (ed.), *National Self-Determination and Secession*. Oxford: Oxford University Press, pp. 62–78.

Miller, David (1999). 'Group Identities, National Identities and Democratic Politics', in John Horton and Susan Mendus (eds.), *Toleration, Identity and Difference*. Basingstoke and New York: Macmillan and St Martin's Press, pp. 103–25.

Miller, J. R. (1989). *Skyscrapers Hide the Heavens*. Toronto: University of Toronto Press.

Milne, David E. (1991). 'Equality or Asymmetry: Why Choose?' in Ronald L. Watts and Douglas M. Brown (eds.), *Options for a New Canada*. Toronto: University of Toronto Press, pp. 285–307.

Milne, David (1994). 'Exposed to the Glare: Constitutional Camouflage and the Fate of Canada's Federation', in F. Leslie Seidle (ed.), *Seeking a New Canadian Partnership: Assymmetrical and Confederal Options*. Montreal: Institute for Research on Public Policy, pp. 107–31.

Miroir, André (1990). 'La Belgique et ses clivages: contradictions structurelles et familles politiques', *Pouvoirs*, April, pp. 5–14.

Mitchell, James (1996). *Strategies for Self-Government: the Campaigns for a Scottish Parliament*. Edinburgh: Polygon.

Mitchell, Paul (1999). 'Futures', in Paul Mitchell and Rick Wilford (eds.), *Politics in Northern Ireland*. Boulder, CO: Westview Press, pp. 265–84.

Mitchell, Paul and Rick Wilford (eds.) (1999). *Politics in Northern Ireland*. Boulder, CO: Westview Press.

Montesquieu (1989). *The Spirit of the Laws*, trans. Anne Cohler, Basia Miller and Harold Stone. Cambridge: Cambridge University Press.

Moore, Margaret (1997). 'On National Self-Determination', *Political Studies* 45: 900–13.

Moore, Margaret (1998). 'The Territorial Dimension of National Self-Determination', in Margaret Moore (ed.), *National Self-Determination and Secession*. Oxford: Oxford University Press, 134–157.

Moreno, Luis (1988). 'Identificación dual y autonomía política', *Revista española de investigaciones sociológicas* 42: 155–74.

Moreno, Luis (1994). 'Ethnoterritorial Concurrence and Imperfect Federalism in Spain', in Bertus De Villiers (ed.), *Evaluating Federal Systems*. Cape Town/Dordrecht: Juta & Co/Martinus Nijhoff Publishers, pp. 162–93.

Moreno, Luis (1995). 'Multiple Ethnoterritorial Concurrence in Spain', *Nationalism and Ethnic Politics* 1: 11–32.

Moreno, Luis. (1997a). *La federalización de España: poder político y territorio*. Madrid: Siglo Veintiuno (English edition 2000: *The Federalization of Spain*. London: Frank Cass).

Moreno, Luis (1997b). *Federalism: the Spanish Experience*. Pretoria: Human Sciences Research Council.

Moreno, Luis and Ana Arriba (1996). 'Dual Identity in Autonomous Catalonia', *Scottish Affairs* 17: 78–97.

Moreno, Luis, Ana Arriba and Araceli Serrano (1998). 'Multiple Identities in Decentralized Spain: the Case of Catalonia', *Regional and Federal Studies* 8.3: 65–88.

Morton, William L. (1979). 'Clio in Canada: the Interpretation of Canadian History', in Ramsay Cook, Craig Brown and Carl Berger (eds.), *Approaches to Canadian History*. Toronto: University of Toronto Press, pp. 42–9.

Mouffe, Chantal (2000). *The Democratic Paradox*. London: Verso.

Murphy, Alexander B. (1988). 'Evolving Regionalism in Linguistically Divided Belgium', in R. J. Johnston, David B. Knight and Eleonore Kofman (eds.), *Nationalism, Self-Determination and Political Geography*. London: Croom Helm, pp. 135–50.

Murphy, Alexander B. (1995). 'Belgium's Regional Divergence: Along the Road to Federation', in Graham Smith (ed.), *Federalism: The Multiethnic Challenge*. London: Longman, pp. 73–100.

Nagel, Thomas (1991). *Equality and Partiality*. New York: Oxford University Press.

Nairn, Tom (1977). 'Scotland and Europe', in Tom Nairn, *The Break-Up of Britain*. London: New Left Books, pp. 92–125.

Newton, Michael T. and Peter J. Donaghy (1997). *Institutions of Modern Spain: a Political and Economic Guide*. Cambridge: Cambridge University Press.

Nielson, Kai (1998). 'Liberal Nationalism, Liberal Democracies, and Secession', *University of Toronto Law Journal* 48: 253–95.

Nietzsche, F. (1994). *On the Genealogy of Morality and Other Essays*, ed. K. Ansell-Pearson, trans. C. Diethe. Cambridge: Cambridge University Press.

Niou, Emerson and Peter Ordeshook (1997). 'Designing Coherent Government', in Larry Diamond and Marc Plattner (eds.), *Consolidating the Third Wave Democracies*. Baltimore: Johns Hopkins University Press, pp. 160–8.

Noël, Alain (1998). 'Le principe fédéral, la solidarité et le partenariat', in Roger Gibbins and Guy Laforest (eds.), *Sortir de l'impasse: les voies de la réconciliation*. Montreal: Institut de recherches en politiques publiques, pp. 263–95.

Nordlinger, Eric A. (1972). *Conflict Regulation in Divided Societies*. Occasional Papers in International Affairs, no. 29. Cambridge, MA: Harvard University.

Norman, Wayne J. (1994). 'Towards a Philosophy of Federalism', in Judith Baker (ed.), *Group Rights*. Toronto: University of Toronto Press, pp. 79–100.

Norman, Wayne (1995). 'The Ideology of Shared Values: a Myopic Vision of Unity in the Multi-Nation State', in Joseph Carens (ed.), *Is Quebec Nationalism Just? Perspectives from Anglophone Canada*. Montreal: McGill-Queen's University Press, pp. 137–59.

Norman, Wayne (1998). 'The Ethics of Secession as the Regulation of Secessionist Politics', in Margaret Moore (ed.), *National Self-Determination and Secession*. Oxford: Oxford University Press, pp. 34–61.

Norman, Wayne (forthcoming). 'Secession and (Constitutional) Democracy', in Ferran Requejo (ed.), *Democracy and National Pluralism*. London: Routledge Press.

Norris, Alexander (1997a). 'Immigrant Students Back Bill 101', *The Gazette*, 29 October.

Norris, Alexander (1997b). 'Learning French Pays Off', *The Gazette*, 26 November.

Norris, Alexander (1998). 'Bilingual Anglo Youth On the Rise. Census Figures Show Strong Trend', *The Gazette*, 24 March.

Nussbaum, Martha (1996a). 'Patriotism and Cosmopolitanism', in Joshua Cohen (ed.), *For Love of Country: Debating the Limits of Patriotism*. Boston: Beacon Press, pp. 2–17.

Nussbaum, Martha (1996b). 'Reply', in Joshua Cohen (ed.), *For Love of Country: Debating the Limits of Patriotism*. Boston: Beacon Press, pp. 131–44.

Ohmae, Kenichi (1995). *The End of the Nation State: the Rise of Regional Economies*. New York: Free Press.

O'Leary, Brendan (1999). 'The Nature of the Agreement', *Fordham International Law Journal* 22: 1628–67.

O'Leary, Brendan, Tom Lyne, Jim Marshall and Bob Rowthorn (1993). *Northern Ireland: Sharing Authority*. London: Institute for Public Policy Research.

O'Neill, Shane (1996). 'The Idea of an Overlapping Consensus in Northern Ireland: Stretching the Limits of Liberalism', *Irish Political Studies* 11 83–102.

O'Neill, Shane. (1997). *Impartiality in Context: Grounding Justice in a Pluralist World*. Albany: State University of New York Press.

O'Neill, Shane. (2000). 'Liberty, Equality and the Rights of Cultures: the Marching Controversy at Drumcree', *British Journal of Politics and International Relations* 2: 26–45.

Oliver, Michael (1991). 'Laurendeau et Trudeau: leurs opinions sur le Canada', in Raymond Hudon and Réjean Pelletier (eds.), *L'engagement intellectuel: mélanges en l'honneur de Léon Dion*. Sainte-Foy: Presses de l'Université Laval, pp. 417–27.

Olling, R. D. and R. Westmacott (eds.)(1988). *Perspectives on Canadian Federalism*. Scarborough, Ont.: Prentice-Hall.

Oneto, G. (1997). *L'invenzione della Padania: la rinascita della communità più antica d'Europa*. Bergamo: Foedus.

Overlegcentrum voor vlaamse verenigingen (OVV) (1993). 'La sécurité sociale: une compétence non fédérale', *La revue nouvelle* , November, pp. 65–8.

Owen, David (1995). *Nietzsche, Politics and Morality*. London: Sage.

Parada, J. Ramón (1996). 'España: ¿Una or Trina?', *Revista de Administración Pública* 141 (Sept.–Dec.), 7–23.

Parekh, Bhikhu (1995). 'Ethnocentricity of the Nationalist Discourse', *Nations and Nationalism* 1: 25–52.

Parfit, Derek (1984). *Reasons and Persons*. Oxford: Clarendon Press.

Paterson, Lindsay (1994). *The Autonomy of Modern Scotland*. Edinburgh: Edinburgh University Press.

Patten, Alan (1996). 'The Republican Critique of Liberalism', *British Journal of Political Science* 26.1: 25–44.

Peeters, Patrick (1994). 'Federalism: A Comparative Perspective – Belgium Transforms from a Unitary to a Federal State', in Bertus de Villiers (ed.) *Evaluating Federal Systems*, Capetown/Dordrecht: Juta and Company/Martinus Nijhoff Publishers, pp. 194–207.

Pérez-Agote, Alfonso (1994). 'Un modelo fenomenológico-genético para el análisis comparativo de la dimensión política de las identidades colectivas en el estado de las autonomías', in J. Beramendi, R. Máiz and X.-M. Núñez (eds.), *Nationalism in Europe. Past and Present*. Santiago de Compostela, pp. 307–23.

Pérez-Diaz, Victore M. (1993). *The Return of Civil Society: the Emergence of Democratic Spain*. Cambridge, MA: Harvard University Press.

Persky, Stan (ed.) (1998). *The Supreme Court of Canada Decision on Aboriginal Title: Delgamuukw*. Vancouver: Greystone Books.

Petschen, Santiago (1993). *La Europa de las regiones*. Barcelona: Generalitat de Catalunya.

Phillips, Anne (1995). *The Politics of Presence: Issues in Democracy and Group Representation*. Oxford: Oxford University Press.

Pierré-Caps, Stéphane (1995). *La Multination: l'avenir des minorités en Europe centrale et orientale*. Paris: O. Jacob.

Pintarits, Sylvia (1995). *Macht, Demokratie und Regionen in Europa: Analysen und Szenarien der Integration und Desintegration*. Marburg: Metropolis.

Pittock, Murray (1991). *The Invention of Scotland: the Stuart Myth and the Scottish Identity, 1638 to the Present*. New York: Routledge.

Platón, Miguel (1994). *La amenaza separatista: mito y realidad de los nacionalismos en España*. Madrid: Ediciones Temas de Hoy.

PNV (1995). Partido Nacionalista Vasco, *Asamblea General, Ponencias aprobadas*.

Polasky, Janet (1981). 'Liberalism and Biculturalism', in Arend Lijphart (ed.), *Conflict and Coexistence in Belgium: the Dynamics of a Culturally Divided Society*. Berkeley: Institute of International Studies, University of California, pp. 34–45.

Pollitt, Christopher (1995). 'Management Techniques for the Public Sector: Pulpit and Practice', in B. Guy Peters and Donald Savoie (eds.), *Governance in a Changing Environment*. Montreal and Kingston: McGill-Queen's University Press, pp. 203–38.

Popper, Karl (1976). 'The Logic of the Social Sciences', in Theodor Adorno et al., *The Positivist Dispute in German Sociology*. London: Heinemann, pp. 87–104.

Porter, Elisabeth (1998). 'Identity, Location, Plurality: Women, Nationalism and Northern Ireland', in Rick Wilford and Robert Miller (eds), *Women, Ethnicity and Nationalism: the Politics of Transition*. London: Routledge, pp. 36–61.

Preuss, Ulrich and Ferran Requejo (1998). *European Citizenship, Multiculturalism and the State*. Baden-Baden: Nomos.

Proudhon, Pierre-Joseph (1979). *The Principle of Federation*, trans. and introd. Richard Vernon. Toronto: University of Toronto Press.

Pryde, George (1950). *The Treaty of Union of Scotland and England, 1707*. Westport, CT: Greenwood Press.

Pujol, Jordi (1980). *Construir Catalunya*. Barcelona: Pòrtic.

Rabushka, Alvin and Kenneth A. Shepsle (1971). 'Political Entrepreneurship and Patterns of Democratic Instability in Plural Societies', *Race* 12.4: 461–76.

Rabushka, Alvin and Kenneth A. Shepsle (1972). *Politics in Plural Societies: a Theory of Political Instability*. Columbus: Merill.

Rawls, John. (1971). *A Theory of Justice*. Cambridge, MA: Bellknap–Harvard University Press.

Rawls, John (1972). *A Theory of Justice*. Oxford: Oxford University Press.

Rawls, John (1995). 'Reply to Habermas', *Journal of Philosophy* 92.3: 132–80.

Rawls, John (1996). *Political Liberalism*. New York: Columbia University Press.

Rawls, John (1999). *The Law of Peoples and the Idea of Public Reason Revisited*. Cambridge, MA: Harvard University Press.

Raz, Joseph (1986). *The Morality of Freedom*. Oxford: Oxford University Press.

Rees, Earl L. (1996). 'Spain's Linguistic Normalization Laws: the Catalan Controversy', *Hispania* 79: 313–21.

Reid, Scott (1992). *Canada Remapped: How the Partition of Quebec will Reshape the Nation*. Vancouver: Pulp Press.

Requejo, Ferran (1994). *Las democracias: democracia antigua, democracia liberal y Estado de Bienestar*. 2nd edn. Barcelona: Ariel.

Requejo, Ferran (1996). 'Diferencias nacionales y federalismo asymétrico', *Claves de Razon Practica* 59: 24–37.

Requejo, Ferran (1997). 'Cultural Pluralism, Nationalism and Federalism: a Revision of Democratic Citizenship in Plurinational States', unpublished paper. Barcelona: Pompeu Fabra University.

Requejo, Ferran (1998a). 'European Citizenship in Plurinational States: Some Limits of Traditional Democratic Theories: Rawls and Habermas', in Ulrich Preuss and Ferran Requejo (eds.), *European Citizenship, Multiculturalism and the State*. Baden-Baden: Nomos, pp. 29–49.

Requejo, Ferran (1998b). *¿Federalisme, per a què?*. Barcelona: L'Hora del Present.

Requejo, Ferran (1998c). *Reconeixement nacional, democràcia i federalisme: alguns límits del model constitucional espanyol*. Barcelona: Fundació Ramon Trias Fargas.

Requejo, Ferran (1998d). 'Los análisis sobre los acuerdos federales. Una revisión', *Agenda. Revista de Gobierno y Politicas Publicas* 1: 9–31.

Requejo, Ferran (1998e). 'L'Estat de les Autonomies, dues dècades després', *Transversal* 5: 24–8.

Requejo, Ferran (1999). 'Cultural Pluralism, Nationalism and Federalism: a Revision of Democratic Citizenship in Plurinational States', *European Journal of Political Research* 35.2: 255–86.

Resnick, Philip (1994a). *Thinking English Canada*. Toronto: Studdart.

Resnick, Philip (1994b). 'Toward a Multinational Federalism: Asymmetrical and Confederal Alternatives', in F. Leslie Seidle (ed.), *Seeking a New Canadian Partnership: Asymmetrical and Confederal Options / A la recherche d'un nouveau contrat politique pour le Canada: options asymétriques et options confédérales*. Montreal: IRPP, pp. 71–89.

Resnick, Philip (1995). 'English Canada: the Nation that Dares Not Speak its Name', in Kenneth McRoberts (ed.), *Beyond Quebec: Taking Stock of English Canada*. Montreal: McGill-Queen's University Press, pp. 81–92.

Richer, Jules (1997). 'Propositions de Calgary: pour Chrétien, la réaction de Bouchard était prévisible', *Le Devoir*, 17 September A4.

Riddell, T. Q. and Morton, F. L. (1998). 'Reasonable Limitations, Distinct Society and the Canada Clause: Interpretive Clauses and the Competition for Constitutional Advantage', *Canadian Journal of Political Science* 31.3: 467–94.

Riker, William (1975). 'Federalism', in Fred Greenstein and Nelson Polsby (eds.), *Handbook of Political Science*, vol. 5. Reading, MA; Don Mills, Ont.: Addison-Wesley, pp. 93–172.

Rimanque, Karel (1989). 'Réflexions concernant la question oratoire: y a-t-il un Etat belge', in Hugues Dumont et al. (eds.), *Belgitude et crise de l'Etat belge*. Brussels: Facultés universitaires Saint-Louis, pp. 63–9.

Rioux, Christian (1998). 'La Catalogne renforce sa loi linguistique', *Le Devoir*, 30 January, pp. A1, A14.

Rocher, François (1992). 'La consécration du fédéralisme centralisateur', in *Référendum, 26 octobre 1992. Les objections de 20 spécialistes aux offres fédérales*. Montreal: Editions Saint-Martin, 87–98.

Rocher, François (1996). 'Nationalisme et projet national', *Virtualités* 3: 46–50.

Rocher, François and Gérard Boismenu (1990). 'New Constitutional Signposts: Distinct Society, Linguistic Duality and Institutional Changes', in Alain-G. Gagnon and James P. Bickerton (eds.), *Canadian Politics: An Introduction to the Discipline*. Peterborough, Ont.: Broadview Press, pp. 222–45.

Rocher, François and Christian Rouillard (1996). 'Using the Concept of Deconcentration to Overcome the Centralization/Decentralization Dichotomy: Thoughts on Recent Constitutional and Political Reform', in Douglas M. Brown and Patrick Fafard (eds.), *Canada: the State of the Federation 1996*. Kingston: Institute of Intergovernmental Relations pp. 99–134.

Rocher, François and Christian Rouillard (1998). 'Décentralization, subsidiarité et néolibéralisme au Canada: lorsque l'arbre cache la forêt', *Canadian Public Policy/Analyse de politiques* 24.2: 233–58.

Rocher, François and Miriam Smith (1997). 'The New Boundaries of Canadian Political Culture', *Journal of History and Politics* 12.2: 36–70.

Rocher, Guy (1997). 'Du pluralisme à l'égalitarisme dans la démocratie canadienne', paper presented to the colloquium 'Quel Québec voulons-nous?' Montreal, 25–6 October.

Rocher, Guy and Bruno Marcotte (1997). 'Politiques linguistiques et identité nationale comparées au Quebec et en Catalogne', in Yvan Lamonde and Gérard Bouchard (eds.), *La nation dans tous ses états: le Quebec en comparaison*. Montreal: L'Harmattan, pp. 251–67.

Rokkan, Stein and Derek Urwin (1983). *Economy, Territory, Identity. Politics of West European Peripheries*. London: Sage.

Roland, Gérard, Toon Vandevelde and Philippe Van Parijs (1997). 'Repenser la solidarité entre régions et nations', *La Revue Nouvelle*, May–June, pp. 144–57.

Rolston, Bill (1998). 'What's Wrong with Multiculturalism: Liberalism and the Irish Conflict', in David Miller (ed.), *Rethinking Northern Ireland*. London: Longman, pp. 253–74.

Roosens, Eugeen (1981). 'The Multicultural Nature of Contemporary Belgian Society: the Immigrant Community', in Arend Lijphart (ed.), *Conflict and Coexistence in Belgium: The Dynamics of a Culturally Divided Society*. Berkeley: Institute of International Studies, University of California, pp. 61–92.

Rossiter, Clinton (ed.) (1961). *The Federalist Papers*. New York: The New American Library.

Roulston, Carmel (1997). 'Women on the Margin: the Women's Movement in Northern Ireland, 1973–95', in Lois West (ed.), *Feminist Nationalism*. London: Routledge, pp. 41–58.

Rousseau, Jean-Jacques (1972). *The Government of Poland*, trans. Willmoore Kendall. Indianopolis: Bobbs-Merrill.

Roy, Fernande (1993). *Histoire des idéologies au Quebec aux XIXe et XXe siècles*. Montreal: Boréal.

Ruane, J. and Todd, J. (1996). *The Dynamics of Conflict in Northern Ireland: Power, Conflict and Emancipation*. Cambridge: Cambridge University Press.

Rudolph, J. and R. Thompson (1985). 'Ethnoterritorial Movements and the Policy Process: Accommodating Nationalist Demands in the Developed World', *Comparative Politics* 17: 291–311.

Rudolph, Jr., Joseph R. and Robert J. Thompson (eds.) (1989). *Ethnoterritorial Politics, Policy and the Western World*. Boulder, CO.: Westview Press.

Russell, Peter H. (1992). *Constitutional Odyssey: Can Canadians Become a Sovereign People?*. Toronto: University of Toronto Press.

Russell, Peter H. (1996). 'Constitution, Citizenship and Ethnicity', in Jean Laponce and William Safran (eds.), *Ethnicity and Citizenship: the Canadian Case*. London: Frank Cass, pp. 96–106.

RVAP (1997). 'Simetría y asimetría en el Estado de las Autonomías', *Revista Vasca de la Administración Pública* 47.2.

Ryan, Claude (1999). 'What if Quebecers Voted Clearly for Secession?' in David Schneiderman (ed.), *The Quebec Decision*. Toronto: James Lorimer and Company, pp. 149–52.

Safran, William (1987). 'Ethnic Mobilization, Modernization, and Ideology: Jacobinism, Marxism, Organicism and Functionalism', *The Journal of Ethnic Studies* 15: 1–31.

Salmond, Alex (1998). 'The Race for Holyrood', *The Electronic Scotsman* (http://www.alba.org.uk).

Sandel, Michael (1982). *Liberalism and the Limits of Justice*. Cambridge: Cambridge University Press.

Sandel, Michael (1984). 'The Procedural Republic and the Unencumbered Self', *Political Theory* 12. 1: 81–96.

Sandel, Michael (1996). *Democracy's Discontent: America in Search of a Public Philosophy*. Cambridge, MA: Belknap Press.

Sanders, Lynn (1997). 'Against Deliberation', *Political Theory* 25.3: 347–76.

Sanmartí Roset, Josep Maria (1996). *Las políticas lingüísticas y las lenguas minoritarias en el proceso de construcción de Europa*. Bilbao: Instituto Vasco de Administracion Publica.

Schmidt, Vivian (1995). 'The New World Order Inc.: the Rise of Business and the Decline of the Nation State', *Daedalus* 124.2: 75–106.

Schneiderman, David (ed.) (1999). *The Quebec Decision*. Toronto: James Lorimer and Company.

Scott, Allen (1998). *Regions and the World Economy*. Oxford: Oxford University Press.

Scott, Paul H. (1979). *1707: the Union of Scotland and England*. Edinburgh: Saltire Society.

Seidle, F. Leslie (ed.) (1994). *Seeking a New Canadian Partnership*. Montreal: Institute for Research on Public Policy.

Senelle, Robert (1989). 'Constitutional Reform in Belgium: From Unitarism Towards Federalism', in Murray Forsyth (ed.), *Federalism and Nationalism*. Leicester: Leicester University Press, pp. 51–95.

Seymour, Michel (1995). 'La fédération décentralisée', *Le Devoir*, 27 March, p. A7.

Sharpe, L. J. (1998). 'British Centralism Revisited', paper presented to the American Political Science Association, Boston.

Shaw, Jo (2000). 'Relating Constitutionalism and Flexibility in the EU', in G. de Burca and J. Scott (eds.); *Constitutional Change in the EU: From Uniformity to Flexibility?* London: Hart Publishing, pp. 337–58.

Simeon, Richard (1998). 'Considerations on the Design of Federations: The South African Constitution in Comparative Perspective', *SA Public Law* 13: 42–71.

Simeon, Richard and David Cameron (2000). 'Intergovernmental Relations and Democratic Citizenship', in B. Guy Peters and Donald Savoie (eds.), *Governance in the Twenty-First Century: Revitalizing Public Service*. Montreal: McGill-Queen's University Press, pp. 58–118.

Simeon, Richard and Ian Robinson (1990). *State, Society, and the Development of Canadian Federalism*. Ottawa: Supply and Services Canada.

Simeon, Richard and Ian Robinson (1994). 'The Dynamics of Canadian Federalism', in James P. Bickerton and Alain-G. Gagnon (eds.), *Canadian Politics*, 2nd edn. Peterborough, Ont.: Broadview Press, pp. 366–88.

Skinner, Quentin (1986). 'The Paradoxes of Political Liberty', in *Tanner Lectures on Human Values VII*, pp. 225–50.

Skinner, Quentin (1992). 'On Justice, the Common Good, and the Priority of Liberty', in Chantal Mouffe (ed.), *Dimensions of Radical Democracy*. London: Verso, pp. 211–24.

Smiley, Donald (1992). 'Language Policies in the Canadian Political Community', in Jean-William Lapierre, Vincent Lemieux and Jacques Zylberberg (eds.), *Etre contemporain. Mélanges en l'honneur de Gérard Bergeron*. Quebec: Presses de l'Université du Québec/Ecole nationale d'administration publique, pp. 271–90.

Smith, Anthony (1971). *Theories of Nationalism*. London: Duckworth.

Smith, Anthony (1981). *The Ethnic Revival*. Cambridge: Cambridge University Press.

Smith, Anthony (1986). *The Ethnic Origins of Nations*. Oxford: Blackwell.

Smith, Anthony (1991). *National Identity*. Harmondsworth: Penguin.

Smith, Graham (ed.) (1995a). *Federalism: the Multiethnic Challenge*. London: Longman.

Smith, Graham (1995b). 'Mapping the Federal Condition: Ideology, Political Practice and Social Justice', in Graham Smith (ed.), *Federalism: the Multiethnic challenge*. London: Longman, pp. 1–28.

Smout, T. Christopher (1989). 'Problems of Nationalism, Identity and Improvement in later Eighteenth-Century Scotland', in T. M. Devine (ed.), *Improvement and Enlightenment*. Edinburgh: J. Donald, pp. 1–21.

Smout, T. Christopher (1994). 'Perspectives on the Scottish Identity', *Scottish Affairs* 6: 101–13.

Snyder, Jack (2000). *From Voting to Violence: Democratization and Nationalist Conflict*. New York: Norton.

Solé, Jordi (1998). 'Nacionalismos contra nacionalismos', *El País*, 4 September.

Sonntag, Selma K. (1993). 'The Politics of Compromise: the Enactment of Regional Unilingualism', *International Journal of the Sociology of Language* 104: 9–30.

Soysal, Yasemin Nuhoglu (1994). *Limits of Citizenship: Migrants and Postnational Membership in Europe*. Chicago: University of Chicago Press.

Spinner, Jeff (1994). *The Boundaries of Citizenship: Race, Ethnicity, and Nationality in the Liberal State*. Baltimore: Johns Hopkins University Press.

Stark, Andrew (1992). 'English Canadian Opposition to Quebec Nationalism', in R. Kent Weaver (ed.), *The Collapse of Canada?* Washington, DC: Brookings Institution, pp. 123–58.

Stark, Andrew (1997). 'Limousine Liberals, Welfare Conservatives', *Political Theory* 25. 4: 475–501.

Statistique Canada (1997). *Le Quotidien*, 2 December.

Steinberg, Jonathan (1996). *Why Switzerland?*, 2nd edn. Cambridge: Cambridge University Press.

Stengers, Jean (1981). 'Belgian National Sentiments', in Arend Lijphart (ed.), *Conflict and Coexistence in Belgium: the Dynamics of a Culturally Divided Society*. Berkeley: Institute of International Studies, University of California, pp. 46–60.

Stengers, Jean (1989). 'La Belgique, un accident de l'histoire?' *Revue de l'Université de Bruxelles* 3–4: 17–34.

Stocker, Laura (1992). 'Interest and Ethics in Politics', *American Political Science Review* 86.2: 369–80.

Storper, M. (1995). 'The Resurgence of Regional Economies, Ten Years Later: the Region as a Nexus of Untraded Dependencies', *European Urban and Regional Studies* 2.3: 191–221.

Strange, Susan (1995). 'The Limits of Politics', *Government and Opposition* 30: 291–311.

Supreme Court of Canada (1981). *A.-G. Manitoba v. A.-G. Canada et al. (Patriation Reference)*, 1 SCR 753.

Supreme Court of Canada (1997). *Delgamuukw v. British Columbia*, 3 SCR 1010. Available http://www.droit.umontreal.ca/doc/csc-scc/en/index.html.

Supreme Court of Canada (1998). *Reference re Secession of Quebec*, 2 SCR 217. Available http://www.droit.umontreal.ca/doc/csc-scc/en/index.html

Swennen, René (1998). 'Wallonie française?' in 'Belgique: l'Etat fédéral, une étape?' *Problèmes politiques et sociaux*, no. 795, pp. 18–20.

Tamir, Yael (1993). *Liberal Nationalism*. Princeton: Princeton University Press.

Tarlton, Charles (1965). 'Symmetry and Asymmetry as Elements of Federalism: a Theoretical Speculation', *Journal of Politics* 27.4: 861–74.

Taylor, Charles (1989). 'Cross-Purposes: the Liberal-Communitarian Debate', in Nancy Rosenblum (ed.), *Liberalism and the Moral Life*. Cambridge, MA: Harvard University Press.

Taylor, Charles (1991a). 'Shared and Divergent Values', in R. L. Watts and D. M. Brown (eds.), *Options for a New Canada*. Toronto: Toronto University Press, pp. 53–76.

Taylor, Charles (1991b). *The Ethics of Authenticity*. Cambridge, MA: Harvard University Press.

Taylor, Charles (1992a). 'The Politics of Recognition', in Amy Gutmann (ed.), *Multiculturalism and the Politics of Recognition*. Princeton: Princeton University Press, pp. 25–73.

Taylor, Charles (1992b). 'Quel principe d'identité collective?' in Jacques Lenoble and Nicole Dewandre (eds.), *L'Europe au soir du siècle: identité et démocracie*. Paris: Editions Esprit, pp. 59–66.

Taylor, Charles (1992c). 'Les avenirs possibles: la légitimité, l'identité et l'aliénation au Canada à la fin du siècle', in *Rapprocher les solitudes*. Sainte-Foy: Presses de l'Université Laval, pp. 69–133.

Taylor, Charles (1993a). *Reconciling the Solitudes: Essays on Canadian Federalism and Nationalism*, ed. Guy Laforest. Montreal and Kingston: McGill-Queen's University Press.

Taylor, Charles (1993b). 'Why Do Nations Have to Become States?' in Charles Taylor, *Reconciling the Solitudes: Essays on Canadian Federalism and Nationalism*. Montreal and Kingston: McGill-Queen's University Press, pp. 40–58.

Thelen, Kathleen and Sven Steinmo (1992). 'Historical Institutionalism in Comparative Politics', in Sven Steinmo, Kathleen Thelen and Frank Longstreth (eds.), *Structuring Politics: Historical Institutionalism in Comparative Analysis*. Cambridge: Cambridge University Press, pp. 1–32.

Thomas, David (1997). *Whistling Past the Graveyard: Constitutional Abeyances, Quebec, and the Future of Canada*. Toronto: Oxford University Press.

Tilly, Charles (1990). *Coercion, Capital and European States, AD 990–1990*. Oxford: Blackwell.

Tilly, Charles (1994). 'Entanglements of European Cities and States', in Charles Tilly and W.P. Blockmans (eds.), *Cities and the Rise of States in Europe, AD 1000 to 1800*. Boulder, CO: Westview, pp. 1–27.

Tilly, Charles and W. P. Blockmans (eds.) (1994). *Cities and the Rise of States in Europe, AD 1000 to 1800*. Boulder, CO: Westview.

Tobias, John L. (1991). 'Protection, Civilization, Assimilation: an Outline History of Canada's Indian Policy', in J. R. Miller (ed.), *Sweet Promises: a Reader on Indian–White Relations in Canada*. Toronto: University of Toronto Press, pp. 127–44.

Tourret, Paul (1994). 'La quête identitaire wallonne', *Hérodote*, January–June, pp. 58–75.

Trudeau, Pierre (ed. Ron Graham) (1998). *The Essential Trudeau*. Toronto: McClelland and Stewart.

Trudeau, Pierre Elliott (1968). *Federalism and the French-Canadians*. New York: St Martin's Press.

Trudeau, Pierre Elliott (1990a). *Pierre Trudeau Speaks Out on Meech Lake*. Toronto: General Paperbacks.

Trudeau, Pierre Elliott (1990b). 'Des valeurs d'une société juste', in Thomas S. Axworthy and Pierre Elliott Trudeau (eds.), *Les années Trudeau: la recherche d'une société juste*. Montreal: Le Jour, pp. 379–407.

Trudeau, Pierre Elliott (1992). *A Mess that Deserves a Big No*. Toronto: Robert Davis Publishers.

Trudeau, Pierre Elliott (1993). *Memoirs*. Montreal: McClelland and Stewart.

Tully, James (1992). 'The Crisis of Identification: the Case of Canada', *Political Studies* 42: 77–96.

Tully, James (1994a). 'Diversity's Gambit Declined', in Curtis Cook (ed.), *Constitutional Predicament: Canada After the Referendum of 1992*. Montreal: McGill-Queen's University Press, pp. 149–98.

Tully, James (1994b). *Philosophy in an Age of Pluralism*. Cambridge: Cambridge University Press.

Tully, James (1995). *Strange Multiplicity: Constitutionalism in an Age of Diversity*. Cambridge: Cambridge University Press.

Tully, James (1999a). 'The Agonic Freedom of Citizens', *Economy and Society* 28: 161–82.

Tully, James (1999b). 'To Think and Act Differently: Foucault's Four Reciprocal Objections to Habermas', in David Owen (ed.), *Foucault contra Habermas*. London: Routledge, pp. 90–141.

Tully, James (2000a). *The Unattained Yet Attainable Democracy: Canada and Quebec Face the New Century*. Montreal: Programme d'études sur le Québec, Université McGill.

Tully, James (2000b). 'The Challenge of Reimagining Citizenship and Belonging in Multicultural and Multinational Societies', in Iain Hampsher-Monk and Catriona McKinnon (eds.), *The Demands of Citizenship*. London: Continuum International Publishing, pp. 212–34.

Tully, James (2000c). 'Aboriginal Peoples: Negotiating Reconciliation', in James Bickerton and Alain-G. Gagnon (eds.), *Canadian Politics*. 3rd edition. Peterborough, Ont.: Broadview Press, pp. 413–43.

Tully, James (2000d). 'The Struggles of Indigenous Peoples for and of Freedom', in Duncan Ivison, Paul Patton and Douglas Saunders (eds.), *Political Theory and the Rights of Indigenous Peoples*. Oakleigh, Victoria: Cambridge University Press (Australia), pp. 36–59.

United Nations (1993). Human Rights Committee, Communications nos. 359/ 1989 and 385/1989, 31 March.

Uyttendaele, Marc (1989). 'L'idée de la Belgique: une nation par défaut', *Revue de l'Université de Bruxelles*, pp. 7–16.

Vagman, Vincent (1994). *Le mouvement wallon et la question bruxelloise*. Brussels: Courrier hebdomadaire CRISP, no 1434–5, pp.

Vaillancourt, François (1996). 'Language and Socioeconomic Status in Quebec: Measurement, Findings, Determinants and Policy Costs', *International Journal on the Sociology of Language* 121: 69–92.

Van Houten, Pieter (1998). 'Regional Assertiveness and Intergovernmental Financial Relations: Illustrations from Belgium and Germany', paper presented at the annual meeting of the American Political Science Association, Boston.

Van Parijs, Philippe (1993). 'La morale d'un graphique', *La revue nouvelle*, November, pp. 69–73.

Van Velthonen, Harry (1987). 'The Process of Language Shift in Brussels: Historical Background and Mechanisms', in Els Witte and Hugo Baetens Beardsmore (eds.), *The Interdisciplinary Study of Urban Bilingualism in Brussels*. Philadelphia: Multilingual Matters, pp. 15–45.

Venne, Sharon (1998). *Our Elders Understand Our Thoughts: Evolving International Law Regarding Indigenous Rights*. Penticton: Theytus Books.

Verhofstadt, Guy (1996). 'Flanders and the Jump Towards the 21st Century', VEV, 1 November.

Vernon, Richard (1988). 'The Federal Citizen', in M. W. Westmacott and R. D. Olling (eds.), *Perspectives on Canadian Federalism*. Scarborough, Ont.: Prentice-Hall, pp. 3–15.

Villers, Y. (1998). 'Opinions et débats', *Le Soir*, 4 April.

Vipond, Robert (1995). 'From Provincial Autonomy to Provincial Equality (Or Clyde Wells and the Distinct Society)', in Joseph Carens (ed.), *Is Quebec Nationalism Just? Perspectives from Anglophone Canada*. Montreal and Kingston: McGill-Queen's University Press, pp. 97–119.

Vos, Louis (1993). 'Shifting Nationalism: Belgians, Flemings and Walloons', in Mikulas Teich and Roy Porter (eds.), *The National Question in Europe in Historical Context*. Cambridge: Cambridge University Press, pp. 203–20.

Waddell, Eric (1986). 'State, Language and Society: the Vicissitudes of French in Quebec and Canada', in Alan Cairns and Cynthia Williams (eds.), *The Politics of Gender, Ethnicity and Language in Canada*. Ottawa: Supply and Services Canada, pp. 67–110.

Walton, Douglas. (1998). *The New Dialectic: Conversational Contexts of Argument*. Toronto: University of Toronto Press.

Walzer, Michael (1992). 'The New Tribalism: Notes on a Difficult Problem', *Dissent* (March), pp. 164–71.

Walzer, Michael (1997). *On Toleration*. New Haven, CT.: Yale University Press.

Watts, Ronald (1991). 'The Federative Superstructure', Ronald Watts and Douglas Brown (eds.), *Options for a New Canada*. Toronto: University of Toronto Press, pp. 309–36.

Watts, Ronald (1995). 'Contemporary Views on Federalism', in Bertus de Villiers (ed.), *Evaluating Federal Systems*. Cape Town and Dordrecht: Juta & Co./Martinus Nijhoff Publishers, pp. 1–29.

Watts, Ronald (1996). *Comparing Federal Systems in the 1990's*. Kingston, Ont.: Institute of Intergovernmental Relations.

Watts, Ronald and Douglas Brown (eds.) (1991). *Options for a New Canada*. Toronto: University of Toronto Press.

Weaver, Sally M. (1981). *Making Canadian Indian Policy: the Hidden Agenda 1968–1970*. Toronto: University of Toronto Press.

Webber, Jeremy (1994). *Reimagining Canada: Language, Culture and the Canadian Constitution*. Montreal and Kingston: Montreal-Queen's University Press.

Whitaker, Reg (1992). *A Sovereign Idea*. Montreal and Kingston: McGill-Queen's University Press.

Whitaker, Reg (1993). 'The Dog that Never Barked: Who Killed Asymmetrical Federalism?' in Kenneth McRoberts and Patrick Monahan (eds.), *The Charlottetown Accord, the Referendum, and the Future of Canada*. Toronto: University of Toronto Press, pp. 107–14.

Whyte, John (1990). *Interpreting Northern Ireland*. Oxford: Clarendon Press.

Wiarda, Howard J. (1993). *Politics in Iberia: the Political Systems of Spain and Portugal*. New York: HarperCollins.

Wilford, Rick (1999). 'Epilogue', in Paul Mitchell and Rick Wilford (eds.), *Politics in Northern Ireland*. Boulder, CO: Westview.

Wilson, C. (1970). 'Note of Dissent', *Scotland's Government: Report of the Scottish Constitutional Committee*. Edinburgh: Scottish Constitutional Committee.

Wilson, Woodrow (1995) [1918]. 'Address to a Joint Session of Congress, January 1918', in Omar Dahbour and Micheline R. Ishay (eds.), *The Nationalism Reader*. Atlantic Highlands, NJ, pp. 306–11.

Witte, Els (1987). 'Socio-Political Aspects: Bilingual Brussels as an Indication of Growing Political Tensions (1960–1985)', in Els Witte and Hugo Baetens Beardsmore (eds.), *The Interdisciplinary Study of Urban Bilingualism in Brussels*. Philadelphia: Multilingual Matters, pp. 47–74.

Witte, Els (1992). 'Belgian Federalism: Towards Complexity and Asymmetry', *West European Politics* 15.4: 95–117.

Woolard, Kathryn (1989). *Double Talk: Bilingualism and the Politics of Ethnicity in Catalonia*. Stanford: Stanford University Press.

Wright, Frank (1987). *Northern Ireland: a Comparative Analysis*. Dublin: Gill and Macmillan.

Young, Iris Marion (1989). 'Polity and Group Difference: a Critique of the Ideal of Universal Citizenship', *Ethics* 99: 250–74.

Young, Iris Marion (1990). *Justice and the Politics of Difference*. Princeton: Princeton University Press.

Young, Iris Marion (1997). 'Difference as a Resource for Democratic Communication', in James Bohman and William Rehg (eds.), *Deliberative Democracy: Essays on Reason and Politics*. Cambridge, MA: MIT Press, 383–406.

Zakaria, Haji Ahmad (ed.) (1987). *The Government and Politics of Malaysia*. Singapore: Oxford University Press.

Zolberg, Aristide (1974). 'The Making of Flemings and Walloons: Belgium, 1830–1914', *Journal of Interdisciplinary History* 5: 179–235.

Zolberg, Aristide (1977). 'Splitting the Difference: Federalization without Federalism in Belgium', in J. E. Milton, *Ethnic Conflict in the Western World*. Ithaca: Cornell University Press, pp. 103–42.

Index